Practical Modern SCADA Protocols: DNP3, 60870.5 and Related Systems

Titles in the series

Practical Cleanrooms: Technologies and Facilities (David Conway)

Practical Data Acquisition for Instrumentation and Control Systems (John Park, Steve Mackay)

Practical Data Communications for Instrumentation and Control (John Park, Steve Mackay, Edwin Wright)

Practical Digital Signal Processing for Engineers and Technicians (Edmund Lai)

Practical Electrical Network Automation and Communication Systems (Cobus Strauss)

Practical Embedded Controllers (John Park)

Practical Fiber Optics (David Bailey, Edwin Wright)

Practical Industrial Data Networks: Design, Installation and Troubleshooting (Steve Mackay, Edwin Wright, John Park, Deon Reynders)

Practical Industrial Safety, Risk Assessment and Shutdown Systems for Instrumentation and Control (Dave Macdonald)

Practical Modern SCADA Protocols: DNP3, 60870.5 and Related Systems (Gordon Clarke, Deon Reynders)

Practical Radio Engineering and Telemetry for Industry (David Bailey)

Practical SCADA for Industry (David Bailey, Edwin Wright)

Practical TCP/IP and Ethernet Networking (Deon Reynders, Edwin Wright)

Practical Variable Speed Drives and Power Electronics (Malcolm Barnes)

Practical Modern SCADA Protocols: DNP3, 60870.5 and Related Systems

Gordon Clarke CP Eng, BEng, MBA, Western Technical Services, Hobart, Australia

Deon Reynders Pr.Eng, BSc(ElecEng)(Hons), MBA, IDC Technologies, Perth, Australia

Edwin Wright BSc, BE(Hons)(Elec), MIPENZ, IDC Technologies, Perth, Australia

ELSEVIER

AMSTERDAM • BOSTON • HEIDELBERG • LONDON • NEW YORK • OXFORD
PARIS • SAN DIEGO • SAN FRANCISCO • SINGAPORE • SYDNEY • TOKYO

Newnes is an imprint of Elsevier

Newnes

Newnes is an imprint of Elsevier
The Boulevard, Langford Lane, Kidlington, Oxford, OX5 1GB, UK
30 Corporate Drive, Suite 400, Burlington, MA 01803, USA

First edition 2004
Reprinted 2008

British Library Cataloguing in Publication Data
A catalogue record for this book is available from the British Library

Library of Congress Cataloging-in-Publication Data
A catalog record for this book is available from the Library of Congress

ISBN: 978-0-7506-5799-0

For information on all Newnes publications
visit our website at www.elsevierdirect.com

Transferred to Digital Printing in 2009

Working together to grow
libraries in developing countries

www.elsevier.com | www.bookaid.org | www.sabre.org

ELSEVIER   BOOK AID
International   Sabre Foundation

Contents

Preface

This is a comprehensive book covering the essentials of SCADA communication systems focusing on DNP3 and the other new developments in this area. It commences with a brief review of the fundamentals of SCADA systems hardware, software and the typical communications systems (such as RS-232, RS-485, Ethernet and TCP/IP) that connect the SCADA operator stations together.

A solid review is then done on the DNP3 and IEC 60870-5 protocol where the features, message structure, practical benefits and applications are discussed. The book is intended to be product independent but examples will be taken from existing products to ensure that all aspects of the protocols are covered.

DNP3 is an open protocol developed by Harris Controls Division, Distributed Automation Products in the early 1990s and released to the industry based DNP3 Users Group in November 1993. Much of the material on DNP3 contained within this text is based substantially on the documentation available from the DNP3 Users Group, with interpretation and presentation by the author. The author has tried to identify cases in the text where material has been reproduced directly from user group standards or other sources, and apology is offered if there are any inadvertent oversights in doing this.

This book provides you with the tools to design your next SCADA system more effectively using open protocols and to draw on the latest technologies.

After reading this you should be able to:

- Explain the fundamentals of DNP3 and associated SCADA protocols
- Demonstrate knowledge of the 'nuts and bolts' about selecting DNP3 based systems
- Apply the best current practice for data communications for SCADA systems
- Have a good working knowledge of the DNP3 and IEC 60870-5 protocols
- Troubleshoot simple problems with the DNP3
- Explain how UCA is structured and works
- Provide a working explanation of SCADA protocols and how they should be structured and applied
- Apply 'best practice' decisions on the best and most cost effective use of SCADA open protocols for your company

A basic working knowledge of SCADA and data communications is useful but not essential.

The structure of the book is as follows.

Chapter 1: *Introduction.* An introduction to DNP3 and IEC 60870-5 and other various SCADA protocols that are in use.

Chapter 2: *Fundamentals of SCADA communications.* The structure of SCADA systems and discussion of RTUs, communication architectures, basic standards such as RS-232 and the OSI model with a few remarks on typical SCADA protocols used.

Chapter 3: *Open SCADA protocols DNP3 and IEC 60870.* An introduction to open SCADA protocols.

Chapter 4: *Preview of DNP3.* A preview of DNP3 with the reasons for its remarkable success in the SCADA business.

Chapter 5: *Fundamentals of distributed network protocol.* The fundamentals of DNP3 with a detailed discussion of its underlying structure.

Chapter 6: *Advanced considerations of DNP3.* DNP3 subset definitions and conformance testing, interoperability and polling and communications options.

Chapter 7: *Preview of IEC 60870-5.* Describing how the protocol is referred by the standards and presenting its structure.

Chapter 8: *Fundamentals of IEC 60870-5.* A detailed presentation of the standards, structure and operation.

Chapter 9: *Advanced considerations of IEC 60870-5.* Presents application level functions, interoperability, provisions and network operations.

Chapter 10: *Differences between DNP3 and IEC 60870.* A discussion on the main differences between the DNP3 and the IEC 60870 standard.

Chapter 11: *Intelligent electronic devices (IEDs).* A description of what an IED is and some issues on installation and commissioning.

Chapter 12: *Ethernet and TCP/IP networks.* The basics of networking, Ethernet and the TCP/IP protocol and their relevance to DNP3.

Chapter 13: *Fieldbus and SCADA communications systems.* The essentials of Fieldbus (such as Profibus and Foundation Fieldbus) and their relevance to DNP3.

Chapter 14: *UCA protocol.* A review of the UCA protocol and its relevance to DNP3.

Chapter 15: *Applications of DNP3 and SCADA protocols.* Discussion of a water industry application.

Chapter 16: *Future developments.* The future developments of DNP3.

Acknowledgements

We would like to acknowledge Mr Ian Wiese, 'SCADA architect extraordinaire' and owner of the valuable SCADA website: www.iinet.net.au/~Ianw, and Mr Andrew West, Chair of the DNP Users Group Technical Committee for their valuable advice, encouragement and assistance in preparing this book. They obviously take no responsibility for the contents.

If you have any further interest in these topics we would like to recommend that you subscribe to:

www.lists.iinet.net.au/cgi-bin/mailman/listsinfo/scada
www.dnp.org

1

Introduction

Objectives

When you have completed study of this chapter you will be able to:

- Describe the essentials of SCADA systems
- Describe why open systems are important
- List the main advantages of using DNP3 and IEC 60870-5
- Describe the essentials of the layered communications architecture

1.1 Overview

This chapter serves to introduce the different topics that will be covered in the manual and gives an overall flavor of the associated training course. Note that this chapter is in many cases an extract from the material in later chapters where the various issues are covered in far greater detail.

It will be broken down into:

- SCADA systems
- Open systems and communication standards
- DNP3
- Local area networks, Ethernet and TCP/IP
- The UCA protocol

1.2 SCADA systems

SCADA (supervisory control and data acquisition system) refers to the combination of telemetry and data acquisition. SCADA encompasses the collecting of the information via a RTU (remote terminal unit), transferring it back to the central site, carrying out any necessary analysis and control and then displaying that information on a number of operator screens or displays. The required control actions are then conveyed back to the process.

In the early days of data acquisition relay logic was used to control production and plant systems. With the advent of the CPU (as part of the microprocessor) and other electronic devices, manufacturers incorporated digital electronics into relay logic equipment, creating the PLC or programmable logic controller, which is still one of the most widely used control systems in industry. As needs grew to monitor and control more devices in the plant, the PLCs were distributed and the systems became more intelligent and smaller in size. PLCs and/or DCS (distributed control systems) are used as shown below. Although initially RTU was often a dedicated device, PLCs are often used as RTUs these days.

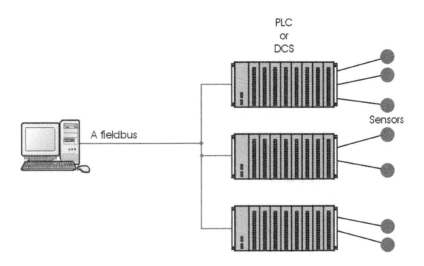

Figure 1.1
PC to PLC or DCS with a fieldbus and sensors

The advantages of the PLC/DCS/SCADA system are:

- The computer can record and store a very large amount of data
- The data can be displayed in any way the user requires
- Thousands of sensors over a wide area can be connected to the system
- The operator can incorporate real data simulations into the system
- Many types of data can be collected from the RTUs
- The data can be viewed from anywhere, not just on site

The disadvantages are:

- The system is more complicated than the sensor to panel type
- Different operating skills are required, such as system analysts and programmer
- With thousands of sensors there is still a lot of wire to deal with
- The operator can see only as far as the PLC

As the requirement for smaller and smarter systems grew, sensors were designed with the intelligence of PLCs and DCSs. These devices are known as IEDs (intelligent electronic devices). The IEDs are connected on a fieldbus such as Profibus, DeviceNet or Foundation Fieldbus to the PC. They include enough intelligence to acquire data, communicate to other devices and hold their part of the overall program. Each of these super smart sensors can have more than one sensor on board. Typically an IED could combine an analog input sensor, analog output, PID control, communication system and program memory in the one device.

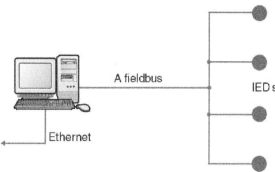

Figure 1.2
PC to IED using a fieldbus

The advantages of the PC to IED fieldbus system are:

- Minimal wiring is needed
- The operator can see down to the sensor level
- The data received from the device can include information such as serial numbers, model numbers, when it was installed and by whom
- All devices are plug and play; so installation and replacement are easy
- Smaller devices mean less physical space for the data acquisition system

The disadvantages of a PC to IED system are:

- The more sophisticated system requires better trained employees
- Sensor prices are higher (but this is offset somewhat by the lack of PLCs)
- The IEDs rely more on the communication system

1.2.1 SCADA hardware

A SCADA system consists of a number of remote terminal units (or RTUs) collecting field data and sending that data back to a master station via a communications system. The master station displays the acquired data and also allows the operator to perform remote control tasks.

The accurate and timely data allows for optimization of the plant operation and process. A further benefit is more efficient, reliable and most importantly, safer operations. This all results in a lower cost of operation compared to earlier non-automated systems.

On a more complex SCADA system there are essentially five levels or hierarchies:

- Field level instrumentation and control devices
- Marshalling terminals and RTUs
- Communications system
- The master station(s)
- The commercial information technology (IT) or data processing department computer system

The RTU provides an interface to the field analog and digital sensors situated at each remote site.

The communications system provides the pathway for communications between the master station and the remote sites. This communication system can be wire, fiber optic, radio, telephone line, microwave and possibly even satellite. Specific protocols and error detection philosophies are used for efficient and optimum transfer of data.

The master station (or sub-masters) gather data from the various RTUs and generally provide an operator interface for display of information and control of the remote sites. In large telemetry systems, sub-master sites gather information from remote sites and act as a relay back to the control master station.

1.2.2 SCADA software

SCADA software can be divided into two types, proprietary or open. Companies develop proprietary software to communicate to their hardware. These systems are sold as 'turn key' solutions. The main problem with these systems is the overwhelming reliance on the supplier of the system. Open software systems have gained popularity because of the interoperability they bring to the system. Interoperability is the ability to mix different manufacturers' equipment on the same system.

Citect and WonderWare are just two of the open software packages available on the market for SCADA systems. Some packages are now including asset management integrated within the SCADA system. The typical components of a SCADA system are indicated in the diagram below.

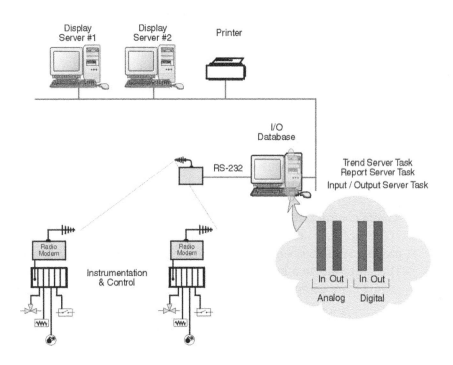

Figure 1.3
Typical SCADA system

1.3 Open systems and communications standards

A communication framework that has had a tremendous impact on the design of communications systems is the open systems interconnection (OSI) model developed by the International Standards Organization (ISO). The objective of the model is to provide a framework for the coordination of standards development and allows both existing and evolving standards activities to be set within that common framework.

The interconnection of two or more devices with digital communication is the first step towards establishing a network. In addition to the hardware requirements, the software problems of communication must also be overcome. Where all the devices on a network are from the same manufacturer, the hardware and software problems are usually easily solved because the system is usually designed within the same guidelines and specifications.

Open systems are those that conform to specifications and guidelines, which are 'open' to all. This allows equipment from any manufacturer, who complies with that standard, to be used interchangeably on the network. The benefits of open systems include multiple vendors and hence wider availability of equipment, lower prices and easier integration with other components.

In 1978 the ISO, faced with the proliferation of closed systems, defined a 'Reference Model for Communication between Open Systems' (ISO 7498), which has become known as the open systems interconnection model, or simply as the OSI model. OSI is essentially a data communications management structure, which breaks data communications down into a manageable hierarchy of seven layers. Each layer has a defined purpose and interfaces with the layers above it and below it. By laying down standards for each layer, some flexibility is allowed so that the system designers can develop protocols for each layer independent of each other. By conforming to the OSI standards, a system is able to communicate with any other compliant system, anywhere in the world.

It should be realized at the outset that the OSI reference model is not a protocol or set of rules for how a protocol should be written but rather an overall framework in which to define protocols. The OSI model framework specifically and clearly defines the functions or services that have to be provided at each of the seven layers (or levels).

The diagram below shows the seven layers of the OSI model.

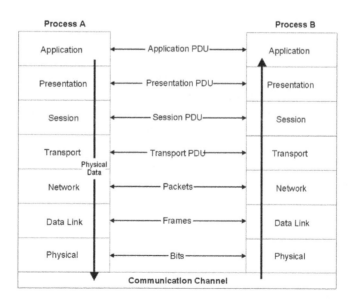

Figure 1.4
Full architecture of OSI model

A brief summary of the seven layers is as follows:

- **Application**
  The provision of network services to the user's application programs.
  Note: the actual application programs do NOT reside here

- **Presentation**
  Primarily takes care of data representation (including encryption)

- **Session**
  Control of the communications (sessions) between the users

- **Transport**
  The management of the communications between the two end systems

- **Network**
  Primarily responsible for the routing of messages

- **Data link**
  Responsible for assembling and sending a frame of data from one system to another

- **Physical**
  Defines the electrical signals and mechanical connections at the physical level

The figure below gives an idea on how transmission of a message is effected by each layer being encapsulated within the layer below it, before it is sent out on the physical data highway. Similarly once the packet (or more strictly speaking – the frame) is received each layer is then stripped off as the packet is pushed to the top where the message is then extracted.

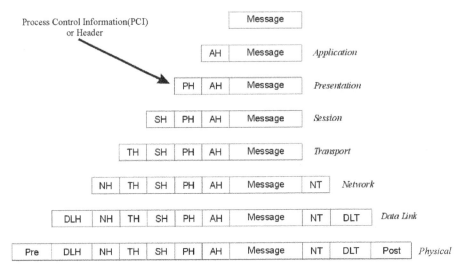

Figure 1.5
OSI message passing

1.4   IEC 60870.5 and DNP3.0

In 1988 the International Electrotechnical Commission (IEC) began publishing a standard entitled 'IEC 870 Telecontrol equipment and systems', of which one part was 'Part 5 Transmission Protocols'. This was developed in a hierarchical manner and published in a number of sub-paths taking from 1990 to 1995 to completely define an open protocol for SCADA communications. The protocol was defined in terms of the open systems interconnection model (OSI) using a minimum sub-set of the layers; the physical, data link, and application layers. This included detailed definition of message structure at the data link level, and a set of application level data structures so that manufacturers could use the protocol to create systems that would be capable of interoperation.

The IEC standard was subsequently renumbered with the prefix 60 and so the IEC standard for transmission protocols is now IEC 60870.5.

The IEC 60870.5 protocol was defined primarily for the telecommunication of electrical system and control information, and accordingly has data structures that are specifically related to this application. Although it includes general data types that could be used in any SCADA application, the use of IEC 60870 has largely been confined to the electricity industry.

During the same period, which IEC 870 was progressively released, the DNP3 protocol was developed and released in North America.

DNP3 is an open protocol developed by Harris Controls Division, Distributed Automation Products in the early 1990s and released to the industry based DNP3 Users Group in November 1993.

Although the protocol is generally referred to as DNP3 or Distributed Network Protocol Version 3.0, it is the telecommunications standard that defines communications between master stations, remote telemetry units (RTUs) and other intelligent electronic devices (IEDs). It was developed to achieve interoperability among systems in the electric utility, oil & gas, water/waste water and security industries.

From its creation for the electrical distribution industry in America, DNP3 has gained significant acceptance in both geographic and industry terms. DNP3 is supported by a large number of vendors and users in electrical, water infrastructure, and other industries in North America, South America, South Africa, Asia, Australia and New Zealand. In Europe DNP3 competes with IEC 60870-5, which is widely used in that region. However, the IEC protocol is confined to the electrical distribution industry, whereas DNP3 has found wider industry applications in the oil & gas, water/waste water and security industries.

A key feature of the DNP3 protocol is that it is an open protocol standard and it is one that has been adopted by a significant number of equipment manufacturers.

DNP3 has been recognized as having a particularly strong compliance system. In addition to having a comprehensive specification of data objects, DNP3 has a detailed compliance certification system. This is based on having defined implementation sub-sets to which devices must be certified. This provides a means for manufacturers to implement reduced function systems that still provide defined levels of functionality.

Both DNP3 and IEC 60870-5 were designed specifically for SCADA (supervisory control and data acquisition) applications. These involve acquisition of information and sending of control commands between physically separate computer devices. They are designed to transmit relatively small packets of data in a reliable manner with the messages involved arriving in a deterministic sequence. In this respect they are different from more general purpose protocols, such as FTP which is part of TCP/IP, which can send quite large files, but in a way that is generally not as suitable for SCADA control.

Key features of these protocols:

- Open protocols, available for use by any manufacturer or user
- Designed for reliable communication of data and control
- Widely supported by manufacturers of SCADA master systems and software, and of RTUs and IEDs

1.5 Local area networks, Ethernet and TCP/IP

Linking computers and other devices together to share information is nothing new. The technology for local area networks (LANs) was developed in the 1970s by minicomputer manufacturers to link widely separated user terminals to computers. This allowed the sharing of expensive peripheral equipment as well as data that may have previously existed in only one physical location.

SCADA master stations and RTUs are increasingly using components of local area networks (such as Ethernet) and TCP/IP in the communications of the real time data. Although the OSI model is generally preferred, a simplified model called the TCP/IP reference model is used and which consists of the following four layers:

- **Layer 1**
  Network interface layer
  Provides the physical link between devices. Also known as the local network or network access layer

- **Layer 2**
  Internet layer
  Isolates the host from specific networking requirements. The Internet protocol (IP) exists here, but does not guarantee delivery

- **Layer 3**
  Service layer
  Supplies the host service requirements. The transmission control protocol (TCP) resides here, providing reliable end-to-end service

- **Layer 4**
  Application layer
  Provides user-to-host and host-to-user processing and applications

LANs (layer 1) are characterized by high-speed transmission over a restricted geographical area. Thick Ethernet (10Base5), for example, operates at 10 Mb/s over a maximum distance of 500 m before the signals need to be boosted.

While LANs operate where distances are relatively small, wide area networks (WANs) are used to link LANs that are separated by large distances that range from a few tens of meters to thousands of kilometers. WANs normally use the public telecommunication system to provide cost-effective connection between LANs.

The way the nodes are connected to form a network is known as its topology. A logical topology defines how the elements in the network communicate with each other, and how information is transmitted through a network. A physical topology defines the wiring layout for a network. This specifies how the elements in the network are connected to each other electrically.

The concept of internetworking allows one to interconnect many different physical networks and make them function as a coordinated unit. Each network may have its own underlying hardware technology – but these are hidden from the user by the Internet technology. The TCP/IP protocol is used to communicate across any two interconnected networks.

The Internet protocol (IP) is at the core of the TCP/IP suite that resides at the Internet layer. It is primarily responsible for routing packets towards their destination, from router to router. This routing is performed on the basis of the IP addresses, embedded in the header attached to each packet forwarded by IP.

The host-to-host communications layer (also referred to as the service layer, or as the transport layer in terms of the OSI model) is primarily responsible for ensuring end-to-end delivery of packets transmitted by the Internet protocol (IP). This additional reliability is needed to compensate for the lack of reliability in IP.

There are only two relevant protocols residing in the host-to-host communications layer, namely TCP (transmission control protocol) and UDP (user datagram protocol). In addition to this, the host-to-host layer includes the APIs (application programming interfaces) used by programmers to gain access to these protocols from the process/application layer.

TCP is a connection-oriented protocol (discussed later) and is therefore reliable. TCP establishes a connection between two hosts before any data is transmitted. It is therefore possible to verify that all packets are received on the other end and to arrange re-transmission in the case of lost packets. Since TCP provides all of these built-in functions, it involves significant additional overhead in terms of processing time and header size.

UDP is a 'connectionless' or non-connection-oriented protocol and does not require a connection to be established between two machines prior to data transmission. It is therefore said to be an 'unreliable' protocol – the word 'unreliable' is used here as opposed to 'reliable' in the case of TCP. As in the case of TCP, it makes use of the underlying IP protocol to deliver its datagrams.

There are a variety of application protocols available with the TCP/IP protocol suite. These are:

- **TELNET**
  This allows a user at one terminal to communicate interactively with an application process on another terminal

- **FTP**
  This allows a user to interact with a remote file system

- **SMTP**
  A network wide mail transfer service

- **SNMP**
  A user can obtain data on the network performance and control a gateway/bridge

To obtain an overall perspective, the following diagram illustrates the interrelation of the various TCP/IP protocol layers with reference to the original four layer ARPA net and the modern OSI-RM.

OSI LAYER	PROTOCOL IMPLEMENTATION						ARPA LAYER
APPLICATION	File Transfer	Electronic Mail	Terminal Emulation	File Transfer	Client/Server	Network Management	PROCESS AND APPLICATION
PRESENTATION	File Transfer Protocol (FTP)	Simple Mail Transfer Protocol (SMTP)	TELNET Protocol	Trivial File Transfer Protocol (TFTP)	Sun Microsystems. Network file Systems Protocol (NFS)	Simple Network Management Protocol (SNMP)	
SESSION	MIL-STD 1780 RFC 959	MIL-STD 1781 RFC 821	MIL-STD 1782 RFC 854	RFC 783	RFC s 1014, 1057 & 1094	RFC 1157	
TRANSPORT	Transmission Control Protocol (TCP) MIL-STD 1778 RFC 793			User Datagram Protocol (UDP) RFC768			HOST TO HOST
NETWORK	Address Resolution ARP RFC 826 & RARP RFC 903		Internet Protocol (IP) MIL STD 1777 & RFC 791		Internet Control Message Protocol (ICMP) RFC 792		INTERNET
DATA LINK	Network Interface Cards: Ethernet, Token-Ring, ARCNET, MAN and WAN. RFC 894, 1042, 1201 and others						NETWORK
PHYSICAL	Transmission Media: Twisted pair cable, Coaxial Cable, Fiber Optics, Wirless Media etc. etc.						INTERFACE

Figure 1.6
TCP/IP and OSI model layers

1.6   UCA protocol

The electric industry, through the Electric Power Research Institute (EPRI) began developing the Utility Communications Architecture (UCATM) in 1988. The result is a complete set of standards allowing UCA compliant monitoring and control devices to inter-operate with utility applications (not just SCADA) in a multi-vendor environment. This protocol is sometimes (incorrectly) regarded as a replacement for DNP3. This is unlikely to happen but both will likely complement each other.

UCA is more than a communications protocol. It is a comprehensive system intended to allow utilities to purchase 'off-the-shelf' UCA compliant devices (such as pole top reclosers, transformers, pumps, valves, flow meters etc) and to have these devices automatically integrated into the SCADA and information technology systems. The industry agreed data relevant to that device will be automatically transferred to SCADA and IT systems identifying themselves as requiring it.

The 'plug and play' concepts, ease of configuration and integration, and predefined data models mean UCA will reduce the costs within the various utility industries, and ensure the success of UCA. UCA is already a fact of life for the electricity industry with many vendors offering UCA compliant products and a large installed base of systems, particularly in the US. Within the water and gas industries it will take a number of years before the data models are agreed and trialled.

Outside the utilities there is little push for UCA, although the concepts are likely to become routine in the SCADA industry.

In 1999, the Institute of Electrical and Electronic Engineers (IEEE) published the UCA Version 2 as an IEEE standard.

EPRI began a successful campaign to have the IEEE oversee UCAs continued development. As a result, the IEEE published UCA Version 2 as an IEEE standard in 1999. UCA-2 addressed the issues that were identified in field testing of the original specification, and it embraced the Internet suite of protocols, which had become widely accepted since the early days of UCA-1.

It is envisaged that DNP3 and UCA will complement each other in the near future.

2

Fundamentals of SCADA communications

Objectives

When you have completed study of this chapter you will be able to:

- Describe the essentials of the SCADA hardware and software
- Describe the key components of an RTU
- List the different communication philosophies used
- Describe the RS-232 and RS-485 standards
- List the key components of the Modbus protocol
- Explain the seven different layers of the OSI model

2.1   SCADA systems

2.1.1   Introduction and brief history of SCADA

SCADA (supervisory control and data acquisition) has been around as long as there have been control systems. The first 'SCADA' systems utilized data acquisition by means of panels of meters, lights and strip chart recorders. Supervisory control was exercised by the operator, who manually operated various control knobs. These devices were and still are used to do supervisory control and data acquisition on plants, factories and power generating facilities. The Figure 2.1 shows a sensor to panel system.

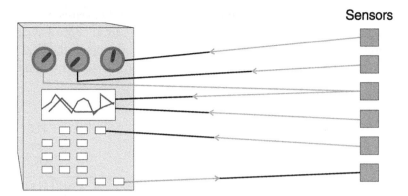

Figure 2.1
Sensors to panel using 4–20 mA or voltage

The sensor to panel type of SCADA system has the following advantages:

- It is simple, no CPUs, RAM, ROM or software programming needed
- The sensors are connected directly to the meters, switches and lights on the panel
- It could be (in most circumstances) easy and cheap to add a simple device like a switch or indicator

This approach has, however, several disadvantages:

- The amount of wire becomes unmanageable after the installation of hundreds of sensors
- The quantity and type of data is minimal and rudimentary
- Installation of additional sensors becomes progressively harder as the system grows
- Re-configuration of the system becomes extremely difficult
- Simulation using real data is not possible
- Storage of data is minimal and difficult to manage
- No off-site monitoring of data or alarms
- Someone has to watch the dials and meters 24 hours a day

2.1.2   Modern SCADA systems

In modern manufacturing and industrial processes, mining industries, public and private utilities, leisure and security industries telemetry is often needed to connect equipment and systems separated by large distances. This can range from a few meters to thousands of kilometers. Telemetry is used to send commands, programs and receive monitoring information from these remote locations.

SCADA refers to the combination of telemetry and data acquisition. SCADA encompasses the collecting of the information, transferring it back to the central site, carrying out any necessary analysis and control and then displaying that information on a number of operator screens or displays. The required control actions are then conveyed back to the process.

In the early days of data acquisition relay logic was used to control production and plant systems. With the advent of the CPU and other electronic devices, manufacturers incorporated digital electronics into relay logic equipment. The PLC or programmable logic controller is still one of the most widely used control systems in industry. As needs grew to monitor and control more devices in the plant, the PLCs were distributed and the systems became more intelligent and smaller in size. PLCs and DCS or (distributed control systems) are used as shown below.

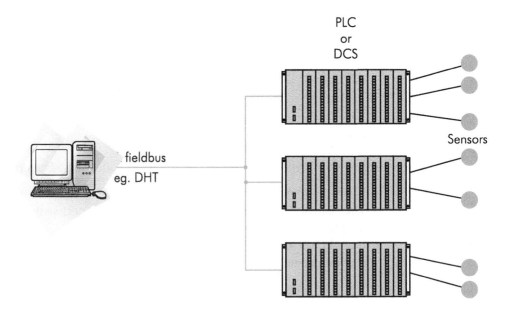

Figure 2.2
PC to PLC or DCS with a plant bus and sensors

The advantages of the PLC/DCS SCADA system are:

- The computer can record and store a very large amount of data
- The data can be displayed in any way the user requires
- Thousands of sensors over a wide area can be connected to the system
- The operator can incorporate real data simulations into the system
- Many types of data can be collected from the RTUs
- The data can be viewed from anywhere, not just on site

The disadvantages are:

- The system is more complicated than the sensor to panel type
- Different operating skills are required, such as system analysts and programmer
- With thousands of sensors there is still a lot of wire to deal with
- The operator can see only as far as the PLC

As the requirement for smaller and smarter systems grew, sensors were designed with the intelligence of PLCs and DCSs. These devices are known as IEDs (intelligent electronic devices). The IEDs are connected on a fieldbus such as Profibus, DeviceNet or Foundation Fieldbus to the PC. They include enough intelligence to acquire data, communicate to other devices and hold their part of the overall program. Each of these super smart sensors can have more than one sensor on board. Typically an IED could combine an analog input sensor, analog output, PID control, communication system and program memory in the one device.

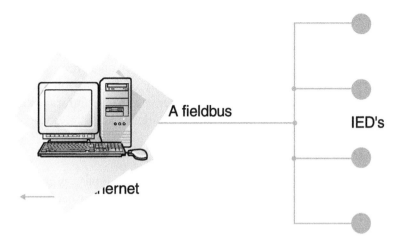

A fieldbus

IED's

..iernet

Figure 2.3
PC to IED using a fieldbus

The advantages of the PC to IED fieldbus system are:

- Minimal wiring is needed
- The operator can see down to the sensor level
- The data received from the device can include information like...serial numbers, model numbers, when it was installed and by whom
- All devices are plug and play, so installation and replacement are easy
- Smaller devices means less physical space for the data acquisition system

The disadvantages of a PC to IED system are:

- The more sophisticated system requires better trained employees
- Sensor prices are higher (but this is offset somewhat by the lack of PLCs)
- The IEDs rely more on the communication system.

2.1.3   SCADA hardware

A SCADA system consists of a number of remote terminal units (or RTUs) collecting field data and sending that data back to a master station via a communications system. The master station displays the acquired data and also allows the operator to perform remote control tasks.

The accurate and timely data allows for optimization of the plant operation and process. A further benefit is more efficient, reliable and most importantly, safer operations. This all results in a lower cost of operation compared to earlier non-automated systems.

On a more complex SCADA system there are essentially five levels or hierarchies:

- Field level instrumentation and control devices
- Marshalling terminals and RTUs
- Communications system
- The master station(s)
- The commercial data processing department computer system

The RTU provides an interface to the field analog and digital sensors situated at each remote site.

The communications system provides the pathway for communications between the master station and the remote sites. This communication system can be wire, fiber optic, radio, telephone line, microwave and possibly even satellite. Specific protocols and error detection philosophies are used for efficient and optimum transfer of data.

The master station (or sub-masters) gather data from the various RTUs and generally provide an operator interface for display of information and control of the remote sites. In large telemetry systems, sub-master sites gather information from remote sites and act as a relay back to the control master station.

2.1.4   SCADA software

SCADA software can be divided into two types, proprietary or open. Companies develop proprietary software to communicate to their hardware. These systems are sold as 'turn key' solutions. The main problem with these systems is the overwhelming reliance on the supplier of the system. Open software systems have gained popularity because of the interoperability they bring to the system. Interoperability is the ability to mix different manufacturers' equipment on the same system.

Citect and WonderWare are just two of the open software packages available on the market for SCADA systems. Some packages are now including asset management integrated within the SCADA system. The typical components of a SCADA system are indicated in the next diagram.

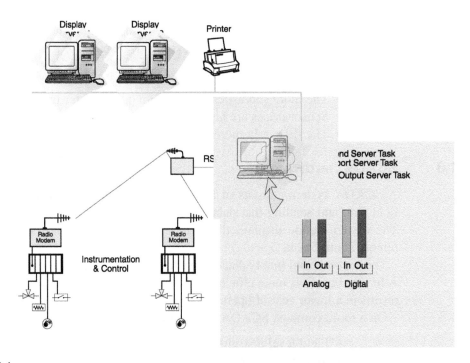

Figure 2.4
Typical SCADA system

Key features of SCADA software include:

- User interfaces
- Graphics displays
- Alarms
- Trends
- RTU (and PLC) interface
- Scalability
- Access to data
- Database
- Networking
- Fault tolerance and redundancy
- Client/server distributed processing

2.1.5   SCADA and local area networks

Local area networks (LAN) are all about sharing information and resources. To enable all the nodes on the SCADA network to share information, they must be connected by some transmission medium. The method of connection is known as the network topology.

Nodes need to share this transmission medium in such a way as to allow all nodes access to the medium without disrupting an established sender.

A LAN is a communications path between computers, file-servers, terminals, work-stations and various other intelligent peripheral equipment, which are generally referred to as devices or hosts. A LAN allows access to devices to be shared by several users, with full connectivity between all stations on the network. A LAN is usually owned and administered by a private owner and is located within a localized group of buildings.

Ethernet is the most widely used LAN today because it is cheap and easy to use. Connection of the SCADA network to the LAN allows anyone within the company with the right software and permission, to access the system. Since the data is held in a database the user can be limited to reading the information. Security issues are obviously a concern, but can be addressed.

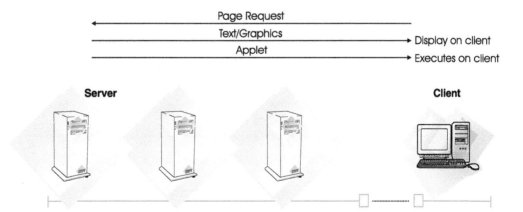

Figure 2.5
Ethernet used to transfer data on a SCADA system

Modem use in SCADA systems

Figure 2.6
PC to RTU using a modem

Often in SCADA systems the RTU (remote terminal unit (PLC, DCS or IED)) is located at a remote location. This distance can vary from tens of meters to thousands of kilometers. One of the most cost-effective ways of communicating with the RTU over long distances can be by dial-up telephone connection. With this system the devices needed are a PC, two dial-up modems and the RTU (assuming that the RTU has a built in COM port). The modems are put in the auto-answer mode and the RTU can dial into the PC or the PC can dial the RTU. The software to do this is readily available from RTU manufacturers. The modems can be bought off the shelf at the local computer store.

Line modems are used to connect RTUs to a network over a pair of wires. These systems are usually fairly short (up to 1 kilometer) and use FSK (frequency shift keying) to communicate. Line modems are used to communicate to RTUs when RS-232 or RS-485 communication systems are not practical. The bit rates used on this type of system are usually slow, 1200 to 9600 bps.

2.1.6 Computer sites and troubleshooting

Computers and RTUs usually run without problems for a long time if left to themselves. Maintenance tasks could include daily, weekly, monthly or annual checks. When maintenance is necessary, the technician or engineer may need to check the following equipment on a regular basis.

- The RTU and component modules
- Analog input modules
- Digital input module
- Interface from RTU to PLC (RS-232/RS-485)
- Privately owned cable
- Switched telephone line
- Analog or digital data links
- The master sites
- The central site
- The operator station and software

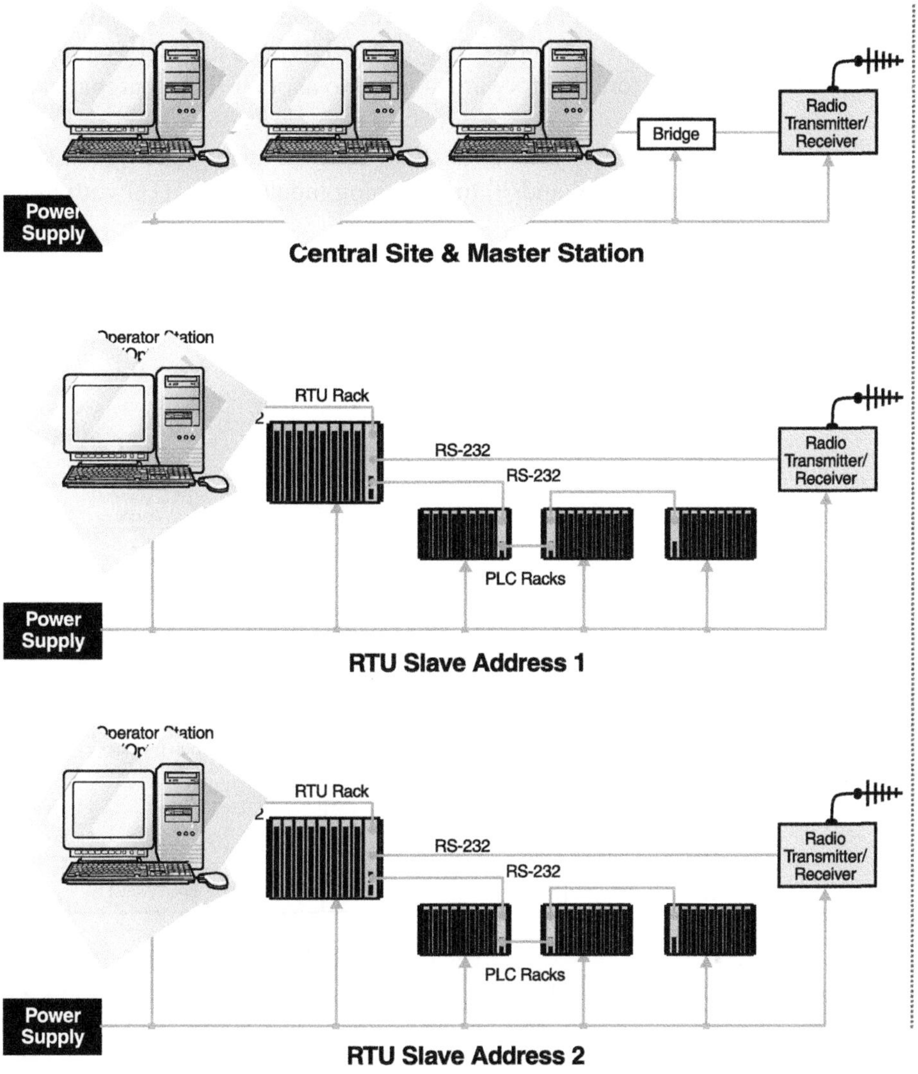

Figure 2.7
Components that could need maintenance in a SCADA system

2.2 Remote terminal units

2.2.1 Introduction

An RTU (sometimes referred to as a remote telemetry unit or remote terminal unit) is a stand-alone data acquisition and control unit, generally microprocessor based, that monitors and controls equipment at a remote location. Its primary task is to control and acquire data from process equipment at the remote location and to transfer this data back to a central station. It generally also has the facility for having its configuration and control programs dynamically downloaded from some central station. Although, traditionally, the RTU communicates back to some central station, it is also possible to communicate on a peer-to-peer basis with other RTUs. The RTU can also act as a relay station (sometimes referred to as a store and forward station) to another RTU that may not be accessible from the central station.

Small RTUs generally have less than 10 to 20 analog and digital signals; medium sized RTUs have 100 digital and 30 to 40 analog inputs. Any RTU with more inputs is referred to as 'large'.

A typical RTU configuration is shown in the figure below:

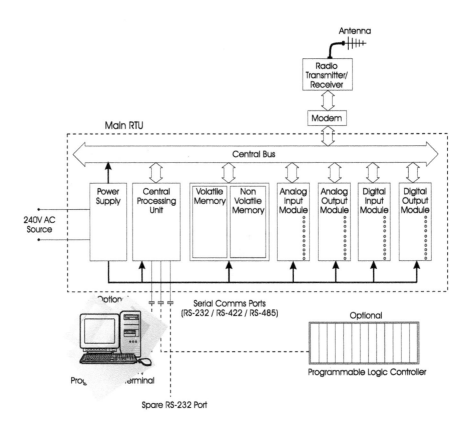

Figure 2.8
Typical RTU hardware structure

Typical RTU hardware modules include a control processor and associated memory, analog inputs, analog outputs, counter inputs, digital inputs, digital outputs, communication interface(s), power supply, as well as an RTU rack and enclosure.

2.2.2 Control processor unit (or CPU)

This is generally microprocessor based (16- or 32-bit) eg 68302 or 80386, and the total memory capacity of 256 kbytes (expandable to 4 Mbytes) broken into three types namely EPROM, RAM and Flash/EEPROM.

Communication ports – typically two or three ports (RS-232/RS-422/RS-485) provide an interface to diagnostics terminals, operator stations, or communications Ethernet link to a central site (e.g. by modem).

Diagnostic LEDs provided on the control unit simplify troubleshooting and diagnosis of problems such as CPU or I/O module failure.

A real-time clock with full calendar is useful for accurate time stamping of events.

A watchdog timer provides a check that the RTU program is executing regularly. The RTU program regularly resets the watchdog time and if this is not done within a certain time-out period the watchdog timer flags an error condition (and can reset the CPU).

2.2.3 Analog input modules

There are five main components making up an Analog input module. They are the input multiplexer, the input signal amplifier, the sample and hold circuit, the A/D converter and the bus interface and board timing system.

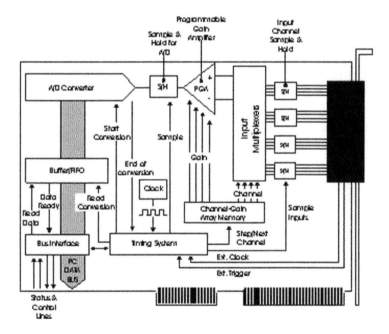

Figure 2.9
Block diagram of a typical analog input module

A multiplexer is a device that samples several (usually 16) analog inputs in turn and switches each to the output in sequence. The output generally goes to an analog to digital converter (also called an A/D converter or ADC), eliminating the need for a converter on each input channel. This can result in considerable cost savings.

Where low-level voltages need to be digitized, they must be amplified to match the input range of the board's A/D converter. If a low-level signal is fed directly into a board without amplification, a loss of precision will be the result. Some boards provide on-board amplification (or gain), while those with a programmable gain amplifier (PGA) make it possible to select – via software – different gains for different channels, for a series of conversions.

Most A/D converters require a fixed time during which the input signal remains constant (the aperture time) in order to perform an A/D conversion. Therefore, a sample-and-hold device is used on the input to the A/D converter. It samples the output signal from the multiplexer or gain amplifier very quickly and holds it constant for the A/D's aperture time.

The A/D converter is the heart of the module. Its function is to measure an input analog voltage and to output a digital code corresponding to the input voltage. There are several types of A/D converters, but the ones used most frequently are the integrating A/Ds and the successive approximation A/Ds.

Integrating (or dual slope) A/Ds are used for very low frequency applications (a few hundred hertz maximum) and may have very high accuracy and precision (e.g. 22 bit). They are found in thermocouple and RTD modules. Other advantages include very low cost and immunity to noise and mains pickup due to the integrating and dual slope nature of the A/D converter.

Successive approximation A/Ds allow much higher sampling rates (up to a few hundred kHz with 12 bits is possible) while still being reasonable in cost. The conversion algorithm is similar to that of a binary search, where the A/D starts by comparing the input with a voltage (generated by an internal D/A converter), corresponding to half of the full-scale range. If the input is in the lower half the first digit is zero and the A/D repeats this comparison using the lower half of the input range. If the voltage had been in the upper half, the first digit would have been 1 and the next comparison in the upper half of the input range. This dividing of the remaining fraction of the input range in half and comparing to the input voltage continues until the specified number of bits of accuracy have been obtained.

Typical analog input modules feature:

- 8 or 16 analog inputs
- Resolution of 8 or 12 bits
- Range of 4–20 mA (other possibilities are 0–20 mA/±10 volts/0–10 volts)
- Input resistance typically 240 kohm to 1 Mohm
- Conversion rates typically 10 microseconds to 30 milliseconds

Inputs are preferably differential rather than single ended for better noise immunity.

2.2.4 Analog output modules

Analog output modules perform the opposite function to that of the analog input modules by converting a digital value (as supplied by the CPU) to an analog value by means of a digital to analog converter (also called a D/A converter or DAC).

Typically the analog output module has the following features:

- 8 analog outputs
- Resolution of 8 or 12 bits
- Conversion rate from 10 μ seconds to 30 milliseconds
- Outputs ranging from 4–20 mA/± 10 volts/0 to 10 volts

Care has to be taken here on ensuring the load resistance is not lower than specified (typically 50 kohm) or the voltage drop will be excessive.

Analog output module designs generally prefer to provide voltage outputs rather than current output (unless power is provided externally), as this places lower power requirements on the backplane.

2.2.5 Digital input modules

These are used to indicate such items as status and alarm signals. Most digital input boards provide groups of 8, 16 or 32 inputs per board.

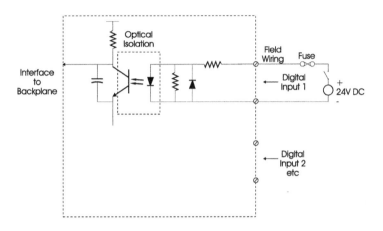

Figure 2.10
Digital input circuit with flow chart of operation

2.2.6 Digital counter or accumulator modules

There are many applications where a pulse-input module is required – for example from a metering panel. This can be a contact closure signal or if the pulse frequency is high enough – solid state relay signals. Pulse input signals are normally dry contacts i.e. the power is provided from the RTU power supply rather than the actual pulse source.

Optical isolation is useful to minimize the effect of externally generated noise. The size of the accumulator is important when considering the number of pulses that will be counted, before transferring the data to another memory location. For example, a 12-bit register has the capacity for 4096 counts whereas 16 bits gives 65 536 pulses.

Typical specifications here are:

- 4 counter inputs
- Four 16-bit counters (65 536 counts per counter input)
- Count frequency up to 20 kHz range

Duty cycle preferably 50% (ratio of mark to space) for the upper count frequency limits.

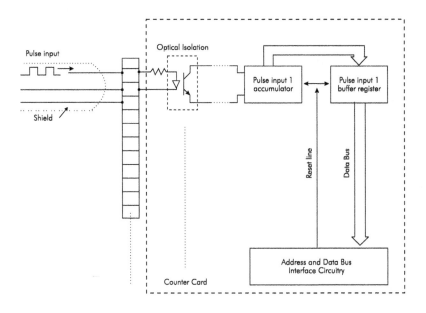

Figure 2.11
Pulse input module

2.2.7   Digital output module

A digital output module drives an output voltage at each of the appropriate output channels with three approaches possible viz. Triac switching, Reed relay switching or TTL voltage outputs.

Typical digital output module specs are:

- 8 digital outputs
- 240 V AC/24 V DC (0.5 amp to 2.0 amp) outputs
- Associated LED indicator for each output to indicate current status
- Optical isolation or dry relay contact for each output

2.2.8   Communication interfaces

The modern RTU should be flexible enough to handle multiple communication media such as:

- RS-232/RS-442/RS-485
- Ethernet
- Dial up telephone lines/dedicated landlines
- Microwave/MUX
- Satellite
- X.25 packet protocols
- Radio via trunked/VHF/UHF/900 MHz

Interestingly enough, the more challenging design for RTUs is the radio communication interface. The landline interface is considered to be an easier design problem.

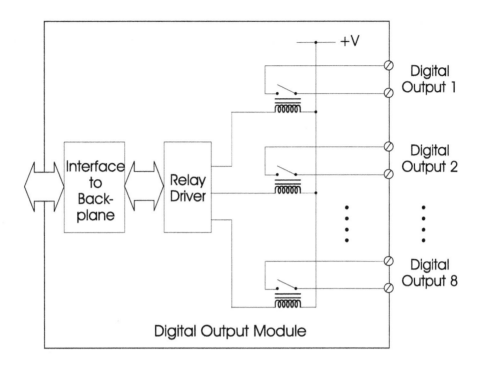

Figure 2.12
Digital output module

2.2.9   Power supply module

The RTU should be able to operate from 110/240 V AC ± 10% 50 Hz or 12/24/48 V DC ± 10% typically. Batteries that should be provided are lead acid or nickel cadmium. Typical requirements here are for 20-hour standby operation and a recharging time of 12 hours for a fully discharged battery at 25°C. Cabinets for batteries are normally rated to IP 52 for internal mounting and IP 56 for external mounting.

2.3   PLCs used as RTUs

A PLC or programmable logic controller is a computer based solid state device that controls industrial equipment and processes. It was initially designed to perform the logic functions executed by relays, drum switches and mechanical timer/counters. Analog control is now a standard part of the PLC operation as well.

The advantage of a PLC over commercially available RTUs is that it can be used in a general-purpose role and can easily be setup for a variety of different functions. PLCs are also physically compact and take up far less space than alternative solutions. However PLCs may not be suitable for specialized requirements such as for radio telemetry applications.

2.4 The master station

A master station has two main functions namely (1) to obtain field data periodically from RTUs and sub-master stations and (2) to control remote devices through the operator station.

There are various combinations of systems possible, as indicated in the diagram below.
Alternative 1

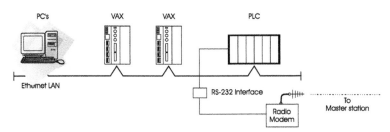

Alternative 2

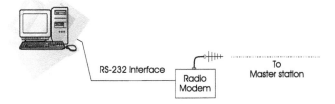

Alternative 3

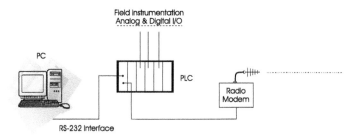

Figure 2.13
Various approaches possible for the master station

It may also be necessary to set up a sub-master station. This is necessary to control sites within a specific region. The sub-master station has the following functions:

- Acquire data from RTUs within the region
- Log and display this data on a local operator station
- Pass data back to the master station
- Pass on control requests from the master station to the RTUs in its region

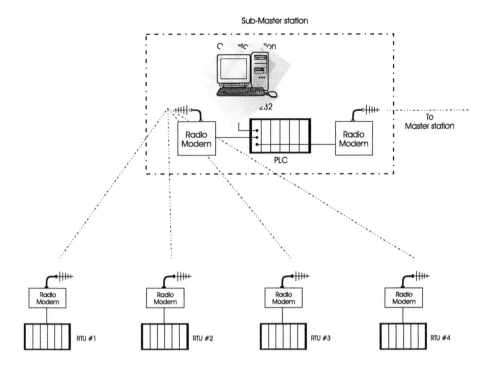

Figure 2.14
Sub-master architecture

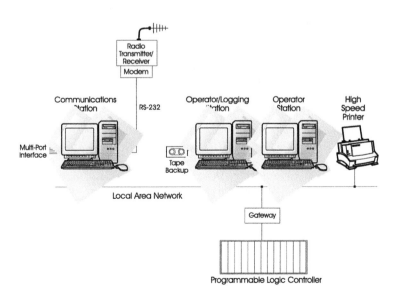

Figure 2.15
Typical structure of the master station

The master station has the following typical functions:

- Establishment of communications, which involves configuring each RTU, initializing each RTU with input/output parameters, as well as downloading control and data acquisition programs to the RTU
- Operation of the communications link, which involves (in a master–slave arrangement) polling each RTU for data and writing to the RTU, logging alarms and events to hard disk (and operator display if necessary), as well as linking inputs and outputs at different RTUs automatically
- Diagnostics, which involve accurate diagnostic information on failure of RTU and possible problems, as well as predicting potential problems such as data overloads

There are three components to the master station software, namely the operating system software, the system SCADA software (suitably configured) and the SCADA application software. There is also the necessary firmware (such as BIOS) which acts as an interface between the operating system and the computer system hardware.

The operating system software will not be discussed further here. Good examples of these are DOS, Windows 95/98/2000, Windows NT, LINUX and UNIX.

The System SCADA software refers to the software put together by the particular SCADA system vendor and then configured by a particular user. Generally it consists of four main modules namely data acquisition, control, archiving (or database storage) and the man machine interface (MMI) which is more politically correctly known as the human machine interface.

2.5   Communication architectures

There are three main physical communication architectures that can be combined in one communication system. They are:

2.5.1   Point-to-point architecture

This is the simplest configuration, where data is exchanged between two stations only. One station can be setup as the master and one as the slave. It is possible for both stations to communicate in full-duplex mode (transmitting and receiving on two separate frequencies) or half-duplex with only one frequency.

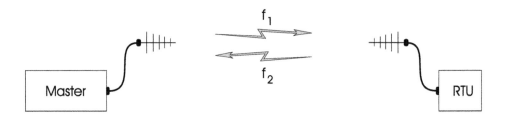

Figure 2.16
Point-to-point (two stations)

2.5.2 Multi-point architecture (Multiple stations)

In this configuration there is generally one master and multiple slaves. Normally data is passed between the master and each of the slaves. If two slaves need to transfer data between each other they would do so through the master that acts as arbitrator or moderator.

Alternatively it is possible for all the stations to act in a peer-to-peer relationship. This is a more complex arrangement requiring sophisticated protocols to handle collisions between two different stations wanting to transmit at the same time.

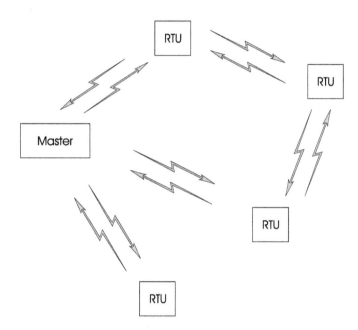

Figure 2.17
Multiple stations

2.5.3 Relay station architecture

There are two possibilities here, namely store and forward or talk-through repeaters.

Store and forward relay operation can be a component of the other approaches discussed above. This takes place where a station retransmits messages to another station that is out of the range of the master station. This intermediate station is often called a store and forward relay station.

There is no simultaneous transmission of the message by the store and forward relay station. It first receives and stores the message, then retransmits it on the same frequency as the one on which it was received from the master station.

This approach is slower than a talk-through repeater as each message has to be sent twice. The advantages are considerable savings in mast heights and costs.

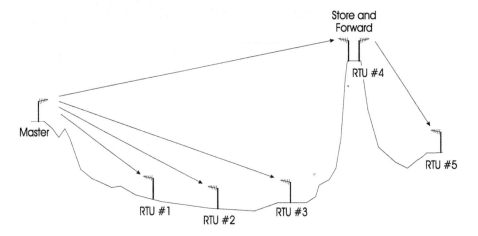

Figurse 2.18
Store and forward station

The use of talk-through repeaters is the generally preferred way of increasing the radio system's range. The repeater, situated on a geographically high point, re-transmits the radio signal received simultaneously on a different frequency. This implies that all the stations repeating the signal must receive and transmit on different frequencies.

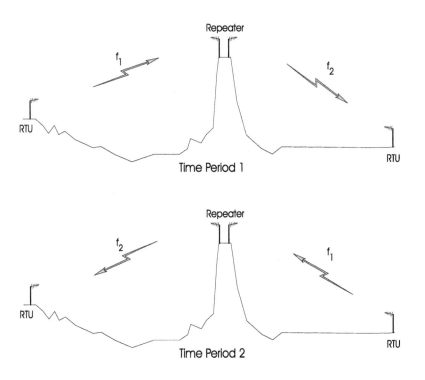

Figure 2.19
Talk through repeaters

2.6 Communication philosophies

There are two commonly used options here, namely a polled approach or a contention approach.

2.6.1 Polled (master–slave)

This can be used in a point-to-point or multi-point configuration and is probably the simplest philosophy to use. The master is in total control of the communication system and makes regular (repetitive) requests for data to be transferred to and from each one of a number of slaves. The slaves do not initiate the transactions but rely on the master. It is essentially a half-duplex approach where the slave only responds on a request from the master. If a slave does not respond in a defined time, the master then retries (typically up to three times) and then marks the slave as unserviceable before trying the next slave node in the sequence. It is possible to retry the unserviceable slave again on the next cycle of polling.

The advantages of this approach are:

- The software is simple and reliable due to the simplicity of the philosophy
- Link failure between the master and a slave node is detected quickly
- No collisions can occur on the network; hence the data throughput is predictable and constant

For heavily loaded systems with each node having constant data transfer requirements this gives a predictable and efficient system.

The disadvantages are:

- Variations in the data transfer requirements of each slave cannot be handled
- Interrupt type requests from a slave requesting urgent action cannot be handled (as the master may be processing some other slave)
- Systems that are lightly loaded with minimum data changes from a slave are quite inefficient and unnecessarily slow
- Slaves needing to communicate with each other have to do so through the master with added complexity in the design of the master station

Two applications of the polled approach are shown in the following implementations.

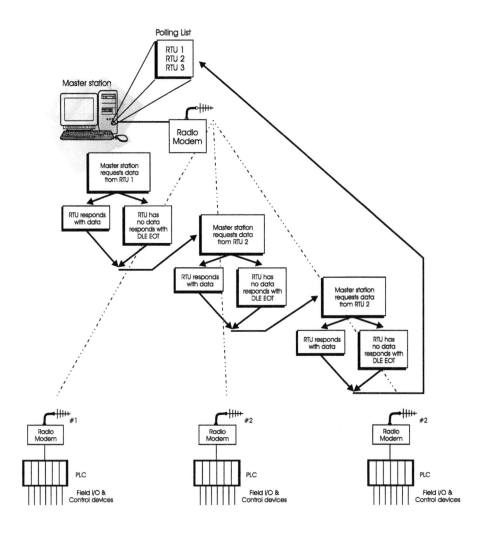

Figure 2.20
Illustration of polling techniques for master station and RTUs

An example of a high and normal priority arrangement is given in the diagram below.

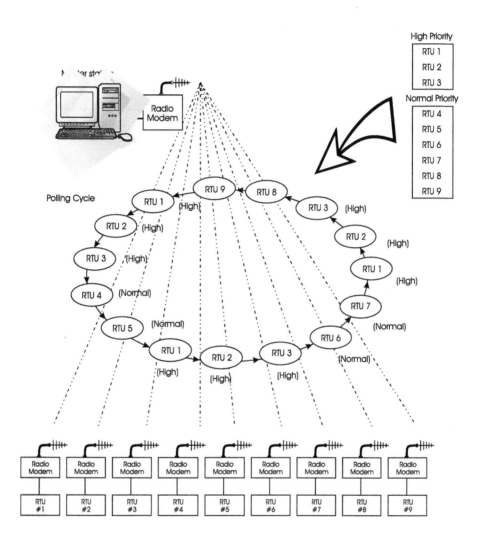

Figure 2.21
High and normal priority arrangement

A priority message sent from the master station can override the standard polling sequence. In this case the master station completes the poll request for a specific station and then sends out the priority request to a specific station (which was not necessarily next in the polling sequence). It then waits a predefined time for a response from this RTU or continues with polling a few more stations in the polling sequence, before requesting a reply from this specific station.

Care should be taken in defining the optimum values for the timers – e.g. a satellite link may have significant delays compared to a leased line communications system.

2.6.2   Contention (peer-to-peer)

A contention method such as carrier sense with multiple access/collision detection (CSMA/CD) can be used in order to control communications. There is no controlling master and individual stations have to contend (compete) for access to the transmission medium. In such an arrangement collisions are unavoidable and stations have to contend with them.

RTU to RTU communication

In a situation where an RTU wants to communicate with another RTU, a technique used is to respond to a poll by the master station with a message with a destination address other than that of the master station.

The master station will then examine the destination address field of the message received from the RTU and if it does not observe its own, retransmits it onto the appropriate remote station.

This approach can be used in a master slave network or a group of stations all with equal status.

The only attempt made in order to avoid collisions is to listen to the medium before transmitting. The systems rely on recovery methods to handle collision problems. Typically these systems are very effective at low capacity rates; as soon as the traffic rises to over 30% of the channel capacity there is an avalanche-type collapse of the system and communications becomes unreliable and erratic.

This technique is used solely on networks where all nodes have access to the same media (within radio range or on a common cable link).

Exception reporting (event reporting)

A technique to reduce the unnecessary transfer of data is to use some form of exception reporting. This approach is popular with the CSMA/CD philosophy but it could also offer a solution for the polled approach where there is a considerable amount of data to transfer from each slave.

The remote station monitors its own inputs for a change of state or data. Only when there is a change of state, the remote station writes a block of data to the master station.

Each analog or digital point that has to be reported back to the central master station has a set of exception reporting parameters associated with it, such as high and low alarm limits of individual analog values.

Polling plus CSMA/CD with exception reporting

A practical approach to combining all the approaches discussed previously is to use the concept of a slot time for each station.

Assume that the architecture includes a master and a number of slaves that need to communicate with the master station. There is no communication between slaves required (except possibly through the master).

The time each station is allowed to transmit is called a slot time. There are two types of slots:

- A slave (or a few slaves) transmitting to a master
- A master transmitting to a slave

A slot time is calculated as the sum of the maximums of modem setup time (e.g. 30 milliseconds) plus radio transmit time (e.g. 100 milliseconds) plus time for protocol message (e.g. 58 milliseconds) plus muting time (e.g. 25 milliseconds) for each transmitter. Typical times are given in brackets.

The master commences operations by polling each slave in turn. Each slave will synchronize in on the master message and will transmit an acknowledge message. Hereafter, slaves will only transmit (using CSMA/CD) during the master receiving time slots, which alternate with the master transmit time slots. On a change in state detected by a slave node, it will transmit the data on the first available master receive time slot. If two remote slaves try to transmit in the same time slot, the message will be corrupted and the slaves will not receive a response from the master. The slaves will then select, at random, a subsequent master receiver time slot and attempt a retransmission of the message. If the master continues to get corrupted messages, it may elect to do a complete poll of all the remote slaves as the CSMA/CD type mechanism is possibly breaking down due to excessive traffic.

2.7   Basic standards: RS-232 and RS-485

RS-232 and RS-485 form the key element in transferring digital information between the RTUs (or operator terminals), and the modems which convert the digital information to the appropriate analog form suitable for transmission over greater distances.

An interface standard defines the electrical and mechanical details that allow communications equipment from different manufacturers to be connected together and to function efficiently. It should be emphasized that RS-232, and the other related EIA standards, define only the electrical and mechanical details of the interface and do not define a protocol.

These standards were designed primarily to transport digital data from one point to another. The RS-232 standard was initially designed to connect digital computer equipment to a modem where the data would then be converted into an analog form suitable for transmission over greater distances. RS-485 has the ability to transfer digital data over distances of over 1200 m.

The most popular (but probably technically the most inferior) of the RS standards is the RS-232C standard. This will be discussed first. The correct representation of RS-232E and RS-485 is actually EIA-232E and EIA-485; however the more popular RS prefix is used in this manual.

2.7.1   RS-232

The RS-232C interface standard for serial data communication (CCITT V.24 Interface Standard) defines the *'Interface between Data Terminal Equipment (DTE) and Data Communications Equipment (DCE) Employing Serial Binary Data Interchange'*.

It was issued in the USA in 1969 by the Engineering Department of the EIA, in cooperation with Bell Laboratories and the leading manufacturers of communications equipment, to clearly define the interface requirements when connecting data terminals to the Bell telephone system. The current revision is EIA-232E (1991).

The RS-232 standard consists of 3 major parts, which define:

- The electrical signal characteristics such as the voltage levels and grounding characteristics of the interchange signals and associated circuitry
- The interface mechanical characteristics of the mechanical interface between DTE and DCE, and
- The functional description of the interchange circuits, such as the function of the data, timing and control signals used at the interface between DTE and DCE

2.7.2 Electrical signal characteristics

The RS-232 interface standard is designed for the connection of two devices called:

- **DTE**
  Data terminal equipment (e.g. a computer or printer). A DTE device communicates with a DCE device and transmits data on pin 2 and receives data on pin 3 on a 25-pin D-type connector

- **DCE**
  Data communications equipment, now also called data circuit-terminating equipment in RS-232D/E (e.g. a computer or Modem). A DCE device transmits data between the DTE and a physical data communications link (e.g. telephone system). It transmits data on pin 3 and receives data on pin 2 on a 25-pin D-type connector

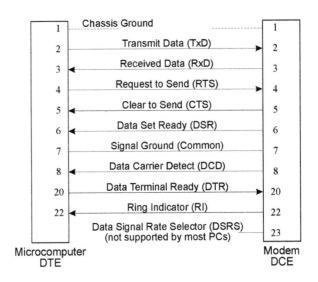

Figure 2.22
The connections between the DTE and DCE

At the RS-232 receiver, the following signal voltage levels are specified:

	Voltage Between		
Logic 0	+3V	And	+25V
Logic 1	-3V	And	-25V
Undefined	-3V	And	+3V

Table 2.1
RS-232 receiver voltages

The RS-232 transmitter has to produce a slightly higher voltage level in the range of +5 volts to +25 volts and -5 volts to -25 volts to overcome the voltage drop along the line. In practice most transmitters operate at voltages between 5 volts and 12 volts.

The RS-232 standard defines twenty-five electrical connections, which are each described later. The electrical connections are divided into the four groups namely data lines, control lines, timing lines and special secondary lines.

The data lines are used for the transfer of data. Pins 2 and 3 are used for this purpose. Data flow is designated from the perspective of the DTE interface, hence the 'transmit line', on which the DTE transmits (and DCE receives), is associated with pin 2 at the DTE end and pin 2 at the DCE end. The 'receive line', on which the DTE receives (and DCE transmits), is associated with pin 3 at the DTE end and pin 3 at the DCE end. Pin 7 is the common return line for the transmit and receive data lines.

The control lines are used for interactive device control, commonly known as 'hardware handshaking' and regulate the way in which data flows across the interface. The four most commonly used control lines are:

- RTS – Request to send
- CTS – Clear to send
- DSR – Data set ready (or DCE ready in RS-232D/E)
- DTR – Data terminal ready (or DTE ready in RS-232D/E)

Note that the handshake lines operate in the opposite voltage sense to the data lines. When a control line is active (logic=1), the voltage is in the range +3 to +25 volts and when deactivated (logic=0), the voltage is zero or negative.

The typical structure of the data frame used for RS-232 applications is as follows. The first bit is the start bit, followed by the data bits, with the least significant bit first. The data bits may be in a packet of 5, 6, 7 or 8 bits. After the last data bit, there is an optional parity bit (even, odd or none) followed by a stop bit. Following the stop bit, there is a marking state of 1-, 1½- or 2-bit periods, to indicate that the sequence of data bits is complete, before the next frame can be sent.

The capacitance (maximum of 2500 pF) in the connecting cable limits the maximum distance of transmission with RS-232 to typically 50 m.

2.7.3 Interface mechanical characteristics

Although not specified by RS-232C, the DB-25 connector (25-pin, D-type) and the DB-9 connector (9-pin D-type) have become so closely associated with RS-232 that they have become the *de facto* standard.

The pin allocation for the DB-9 connector is not the same as for the DB-25; but is as follows:

Data transmit	:	Pin 3
Data receive	:	Pin 2
Signal common	:	Pin 5

2.7.4 Functional description of the interchange circuits

The EIA circuit functions are defined, with reference to the DTE, as follows:

Pin 1 – Protective ground (shield)

A connection is seldom made between the protective ground pins at each end. Their purpose is to prevent hazardous voltages, by ensuring that the DTE and DCE chassis are at the same potential at both ends. There is, however, a danger that a path could be established for circulating earth currents. Consequently the cable shield is usually connected at one end only.

Pin 2 – Transmitted data (TXD)

This line carries serial data from pin 2 on the DTE to pin 2 on the DCE. The line is held at MARK (or a negative voltage) during periods of line idle.

Pin 3 – Received data (RXD)

This line carries serial data from pin 3 on the DCE to pin 3 on the DTE.

Pin 4 – Request to send (RTS)

See Clear to send.

Pin 5 – Clear to send (CTS)

When a half-duplex modem is receiving, the DTE keeps RTS inhibited. When it becomes the DTE's turn to transmit, it advises the modem by asserting the RTS pin. When the modem asserts the CTS it informs the DTE that it is now safe to send data. The procedure is reversed when switching from transmit to receive.

Pin 6 – Data set ready (DSR)

This is also called DCE ready. In the answer mode, the answer tone and the DSR are asserted two seconds after the telephone goes off hook.

Pin 7 – Signal ground (common)

This is the common return line for the data transmit and receive signals. The connection, pin 7 to pin 7 between the two ends, is always made.

Pin 8 – Data carrier detect (DCD)

This is also called the received line signal detector. Pin 8 is asserted by the modem when it receives a remote carrier and remains asserted for the duration of the link.

Pin 20 – DTE ready (or data terminal ready)

DTE ready enables, but does not cause, the modem to switch onto the line. In originate mode, DTE ready must be asserted in order to auto dial. In answer mode, DTE ready must be asserted to auto answer.

Pin 22 – Ring indicator

This pin is asserted during a ring on the line.

Pin 23 – Data signal rate selector (DSRS)

When two data rates are possible, the higher is selected by asserting pin 23.

2.7.5 The sequence of asynchronous operation of the RS-232 interface

Asynchronous operation is arguably the more common approach when using RS-232 and will be examined in this section using the more complex half-duplex data interchange. It should be noted that the half-duplex description is given as it encompasses that of full-duplex operation.

Figure 2.23 gives a graphical description of the operation with the initiating user terminal (or DTE) and its associated modem (or DCE) on the left of the diagram and the remote computer and its modem on the right.

The following sequence of steps occur:

- The initiating user manually dials the number of the remote computer
- The receiving modem asserts the ring indicator line (RI – pin 22) in a pulsed ON/OFF fashion as per the ringing tone. The remote computer already has its data terminal ready line (or DTR – pin 20) asserted to indicate that it is ready to receive calls. (Alternatively the remote computer may assert the DTR line after a few rings.) The remote computer then sets its request to send line (RTS – pin 4) to ON
- The receiving modem then answers the telephone and transmits a carrier signal to the initiating end. It also asserts the DCE ready (DSR – pin 6) after a few seconds
- The initiating modem then asserts the data carrier detect line (DCD – pin 8). The initiating terminal asserts its DTR (if it is not already high). The modem then responds by asserting its data set ready line (DSR – pin 6)
- The receiving modem then asserts its clear to send line (CTS – pin 5) which permits the transfer of data from the remote computer to the initiating side
- Data is then transferred from the receiving DTE on pin 2 (transmitted data) to the receiving modem. The receiving remote computer can then transmit a short message to indicate to the originating terminal that it can proceed with the data transfer. The originating modem transmits the data to the originating terminal on pin 3

- The receiving terminal then sets its request to send line (RTS – pin 4) to OFF. The receiving modem then sets its clear to send line (CTS – pin 5) to OFF as well
- The receiving modem then switches its carrier signal OFF
- The originating terminal detects that the data carrier detect signal has been switched OFF on the originating modem and then switches its RTS line to the ON state. The originating modem then indicates that transmission can proceed by setting its CTS line to ON
- Transmission of data then proceeds from the originating terminal to the remote computer
- When the interchange is complete, both carriers are switched OFF (and in many cases the DTR is set to OFF). This means that the CTS, RTS and DCE ready (or DSR) lines are set to OFF

Note that full-duplex operation requires that transmission and reception occur simultaneously. In this case there is no RTS/CTS interaction at either end. The RTS line and CTS line are left ON with a carrier to the remote computer.

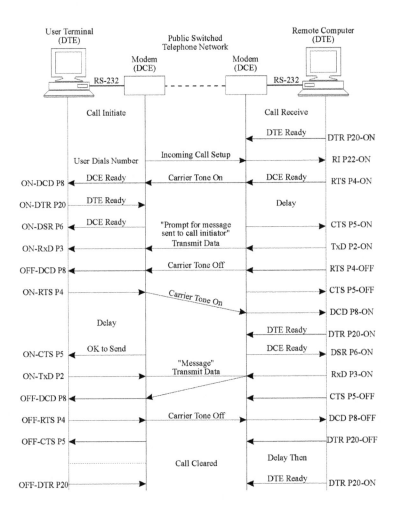

Figure 2.23
Typical operation of a half-duplex RS-232 data interchange

2.7.6   Synchronous communications

The major difference between asynchronous and synchronous communications with modems is the need for timing signals.

A synchronous modem outputs a square wave on pin 15 of the RS-232 DB-25 connector. This pin 15 is called the transmit clock pin or more formally the DCE transmitter signal element timing pin. This square wave is set to the frequency of the modem's bit rate. The attached personal computer (the DTE) then synchronizes its transmission of data from pin 2 to the modem.

There are two interchange circuits that can be employed to change the operation of the attached communications device.

These are:

Signal quality detector (CG, pin 21)

If there is high probability of error in the received data to the modem because of poor signal quality this line is set to OFF.

Data signal rate selector (CH/CI, pin 23)

If the signal quality detector pin indicates that the quality of the signal is unacceptable (i.e. it is set to OFF), the terminal may set the pin 23 to ON to select a higher data rate; or OFF to select a lower data rate. This is called the CH circuit.

If, however, the modem selects the data rate and advises the terminal on pin 23 (ON or OFF), the circuit is known as circuit CI.

Disadvantages of the RS-232 standard

System designers have tended to look for alternative approaches (such as the RS-422 and RS-485 standards) because of the following limitations of RS-232:

- The restriction of point-to-point communications is a drawback when many devices have to be multidropped together
- The distance limitation (typically 50 meters) is a limitation when distances of 1000 m are needed
- The 20 kbps baud rate is too slow for many applications
- The voltages of –3 to –25 volts and +3 to +25 volts are not compatible with many modern power supplies (in computers) of +5 and +12 volt
- The standard is an example of an unbalanced standard with high noise susceptibility

2.7.7   RS-485

RS-485 permits multidrop network connection on two wires and provides for reliable serial data communication for:

- Distances of up to 1200 m
- Data rates of up to 10 Mbps

Up to 32 line drivers permitted on the same line and up to 32 line receivers are permitted on the same line.

The line voltages range between –1.5 V to –6 V for logic '1' and +1.5 V to +6 V for Logic '0'. As with RS-422, the line driver for the RS-485 interface produces a 5-volt differential voltage on two wires. For full-duplex systems, five wires are required. For a half-duplex system, only three wires are required. The additional wire (5 rather than 4, 3 rather than 2) is to provide a common reference voltage for all devices on the system.

The major enhancement of RS-485 is that a line driver can operate in three states (called tri-state operation), namely logic '0', logic '1' and 'high-impedance', where it draws virtually no current and appears not to be present on the line. This latter state is known as the 'disabled' state and can be initiated by a signal on a control pin on the line driver integrated circuit. This allows 'multidrop' operation, where up to 32 transmitters can be connected on the same line, although only one can be active at any one time. Each terminal in a multidrop system must therefore be allocated a unique address to avoid any conflict with other devices on the system. RS-485 includes current limiting in cases where contention occurs.

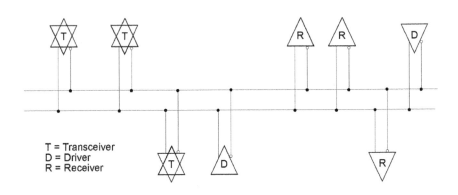

Figure 2.24
The RS-485 multi-point interface standard

2.8 SCADA protocols

Two protocols commonly used for SCADA applications will be discussed here, namely HDLC and MODBUS. They are increasingly being replaced by DNP3, Ethernet and TCP/IP protocol.

2.8.1 HDLC

HDLC (high level data link control) has been defined by the International Standards Organization for use on both multi-point and point-to-point links. Other descriptions of it include SDLC (synchronous data link control used by IBM) and ADCCP (advanced data communication control procedure used by ANSI). HDLC will be the reference used throughout the following text. In contrast to the BSC, a character-based protocol, HDLC is a bit-based protocol. It is interesting to note that it is a predecessor to the local area network protocols such as Ethernet.

The two most common modes of operation for HDLC are:

- Unbalanced normal response mode (NRM). This is used only on a primary (or master) station initiating all transactions
- Asynchronous balanced mode (ABM). In this mode each node has equal status and can act as either a primary or secondary node

HDLC frame format

The standard format is indicated in Figure 2.25. The three different classes of frames used are as follows:

- **Unnumbered frames**
  Used for setting up the link or connection and to define whether NRM or ABM is to be used. They are called unnumbered frames because no sequence numbers are included

- **Information frames**
  Used to convey the actual data from one node to another

- **Supervisory frames**
  Used for flow control and error control purposes. They indicate whether the secondary station is available to receive the information frames; they are also used to acknowledge the frames. There are two forms of error control used: a selective retransmission procedure because of an error, or a request to transmit a number of previous frames

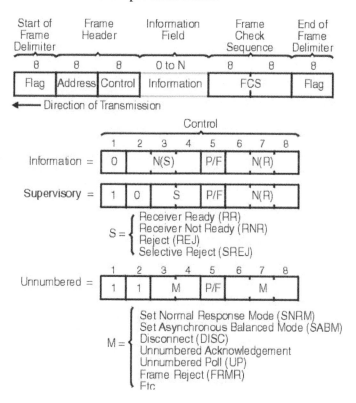

Figure 2.25
HDLC frame format and types

Frame contents

The frame contents are as follows:

- The flag character is a byte with the value 01111110. To ensure that the receiver always knows that the character it receives is unique (rather than merely some other character in the sequence), a procedure called zero insertion is adopted. This requires the transmitter to insert a 0 after a sequence of five 1s in the text, so that the flag character can never appear in the message text. The receiver removes the inserted zeros
- The frame check sequence (FCS) uses the CRC-CCITT methodology, except that sixteen 1s are added to the tail of the message before the CRC calculation proceeds, and the remainder is inverted
- The address field can contain one of three types of address for the request or response messages to or from the secondary node. They are:
    - Standard secondary address
    - Group addresses for groups of nodes on the network
    - Broadcast addresses for all nodes on the network (here the address contains all 1s)
- Where there are a large number of secondaries on the network, the address field can be extended beyond eight bits by encoding the least significant bit as a 1. This then indicates that there is another byte to follow in the address field

Note: The send and receive sequence numbers are important for the detection and correction of errors in the messages. The P/F bit is the poll/final bit and when set to 1 indicates to the receiver that it must respond or acknowledge this frame (again with the P/F bit set to 1).

2.8.2   Protocol operation

A typical sequence of operations for a multidrop link is given below:

- The primary node sends a normal response mode frame, with the P/F bit set to 1, together with the address of the secondary node
- The secondary node responds with an unnumbered acknowledgment with the P/F bit set to 1. If the receiving node is unable to accept the setup command, a disconnected mode frame is returned instead
- Data is transferred with the information frames
- The primary node sends an unnumbered frame containing a disconnect in the control field
- The secondary node responds with an unnumbered acknowledgment

A similar approach is followed for a point-to-point link using asynchronous balanced mode, except that both nodes can initiate the setting up of the link and the transfer of information frames, and the clearing of the point-to-point link.

The following differences also apply:

- When the secondary node transfers the data, it transmits the data as a sequence of information frames with the P/F bit set to 1 in the final frame of the sequence
- In NRM mode, if the secondary node has no further data to transfer, it responds with a receiver not ready frame with the P/F bit set to 1

2.8.3   Error control/flow control

For a half-duplex exchange of information frames, error control is by means of sequence numbers. Each end maintains a transmit sequence number and a receive sequence number. When a node successfully receives a frame, it responds with a supervisory frame containing a receiver ready (RR) indication and a receive sequence number. The number is that of the next frame expected, thus acknowledging all previous frames.

If the receiving node responds with a negative acknowledgment (REJ) frame, the transmitter must transmit all frames from the receive sequence number in the REJ frame. This happens when the receiver detects an out-of-sequence frame.

It is also possible for selective retransmission to be used. In this case the receiver would return a selection rejection frame containing only the sequence number of the missing frame.

A slightly more complex approach is required for a point-to-point link using asynchronous balanced mode with full-duplex operation, where information frames are transmitted in two directions at the same time. The same philosophy is followed as for half-duplex operation except that checks for correct sequences of frame numbers must be maintained at both ends of the link.

Flow control operates on the principle that the maximum number of information frames awaiting acknowledgment at any time is seven. If seven acknowledgments are outstanding, the transmitting node will suspend transmission until an acknowledgment is received. This can be either in the form of a receiver ready supervisory frame, or piggy-backed in an information frame being returned from the receiver.

If the sequence numbers at both ends of the link become so out of sequence that the number of frames awaiting acknowledgment exceeds seven, the secondary node transmits a frame reject or a command reject frame to the primary node. The primary node then sets up the link again, and on an acknowledgment from the secondary node, both sides reset all the sequence numbers and commence the transfer of information frames.

It is possible for the receiver to run out of buffer space to store messages. When this happens it will transmit a receiver not ready (RNR) supervisory frame to the primary node to instruct it to stop sending any more information frames.

2.8.4   Modbus protocol

General overview

The Modbus transmission protocol was developed by Gould Modicon (now Schneider) for process control systems. In contrast to the many other buses discussed, no interface is defined. The user can therefore choose between EIA-232, EIA-422, EIA-485 or 20 mA current loop, all of which are suitable for the transmission rates which the protocol defines.

Although Modbus is relatively slow in comparison with other buses, it has the advantage of wide acceptance among instrument manufacturers and users. About 20 to 30 manufacturers produce equipment with the Modbus protocol and many systems are in industrial operation. It can therefore be regarded as a *de facto* industrial standard with proven capabilities. A recent survey in the well-known American *Control Engineering* magazine indicated that over 40% of industrial communication applications use the Modbus protocol for interfacing.

Besides the standard Modbus protocol, there is another Modbus protocol, called Modbus Plus.

The Modbus is accessed on the master/slave principle, the protocol providing for one master and up to 247 slaves. Only the master initiates a transaction.

Transactions are either a query/response type where only a single slave is addressed, or a broadcast/no response type where all slaves are addressed. A transaction comprises a single query and single response frame or a single broadcast frame.

Certain characteristics of the Modbus protocol are fixed, such as frame format, frame sequences, handling of communications errors and exception conditions and the functions performed. Other characteristics are selectable. These are transmission medium, transmission characteristics and transmission mode, RTU or ASCII. The user characteristics are set at each device and cannot be changed when the system is running.

The Modbus protocol provides frames for the transmission of messages between master and slaves. The information in the message is the address of the intended receiver, what the receiver must do, the data needed to perform the action and a means of checking errors. The slave reads the messages, and if there is no error it performs the task and sends a response back to the master. The information in the response message is the slave address, the action performed, the result of the action and a means of checking errors. If the initial message was of a broadcast type, there is no response from the slaves.

Normally, the master can send another query as soon as it has received the response message. A timeout function ensures that the system still functions when the query is not received correctly.

Data can be exchanged in two transmission modes:

- ASCII – readable, used e.g. for testing
- RTU – compact and faster; used for normal operation (hex)

The RTU mode (sometime also referred to as Modbus-B for Modbus Binary) is the preferred Modbus mode and will be discussed in this section. The ASCII transmission mode has a typical message that is about twice the length of the equivalent RTU message.

The Modbus also provides an error check for transmission and communication errors. Communication errors are detected by character framing, a parity check, a redundancy check or CRC. The latter varies depending on whether the RTU or ASCII transmission mode is being used.

Modbus functions

All functions supported by the Modbus protocol are identified by an index number.

They are designed as control commands for field instrumentation and actuators and are as follows:

- Coil control commands for reading and setting a single coil or a group of coils
- Input control commands for reading input status of a group of inputs
- Register control commands for reading and setting one or more holding registers
- Diagnostics test and report functions
- Program functions
- Polling control functions
- Reset

Protocol specifics

This section reviews the Modbus protocol in detail and is broken down into the following sections:

- Message format
- Synchronization
- Memory location
- Function codes
- Exception responses

Message format

A transaction consists of a single request from the host to a specific secondary device and a single response from that device back to the host. Both of these messages are formatted as Modbus message frames. Each such message frame consists of a series of bytes grouped into four fields as described in the following paragraphs. Note that each of these bytes indicated here are in Hex format (not ASCII).

Address Field	Function Field	DATA Data Field	Error Check Field
1 Byte	1 Byte	Variable	2 Bytes

Figure 2.26
Format of Modbus message frame

The first field in each message frame is the address field, which consists of a single byte of information. In request frames, this byte identifies the controller to which the request is being directed. The resulting response frame begins with the address of the responding device. Each slave can have an address field between 1 and 247, although practical limitations will limit the maximum number of slaves. A typical Modbus installation will have one master and two or three slaves.

The second field in each message is the function field, which also consists of a single byte of information. In a host request, this byte identifies the function that the target PLC is to perform.

If the target PLC is able to perform the requested function, the function field of its response will echo that of the original request. Otherwise, the function field of the request will be echoed with its most-significant bit set to one, thus signaling an exception response. Table 2.2 summarizes the typical functions used.

The third field in a message frame is the data field, which varies in length according to which function is specified in the function field. In a host request, this field contains information the PLC may need to complete the requested function. In a PLC response, this field contains any data requested by that host.

The last two bytes in a message frame comprise the error-check field. The numeric value of this field is calculated by performing a cyclic redundancy check (CRC-16) on the message frame. This error checking assures that devices do not react to messages that may have been changed during transmission.

Synchronization

In order to achieve reliable communication, the reception of a message must be synchronized with its transmission. In other words, the receiving device must be able to identify the start of a new message frame. Under the Modbus RTU protocol, frame synchronization is established by limiting the idle time between successive characters within a message frame. If three character times (approximately three milliseconds) elapse without the receiving device detecting a new character, the pending message will be flushed. The next byte will then be interpreted as the address field of a new message line.

Memory notation

The memory notation allows for four different data types: coils, discrete inputs, input registers and holding registers. Register variables consist of two bytes, while coils and discrete inputs are single bytes.

Each function references only one type of data. This allows message-frame memory references to be expressed as offsets relative to the lowest possible address for that data type. For example, holding register 40001 is referenced as 0000.

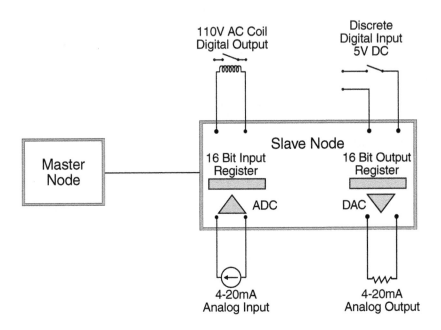

Figure 2.27
Diagram illustrating Modbus data types

Table 2.2 lists the address range and offsets for these four data types, as well as the function codes which apply to each. The diagram above also gives an easy reference to the Modbus data types.

Function codes

Each request frame contains a function code that defines the action expected for the target controller. The meaning of the request data fields is dependent on the function code specified.

The following paragraphs define and illustrate most of the popular function codes supported. In these examples, the contents of the message-frame fields are shown as hexadecimal bytes.

Data Type	Absolute Addresses	Relative Addresses	Function Codes	Description
Coils	00001 to 09999	0 to 9998	01	Read Coil Status
Coils	00001 to 09999	0 to 9998	05	Force Single Coil
Coils	00001 to 09999	0 to 9998	15	Force Multiple Coils
Discrete Inputs	10001 to 19999	0 to 9998	02	Read Input Status
Input Registers	30001 to 39999	0 to 9998	04	Read Input Registers
Holding Registers	40001 to 49999	0 to 9998	03	Read Holding Register
Holding Registers	40001 to 49999	0 to 9998	06	Preset Single Register
Holding Registers	40001 to 49999	0 to 9998	16	Preset Multiple Registers
-	-	-	07	Read Exception Status
-	-	-	08	Loopback Diagnostic Test

Table 2.2
Modicon data types supported

Read coil or digital output status (function code 01)

This function allows the host to obtain the ON/OFF status of one or more logic coils in the target device.

The data field of the request consists of the relative address of the first coil followed by the number of coils to be read. The data field of the response frame consists of a count of the coil bytes followed by that many bytes of coil data.

The coil data bytes are packed with one bit for the status of each consecutive coil (1=ON, 0=OFF). The least significant bit of the first coil data byte conveys the status of the first coil read. If the number of coils read is not an even multiple of eight, the last data byte will be padded with zeros on the high end. Note that if multiple data bytes are requested, the low order bit of the first data byte in the response of the slave contains the first addressed coil.

In the following example, the host requests the status of coils AH (00011) and BH (00012). The target device's response indicates both coils are ON.

Request Message

Address	Function Code	Initial Coil Offset		Number of Points		CRC
		Hi	Lo	Hi	Lo	
01	01	00	0A	00	02	9D C9

Response Frame

Address	Function Code	Byte Count	Coil Data	CRC
01	01	01	03	11 89

Figure 2.28
Example of read coil status

Read digital input status (function code 02)

This function enables the host to read one or more discrete inputs in the target device.

The data field of the request frame consists of the relative address of the first discrete input followed by the number of discrete inputs to be read. The data field of the response frame consists of a count of the discrete input data bytes followed by that many bytes of discrete input data.

The discrete-input data bytes are packed with one bit for the status of each consecutive discrete input (1=ON, 0=OFF). The least significant bit of the first discrete input data byte conveys the status of the first input read. If the number of discrete inputs read is not an even multiple of eight, the last data byte will be padded with zeros on the high end. The low order bit of the first byte of the response from the slave contains the first addressed digital input.

In the following example, the host requests the status of discrete inputs 10001 and 10002. The target device's response indicates that discrete input 10001 is OFF and 10002 is ON.

Request Message

Address	Function Code	Initial Coil Offset		Number of Points		CRC
		Hi	Lo	Hi	Lo	
01	02	00	00	00	02	F9 CB

Response Frame

Address	Function Code	Byte Count	Input Data	CRC
01	02	01	02	20 49

Figure 2.29
Example of read input status

Read holding registers (function code 03)

This function allows the host to obtain the contents of one or more holding registers in the target device.

The data field of the request frame consist of the relative address of the first holding register followed by the number of registers to be read. The data field of the response time consists of a count of the register data bytes followed by that many bytes of holding register data.

The contents of each requested register are returned in two consecutive register-data bytes (most significant byte first).

In the following example, the host requests the contents of holding register 40003. The controller's response indicates that the numerical value of the register's contents is 2047. The first byte of the response register data is the high order byte of the first addressed register.

Request Message

Address	Function Code	Starting Register		Register Count		CRC
		Hi	Lo	Hi	Lo	
01	03	00	02	00	01	25 CA

Response Frame

Address	Function Code	Byte Count	Register Data		CRC
			Hi	Lo	
01	03	02	07	FF	FA 34

Figure 2.30
Example of reading holding register

Reading input registers (function code 04)

This function allows the host to obtain the contents of one or more input registers in the target device.

The data field of the request frame consists of the relative address of the first input register followed by the number of registers to be read. The data field of the response frame consists of a count of the register-data bytes followed by that many bytes of input-register data.

The contents of each requested register are returned in two consecutive register-data bytes (most-significant byte first). The range for register variables is 0 to 4095.

In the following example, the host requests the contents of input register 30001. The PLC's response indicates that the numerical value of that register's contents is 03FFH, which would correspond to a data value of 25.6 per cent (if the scaling of 0 to 102.4 per cent is adopted).

Request Message

Address	Function Code	Starting Register		Register Count		CRC	
		Hi	Lo	Hi	Lo		
01	04	00	00	00	01	31	CA

Response Frame

Address	Function Code	Byte Count	Register Data		CRC	
			Hi	Lo		
01	04	02	03	FF	F9	80

Figure 2.31
Example of reading input register

Force single coil (function code 05)

This function allows the host to alter the ON/OFF status of a single logic coil in the target device.

The data field of the request frame consists of the relative address of the coil followed by the desired status for that coil. A status value of 65280 (FF00H) will activate the coil, while a status value of zero (0000H) will deactivate it. Any other status value is illegal.

If the controller is able to force the specified coil to the requested state, the response frame will be identical to the request. Otherwise an exception response will be returned.

If the address 00 is used to indicate broadcast mode, all attached slaves will modify the specified coil address to the state required.

The following example illustrates a successful attempt to force coil 00011 OFF.

Request Message

Address	Function Code	Coil Offset		New Coil Status		CRC	
		Hi	Lo	Hi	Lo		
01	05	00	0A	00	00	ED	C8

Response Frame

Address	Function Code	Coil Offset		New Coil Status		CRC	
		Hi	Lo	Hi	Lo		
01	05	00	0A	00	00	ED	C8

Figure 2.32
Example of forcing a single coil

Preset single register (function code 06)

This function enables the host to alter the contents of a single holding register in the target device.

The data field of the request frame consists of the relative address of the holding register followed by the new value to be written to that register (most-significant byte first).

If the controller is able to write the requested new value to the specified register, the response frame will be identical to the request. Otherwise, an exception response will be returned.

The following example illustrates a successful attempt to change the contents of holding register 40003 to 3072 (0C00 Hex).

When slave address is set to 00 (broadcast mode), all slaves will load the specified register with the value specified.

Request Message

Address	Function Code	Register Offset		Register Value		CRC
		Hi	Lo	Hi	Lo	
01	06	00	02	0C	00	2D 0A

Response Frame

Address	Function Code	Register Offset		Register Value		CRC
		Hi	Lo	Hi	Lo	
01	06	00	02	0C	00	2D 0A

Figure 2.33
Example of presetting a single register

Read exception status (function code 07)

Request Message

Address	Function Code	CRC
11	07	.. ..

Response Frame

Address	Function Code	Coil Station	CRC
11	07	02	.. ..

Figure 2.34
Read exception status query message

This is a short message requesting the status of eight digital points within the slave device.

This will provide the status of eight predefined digital points in the slave. For example this could be items such as the status of the battery, whether memory protect has been enabled or the status of the remote input/output racks connected to the system.

Loopback test (function code 08)

The objective of this function code is to test the operation of the communications system without affecting the memory tables of the slave device. It is also possible to implement additional diagnostic features in a slave device (should this be considered necessary) such as number of CRC errors, number of exception responses etc.

The most common implementation will only be considered in this section; namely a simple return of the query message.

Request Frame

Address	Function Code	Data Diagnostic Code		Data		CRC
		Hi	Lo	Hi	Lo	
11	08	00	00	A5	37	.. ..

Response Frame

Address	Function Code	Data Diagnostic Code		Data		CRC
		Hi	Lo	Hi	Lo	
11	08	00	00	A5	37	.. ..

Figure 2.35
Loopback test message

Force multiple coils or digital outputs (function code 15)

This forces a contiguous (or adjacent) group of coils to an ON or OFF state. The following example sets 10 coils starting at address 01 Hex (at slave address 01) to the ON state. If slave address 00 is used in the request frame broadcast mode will be implemented resulting in all slaves changing their coils at the defined addresses.

Request Frame

Address	Function Code	Address		Byte Count	Data Coil Status		CRC
		Hi	Lo		Hi	Lo	
01	0F	00	01	0F	FF	03	.. ..

Response Frame

Address	Function Code	Address		Number of Coils		CRC
		Hi	Lo	Hi	Lo	
01	0F	00	01	00	0A	.. ..

Figure 2.36
Example of forcing multiple coils

Force multiple registers (function code 16)

This is similar to the preset of a single register and the forcing of multiple coils. In the example below, a slave address 01 has 2 registers changed commencing at address 10.

Request Frame

Address	Function Code	Address		Quantity		Byte Count	First Register		Second Register		CRC
		Hi	Lo	Hi	Lo		Hi	Lo	Hi	Lo	
01	10	00	0A	00	02	04	00	0A	01	02	.. ..

Response Frame

Address	Function Code	Address		Quality		CRC
		Hi	Lo	Hi	Lo	
01	10	00	0A	00	02	.. ..

Figure 2.37
Example of presetting multiple registers

Exception responses

Request frames containing parity or checksum errors are ignored – no response is sent by any device. If an otherwise valid request frame contains an illegal request (one not supported by the target slave unit), an exception response will be returned to the host.

The four fields of an exception response contain:

- The address of the responding controller
- The requested function number with its most-significant bit set to one
- An appropriate exception code
- The CRC-16 checksum

The following table lists most important exception codes that may be returned.

Code	Name	Description
01	Illegal Function	Requested function is not supported.
02	Illegal Data Address	Requested data address is not supported
03	Illegal Data Value	Specified data value is not supported
04	Failure in Associated Device	Slave PLC has failed to respond to a message
05	Acknowledge	Slave PLC is processing the command
06	Busy, rejected message	Slave PLC is busy

Table 2.3
Abbreviated list of exception codes returned

An example of an illegal request and the corresponding exception response is shown below. The request in this example is to REAL COIL STATUS of points 514 to 521 (eight coils 00000 beginning an offset 0201H). These points are not supported in this particular slave device.

Request Message

Address	Function Code	Starting Point	Number of Points	CRC
01	01	02 01	00 08	6D B4

Exception Response Message

Address	Function Code	Exception Code	CRC
01	81	02	C1 91

Figure 2.38
Example of an illegal request

2.9   The open systems interconnection model

Overview

A communication framework that has had a tremendous impact on the design of communications systems is the open systems interconnection (OSI) model developed by the International Standardization Organization. The objective of the model is to provide a framework for the coordination of standards development and allows both existing and evolving standards activities to be set within that common framework.

The interconnection of two or more devices with digital communication is the first step towards establishing a network. In addition to the hardware requirements, the software problems of communication must also be overcome. Where all the devices on a network are from the same manufacturer, the hardware and software problems are usually easily solved because the system is usually designed within the same guidelines and specifications.

When devices from several manufacturers are used on the same application, the problems seem to multiply. Systems that are specific to one manufacturer and which work with specific hardware connections and protocols are called closed systems. Usually, these systems were developed at a time before standardization or when it was considered unlikely that equipment from other manufacturers would be included in the network.

In contrast, open systems are those that conform to specifications and guidelines which are 'open' to all. This allows equipment from any manufacturer, who complies with that standard, to be used interchangeably on the network. The benefits of open systems include multiple vendors and hence wider availability of equipment, lower prices and easier integration with other components.

In 1978 the ISO, faced with the proliferation of closed systems, defined a 'Reference Model for Communication between Open Systems' (ISO 7498), which has become known as the open systems interconnection model, or simply as the OSI model. OSI is essentially a data communications management structure, which breaks data communications down into a manageable hierarchy of seven layers. Each layer has a defined purpose and interfaces with the layers above it and below it. By laying down standards for each layer, some flexibility is allowed so that the system designers can develop protocols for each layer independent of each other. By conforming to the OSI standards, a system is able to communicate with any other compliant system, anywhere in the world.

It should be realized at the outset that the OSI reference model is not a protocol or set of rules for how a protocol should be written but rather an overall framework in which to define protocols. The OSI model framework specifically and clearly defines the functions or services that have to be provided at each of the seven layers (or levels).

Since there must be at least two sites to communicate, each layer also appears to converse 'horizontally' with its peer layer at the other end of the communication channel in a virtual (logical) communication. The OSI layering concept is shown in Figure 2.39.

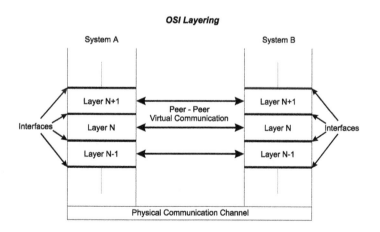

Figure 2.39
OSI layering concept

The actual functions within each layer are provided by entities such as programs, functions, or protocols, and implement the services for a particular layer on a single machine. Several entities, for example a protocol entity and a management entity, may exist at a given layer. Entities in adjacent layers interact through the common upper and lower boundaries by passing physical information through service access points (SAPs). A SAP could be compared to a pre-defined 'postbox' where one layer would collect data from the previous layer. The relationship between layers, entities, functions and SAPs is shown in Figure 2.39.

In the OSI model, the entity in the next higher layer is referred to as the N+1 entity and the entity in the next lower layer as N-1. The services available to the higher layers are the result of the services provided by all the lower layers.

The functions and capabilities expected at each layer are specified in the model. However, the model does not prescribe how this functionality should be implemented. The focus in the model is on the 'interconnection' and on the information that can be passed over this connection. The OSI model does not concern itself with the internal operations of the systems involved.

The diagram below shows the seven layers of the OSI model.

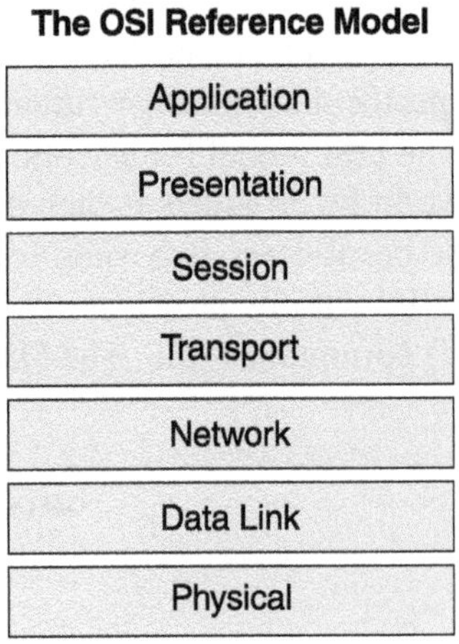

The OSI Reference Model

Application
Presentation
Session
Transport
Network
Data Link
Physical

Figure 2.40
The OSI reference model

Typically, each layer on the transmitting side adds header information, or protocol control information (PCI), to the data before passing it on to the next lower layer. In some cases, especially at the lowest level, a trailer may also be added. At each level, this combined data and header 'packet' is termed a protocol data unit or PDU. The headers are used to establish the peer-to-peer sessions across the sites and some layer implementations use the headers to invoke functions and services at the layers adjacent to the destination layer.

At the receiving site, the opposite occurs with the headers being stripped from the data as it is passed up through the layers. These header and control messages invoke services and a peer-to-peer logical interaction of entities across the sites. Generally, layers in the same site (i.e. within the same host) communicate in software with parameters passed through primitives, whilst peer layers at different sites communicate with the use of the protocol control information, or headers.

At this stage, it should be quite clear that there is NO connection or direct communication between the peer layers of the network. Rather, all physical communication is across the physical layer, or the lowest layer of the stack. Communication is down through the protocol stack on the transmitting stack and up through the stack on the receiving stack. As will be realized, the net effect of this extra information is to reduce the overall bandwidth of the communications channel, since some of the available bandwidth is used to pass control information.

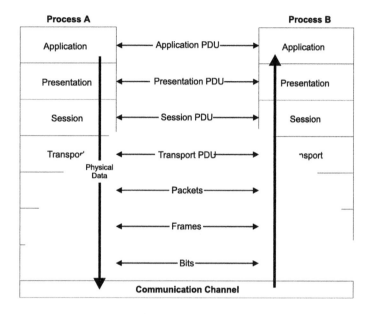

Figure 2.41

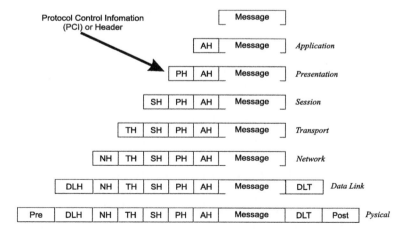

Figure 2.42
OSI message passing

The services provided at each layer of the stack are as follows:

Application layer

The application layer is the topmost layer in the OSI reference model. This layer is responsible for giving applications access to the network. Examples of application-layer tasks include file transfer, electronic mail (e-mail) services, and network management. Application-layer services are much more varied than the services in lower layers, because the entire range of application possibilities is available here. Application programs can get access to the application-layer services in software through application service elements (ASEs). There is a variety of such application service elements; each designed for a class of tasks. To accomplish its tasks, the application layer passes program requests and data to the presentation layer, which is responsible for encoding the application layer's data in the appropriate form.

Presentation layer

The presentation layer is responsible for presenting information in a manner suitable for the applications or users dealing with the information. Functions such as data conversion from EBCDIC to ASCII (or vice versa), use of special graphics or character sets, data compression or expansion, and data encryption or decryption are carried out at this layer. The presentation layer provides services for the application layer above it, and uses the session layer below it. In practice, the presentation layer rarely appears in pure form, and it is the least well defined of the OSI layers. Application- or session-layer programs will often encompass some or all of the presentation layer functions.

Session layer

The session layer is responsible for synchronizing and sequencing the dialogue and packets in a network connection. This layer is also responsible for making sure that the connection is maintained until the transmission is complete, and ensuring that appropriate security measures are taken during a 'session' (that is, a connection). The session layer is used by the presentation layer above it, and uses the transport layer below it.

Transport layer

In the OSI reference model, the transport layer is responsible for providing data transfer at an agreed-upon level of quality, such as at specified transmission speeds and error rates. To ensure delivery, outgoing packets are sometimes assigned numbers in sequence. These numbers are then included in the packets that are transmitted by lower layers. The transport layer at the receiving end subsequently checks the packet numbers to make sure all have been delivered and to put the packet contents into the proper sequence for the recipient. The transport layer provides services for the session layer above it, and uses the network layer below it to find a route between source and destination. The transport layer is crucial in many ways, because it sits between the upper layers (which are strongly application-dependent) and the lower ones (which are network-based).

The layers below the transport layer are collectively known as the 'subnet' layers. Depending on how well (or not) they perform their function, the transport layer has to interfere less (or more) in order to maintain a reliable connection.

Three types of subnet service (i.e. the service supplied by the underlying physical network between two hosts) are distinguished in the OSI model:

- Type A: Very reliable, connection-oriented service
- Type B: Unreliable, connection-oriented service
- Type C: Unreliable, possibly connectionless service

To provide the capabilities required for the above service types, several classes of transport layer protocols have been defined in the OSI model:

- TP0 (transfer protocol class 0), which is the simplest protocol. It assumes type A service; that is, a subnet that does most of the work for the transport layer. Because the subnet is reliable, TP0 requires neither error detection or error correction. Because the connection is connection-oriented, packets do not need to be numbered before transmission
- TP1 (transfer protocol class 1), which assumes a type B subnet; that is, one that may be unreliable. To deal with this, TP1 provides its own error detection, along with facilities for getting the sender to retransmit any erroneous packets
- TP2 (transfer protocol class 2), which also assumes a type A subnet. However, TP2 can multiplex transmissions, so that multiple transport connections can be sustained over the single network connection
- TP3 (transfer protocol class 3), which also assumes a type B subnet. TP3 can also multiplex transmissions, so that this protocol has the capabilities of TP1 and TP2
- TP4 (transfer protocol class 4), which is the most powerful protocol, in that it makes minimal assumptions about the capabilities or reliability of the subnet. TP4 is the only one of the OSI transport-layer protocols that supports connectionless service

Network layer

The network layer is the third lowest layer, or the uppermost subnet layer. It is responsible for the following tasks:

- Determining addresses or translating from hardware to network addresses. These addresses may be on a local network or they may refer to networks located elsewhere on an internetwork. One of the functions of the network layer is, in fact, to provide capabilities needed to communicate on an internetwork
- Finding a route between a source and a destination node or between two intermediate devices
- Fragmentation of large packets of data into frames which are small enough to be transmitted by the underlying data link layer (fragmentation). The corresponding network layer at the receiving node undertakes re-assembly of the packet

Data link layer

The data link layer is responsible for creating, transmitting, and receiving data packets. It provides services for the various protocols at the network layer, and uses the physical layer to transmit or receive material. The data link layer creates packets appropriate for the network architecture being used. Requests and data from the network layer are part of the data in these packets (or frames, as they are often called at this layer). These packets are passed down to the physical layer and from there, the data is transmitted to the physical layer on the destination machine. Network architectures (such as Ethernet, ARCnet, Token Ring, and FDDI) encompass the data link and physical layers, which is why these architectures support services at the data link level. These architectures also represent the most common protocols used at the data link level.

The IEEE (802.x) networking working groups have refined the data link layer into two sub-layers: the logical-link control (LLC) sub-layer at the top and the media-access control (MAC) sub-layer at the bottom. The LLC sub-layer must provide an interface for the network layer protocols, and control the logical communication with its peer at the receiving side. The MAC sub-layer must provide access to a particular physical encoding and transport scheme.

Physical layer

The physical layer is the lowest layer in the OSI reference model. This layer gets data packets from the data link layer above it, and converts the contents of these packets into a series of electrical signals that represent 0 and 1 values in a digital transmission. These signals are sent across a transmission medium to the physical layer at the receiving end. At the destination, the physical layer converts the electrical signals into a series of bit values. These values are grouped into packets and passed up to the data link layer.

The mechanical and electrical properties of the transmission medium are defined at this level. These include the following:

- The type of cable and connectors used. Cable may be coaxial, twisted pair, or fiber optic. The types of connectors depend on the type of cable
- The pin assignments for the cable and connectors. Pin assignments depend on the type of cable and also on the network architecture being used
- Format for the electrical signals. The encoding scheme used to signal 0 and 1 values in a digital transmission or particular values in an analog transmission depend on the network architecture being used. Most networks use digital signaling, and most use some form of Manchester encoding for the signal

Note that this layer does NOT include the specifications of the actual medium used, but rather WHICH medium should be used, and HOW. The specifications of, for example unshielded twisted pair as used by Ethernet is contained in specification EIA/TIA 568.

3

Open SCADA protocols DNP3 and IEC 60870

3.1 Interoperability and open standards

Historically, SCADA system communication protocols have been developed as proprietary protocols, each created by a manufacturer as part of a proprietary system, to meet the specific needs of a particular industry. This was a matter of necessity, as suitable standards had not hitherto existed. However, proprietary protocols have disadvantages for the user. As a system is developed over time the owner is either locked in to expansion using the same proprietary system, or is compelled to replace substantial parts of the system to change to another manufacturer's protocol.

Arising from this underlying disadvantage and the increasing use of SCADA systems generally, the need for open standards became recognized. This recognition has translated into efforts by a number of organizations in a number of countries. However, the emergence of standards that have wide acceptance has been a slow process.

The key benefit of an open standard is that it provides for interoperability between equipment from different manufacturers. This means for example that a user can purchase system equipment such as a master station from one manufacturer, and be able to add RTU equipment sourced from another manufacturer. The RTU in turn may have a number of control relays connected to it which are intelligent electronic devices and also use the protocol. All of this equipment may be sourced from different manufacturers, either in an initial installation, or progressively as the system is developed over time. Some of the different benefits arising from the use of open protocols are listed below, grouped into immediate and long-term effects.

3.1.1 Immediate benefits

- Interoperability between multi-vendor devices
- Fewer protocols to support in the field
- Reduced software costs
- No protocol translators needed
- Shorter delivery schedules
- Less testing, maintenance and training

- Improved documentation
- Independent conformance testing may be provided

3.1.2 Long-term benefits

- Easy system expansion
- Long product life
- More value-added products from vendors
- Faster adoption of new technology
- Major operations savings

3.1.3 Realizing the benefits of interoperability

To realize the potential benefits of interoperability, of course there must be available a suitable number of products supporting the protocol available to the user.

- How many manufacturers support the protocol?
- Are they increasing or declining?
- Do they provide the products you require?
- Are their products truly interoperable?

These issues, together with an understanding of factors that may affect interoperability of particular equipment, are important to realizing the available benefits, and will be considered further in the subsequent chapters.

3.2 Development of standards

Arising from recognition of the need for open SCADA communication protocol standards, work was carried out by standards organizations on a number of fronts over a period of some years. These led by the end of the 1990s to two open SCADA communications protocols, known as DNP3 and IEC 60870.

3.2.1 Early standards

In the late 1980s and early 1990s the following publications by IEEE emerged:

- The standard ANSI/IEEE C37.1 – 1987 is entitled 'Design, Specification and Analysis of Systems used for Supervisory Control, Data Acquisition, and Automatic Control'. It contained a number of sections on telecommunications, however it did not define a message standard between master stations and RTUs
- The IEEE Recommended Practice for SCADA Communication P999-1992 contained a basic message format, but this has not gained widespread application. In particular, although this recommended practice dealt with message framing, it did not define application level message formats. It could not therefore provide a basis for interoperability between different manufacturers' systems

Around the same time, a hierarchical communications model based on the ISO Open Systems Interconnection 7 layer model emerged. A three layer version of this model was proposed by the IEC to provide a simplified hierarchical model that would be suitable as a basis for SCADA communications. This is known as the Enhanced Performance Architecture (EPA) model.

3.2.2 DNP 3.0 and IEC 60870 protocols

In 1990 the 3 layer EPA model was adopted as the basis for telemetry data transmission in standard IEC 870, Telecontrol Equipment and Systems. The main parts of this standard were developed and published between 1990 and 1993. One of the early parts was IEC 870-5 Transmission Protocols. Section 1, entitled Transmission Frame Formats, published in 1990. This document included the specification of four frame formats, or message structures, that would be suitable for telecontrol applications. These were defined as the FT1.1, FT1.2, FT2 and FT3 frames.

It was at this time that the DNP 3.0 standard was developed by Harris Controls. DNP also used one of the four frame formats specified by IEC 870-5, the FT3 format. The IEC 870 standard continued to be developed from this time. In particular, IEC 60870-5-101 Basic Telecontrol Tasks, published in November 1995 specified use of the FT1.2 frame format.

Thus during the early 1990s two separate protocols were developed in parallel by different organizations, working from a common point provided by the early IEC 870-5 documents. These provided both protocols with some areas of similarity in their procedures for handling communications at the lower data link level. In their higher level functionality and data objects though, they are entirely different.

In summary, two open protocol standards have emerged from the EPA model and the specification of frame formats in IEC 60870. These are:

- DNP 3.0
- IEC 60870-5-101

These are the two open communication protocols that provide for interoperability between systems for telecontrol applications that are now competing within the world market. Today DNP has a strong following in North America, South America, South Africa, Asia and Australia, while IEC 60870-5-101 is strongly supported in the European region.

In subsequent chapters each of these protocols will be examined in detail, providing the reader an in-depth understanding of each.

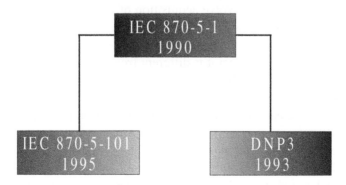

Figure 3.1
Development of standards

4

Preview of DNP3

4.1   What is DNP3?

DNP3 or Distributed Network Protocol Version 3.3 is a telecommunications standard that defines communications between master stations, remote telemetry units (RTUs) and other intelligent electronic devices (IEDs). It was developed to achieve interoperability among systems in the electric utility, oil & gas, water/waste water and security industries.

DNP3 was created as a proprietary protocol by Harris Controls Division initially for use in the electrical utility industry. In November 1993 the protocol was made available for use by third parties by transferring its ownership to the DNP3 User Group. Through the DNP3 User Group, which may be joined for a nominal fee, the full specification of the protocol may be obtained by any person or company.

DNP3 was designed specifically for SCADA (supervisory control and data acquisition) applications. These involve acquisition of information and sending of control commands between physically separate computer devices. It is designed to transmit relatively small packets of data in a reliable manner with the messages involved arriving in a deterministic sequence. In this respect it is different from more general purpose protocols, such as FTP which is part of TCP/IP, which can send quite large files, but in a way that is generally not as suitable for SCADA control.

From its creation for the electrical distribution industry in America, DNP3 has gained significant acceptance in both geographic and industry terms. DNP3 is supported by a large number of vendors and users in electrical, water infrastructure, and other industries in North America, South America, South Africa, Asia and Australia. In Europe DNP3 competes with the IEC 60870-5-101 protocol which is widely used in that region, and which shares a common origin with DNP3. However, the IEC protocol is confined to the electrical distribution industry, whereas DNP3 has found wider industry applications in the oil & gas, water/waste water and security industries.

4.2   Interoperability and open standard

A key feature of the DNP3 protocol is that it is an open protocol standard and it is one that has been adopted by a significant number of equipment manufacturers. As will be discussed in the following section on Background and development, DNP3 is one of the open protocols for SCADA communications that have emerged from the era of proprietary protocols.

The benefit of an open standard is that it provides for interoperability between equipment from different manufacturers. This means for example that a user can purchase system equipment such as a master station from one manufacturer, and be able to add RTU equipment sourced from another manufacturer. The RTU in turn may have a number of control relays connected to it which are intelligent electronic devices and also use the DNP3 protocol. All of this equipment may be sourced from different manufacturers, either in an initial installation, or progressively as the system is developed over time.

Of course the benefits that are realizable are dependent on a number of factors. Some of these are shown below.

Realizing the benefits of interoperability:

- How many manufacturers support the protocol?
- Are they increasing or declining?
- Do they provide the products you require?
- Are their products truly interoperable?

Looking at the list of implementers and users of DNP3 shows that there is a substantial level of support for the protocol across a substantial number of SCADA systems, RTUs, and many different intelligent electronic devices such as relays, instruments, protocol converters, and other devices. A list of implementers of DNP3 is available on the DNP3 User Group internet website (at http://www.dnp.org/). A list of SCADA master and RTU implementers has been included in the appendix.

Some of the well-known implementers are shown in Table 4.1.

DNP3 has been recognized as having a particularly strong compliance system. In addition to having a comprehensive specification of data objects, DNP3 has a detailed compliance certification system. This is based on having defined implementation sub-sets to which devices must be certified. This provides a means for manufacturers to implement reduced function systems that still provide defined levels of functionality.

Some Manufacturers for SCADA and RTUs supporting DNP 3.0

Company	Product
ABB	ABB Power RICH System ABB DPU2000 Relay Master Station
Advanced Control Systems	HPM 9000/ SCADA Master, EMS, DMS MPR-7575 Pole-top RTU MPR-7010 Substation RTU
CI Technologies Inc	PC Based SCADA Systems
Control Microsystems	SCADAPack RTUs/PLCs
Cybectec Inc.	RTU, SMP, PAC
Foxboro	C50 Pole-top RTU
GE Harris Energy Control Systems	Powerlink PC-master, Enmac DMS, XA/21 EMS Dart, SCD
GE Fanuc	CIMPLICITY Software D20, D25 Multifunction IED
GE Harris Energy Control Systems	PowerLink PC-base SCADA Master. DNP over UDP/IP for LAN applications
Hunter Watertech Pty. Ltd.	PDS Telemetry Products PDS 500, PDS Compact, Multipurpose RTUs
Intellution	FIX Software for WIN 95/98/NT
Landis & Gyr Energy Mgt, Inc.	Telegyr/5700
Mitsubishi Electric Corporation	MELSCADA, MELRTU
Motorola	MOSCAD RTUs
National Instruments Corporation	SCADA Master
PC Soft International - Wizcon	Wizcon SCADA/HMI and Wizcon for Internet
Rockwell Software	RSView32 Scada Master
Schneider Electric	Talus 100 RTU and Talus 200 RTU Talus 2000 RTU
Siemens Power & Transmission Distribution	SICAM SCADA - NT Based SCADA SICAM SAS, Poletop RTUs
SUBNET Solution Inc.	SUBSTATION EXPLORER, Windows based Substation HMI
Telegyr Systems, Inc.	Telegyr NMS on NT SCADA System Telegyr 8000 SCADA System
QEI Inc	Quics 4 Master Station Substation RTUs
Quindar Products Ltd.	QUICS IV Master Station XPPB,XPAC,XPDC, XPPQ RTUs

Table 4.1
Some manufacturers for SCADA and RTUs supporting DNP3

4.3 Benefits of DNP3

The following list presents features of DNP3 that provide benefits to the user:

- Open standard
- Supported by an active DNP3 User Group
- A protocol that is supported by a large and increasing number of equipment manufacturers
- Layered architecture conforming to IEC enhanced performance architecture model
- Optimized for reliable and efficient SCADA communications
- Supported by comprehensive implementation testing standards
- Has defined protocol subsets for particular applications
- The ability to select from multiple vendors for future system expansion and modification

The DNP3 User Group documentation identifies the benefits offered by DNP3 in terms of short-term or immediate, as well as longer term. This gives an appropriate focus on the whole-of-life cost/benefit equation which has underpinned the emergence of open standards based systems. The benefits identified by the DNP3 documentation are as follows:

4.3.1   Immediate benefits

- Interoperability between multi-vendor devices
- Fewer protocols to support in the field
- Reduced software costs
- No protocol translators needed
- Shorter delivery schedules
- Less testing, maintenance and training
- Improved documentation
- Independent conformance testing
- Support by independent users group and third-party sources

4.3.2   Long-term benefits

- Easy system expansion
- Long product life
- More value-added products from vendors
- Faster adoption of new technology
- Major operations savings

4.4   Features of DNP3

DNP3 offers substantial features as well as flexibility and security. These are summarized in the following list:

- Supports time stamped messages for sequence of event (SOE) recording
- Breaks messages into multiple frames to provide optimum error control and rapid communication sequences
- Allows peer–peer topology as well as master–slave
- Allows multiple master topology
- Provides user definable objects
- Provides for reporting by exception/event without polling by master
- Provides for 'changed data' only responses
- Broadcast messages
- Secure configuration/file transfers
- Addressing for over 65 000 devices on a single link
- Provides time synchronization and time-stamped events
- Data link and application layer confirmation

4.5   System topology

System topologies include:

- Master–slave
- Multidrop from one master
- Hierarchical with intermediate data concentrators
- Multiple master

These are illustrated in the following drawing.

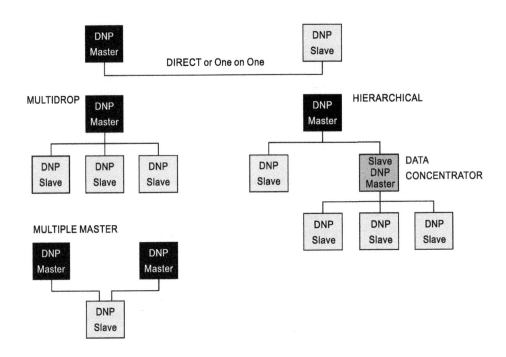

Figure 4.1
DNP3 network topologies

DNP3 supports multiple-slave, peer-to-peer and multiple-master communications. It supports the operational modes of polled, and quiescent operation. The latter is also referred to as reporting by exception. Quiescent operation is so called because polls to check for changes are not required. This is because the master station can rely on the outstation to send an 'unsolicited response' when it has a change that needs to be reported. Thus, in the absence of change the system remains quiescent, or in a quiet state, with neither polls from the master station, nor responses from the outstations. This mode of operation provides for better use of the communications system capacity.

In a quiescent system, generally a periodic background poll is still used, perhaps at hourly intervals, to guard against undetected communications failure. If this was not done, the master station would have no way of detecting the failure of communications with the outstation should it occur. It would just assume that nothing had changed.

The capability to support peer–peer and quiescent operation requires that stations which are not designated as master stations can initiate communications. This is sometimes referred to as 'balanced' communications, which means that any station can act as a primary (or sending) and as a secondary (responding) station at the same time.

Despite the ability for non-master stations to initiate communications within DNP3, only master stations can initiate requests for data, or issue commands, to other stations. Thus, although the term balanced is applied to the communications system, the differentiation between master and slave stations remains necessary. Sometimes the terms master and outstation are used to more appropriately reflect the capabilities of the system.

Architectures may also involve the use of protocol converters to interface to one or more devices using a different communications protocol. A protocol converter might be used in the case of a hierarchical topology, where the outstation devices only use DNP3, and the SCADA master might use a different communications system.

In the case of DNP3 devices with a network port, DNP3 is encapsulated within TCP/IP Ethernet packets. Although this does add the overhead associated with these packets, it provides an effective means of using local or wide area networks to cater for SCADA communications. In some cases, this may allow the efficient extension of a SCADA system by making use of an existing corporate network.

4.6   Background and development

In Chapter 3, the simultaneous development of DNP3 and IEC 60870.5 was introduced. This showed that the DNP3 protocol was developed during the early 1990s at the same time as IEC 60870, and in fact drew on the some of the early definitions of the IEC standard.

DNP3 used one of the four frame formats specified by IEC 870-5, the FT3 format. The IEC 870 standard continued to be developed from this time. In particular, IEC 870-5-101 Basic Telecontrol Tasks, published in November 1995 specified the use of the FT1 frame format.

An important point to note is that DNP3 was developed and released during the period when the IEC 870 standard was also being developed and progressively released. DNP3 is based on the enhanced performance architecture arising from the work of IEC TC57. Also, the DNP3 framing is based on the FT3 format defined by IEC 870-5-1. However, *DNP3 is not compliant with IEC 870-5*, (now IEC 60870-5). It should be noted that aside from the common point of their origin, the two standards also differ in the physical, data link and application functions as these were all defined completely separately and subsequently to their common origin.

Following release of the protocol to the DNP3 Users Group, a DNP3 Technical Committee was formed in January 1995. This body developed the DNP3 sub-set definitions document, which defines different levels of implementation of the standard. This allows for levels of implementation ranging from basic to more comprehensive.

The DNP3 Users Group and Technical Committee is an active body that is providing ongoing support and development of the protocol, and furtherance of its underlying objectives. Examples of this include the ongoing development of independent conformance testing, and in the extension of the standard to cover transmission over networked systems.

4.7   Why use DNP3?

DNP3 is an open protocol that is gaining widespread acceptance and usage across a number of industries and countries. It is optimized for SCADA communications, and provides secure and efficient communications for the types of messages transferred by these systems.

The reasons for the adoption of DNP3 by users are primarily:

- It is an open protocol
- It is optimized for SCADA communications
- It provides interoperability between different vendor's equipment
- It is supported by a substantial number of SCADA equipment manufacturers
- It will provide immediate and long-term benefits to users

5

Fundamentals of distributed network protocol

Objectives

When you have completed study of this chapter you should be able to:

- Relate the DNP3 model to the appropriate layers of the OSI model
- Describe the DNP3 protocol message structure
- Describe the operation of DNP3

5.1 Fundamental concepts

5.1.1 The OSI 7 layer model

The open systems interconnection model was defined by the International Standards Organization (ISO). This model was a significant step in the development of standardization of data communications systems. The OSI model presents data communications in a hierarchical manner, starting at the bottom with the physical layer (layer 1), and moving to the application layer (layer 7) at the top.

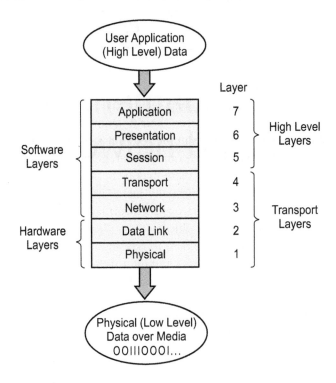

Figure 5.1
ISO open systems interconnection model (OSI)

The direction of data flow during transmission from a source is depicted in Figure 5.1. It shows the high level data, which is generated by the user application, at the top. In transmission this data is passed down through the hierarchy, with each layer modifying the data in some way. The resulting bit stream on the physical media is depicted at the bottom of the figure. A feature of the model is that each layer of the model communicates via the lower levels and the communication medium to the same layer at the receiving end. Whatever message is passed to the lower levels, that same message emerges from the lower levels at the other end of the transmission, ie at the destination.

It is important to realize that the OSI model is not a protocol specification. It provides a framework for the development of communications protocols, and a means of defining and differentiating the functions performed by those protocols. It defines the interfaces between increasingly high level functions, in terms of the data types passing across the interfaces, and the functions and services provided by each layer. It does not specify what these are.

It may be seen that the bottom four layers can be referred to as the transport layers, and the top three as the high level layers. Also, the layers may be characterized into hardware and software, representing the way the functions of the layers are provided.

In the area of SCADA and IED communications, there was a need for a simplified model that omits some of the higher level functions. Such a model was created by the International Electrotechnical Commission (IEC) who defined a 3 layer model. This is known as the enhanced performance architecture (EPA) model . It is this model on which DNP3 is based. The functions of each of the layers used by DNP3 are discussed in the next section.

Before moving to the EPA model, we will use the general OSI reference model to illustrate message buildup. This will demonstrate the general principle and introduce the idea of message headers. These concepts will assist us in understanding the details of message construction under DNP3.

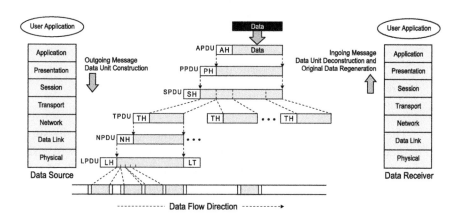

Figure 5.2
Generic message buildup using the OSI 7 layer model

Some of the features and terminology illustrated by the message buildup are now discussed.

Data flow during message construction is from the application level down to the physical level, then across the physical medium, then at the receiving device up through the model layers until the original message is regenerated.

The application data is given an application header by the application layer. This forms the application protocol data unit or APDU. The APDU is the data unit used by the next layer, the presentation layer. This adds its own header, and so on.

The data may be split into smaller size units during the process of message construction. In this example, the session protocol data unit (SPDU) is broken into multiple data units at the transport level.

The data link layer adds both a header, and a trailer section containing an error detection code, forming the link protocol data unit (LPDU). At the physical layer this is broken down into 8-bit blocks, each with start and stop bits appended for asynchronous transmission.

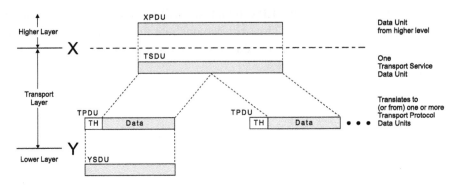

Figure 5.3
Definition of service data unit versus protocol data unit

The drawing shows a distinction in terminology between the service data unit and the protocol data unit, which is worth being aware of because it will assist in understanding of terms like TSDU and TPDU when used in relation to DNP3. The TSDU is the data unit used to communicate with the higher level, that is, to provide the service to the higher level. The TPDU is the data unit exchanged with the level below.

The drawing illustrates in this case the transport level breaking down the higher level data unit into multiple data units to be passed down to the next level.

5.1.2   Enhance performance architecture

The enhanced performance architecture model developed by IEC Technical Committee 57 is a 3 layer sub-set of the OSI 7 layer model. The layers used in this model are the two hardware layers and the top software layer, the application layer.

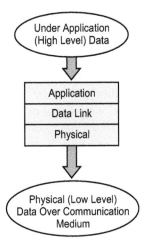

Figure 5.4
Enhanced performance architecture (EPA) model

As for the OSI 7 layer model, during transmission high level data is passed from the user application to the application level, and from there down through the hierarchy to produce a stream of data over the physical communications medium. In the process, the data may be converted from a single user application data unit into smaller chunks and ultimately to a bit stream. On reception at its destination the reverse process is applied, and leading to regeneration of the original application level data unit.

DNP3 uses these three layers, but adds some transport functions. These are often referred to as the pseudo-transport layers, and are sometimes depicted as corresponding to the transport and network layers in a limited manner. This relationship is shown in the following drawing.

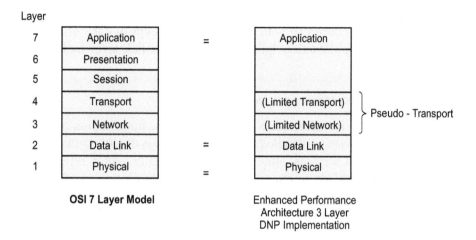

Figure 5.5
Relationship of EPA model to OSI 7 layer model

This drawing shows the relationship between the 3 layer Enhanced performance architecture (EPA), as implemented by DNP3, and the OSI reference model.

In the following section the message structure will be analyzed in terms of the EPA model. Before looking at that, a brief review of the general functions of each of the layers will be made.

5.1.3 Functions of the model layers

The functions of each layer of the EPA model are described briefly in the following paragraphs. The network and transport layer functions have included as the pseudo-transport layer, as limited transport and network functions are supported by the DNP3 protocol.

Physical layer

The physical layer is the physical media over which the protocol is transmitted. The definition of this the physical interface characteristics in terms of electrical specifications, timing, pin-outs and so on. The data element at this level is essentially the bit, ie it is concerned with how to pass one bit of data at a time across the physical media. Definition of the physical layer also includes the functions for controlling the media, such as details required to establish and maintain the physical link, and to control data flow.

The actual specification of this layer is normally a separate standard such as ITU-T X.21 or V.24, EIA RS-232 or others.

The physical layer specification for DNP3 is covered in greater detail later in this text, but it is noted here that EIA RS-232C was originally specified for voltage levels and control signals, and ITU-T (formerly CCITT) V.24 for DTE-DCE signaling.

Other communications media such as over Ethernet are in the process of being defined for use by the DNP3 User Group Technical Committee.

Data link layer

The data link layer provides for reliable transmission of data across the physical medium. While the physical layer is concerned with the passage of a signal, or a bit of data, the data link layer is concerned with the passage of groups of data. These groups may be referred to as a frame. Functions provided by the data link layer include flow control and error detection.

The pseudo-transport layer

This layer is included in DNP3 to allow for the transmission of larger blocks of data than could otherwise be handled. Some writers have described this in terms of both network and transport services, although these are usually simply referred to as pseudo-transport services. Network functions are concerned with routing and flow control of data packets over networks. Transport functions provide network transparent end-to-end delivery of whole messages, including disassembly and reassembly, and error correction.

Application layer

The application layer is the level where the data is generated for sending, or requested to be sent. It is the layer that interfaces to the lower levels to achieve the result of end-end transmission of required information. In turn, the DNP3 application layer provides its services to the user application programs, such as an HMI system, an RTU, or other system.

5.2   Understanding DNP3 message structure

In the preceding sections, the buildup of a generic OSI 7 layer model message was shown and the enhanced performance architecture was introduced. In this section, the buildup of a DNP3 message will be examined. This will provide an introduction to the overall structure of the DNP3 message. At this point we need not be concerned with the detailed meaning of each part of the message. Detailed descriptions of the meaning of the data added at each layer will be given in later sections.

5.2.1   DNP3 message buildup

The figure below shows how the transmitted message is built up in DNP3. Each layer of the model takes the information passed from the higher layer, and adds information connected with the services performed by that layer. The additional information is usually added as a header, that is, in front of the original message.

Thus during message assembly, the message will grow in size with each layer that it passes down through. It is also disassembled in this process into smaller units of data.

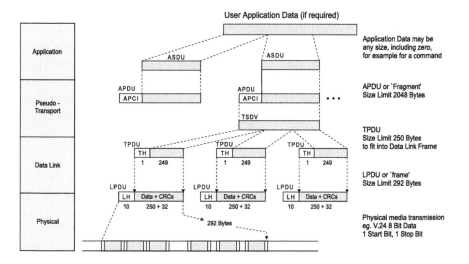

Figure 5.6
Buildup of DNP3 message

The message buildup illustrated in the drawing is now briefly described for each layer. It is described here from the highest level, the application level, downwards. This reflects the sequence of message building during sending. Of course the sequence at the other end is in reverse, as the message is passed over the physical medium, into the data link layer, and up to the application layer.

5.2.2   Application layer

The user data is the data arising from the user application. The user application can be visualized as a layer above the application layer, and could for example be a human machine interface (HMI) program such as 'Citect' or 'Intellution Fix', or it could be an embedded program, such as a C+ application program. The data could be alarm and event data, digital status data, or even a data file such as a configuration file being passed from a master station to an RTU or an IED. On the other hand, in the case of many types of command being issued by a master station, there may be no data at all. A key point is that this data can be of any size. The total data size is not limited by the protocol.

The application layer initially forms the data into manageable sized blocks. These are called application service data units or ASDUs. The application layer then creates the application protocol data unit APDU by combining a header with the ASDU data. The application header is referred to as the application protocol control information, or APCI. This is either 2 bytes or 4 bytes in length, depending on whether the message is a request or a response. In the case of a command or other user request requiring no additional data, there is only a header, and no ASDU.

Depending on the total size of the data to be transmitted (the size of the ASDU), one or more APDUs are created. In the case that multiple APDUs are required, these are each termed fragments. Whilst the number of fragments required to represent an ASDU is not limited, the size of each fragment is limited to a maximum of 2048 bytes.

5.2.3 The pseudo-transport layer

The APDU from the application layer may be referred to as the transport service data unit within the pseudo-transport layer. It is interpreted purely as data to be transported by the transport layer. The transport layer breaks the TSDU down into smaller units termed transport protocol data units or TPDUs. These are made up of a one byte header, followed by a maximum of 249 bytes of data.

The overall size of the TPDUs, which is 250 bytes, was determined so that each TPDU will fit within one 'frame' or LPDU at the data link layer.

5.2.4 The data link layer

This layer takes the TPDUs from the pseudo-transport layer and adds a 10 byte header to each. As the data link layer is also responsible for providing error detection and correction functions, error checking codes are introduced here. A 16-bit cyclic redundancy code (CRC) is used. Each TPDU is converted to a frame of up to 292 bytes in length.

It is worth noting at this point that the frame format is known as the FT3 frame format, which was originally described by IEC 870-5-1. This frame format represents a historical point of common ground between DNP3 and IEC 870-5. This frame format will be returned to in the next section.

5.2.5 The physical layer

The physical layer converts each frame into a bit stream over the physical media. In the original DNP3 documentation, a bit-serial asynchronous physical layer is specified. It calls for 8-bit data, 1 start bit, 1 stop bit, no parity, and RS-232C voltage levels and control signals.

5.2.6 Summary of message buildup

The buildup of DNP3 messages has been shown from a top-down perspective to have the following features:

- Application functions may or may not require the passage of data
- Commands will often require no data
- The application layer parses the data into APDUs
- The APDU maximum size is 2048 bytes
- The pseudo transport layer parses the APDU into smaller TPDUs
- TPDU maximum size is 250 bytes
- The data link layer adds headers and CRCs to form the LPDU
- LPDU maximum size is 292 bytes, of which 250 bytes are data

In the following sections the detailed functioning of each of the model layers will be examined. Looking at the functionality of each layer it will be necessary to examine and understand the message header sections applied at each layer, and to see how the functions of the layer are performed using them.

5.3 Physical layer

The physical layer may be described in terms of the network topology as well as the characteristics of the communication paths.

As previously noted, the physical layer defines the physical interface characteristics in terms of electrical specifications, timing, pin-outs and so on. This includes details required to establish and maintain the physical link. The data element at this level is essentially the bit, ie it is concerned with how to pass one bit of data at a time.

5.3.1 Description of physical layer

The physical layer originally recommended for DNP3 has the following specification:

- Bit serial asynchronous
- 8 data bits
- 1 start bit, 1 stop bit
- No parity
- RS-232C voltage levels and control signals
- CCIT V.24 hardware protocol for DTE/DCE communications

The DNP3 Users Group Technical Committee subsequently produced a standard for transmission of DNP3 over networks. This provides an alternative definition of the physical layer for that situation.

5.3.2 Services provided by physical layer

The physical layer must provide these functions:

- Connect
- Disconnect
- Send
- Receive
- Status

5.3.3 Topologies

As previously described, DNP3 supports either master-slave or peer-to-peer communications, with either one-on-one or multidrop topologies.

- Point-to-point
- Multidrop from one master
- Hierarchical with intermediate data concentrators
- Multiple master

Point-to-point, or direct topology refers to the case of two DNP3 devices connected together, either directly with a cable, or via modems and a communications path. This could be via a leased line, via radios, or via the public switched telephone network (PSTN).

A serial bus topology is the alternative to a direct topology. This may also be referred to as multidrop. In this case multiple devices are connected to the same communications path.

5.3.4 Physical layer procedures

Procedures must be provided to support both half-duplex and full-duplex communications. The specific procedures used will depend on the topology as well as whether half- or full-duplex transmission is available. One particular role of the procedures is to manage the event of message collision, where it can occur. Because DNP3 supports peer–peer communications, any station can act as a primary, or message initiator. Because of this, messages can be sent from two stations simultaneously, causing a collision.

Before discussing the physical layer procedures, a brief review of the terminology is given in the following table.

Simplex:	Communications are in one direction only
Half duplex:	Two-way communication is possible, but only in one direction at a time. This is because only one communication path or channel is used. To effect communication a protocol for handing over the channel is required.
Full duplex:	Simultaneous two-way communication is possible. Two channels are provided to do this.
Two-wire	A two-wire connection will provide one communication channel. A PSTN line is an example of this. Therefore, half-duplex communications only are possible via this channel.
Four-wire	A four-wire connection will provide two channels, and is capable of supporting duplex communications.

In the following procedures, the data carrier detect (DCD) indication is used to determine if the communications medium is free. Generally a time delay must be used to prioritize access to the channel once it has become free.

5.3.5   Half-duplex procedures

Direct link

With a direct, or point-to-point link, the delay from DCD clear needs to be just sufficient to allow the master station to detect loss of DCD and begin transmission. Note that if a dial-up connection is being used, the DCD signal indicates the establishment of a link rather than the presence of data. In this case the RTS and CTS signals must be used. DNP3 must assert the RTS signal and await the CTS signal before transmitting each frame.

Multidrop link

In the case of a multidrop link, time delays must be used to ensure that stations get access to the medium. This is accomplished by providing a back-off time made of a fixed delay plus a variable delay. These delay times are configurable by the user. Normally the master station will be given a zero fixed delay time, so that it can always gain access in a half-duplex environment. Prioritization of slave stations can be accomplished by this method. Again, the minimum delay must be long enough for the master station to be able to gain control of the medium before any outstation.

5.3.6   Full-duplex procedures

Direct link

No collision can occur as both master and slave have their own channel to each other.

Multidrop link

Time delays are used as for half-duplex multidrop, except that the fixed time delay may be reduced, as it is not necessary to provide this for the master. In the full-duplex multidrop environment, the master has its own channel to all receivers.

5.4   Data link layer

5.4.1   Description of data link layer

The purpose of the data link layer is to establish and maintain reliable communication of data over the physical link.

Link establishment involves setting up the logical communications link between sender and receiver. DNP3 is capable of supporting either connection oriented or connection-less operation. Thus, if a channel operates over a PSTN line and requires connection by dialling before communication can commence, the data link layer manages this without any direction from higher levels.

As seen previously, the data unit at the link layer level may be called the frame. The frame has a maximum size of 292 bytes including CRC codes, and carries a total of 250 bytes of information from the higher levels. The frame includes 16-bit source and destination addresses in its header. These provide for 65 536 different addresses. The address range FFF0–FFFF is reserved for broadcast messages, which are intended to be processed by all receivers. Note that addresses are logical in the sense that it is possible for one physical device to have more than one logical address. In such a case the different addresses would appear as separate devices to the master station.

The frame header also contains a function code. The functions supported by this are those required to initialize and test the operation of each logical link between sender and receiver. As an additional security feature every frame transmitted can request a confirmation of receipt. This is termed link layer confirmation.

These services and functions are expanded upon in the following sections.

5.4.2   Services provided

The following services are all provided by the data link layer. Understanding how these are provided begins with examining the frame format. The frame format includes necessary control bits for controlling message flow, functions, error detection and correction.

Services provided by the data link layer:

- Establish and maintain the communication channel
- Report on link status to higher layers
- Detect and correct errors that may occur during transmission
- Conversion of data between LSDUs and LPDUs
- Error notification to higher levels
- Sequencing and prioritized delivery of LSDUs

5.4.3   Some terminology

Communications in a SCADA system will generally have a structure where some stations may be identified as master stations, and others as slave stations, sub-master stations, or outstations. In a hierarchical structure, there may be some devices that act both as slave stations and master stations.

At the data link level, the terms balanced and unbalanced are used to describe whether all stations may initiate communications or not. In 'unbalanced' systems, only master stations will initiate communications. That is, only a master station will be a primary, or originating, station, and slave stations will always be secondary, or responding, stations. In these systems when a slave station has data that it needs to transmit to the master, it must wait until the master station polls it.

The DNP3 protocol support balanced communications at the data link level. This provides greater flexibility by allowing non-master stations to initiate communications. In DNP3 any station can be an originator or primary station.

The terminology 'balanced' and 'unbalanced' can be confused with the terms 'master' and 'slave'. This confusion can arise because it is easy to imagine that in a balanced system, all stations must be equal. This is not the case, however. The reason is that the terms balanced and unbalanced apply only to the lower data link level communications, whereas the master/slave distinction applies at the application level. In DNP3 the terms master and slave have real meaning, and a station is configured as one or the other. The key to understanding is that only a master station can issue a request, and only a slave can provide a response. These are each application level messages.

In the case of an outstation (a slave station) having unsolicited data to send to the master station, it issues an unsolicited response to the master. At the application level this is a different type of message to a request. At the data link level, however, the message frame appears no different from any other message frame whether issued by a master or a slave. These concepts are illustrated in the following communication sequence diagram.

The diagram below shows how these terms relate to the communication process. The diagram illustrates a request for data from a master station to a non-master station. This could be a poll for current data, a 'static' poll. The diagram illustrates the communication sequence by showing the parties on each side, with message directions shown between them. The time sequence is shown from top to bottom.

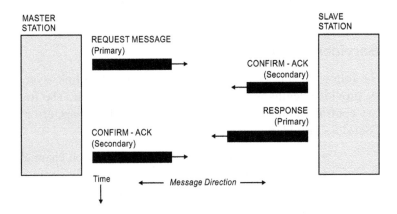

Figure 5.7
Example of communication sequence diagram

In the diagram the designated master station initiates a communication with a non-master station. The request message itself is contained in the application layer information within the message. The designated master station has initiated this communication and is therefore the primary station. A response is required to this message at the data link level, ie a confirmation of receipt is expected. The non-master station sends an acknowledgment. This is a secondary message, ie a data-link response to the primary message. Note that at the data link level, this transaction is now completed.

Because the last transaction contained an application level request for the transmission of data, the non-master station then initiates a communication with the requested data. Now the non-master station is initiating the communication, and it is the primary station for this transaction. This is a new communication sequence, or transaction, at the data link level. Although it is related to the prior transaction at the application level, it is unrelated at this level.

It can be seen from this example that the terms primary and secondary relate to the station initiating a transaction at the data link level, and not to whether the stations are master or non-master.

Although the communications are balanced, and therefore any station can be a primary station and initiate messages, it is incorrect to believe that the terms master and non-master have no meaning. In DNP3 stations may be defined as either master or non-master. This information is used at the link level to determine the setting of a message direction bit, the DIR bit. The direction bit is set for messages from a master, and cleared for messages from a non-master station.

A final definition that is important to understand is the 'data link' or just 'link'. The link refers to the logical connection between a primary station and a secondary station. It is therefore a one-way communication path. To establish two way communications between two devices, it is necessary to establish the links in each direction. The logic in this may be better understood by recognizing that a communication channel between two devices can be duplex, using two entirely separate physical media, one in each direction. The simplest example of this is of course a four-wire connection.

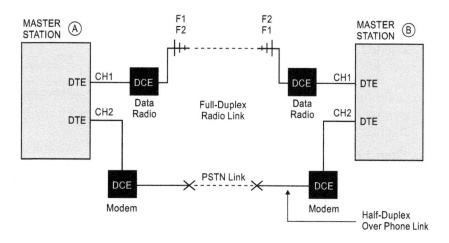

Figure 5.8
Example of communication channels

The drawing shows two communication channels between the master and non-master stations. The first channel uses a data radio, and is full-duplex. The second channel is a backup using modems and the public switched telephone network.

The second channel is half-duplex, although parts of it are in fact full-duplex. In this example there are four links, as follows:

- Channel 1 A to B
- Channel 1 B to A
- Channel 2 A to B
- Channel 2 B to A

5.4.4 How it does it

DNP3 controls transmission at the link layer level by using defined transmission procedures. These procedures make use of a control byte contained within the message frame to control transmission. It is important to realize that neither the control byte nor the procedures can by themselves do this. The procedures define what actions are taken at each end, and the control byte provides the coordination between them. It defines what type of transmission is being sent, ie the frame type, and where in the process the frame fits.

In order to understand how the overall process works, it is necessary to examine the structure of the frame, the meaning of the information in the control byte, and finally the procedures themselves.

The FT3 frame format

The LPDU or frame format was based on the FT3 format specified by IEC 870-5-1. This was one of four possible frame formats specified by IEC 870-5-1. The others are FT1.1, FT1.2 and FT2. These will be discussed further when comparing DNP3 with IEC 870.

The format specifies a 10 byte header, followed optionally by up to 16 data blocks. The overall message size is limited to 292 bytes, which provides for a maximum data capacity of 250 bytes. Thus a fully packed frame will comprise the header plus 16 data blocks, with the last block containing 10 data bytes.

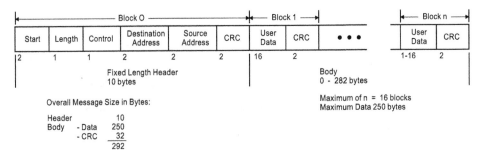

Figure 5.9
FT3 frame format

- **START**
  2 bytes: 0564 (hex)

- **LENGTH**
  Count of user data in bytes, plus 5, not counting CRC bytes. This represents all data, excluding CRC codes following the LENGTH count byte. Its range is

0–255. This is convenient as it is the largest length count that may be represented by 1 byte (=FF hex)

- **CONTROL**
  Frame control byte. See later section

- **DESTINATION**
  2 byte destination address (LSB, MSB)

- **SOURCE**
  2 byte source address (LSB, MSB)

- **CRC**
  2 byte cyclic redundancy check code

- **USER DATA**
  Each block has 16 bytes of user data. Last block has 1–16 as required. In case of a full frame the last block will have 10 bytes of user data

Control byte

The control byte follows the start and length bytes in the frame format. It provides for control of data flow over the physical link, identifies the type, and indicates the direction. The interpretation of most of the control byte is dependent on whether the communication is a primary or a secondary message.

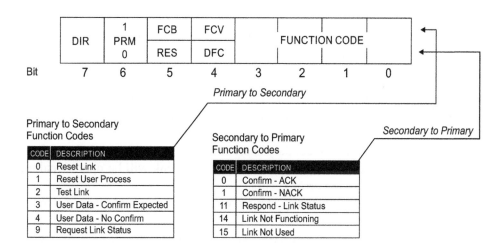

Figure 5.10
Control byte

DIR	Direction
	1 = A to B
	0 = B to A
PRM	Primary message
	1 = frame from primary (initiating station)
	0 = frame from secondary (responding station)
FCB	Frame count bit

FCV	Frame count bit valid
	0 = ignore FCB
	1 = FCV is valid
RES	Reserved = 0
DFC	Data flow control bit. Set to 1 by secondary station if further send of user data will cause buffer overflow.
FC	Function code

The operation of the single bits is now presented in more detail.

Direction bit

The DIR bit indicates the message direction between master and non-master stations. If a message is from a designated master station, this bit is set. Otherwise it is cleared.

Primary bit

The PRM bit is set if the frame is primary (initiating) or a secondary (responding). This is used directly in interpreting the function code. There are six valid function codes for primary frames, and five valid function codes for secondary frames.

Frame count bits

These are the frame count bit (FCB) and the frame count valid bit (FCV). These bits are only used for primary messages. The frame count bit is used to detect losses or duplication of frames to a secondary station. The frame count valid bit enables the use of the FCB. When the FCV bit is true, the FCB is toggled for each successful SEND-CONFIRM transaction between the same primary and secondary stations.

How they work is like this:

- Following data link start-up or a failed transaction, a secondary station will not accept any primary SEND-CONFIRM frames with FCV = 1 until a reset transaction is completed. This means it will only accept either a RESET link or a RESET user process command
- After a secondary station receives a RESET Link frame from a primary and it responds with a CONFIRM, that link will be operational until a frame transmission error occurs
- The secondary station will expect the next frame to contain FCV = 1 and FCB = 1
- The next primary SEND–CONFIRM message will have FCV = 1 and FCB = 1. The secondary station will accept this as the FCB is valid and is set, as expected
- Each subsequent primary SEND–CONFIRM message will have the FCB cleared or set in turn

Data flow control bit

The data flow control bit (DFC) is included in secondary frames. The secondary station will set DFC = 1 if a further SEND of user data will cause its buffer to overflow. On receipt of a frame with DFC = 1 a primary station will cease to send data, but will request link status until DFC = 0.

Data link function codes

The tables below show the detailed meanings for different values of the function code byte. The meanings are different depending on whether the message is a primary or a secondary transmission.

Function Codes from Primary Station

Function Code	Frame Type	Service Function	FCV Bit
0	SEND – CONFIRM expected	Reset of remote link	0
1	SEND – CONFIRM expected	Reset of user process	0
2	SEND – CONFIRM expected	Test function for link	1
3	SEND – CONFIRM expected	User data	1
4	SEND – NO REPLY expected	Unconfirmed user data	0
9	REQUEST – RESPOND expected	Request Link Status	0

Codes 5-8, 10-15 are not used

Function Codes from Secondary Station

Function Code	Frame Type	Service Function
0	CONFIRM	ACK – positive acknowledgement
1	CONFIRM	NACK – Message not accepted, link busy
11	RESPOND	Status of link (DFC = 0 or 1)
14		Link service not functioning
15		Link service not used or implemented

Codes 2-10, 12-13 are not used

The following shortened version of the function codes is included in the sequence diagrams. The codes are preceded with a P or an S, representing primary or secondary codes.

Function code key

P0	Reset link	S0	Confirm – ACK
P1	Reset user process	S1	Confirm – NACK
P2	Test link	S11	Link status
P3	User data – confirm	S14	Not functioning
P4	User data – no confirm	S15	Not implemented
P9	Request link status		

The use of the function codes by the transmission procedures is described in the following sections.

Error control

Error control is effected by the use of an error detection code and by the transmission procedures.

The first part of error control is detecting when an error has occurred in a message. DNP3 uses a 16-bit cyclic redundancy code or CRC to do this. The CRC is transmitted once in the frame header, and thereafter once for every block of up to 128 bits of user data being transmitted. By calculating a CRC for each block of data received, and comparing it to the transmitted CRC for that block, errors will be detected if they occur. If the CRCs do not agree, then an error is indicated. This technique is not foolproof, as it is possible to obtain equal CRCs for different data blocks, but the probability of this is very low.

The second part of error control is the action is performed when an error is detected. In every case where there is an error detected in any part of a frame, the frame is rejected by the receiving data link layer.

For all primary frame types except for SEND – NO REPLY, an error will result in a negative acknowledgment and subsequent re-sending of the frame by the primary. The SEND – NO REPLY frame type is used for sending low priority user data, which does not require confirmations. This type of data will simply be lost in the event of error.

The calculation of the CRC and processing on sending and receipt is a moderately complex operation using binary modulo-2 division. Although tricky for people to actually do, it is accomplished readily by computational devices. The algorithm for CRC processing is presented as a separate section.

5.4.5 Transmission procedures

Link reset

A link reset is required to enable communications between a primary and secondary station. A primary station must send the reset frame on power-up, or after a link is placed on-line.

Main points

- Must be used after a start, restart, or any link failure
- It is the responsibility of the primary station to perform the reset (of it's linked to a secondary station)
- Initiates the primary and secondary stations for further SEND–CONFIRM transactions
- Synchronizes the FCB so that FCB=1 is expected by the secondary for the transaction following the reset

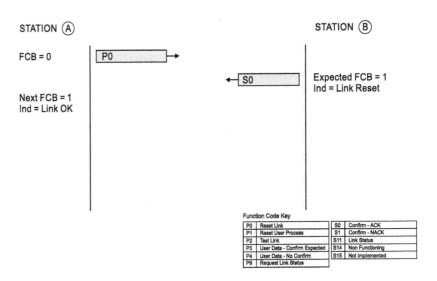

Figure 5.11
Reset link

In the communication sequence diagram above the link reset transaction is represented. Blocks are shown representing the actual frames transmitted. The primary station is shown on the left and the secondary station is on the right. States are shown for the FCB (frame control bit) at the primary, and the expected value of the FCB, at the secondary station. User indications are noted for each station also. These are indications on link status provided to service users.

In the following diagram, the same example is presented showing the actual byte pattern that would be seen if the transaction was captured by a protocol analyzer.

Primary to secondary (A to B)

<05 64 05 C0 01 00 0C 00 CF A0>

Link header	0564	
Length	05	
Control byte	C0	; DIR=1, PRI=1, FCV=0, FC=RESET
Destination address	0001	
Source address	000C	
CRC value	CFA0	

Secondary to primary (B to A)

<05 64 05 00 0C 00 01 00 FD E9>

Link header	0564	
Length	05	
Control byte	00	; DIR=0, PRI=0, FC=ACK
Destination address	000C	
Source address	0001	
CRC value	FDE9	

Figure 5.12
Data link transaction detail – reset

It may be noticed that the primary DIR bit is set in the primary frame, and cleared in the secondary frame. This shows that this transaction is between a master and a non-master. This is coincidental, as it could equally have been the other way (eg as for the return link between B and A).

Reset user process

The reset user process function code has been discontinued. The original DNP3 documentation defined the following functionality:

- Used to reset the link user process
- An ACK is sent if accepted by the user process
- Otherwise a NACK response is sent

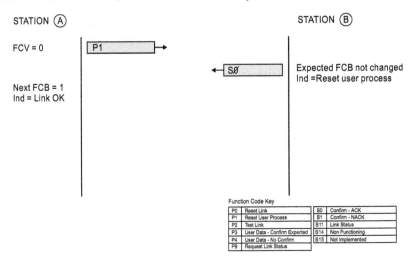

Figure 5.13
Reset user process

Test

The test procedure is used by the primary station to test the link. If the FCBs do not match, the secondary station should re-send the last secondary confirm frame.

If the FCBs do match, it should send a CONFIRM–ACK frame and toggle the FCB. The data flow control bit DFC should be set accordingly in the return frame.

Summary

- Used to test the link
- Secondary station checks FCB to expected FCB
- If FCBs match it sends ACK and toggles expected FCB
- If FCB does not match it re-sends the last confirm frame

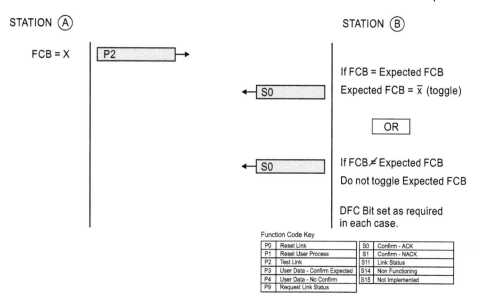

Figure 5.14
Test

Confirmed send user data

This procedure is used for sending frames with user data that require confirmation of receipt. The link must be initially reset before the user data function may be used.

Summary

- The user data function is the most common message
- Link must be reset prior to use
- It carries the user data
- Provides reliable transfer of user data by re-sending frames with errors

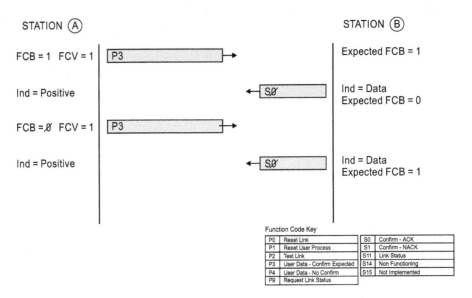

Figure 5.15
User data

The diagram shows the transmission of two consecutive user data frames by the primary station. On the successful receipt of the first user data frame an ACK (confirm–acknowledge) response is sent by the secondary station. The station also indicates the receipt of user data and toggles the expected FCB. On receipt of the confirmation by the primary, the FCB flag is toggled and another user data frame is sent.

In the event of an error in the received message, the frame is ignored and therefore no confirmation is sent. In this case the primary will re-send the message after an appropriate re-try delay time.

Unconfirmed send user data

This procedure is used for sending user data without requiring confirmation from the secondary station. It may be used where the data is of low priority. The advantage is that data can be transmitted at a greater rate, thus providing a better use of bandwidth.

However, the disadvantage is that errors in transmission will result in lost frames. A frame found to have an error (by CRC checking) will be rejected by the secondary station, but as no confirmation was expected by the primary there will be no way for the primary to know that the message was unsuccessful.

Summary

- Used for low priority user data
- No confirmations are sent by secondary
- More efficient use of bandwidth

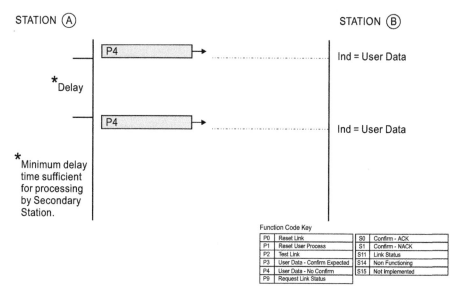

Figure 5.16
Unconfirmed send user data

Request link status

The request link status frame is used following receipt of a NACK or an ACK with DFC=1 during transmission. The DFC (data flow control) bit is set by the secondary station if its buffers are full or if for any other reason it cannot process further data. The request link status is then used to determine when the link can again accept data.

Summary

- Sent to request the status of the secondary station
- Used after a NACK or an ACK with DFC=1 is received
- Response frame will have DFC either set or cleared to give status

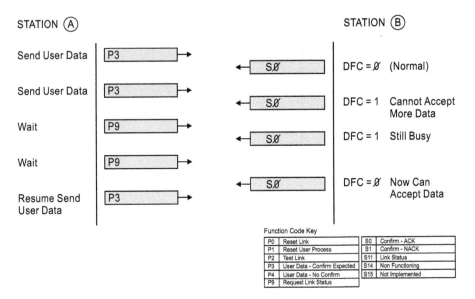

Figure 5.17
Request link status

In the diagram the secondary station's buffer is full after the second user data frame. The secondary responds with an ACK containing the data flow control DFC bit set to 1. The primary station now waits and at intervals sends a request link status frame. When this is acknowledged with DFC=0 the user data transmission is resumed.

CRC error code

The use of the cyclic redundancy code for detection of errors within transmitted frames has been introduced in terms of its function. This section examines the detail of the CRC processing.

DNP3 defines a 16-bit cyclic redundancy check code (or CRC) for error detection. The 16-bit CRC is provided for the 64-bit header data, and for each 128-bit (16 byte) block of user data transmitted.

The CRC code is generated by the following simple algorithm illustrated in the diagram and described in the following.

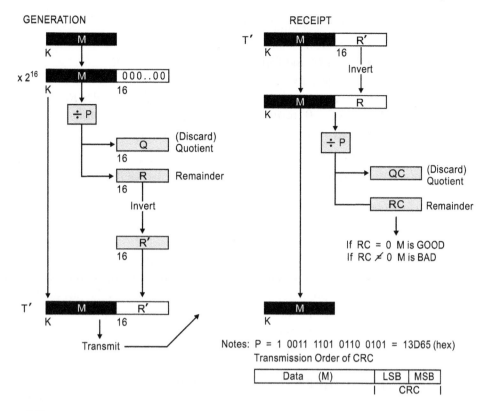

Figure 5.18
CRC code processing

Generation of message:

- Start with user data block M of k bits ($k = 64$ for header, 8–128 for blocks in body)
- Multiply by 2^{16} (ie append 16 zeros to end to form k + 16-bit number)
- Divide by generator polynomial P to obtain quotient Q and remainder R modulo-2 division is used)
- Discard Q, keep R
- Invert R to obtain R'
- Append R' to M forming message T' to be transmitted

Where generator polynomial:
$P = x^{16} + x^{13} + x^{12} + x^{10} + x^8 + x^5 + x^2 + 1$
This forms a 17-bit number which is 13D65 (in hex)

Processing on receipt of message:

- Receive $T' = M$ followed by R'
- Invert R' and form $T = M$ appended with R
- Divide T by P (using modulo-2 division)
- Discard quotient QC, keep calculated remainder RC
- If $RC = 0$, result is GOOD, copy M to data output
- If RC not $= 0$, result is BAD, reject message

It is noted that this CRC has a 'Hamming distance' of 6. This means that at least 6 bits must have been received in error to obtain a false GOOD DATA result.

Summary of data link operation

Summary of data link layer:

- Receives link service data units from higher layer
- Forms the LPDU by including addresses, the control byte, and CRC codes
- Uses procedures to deliver the frame across the physical layer
- Function codes provide for link initialization and error recovery
- Reassembles LSDU at secondary station
- Provides status indications to higher levels

5.5 Transport layer (pseudo-transport)

5.5.1 Description of transport layer

The primary function of the transport layer in DNP3 is to implement message disassembly and reassembly. This allows for the transmission of larger blocks of data than can be handled by the data link layer. Because this functionality is fairly limited compared to the wider OSI definition of the transport layer, the prefix 'pseudo' is often used. For simplicity the layer is referred to in this text as the transport layer.

5.5.2 The transport protocol data unit

The transport layer takes the user data, the transport service data unit (TSDU) and breaks it down into one or more transport protocol data units (TPDUs) and sends each to the data link layer for sending. The TPDUs become the user data within the data link layer, that is the LSDUs.

Recalling that the LSDUs can be a maximum of 250 bytes of user data, this defines the maximum size of the LPDU, including any transport layer overheads. In fact the transport functions are accomplished with a single header byte, leaving 249 bytes for carrying data. This is pictured in the diagram following.

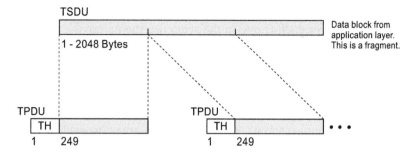

This TSDU is broken down into multiple TPDUs each
containing a 1 byte header and up to 249 bytes of user data.

Each TPDU will fit into one frame format in the DataLlink Layer.

Figure 5.19
Transport protocol data unit

In a receiving, or secondary station, the incoming TPDUs are reformed into the TSDU
for use by the application layer. The transport header bytes are stripped off and the TSDU
is reformed from the multiple TPDMs. The transport layer is responsible for ensuring that
the TSDU is reassembled in the correct sequence.

5.5.3 The transport header

The single byte transport header contains two bits that identify the start and end of
a sequence of frames (TPDUs), plus a six-bit sequence counter.

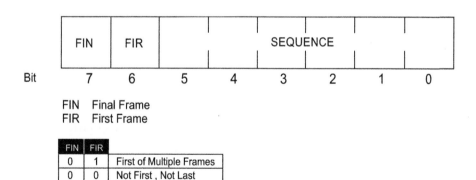

Figure 5.20
Transport header byte

Rules

- If a secondary station receives a frame with the FIR bit set, any previous
  incomplete sequence of frames is discarded
- If a frame is received without the FIR bit set, and no sequence is in progress,
  then this frame is ignored

- Sequence number may be any value 0–63 for first frame, and must increment for each frame in the sequence thereafter
- Sequence number rolls over from 63 to 0

5.5.4 Summary of transport layer

Summary

- Takes TSDU fragments up to 2048 bytes and breaks them into multiple TPDUs
- Includes a 1 byte header
- TPDU can carry 249 bytes of user data
- The TPDU can fit into one FT3 frame format (LSDU)
- Header has FIR and FIN bits and 6-bit sequence number
- Passes TPDUs to and from data link layer
- Assembles incoming TPDUs into TSDU

5.6 Application layer message handling

5.6.1 Description of the application layer

The application layer is the highest level of the protocol, and communicates directly with the user application program. Master stations generate application level request messages for transmission to outstations, and outstations generate application level responses for transmission to the master station. These messages may contain commands, or requests for provision of data, or they may perform other functions such as time synchronization.

Summary

- Forms request messages to outstations
- Request messages may be commands, send data, or request data
- Accepts data from user application to send to master or to outstation
- Breaks user data down into multiple ASDUs
- Adds control information (APCI) to form APDUs
- Multiple APDUs are called fragments
- Fragments do not exceed 2048 bytes
- Fragments contain data objects
- Each fragment must be processable on its own

The fragment size and data content requirements have been specified so that a fragment is always processable on its own. This means that a fragment buffer size of 2048 bytes should be sufficient to allow receipt of a fully processable piece of information. The buffer can then be left empty for receipt of the next fragment.

5.6.2 Application message sequences

At the application level, there are two basic message types in DNP3. These are requests and responses. Only a master station can send a request, and only an outstation can send a response. However, there is a special class of response called an 'unsolicited response'. This allows an outstation to send information to a master station or to a peer (another non-master station).

The message sequences are shown in the following drawings.

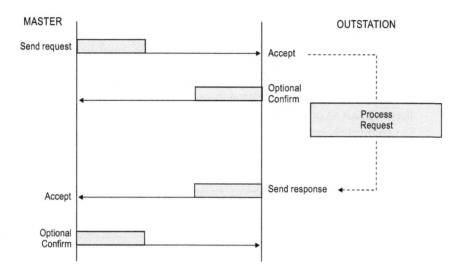

Figure 5.21
Application message sequences

In the above sequence, the outstation receives a request from the master station. If the master station has set a 'confirm' bit, the outstation will send a confirm message. It will at the same time commence processing the request. Once it has assembled the necessary information it will send its response. The master station will send a confirmation if the confirm bit is set in the response.

The case of an unsolicited response is shown below. An event or defined process change is detected, causing the generation of a message by the outstation.

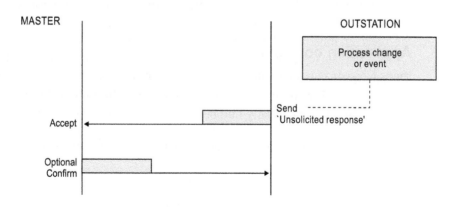

Figure 5.22
Unsolicited response message

Whilst the message sequences appear simple enough, complexities arise from various causes. This includes the need to generate multi-fragment messages, and the need to handle crossovers in communications such as might arise if both a master and an out-station send messages simultaneously. These complexities are catered for by 'flow control' and the APCI, discussed in the following sections.

5.6.3   Application message formats

As noted previously, application messages are of two types, request and response. Each of these appear as one or more APDUs. Each APDU is made up of a header which is termed the application protocol control information, and optional data, the ASDU.

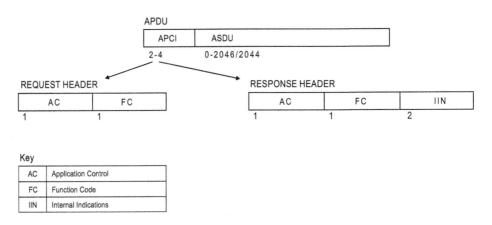

Figure 5.23
Application message format

The request and response headers differ by one field. The response header includes an additional two-byte field designated internal indications (IIN). The content of the ASDU is not depicted in this drawing, but it is made up of data objects, each with an object header. These will be presented in detail later. For now the ASDU may be thought of merely as data.

5.6.4   Application control field

The application control field is the first byte of the control information, or APCI. It is used to control the communication flow. It has three bits or flags, plus a sequence number which is used to sequentially number fragments.

Bit	7	6	5	4	3	2	1	0
	FIR	FIN	CON		SEQUENCE			

Key

FIR	First fragment of multi-fragment message
FIN	Final fragment of multi-fragment message
CON	Confirmation required
Sequence	Fragment sequence number 0 - 15 Master station requests and outstation respones (solicited) 16 - 31 Outstation unsolicited responses

Figure 5.24
Application control field

Key

FIR   First fragment of multi-fragment message
FIN   Final fragment of multi-fragment message
CON   Confirmation required
Sequencefragment sequence number
                       0–15   Master station requests and outstation responses (solicited)
                       16–31   Outstation unsolicited responses

Flow control is implemented by:

- The FIR and FIN bits
- The CON bit
- Master and outstation response timeouts
- Master and outstation re-try counts (optional)

Using the following rules:

- If CON = 1 a confirmation must be sent
- Sequence number is incremented for each fragment
- Sequence number rolls-over from 15 to 0, or 31 to 16
- Response fragment has same sequence number as request fragment
- If multiple request fragments, response starts at last request fragment number
- Increment sequence number for each extra response fragment
- A retransmitted response uses the original sequence number
- Outstation must process one request before starting a second request

These are further detailed in the following sub-sections

Message confirmations

- If the CON bit is set, then a confirmation is required
- A confirmation response to a request has the same sequence number as the request
- If two confirmation messages are received with same sequence number, ignore the second

Sequence numbers

- Sequence number is 0–15 for requests, outstation responses, and the associated confirmations
- Number rolls over from 15 to 0
- Sequence number is 16–31 for unsolicited responses and confirmations
- Confirmations have same sequence number as request or response
- The first fragment of a response has the same sequence number as the request, or as the last fragment of a multi-fragment request
- For a single fragment request re-try, the re-try has the same sequence number as the original request
- For a multi-fragment request re-try, the re-try commences with the sequence number of the last fragment of the previous request

Identical sequence numbers

- If two messages are received with the same sequence number, it usually means that the response message was not received by the other station. Re-transmit response
- If two confirmation responses are received with the same sequence number, ignore the second response

5.6.5   Message transaction flow diagrams

The DNP3 Basic Four documentation includes a number of diagrams illustrating typical message transactions. These are very useful in understanding the transaction sequences. These are represented in the following diagrams, although the layout has been altered.

In these diagrams the transaction sequence is represented by showing the Application Control (AC) information in each message passing between master station and outstation. The time sequence in the diagrams is from top to bottom.

The AC information is shown in the form:

[FIR   FIN   CON   SEQ Number]

Receipt of a message fragment is depicted by an equals sign (=) in the diagrams, indicating the received message was as sent. Where a message is not received, a timeout may subsequently occur.

It should be remembered that at this point the diagrams are concentrating on only the AC part of the message, which is the first byte of the message, as this is the part that is controlling the message flow. Of course, in the whole message the AC byte is followed by the function code FC, the internal indications for response messages, and the data if present. Nevertheless, it is only the AC information that is of importance to the flow control.

Typical message transaction

Case One: Typical Message Transaction Flows

Master AC	Outstation AC	Description
[110 7]	=	Request, no confirm required
=	[111 7]	Response to master request
[110 7]	=	Confirm
=	[111 24]	Unsolicited response
[110 24]	=	Confirm

[FIR FIN CON SEQ]

Case One shows an initial master request without the confirmation bit set. The outstation responds without a prior confirmation. As the outstation's response has CON set, the master sends a confirmation on receipt. Later, the outstation makes an unsolicited response. It uses a sequence number in the range 16–31. The master station responds using the same sequence number.

Case Two: Request with confirm

Master AC	Outstation AC	Description
[111 2]	=	Request
=	[110 2]	Confirm
=	[111 2]	Response to master request
[110 2]	=	Confirm

[FIR FIN CON SEQ]

Case Two shows a typical request–response with confirmation sequence. Notice that the sequence number is unchanged for the whole transaction.

Multi-fragment response

Case Three: Multi-fragment Response

Master AC	Outstation AC	Description
[110 2]	=	Request, no confirm required
=	[101 2]	Response, fragment 1, first
[110 2]	=	Confirm
=	[011 3]	Response, fragment 2, last
[110 3]	=	Confirm
[110 4]	=	Request (new request)

[FIR FIN CON SEQ]

Case Three shows a single-fragment request, without confirmation, requiring a multi-fragment response. Two response fragments were required. The master station increments its sequence number for the subsequent transaction, shown as the 'new request'.

Confirmation timeouts

Case Four: **Outstation Confirmation Timeout**

Master AC	Outstation AC	Description
[110 3]	=	Request
	[111 3]	Response to master request, not received by master
	Timeout	Confirmation not received
=	[111 3]	Resend response
[110 3]	=	Confirm

[FIR FIN CON SEQ]

In Case Four the outstation response was not received by the master station and so no confirmation was issued by the master. After the confirmation timeout period at the outstation, it re-sends its response. Note that it has used the same sequence number.

Case Five: **Confirmation Lost**

Master AC	Outstation AC	Description
[110 5]	=	Request
=	[111 5]	Response to master request
[110 5]		Confirm sent, not received
	Timeout	Confirmation timeout
=	[111 5]	Resend response
[110 5]	=	Confirm

[FIR FIN CON SEQ]

Case Five appears identical to case four at the outstation. In this case the master station did receive its response, but the confirmation it sent was garbled and lost. After its confirmation timeout operates, the outstation re-sends its response. The master station on receiving a second response with the same sequence number just re-sends the confirmation. It does not reprocess the information as it already has that.

Case Six: **Master Request Timeout**

Master AC	Outstation AC	Description
[110 8]		Request, not received
Timeout		Master station timeout
[110 8]	=	Request resent by master
=	[101 8]	Response sent
[110 8]	=	Confirm
=	[011 9]	Second fragment
[110 9]	=	Confirm

[FIR FIN CON SEQ]

Case Six shows the loss of a master station request. After a request timeout period, the master station re-sends its request using the same sequence number.

Effects of network delays

In the following cases delays in the network cause transmissions to arrive after timeouts have operated. Such cases might occur for example when a store and forward device becomes heavily loaded.

Case Seven: Master Station Timeout

Master AC	Outstation AC	Description
[110 12]	=	Request
	[111 12]	Response to master delayed
Timeout		Master Station Timeout
[110 12]	=	Request resent
	[111 12]	Resend response
=(1st)		First response received
[110 12]	=	Confirm
=(2nd)		Second response received
[110 12]	=	Confirmation resent
		Confirmation ignored by RTU

[FIR FIN CON SEQ]

In Case Seven the outstation response has been delayed in the network. The master station times out and then re-sends its request using the same sequence number. The outstation re-sends its response. The first response is received by the master and a confirmation is sent. When the master receives a second response it does not process the data, but sends a confirmation. The outstation receives the second confirmation and discards it.

In general, message delays lead to timeouts and re-sending of either requests or messages. When the delayed message subsequently arrives it is recognized as being part of the current transaction because of its sequence number. If it is a repeat message requiring a confirmation, the confirmation is sent but the message itself is not acted on further. If it is a delayed confirmation that is received, this is simply discarded.

Case Eight: Delayed Confirmation from Outstation

Master AC	Outstation AC	Description
[111 12]	=	Request, No Response Expected eg freeze command
	[110 12]	Confirm sent, delayed in network
Timeout		
[111 12]	=	Request resent and received
=	[110 12]	Confirm
=(1st)		Delayed first confirm received, ignored by master

[FIR FIN CON SEQ]

Case Eight shows a repeat message being sent by the master after the confirmation is delayed. When the confirmation to the first request is received it is discarded by the master station.

Case Nine: Master Request Timeout

Master AC	Outstation AC	Description
	[111 28]	Unsolicited message sent, but delayed in network
	Timeout	Confirmation timeout
=	[111 28]	Message resent
[110 28]	=	Confirm
=(1st)		Delayed first message received
[110 28]	=	Confirm, outstation ignores this

[FIR FIN CON SEQ]

In Case Nine the unsolicited message is delayed in the network. After confirmation timeout, the outstation re-sends the message. This time it is received directly and a confirmation is sent. If the master subsequently receives the original message it ignores it but sends a confirmation. This confirmation is ignored by the outstation. The situation is no different if the messages are received in the opposite order, ie the delayed 1st message arrives first, but after the outstation confirmation timeout.

Collision with unsolicited response

If outstations are configured and enabled to provide unsolicited responses, then there will be the possibility of these occurring at the same time as a master station request. Special features are provided to handle the cases of these transactions becoming intermingled. The first feature is the use of different sequence numbers for unsolicited response transactions. Because these use only the numbers 16–31, these transactions are differentiated by the sequence number.

A second feature is provided to ensure that data is not lost or duplicated arising from an inappropriate sequence of actions. This feature is termed process mode, for which two modes are defined. These are the 'immediate mode', and the 'process after confirm' mode. Immediate mode is used for all transactions except for a master station read request to an outstation, when an unsolicited response transaction is in progress. When an outstation is waiting for confirmation for an unsolicited response, it will delay processing a read request until the confirmation is received. This is the process after confirm mode.

Rules for unsolicited message transactions

- Master station always processes an unsolicited response immediately, even if waiting for a response to a previous message
- If a confirmation for the unsolicited response is requested it is issued immediately by master
- Outstation will process most requests immediately, even if waiting for a response to a previous unsolicited response. This is 'immediate mode'
- Outstation will not process a master station Read request if it is waiting for confirmation of a previous unsolicited response. This is 'process after confirm' mode

These rules are illustrated in the following transactions.

Case Ten: Simultaneous Transactions

Master AC	Outstation AC	Description
[110 7]	[110 24]	Both master and outstations transmit simultaneously
=	=	
=	[111 7]	Response to master station
[110 7]	=	Confirmation to outstation response
[110 24]	=	Confirmation to unsolicited message

[FIR FIN CON SEQ]

In Case Ten both master and outstation transmit messages at the same time. The outstation responds immediately to the master station. Because it responded immediately, it may be deduced that this was an immediate mode request, that is, the master station had not made a read request.

Note that the order of receipt of confirmations at the outstation is unimportant.

Case Eleven: Unsolicited Response without Confirm

Master AC	Outstation AC	Description
[111 2]	[110 22]	Both master and outstations transmit simultaneously
=	=	
		Master stores and processes unsolicited response. No confirm was requested.
=	[110 2]	Confirmation to master station request
=	[111 2]	Response to master station request
[110 2]		Confirm

[FIR FIN CON SEQ]

In Case Eleven a normal message sequence is shown in which an unsolicited message does not require a confirmation. A simultaneous master station request is serviced by the outstation.

Note that sending unsolicited responses without requesting confirmation is not recommended, as this may lead to data loss. Considering this situation leads to understanding when the use of non-confirmed messages is appropriate. This is when timeouts will function to ensure that a missed transaction is re-attempted. For example, requests from the master station requiring responses will be repeated if a response is not received. In this case the message response timeout will cause re-sending of the message when a response is not obtained.

Case Twelve: Simultaneous Transactions Multi-fragment

Master AC	Outstation AC	Description
[110 2]	[111 18]	Master and outstation send messages simultaneously
=	=	
=	[101 2]	Fragment 1 of response
[110 2]	=	Confirm for fragment 1
=	[011 3]	Fragment 2 of response
[110 18]	=	Confirm for unsolicited response
[110 3]	=	Confirm for fragment 2

[FIR FIN CON SEQ]

In Case Twelve the unsolicited response is confirmed during the course of a multi-fragment transaction.

Case Thirteen: Simultaneous Transactions

Master AC	Outstation AC	Description
[110 3]	[111 28]	Master and outstation send messages simultaneously. Unsolicited response not received.
	=	
=	[111 3]	Response to request from master
[110 3]	=	Confirm
	Timeout	Confirmation timeout
=	[111 28]	Unsolicited message resent
[110 28]	=	Confirm

[FIR FIN CON SEQ]

In Case Thirteen an unsolicited response from the outstation is lost or garbled. The outstation responds to a separate transaction from the master station, but re-sends the unsolicited response after its confirmation timeout expires.

Case Fourteen: Process After Confirm Mode (1)

Master AC	Outstation AC	Description
[110 2]	[111 18]	Master and outstation send messages simultaneously. Request is for read data.
=	=	
		Outstation waits for confirmation
[110 18]	=	Confirm for unsolicited response
		RTU now processes master request
=	[111 2]	Response
[110 2]	=	Confirm

[FIR FIN CON SEQ]

Case Fourteen shows the process after confirm mode. The outstation receives a master station read request after it has commenced an unsolicited response. It waits until it has received a confirmation for its unsolicited response before proceeding.

Case Fifteen: Process After Confirm Mode (2)

Master AC	Outstation AC	Description
[110 3]	[111 28] =	Master and outstation send messages simultaneously. Request is for read data. Master does not receive unsolicited response.
		Outstation waits for confirmation
	Timeout	Outstation confirmation timeout
=	[111 28]	Resends unsolicited response
[110 28]	=	Confirm for unsolicited response
		RTU now processes master request
=	[111 3]	Response
[110 3]	=	Confirm

[FIR FIN CON SEQ]

Case Fifteen is similar to Case Fourteen except that the unsolicited response is not received. Again the outstation completes the unsolicited response transaction prior to responding to the master station's read request.

5.7   Application layer message functions

5.7.1   General introduction

In the previous section entitled application layer message handling we have been concerned purely with the flow control of application layer messages. We have seen how the first byte of the application protocol control information (APCI) is used in managing the sequence of application level messages between master and outstation.

In doing this, almost no reference has been made to the actual content of the messages. In this and the following sections we turn the focus on to the actual messages and the information they carry.

In general terms, as we are dealing with SCADA systems, we expect that messages will be capable of sometimes carrying commands, and other times carrying data, which may be generated in response to commands. This is, after all, the high level functionality provided by a SCADA system; control, and data acquisition. Not surprisingly then, the messages contain both function codes, and data objects. Function codes define exactly what the meaning and purpose of a message is. They may, for example, tell an outstation to perform a particular operation, like freeze some counters, or to send some data. The data objects define the structure and interpretation of the data itself.

The reader might at this point wonder why the data should need any predefined formats, that is to have any specific 'data object' definition. Why cannot the outstation simply send data in any format that will be understood by the particular user application? The answer to this lies in the purpose of the protocol in the first place. The protocol is not just intended to provide a means for communication between devices from different manufacturers, but it is intended to make that data meaningful across different platforms. The data is not just unspecified data therefore, but it is specific data types like digital inputs, analog values and so on, each of which has a defined type under DNP3. For all this to work therefore, very specific definitions of the purposes and meaning of the message content are necessary.

We will examine these now. We will begin with the function codes, and then look at the data objects defined under DNP3.

5.7.2   Application function codes

The function code is the second byte of the application protocol control information. It follows the application control byte in both request headers from master stations, and response headers from outstations. The function code indicates what function is required to be performed.

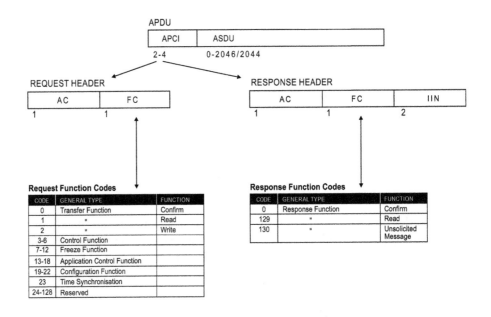

Figure 5.25
Application function codes

Overview of function codes

Request Function Codes

Code	General Type	Function
0	Transfer Function	Confirm
1		Read
2		Write
3-6	Control Function	
7-12	Freeze Function	
13-18	Application Control Function	
19-22	Configuration Function	
23	Time Synchronisation	
24 -128	Reserved	

Response Function Codes

Code	General Type	Function
0	Response Function	Confirm
129		Read
130		Write

The specific actions required for each function code are included in the following tables. The information in these is reproduced directly from that presented in the DNP3 Basic Four documentation, DNP3 Application Layer, Section 3.5 Function Codes.

Many of the functions need to identify specific data on which they operate. They do this with data object references that are included in the data within the ASDU, which follows the APCI header. In this section only the function codes themselves will be examined, with the referencing of the data objects being presented in following sections. In the function descriptions these data objects are referred to as 'specified data objects'.

Request function codes

Transfer Functions			
Code	Function	Action	Response
0	Confirm	Message fragment confirmation. Used by both requests and responses.	No further response required.
1	Read		Respond with requested data objects
2	Write	Store specified data objects in outstation	Respond with status of operation

Transfer functions are those concerned with transferring defined data objects. These are the functions that acquire data from the outstation, or write control information to it.

Control Functions			
Code	**Function**	**Action**	**Response**
3	Select	Select or arm points, but do not produce any control action, or change of setpoint. The Operate function code must be subsequently received to activate these outputs.	Respond with the status of the selected control points.
4	Operate	Set or produce the output actions on the points previously selected by the Select function.	Respond with the status of the control points following action.
5	Direct Operate	Select and operate the specified outputs or control points.	Respond with the status of the control points following action.
6	Direct Operate, no Ack	Select and operate the specified outputs or control points.	No response message to be sent.

The control functions are used to operate or change control points in an outstation. These may be control relay outputs, ie digital points, or analog setpoint values. These may be operated directly, with or without acknowledgment, or with the select before operate sequence.

The select before operate sequence is a security feature that is well known in the electrical supply industry. It provides an additional level of security to ensure against misoperation arising from a corrupted message, or a human error such as selecting the wrong device from a group of similar devices shown on an HMI screen.

Select before operate sequence requires the following to occur:

- Selection of the control points is made
- The outstation responds with the identity and status of the selected points
- The outstation starts a select–operate timer
- The HMI displays the selected points differently, showing they have been selected
- The operate function is sent for the selected points
- The outstation will reject the operate message if the point identities do not match those of the previously selected points.
- The outstation will de-select the points if the select–operate timer expires before the operate function is received

Freeze Functions			
Code	**Function**	**Action**	**Response**
7	Immediate Freeze	Copy specified objects to a freeze buffer.	Respond with status of operation. Note that the data themselves are not returned.
8	Immediate Freeze – No Ack	Copy specified objects to a freeze buffer.	No response to be sent.
9	Freeze and Clear	Copy specified objects to a freeze buffer, then clear the objects.	Respond with status of operation. Note that the data themselves are not returned.
10	Freeze and Clear – No Ack	Copy specified objects to a freeze buffer, then clear the objects.	No response to be sent.
11	Freeze with Time	Copy specified objects to a freeze buffer at the specified time and thereafter at intervals (if) specified.	Respond with status of operation. Note that the data themselves are not returned.
12	Freeze with Time – No Ack	Copy specified objects to a freeze buffer at the specified time and thereafter at intervals (if) specified.	No response to be sent.

Freeze functions are typically used for the following:

- Record system-wide state data at a common time (eg midnight)
- Record status or value of specific point at regular intervals (eg for trending a flowrate)

Application Control Functions			
Code	Function	Action	Response
13	Cold Restart	Restart application on completion of communication sequence.	Respond with time until outstation availability following restart.
14	Warm Restart	Partial restart on completion of communication sequence.	Respond with time until outstation availability following restart.
15	Initialise Data to Defaults	Initialise specified data to initial or default settings.	Respond with status of operation.
16	Initialise Application	Initialise specified applications.	Respond with status of operation.
17	Start Application	Start specified applications.	Respond with status of operation.
18	Stop Application	Stop specified applications.	Respond with status of operation.

The application control functions are coded in order of decreasing effect. The cold restart is a complete restart of the outstation, as if it had been de-powered and then re-powered up. The warm restart may be used to reset the DNP3 application, but not necessarily to reset other application programs. Typically the warm restart is used to initialize its configuration and clear events stored in its buffers. Once either a cold or warm restart has been initiated, the master station should not attempt to communicate with the outstation until the restart time interval returned in the outstation's response has elapsed.

The initialize data to defaults could for example setup standard setpoints, and clear counters. The specific data objects to be initialized are identified in the request, but not the default values themselves. These are stored locally in the outstation, as fixed read-only data, or as parameters in non-volatile memory, for example.

Configuration Functions			
Code	Function	Action	Response
19	Save Configuration	Save the specified configuration to non-volatile memory.	Respond with time outstation availability.
20	Enable Unsolicited Messages	Enable spontaneous reporting of the specified data objects.	Respond with status of operation.
21	Disable Unsolicited Messages	Disable spontaneous reporting of the specified data objects.	Respond with status of operation.
22	Assign Class	Assign specified data objects to a particular class.	Respond with status of operation.

The configuration referred to by these functions is the state of the parameters and settings that collectively determine the behavior of the outstation. It is not referring to a complete program or 'configuration' download. The save configuration function causes storing in a specified non-volatile memory location the settings that define the system's configuration.

The enable and disable of unsolicited messages allows for a live change to this configuration aspect.

The assign class function allows for live assignment of data objects to classes. These are discussed later in the text. The effect of classes is to provide a broad means of referencing data, for example by allowing a read of all data in a particular class.

Time Synchronisation Function			
Code	Function	Action	Response
23	Delay Measurement	Allows measurement of the path delay between the master and the outstation. The value determined is used as an offset when setting the system time at the outstation.	Response message with time delay between receipt and response, ie outstation processing delay time.
24	Record Current Time	Causes outstation to record the time of its clock on completion of receipt of this command message	Respond with status (internal indications bits).

The delay measurement function is used immediately prior to performing a time setting by writing to the outstation clock. It is used over asynchronous serial links, for which the message transmission time is significant in comparison to the one-millisecond clock resolution. The outstation measures the time in milliseconds that it takes to turnaround the message, that is, the time from message receipt to sending the response to the master. The master station subtracts this time from the turnaround time it sees, to determine the time the messages spent in the communication system. It then divides that time by two to obtain an approximation of the one-way message delay from master station to outstation.

The record current time function is used when performing a time setting over a LAN. In this case the transmission occurs essentially instantaneously, so no turnaround time measurement is needed. Both the master station and the outstation record the current values of their own clocks at the time this message is sent. Subsequently, the master sends its recorded time to the outstation, which calculates the time error from the difference between the recorded values.

File Functions			
Code	Function	Action	Response
25	Open File	The required file is locked to prevent use by other processes, and opened.	Respond with File Command Status (Object Group 70, Variation 4)
26	Close File	The file is closed and released for use by other processes.	Respond with File Command Status (Object Group 70, Variation 4)
27	Delete File	The required file is deleted, provided that it is not open. If it is open the command is not executed.	Respond with File Command Status (Object Group 70, Variation 4)
28	Get File Information	Provide file information: Type, Size, Time of Creation, Permissions	Respond with File Descriptor Object (Object Group 70, Variation 7)
29	Authenticate	Requests an authentication key from the outstation, if required, to allow file change operations.	Respond with Authentication Object (Object Group 70, Variation 2)
30	Abort	Immediately abort a file transfer operation in progress, and close the associated file without saving changes.	Respond with File Command Status (Object Group 70, Variation 4)

The file function codes provide for file operations with configuration and other files in outstation devices. Some devices may implement security features to control file access. Where required, these make use of an authentication step, where the master station submits a user name and password with the authenticate function. The outstation responds with a one-time use key which is then used by the master in conjunction with file change operations.

Response function codes

Response Functions			
Code	Function	Action	Response
0	Confirm	Message fragment confirmation. Used by both requests and responses.	No further response required.
129	Response	Respond to request.	Master station will respond with confirm if CON bit set.
130	Unsolicited Message	Unsolicited message from outstation.	Master station will respond with confirm if CON bit set.

The response function codes apply for all messages from outstations, ie stations that are not designated as master stations. The only response these messages require (of the master station) is an optional confirmation on receipt by the master station.

5.7.3   Internal indications

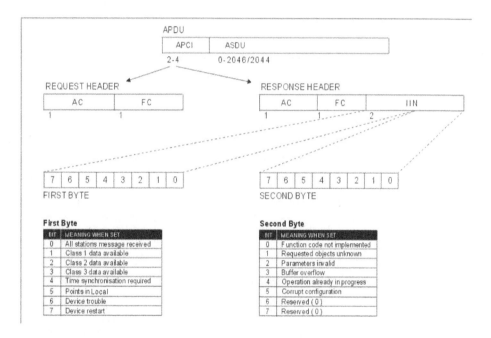

Figure 5.26
Internal indications

The internal indications (IIN) field is a two-byte field that follows the function code in all responses. It is by using the internal indications that the outstation status is reported to the master following a request. Each bit in the field has a specific meaning, in accordance with the table. An outstation would have defined flags within its dynamic memory to correspond to the IIN field bits. These flags would then be copied in each response message.

Descriptions of the detailed meaning of each bit are included in the following table.

First Byte

Bit	Meaning When Set	Notes
0	All stations message received	Set when an address in the range FFF0 - FFFF is received. Cleared after next response. Used to confirm that a broadcast message was received by this station.
1	Class 1 data available	Indicates that data of specified class is available. Master should request this data.
2	Class 2 data available	
3	Class 3 data available	
4	Time synchronisation required	After a restart this will be set. It is cleared during time synchronisation, or by a direct write to the outstation II object.
5	Points in local	Set when one or more points are in local mode and therefore cannot be controlled remotely.
6	Device trouble	Used when an abnormal condition is present, and this cannot be described by the other II bits.
7	Device restart	Set when the user application restarts. Will be cleared when the master writes a 0 directly to this bit of the outstation II object.

Second Byte

Bit	Meaning When Set	Notes
0	Function code not implemented	This function code is not available at this outstation.
1	Requested objects unknown	There are no objects as specified or in the specified class.
2	Parameters invalid	Parameters in the qualifier, range, or data fields are not valid or are out of range.
3	Buffer overflow	Event or other application buffers have overflowed.
4	Operation already in progress	This operation is already executing.
5	Corrupt configuration	This is a specific problem indication showing that the master will have to download a new configuration.
6	Reserved (0)	Always to return 0.
7	Reserved (0)	Always to return 0.

5.7.4   The object header

In DNP3 the data is always comprised of two parts, object headers, and data objects. The object headers identify the data object types, and specific instances of those data that are being referenced by the message. These data may not necessarily be contained in the message, for example a read request carries only the references identifying which data is required. The response to the read request will contain both the data identification and the data itself. The position of the object headers and data objects within the application protocol data unit, or message frame, is shown in the following drawing.

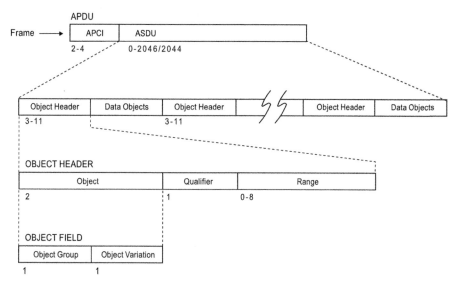

Figure 5.27
The object header

The ASDU is made up of one or more object header and data object fields, up to a maximum frame size of 2048 bytes including the frame header (the APCI).

The object header is between three and eleven bytes in length, and is made up of the object, qualifier and range fields. The object field is further subdivided into two bytes, which are the object group and object variation respectively. The range is between 0 and 8 bytes.

The object field

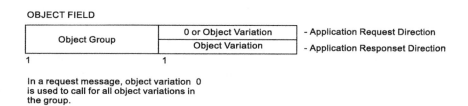

Figure 5.28
The object field

The object field is made up of the object group and the object variation bytes. The group specifies the general type of data, such as analog inputs. The variation specifies a particular variation of that type of data. A list of the object groups is shown in the table below. Full details of these and the object variations for each group are included under Section 5.8 Data object library.

Table of Object Groups

Group Range	Object Group Description
0-9	Binary Input Objects
10-19	Binary Output Objects
20-29	Counter Objects
30-39	Analog Input Objects
40-49	Analog Output Objects
50-59	Time Objects
60-69	Class Objects
70-79	File Objects
80-89	Device Objects
90-99	Application Objects
100+	Alternate Numeric Objects

It can be seen from the table that the object groups are organized into decade ranges. Within each decade there may be more than one object group. Each of these groups has its variations, making altogether a substantial number of individual objects.

Object variation zero

Object variation zero (0) is not used within any group, because this is reserved for a special purpose. When a master station specifies object variation zero in a request message, this is defined to mean all variations of that particular object group. This allows the master station to obtain all object variations without identifying each one.

5.7.5   The qualifier and range fields

In the following sub-sections the operation of the qualifier and range fields is presented. After looking at the structure of these fields, and the meaning of the codes they contain, the different means of referencing data are presented. In the discussion, use is made of referencing 'modes'. It is noted that the mode labels used here are not included within the DNP3 documentation, but are applied here to assist understanding of this complicated area.

It is noted that the reader may find point referencing in DNP3 somewhat difficult to grasp. This arises from the flexibility of referencing that has been provided for by the protocol. At the same time, it may be observed that although a number of different referencing modes and variations for each are defined in DNP3, in practice only a small number are generally used.

Purpose and structure

The qualifier and range fields follow the object field in the object header. These fields are used to identify the specific data points of each object group and variation that are being referred to. For example, this may simply be a range of consecutive points, in which case the start and stop point indexes will be included in the range field. Alternatively, a list of non-consecutive points may be required, and in this case the list of points must be provided seperately. These cases, and others are all handled by the qualifier and range field values.

The qualifier and range fields are used both in request messages from master stations, and in response messages from outstations. For request messages, only identification of the data may be required. In response messages the data objects themselves may be included in the message.

The structure of the qualifier field is shown in the diagram following.

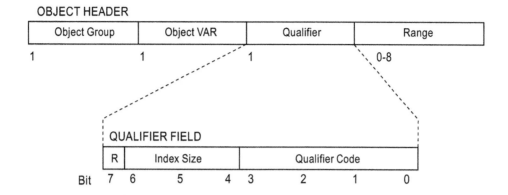

Figure 5.29
The qualifier field

The qualifier field is made up of two sub-fields. These are the qualifier code (or Q-code) and the index size (or I-size). The primary meaning of the qualifier field is provided by the qualifier code value. The index size sub-field provides additional information required for some qualifier code values. These sub-fields, together with the following range field act to fully identify the data object that follows each object header.

5.7.6   Qualifier codes

In the following table, a summary of the qualifier codes is presented. Understanding the meaning of the table hinges on understanding the different modes of referencing that are used. These are explained in the sub-sections following the table.

Qualifier Code Table

Q Code	Interpretation of Qualifier Code		
	Range Value Size (Bits)	Referencing Mode	Notes
0	8	Range - Index Mode	The range field contains start and stop indexes. points are I1 to I2. I-size = 0, or 4-6 for individual object size prefixes.
1	16		
2	32		
3	8	Range – Absolute Mode	The Range field contains start and stop absolute memory addresses in outstation. Data are Bytes B1 to B2. I-size = 0, or 4-6 for individual object size prefixes (response messages only).
4	16		
5	32		
6	-	All Object Mode	Specifies all objects in the referenced group/variation. Only used for requests. There is no range field with this mode. I-size must = 0.
7	8	Non-Ranged Mode	Specifies a list of unrelated points. The Range field contains the number of points referenced. I-size = 0: No indexes, points only. I-size = 1: Indexes are 8 Bit. I-size = 2: Indexes are 16 Bit. I-size = 3: Indexes are 32 Bit
8	16		
9	32		
11	As for I-size	Object Identifier Mode	The Range field contains the number of Object Identifiers following. Each Object Identifier is preceded by a 'Size' field. The size of the Size and Range fields depends on I-size: I-size = 1: Fields are 8 Bit. I-size = 2: Fields are 16 Bit. I-size = 3: Fields are 32 Bit

From the qualifier code table it may be seen that there are five different referencing modes, or ways of referencing or identifying the data objects contained within messages. Also, for some of the referencing modes there are three Q-codes applicable. These allow for three different bit-sizes for the numbers in the range field.

The index-size sub-field

For most of the referencing modes, additional information is provided by the I-size sub-field. The specific meaning of the sub-field is dependent on the referencing mode. In each case where the I-size sub-field is used (ie is non-zero), it gives the size of additional fields that are given for each data object. Depending on the referencing mode, these extra fields contain either an identifier, an index, or a number giving the object size in bytes.

The I-size codes are shown in the table below. The use of these is demonstrated in the following sub-sections for each referencing mode.

Table of Index-Size Codes

I-size Code	Size in bits	Meaning in Request with Q-code = 11	Meaning in Request or Response containing Data Objects
0	no index		No indexing. Objects are packed directly.
1	8	Identifier Field Size	Objects are prefixed with an index of this length.
2	16		
3	32		
4	8		Objects are prefixed with an object size field of this length.
5	16		
6	32		

Range-index mode

The range-index mode is indicated by Q-codes 0, 1 and 2.

In this mode the range field contains two numbers. These are the start and stop index values for the data objects.

Index values imply that in the outstation there is an index giving a one-to-one correspondence between the value of the index, and the actual locations within the device memory of the data objects. The use of indexes simplifies referencing of data objects because regardless of the object's size, each consecutive number represents successive data objects. If the start and stop numbers are I1 and I2, then there are a total of I2–I1+1 data objects being referenced.

In the diagrams following, Q-code 0 is used, defining the range-index mode with eight-bit indexes. These can reference a maximum of 256 data objects. In the request message only the header is present. In the response message, the data objects follow the message.

In the response message only, it is possible to prefix each data object returned with an object size identifier. When this is desired, the I-size field is used to specify the size of the object size fields. This would only be required if the object sizes were variable within an object variation group. When object size fields are not required, the I-size field is set to zero, meaning the objects are packed in sequence without size fields. The diagrams following show the structure of the messages for each of these cases.

REQUEST MESSAGE OBJECT GROUP

			RANGE	
GROUP G	VARIATION V	QUALIFIER 0 0	START I1	STOP I2
1	1	1	1	1

I-size   = 0

Q-code = 0   =>   8-Bit start and stop values

RESPONSE MESSAGE OBJECT GROUP

			RANGE		DATA OBJECTS				
GROUP G	VARIATION V	QUALIFIER 0 0	START I1	STOP I2	DO I1	DO I1+1	DO I1+2	. . .	
1	1	1	1	1	x	x	x		

Note: Size of data objects x = determined by object group / variation definition

Qualifier Codes for Range-Index Mode

Q Code	Interpretation of Qualifier Code		
	Range Value Size (Bits)	Referencing Mode	Notes
0	8	Range – Index Mode	The Range field contains start and stop indexes. Points are I1 to I2. I-size = 0, or 4-6 for individual object size prefixes.
1	16		
2	32		

- Non-zero index-size is valid only with response messages (for this mode)
- It is used when object size prefixes are required before each data object
- The I-size codes 4, 5, and 6 are valid
- They define 8-, 16- and 32-bit object size fields respectively

RESPONSE MESSAGE OBJECT GROUP

			RANGE		DATA OBJECTS						
GROUP	VARIATION	QUALIFIER	START	STOP	Size	DO	Size	DO		. . .	Size
G	V	4 0	I1	I2	I1	I1	I1+1	I1+1			I2
1	1	1	1	1	1		1				1

Note: Size of data objects is determined individually by each object size prefix

Qualifier Codes for Range-Index Mode

Q Code	Interpretation of Qualifier Code		
	Range Value Size (Bits)	Referencing Mode	Notes
0	8	Range – Index Mode	The Range field contains start and stop indexes. Points are I1 to I2. I-size = 0, or 4-6 for individual object size prefixes (response messages only).
1	16		
2	32		

Range-absolute mode

The range-absolute mode is indicated by Q-codes 3, 4 and 5.

This mode is similar to the range-index mode in that the range field contains start and stop values. However, these values represent absolute memory addresses rather than index numbers. This mode is intended for use as a diagnostic tool during manufacturing. This is because use of this mode requires detailed knowledge of the memory structure to interpret the information returned.

In the example following, Q-code 4 is used, defining the absolute-index mode with sixteen-bit indexes. These can reference a maximum of 65 536 data objects. It is noted when multi-byte indexes are used, they are given in order of lowest significant byte to highest significant byte, ie LSB, MSB.

As for the range-index mode, it is also possible to use object size prefixes in the response message. To do this the I-size code is set to 4, 5 or 6 to select 6-, 16- or 32-bit object size prefixes. These have not been illustrated, as the concept has already been demonstrated for the range-index mode.

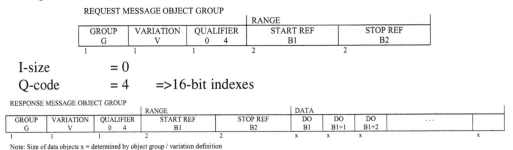

REQUEST MESSAGE OBJECT GROUP

			RANGE	
GROUP	VARIATION	QUALIFIER	START REF	STOP REF
G	V	0 4	B1	B2
1	1	1	2	2

I-size = 0

Q-code = 4 =>16-bit indexes

RESPONSE MESSAGE OBJECT GROUP

			RANGE		DATA					
GROUP	VARIATION	QUALIFIER	START REF	STOP REF	DO	DO	DO		. . .	
G	V	0 4	B1	B2	B1	B1+1	B1+2			
1	1	1	2	2	x	x	x			x

Note: Size of data objects x = determined by object group / variation definition

Q Code	Interpretation of Qualifier Code		
	Range Value Size (Bits)	Referencing Mode	Notes
3	8	Range – Absolute Mode	The Range field contains start and stop absolute memory addresses in outstation. Data are Bytes B1 to B2. I-size = 0, or 4-6 for individual object size prefixes (response messages only).
4	16		
5	32		

All-object mode

The all-object mode is indicated by Q-code = 6.

This mode specifies all data objects of the referenced group and variation. No range field is used with this mode as no additional information is required.

It is important to note that this mode is only valid with requests. Clearly when the data objects are returned in a response message, they must carry identifiers to let the system know which points they represent. Therefore one of the other data object referencing modes is used in the response to an all-object request.

- Only used in request messages
- Asks for all objects in the object/variation group specified

REQUEST MESSAGE OBJECT GROUP

GROUP G	VARIATION V	QUALIFIER 0 6
1	1	1

I-size $\quad = 0$

Q-code $\quad = 6 \quad => \quad$ (no indexes)

Q Code	Interpretation of Qualifier Code		
	Range Value Size (Bits)	Referencing Mode	Notes
6	-	All Object Mode	Specifies all objects in the referenced group/variation. Only used for requests. There is no range field with this mode. I-size must = 0.

Non-ranged mode

The non-ranged mode is indicated by Q-codes 7, 8 and 9.

This mode may be used to identify a number of non-consecutive data objects. For these data objects, it is not possible to simply provide start and stop indexes to identify a range. If the data objects contain sufficient identifying information so that they do not require individual identifiers, then it is necessary only to indicate how many data objects there are.

In the non-ranged mode, the range field is used to provide the number of data objects that are being identified or supplied. The Range field is 8, 16 or 32 bits in length, corresponding to Q-codes 7, 8 and 9.

If the data objects do require identification, then this is done using indices. As noted for the range-index mode, there is an index giving a one-to-one correspondence between values of the index (indices), and the actual locations within the device memory of the data objects. In a request message, values of the index are given only, and these are used at the outstation to find the actual data points.

The provision of the index references for each point follows the header. In the case of a request message, only a list of indices is needed, to identify the data objects required. For a response message, the index value for each data object is included with the data. In the response, each index value is included immediately in front of its data object.

In the non-ranged mode, the size of the indices is specified by the index size qualifier sub-field. The valid values for this mode are 0, 1, 2 and 3. The meanings of these are summarized for convenience in the table below.

Table of Index-Size Codes for Non-Ranged Mode

I-size Code	Size in bits	Meaning in Request or Response containing Data Objects
0	no index	No indexing. Objects are packed directly.
1	8	Objects are prefixed with an index of this length.
2	16	
3	32	

The application of the non-ranged mode differs depending on whether the I-size code is zero or non-zero.

For I-size = 0, the specified number of objects are called for, or provided. This method is useful for requesting or responding with a limited amount of data at one time, perhaps if the outstation could provide more information than could be handled at once by the master station.

For I-size = 1, 2 or 3 a list of specific data objects is provided. This is used when particular data objects, or points, are required rather than a whole range of data objects.

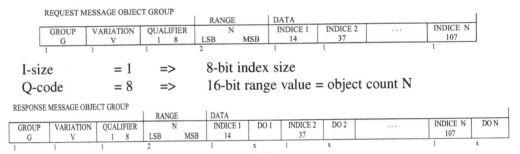

Q Code — Interpretation of Qualifier Code

Q Code	Range Value Size (Bits)	Referencing Mode	Notes
7	8	Non-Ranged Mode	Specifies a list of unrelated points. The Range field contains the number of points referenced.
8	16		I-size = 0: No indexes, points only I-size = 1: Indexes are 8 Bit
9	32		I-size = 2: Indexes are 16 Bit I-size = 3: Indexes are 32 Bit

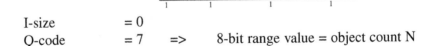

Q Code	Range Value Size (Bits)	Referencing Mode	Notes
7	8	Non-Ranged Mode	Specifies a list of unrelated points. The Range field contains the number of points referenced.
8	16		I-size = 0: No indexes, points only I-size = 1: Indexes are 8 Bit
9	32		I-size = 2: Indexes are 16 Bit I-size = 3: Indexes are 32 Bit

Object identifier mode

The object identifier mode is indicated by Q-code 11.

This mode provides for free-format object identifiers that are not interpreted in any particular way by the DNP3 application. This mode can be used when the other modes of referencing are unable to uniquely specify the data objects involved.

In this mode the range field contains a one-byte number which specifies the number of object identifiers.

This method is useful for reading file objects, and is the only way to request a data object that is larger than one fragment in size.

REQUEST MESSAGE OBJECT GROUP

			RANGE	DATA						
GROUP G	VARIATION V	QUALIFIER 5 11	N	SIZE ID 1	OBJECT ID 1	SIZE ID2	OBJECT ID 2	. . .	SIZE ID N	OBJECT ID N
1	1	1	1	2	size ID 1	2	size ID 2			size ID N

I-size   = 5   =>   Size ID fields are 16 bit (required for Q-code 11)

Q-code   = 11   =>   Object Identifier mode

RESPONSE MESSAGE OBJECT GROUP

			RANGE	DATA OBJECTS EACH PRECEDED BY IDENTIFIER SIZE, AND IDENTIFIERS								
GROUP G	VARIATION V	QUALIFIER 5 11	N	SIZE ID 1	OBJECT ID 1	DO 1	SIZE ID2	OBJECT ID 2	DO 2	. . .	SIZE ID N	OBJECT ID N	DO N
1	1	1	1	2	size ID 1		2	size ID 2				size ID N

Note: Size of data objects determined by object group / variation definition.

Q Code	Range Value Size (Bits)	Referencing Mode	Notes
11	As for I-size	Object Identifier Mode	The 1-byte Range field contains the number of Objects Identifiers (and objects in response) following. Each Object Identifier is preceded by a 'Size' field. The size of the Size field is 2-bytes and this is indicated by I-Size = 5. Devices produced prior to mid-1999 may use the following I-size codes which are now obsolete with Q-code 11: I-size = 1: Fields are 8 Bit I-size = 2: Fields are 16 Bit I-size = 3: Fields are 32 Bit

- Object identifier mode (Q-code = 11) is the only mode to handle multi-fragment size data objects
- The data must be broken down into pieces that will fit into fragments
- Each piece needs an object identifier

RESPONSE MESSAGE OBJECT – FRAGMENT 1

			RANGE	DATA OBJECT		
GROUP G	VARIATION V	QUALIFIER 5 11	N =1	SIZE	OBJECT ID	DATA FOR PIECE 1
1	1	1	1	2	size ID 1	

RESPONSE MESSAGE OBJECT – FRAGMENT 2

			RANGE	DATA OBJECT		
GROUP G	VARIATION V	QUALIFIER 5 11	N =1	SIZE	OBJECT ID	DATA FOR PIECE 2
1	1	1	1		size ID 1	

RESPONSE MESSAGE OBJECT – FRAGMENT 3

			RANGE	DATA OBJECT		
GROUP G	VARIATION V	QUALIFIER 5 11	N =1	SIZE	OBJECT ID	DATA FOR PIECE 3
1	1	1	1	2	size ID 1	

Point indexes

In the previous sub-sections, reference has been made to the point indexes, or simply indexes, that identify each particular object within an object group. The point indexes are assigned by the manufacturer of a device for each of the points provided by the device. These may be associated directly with physical inputs or outputs, or with internal points such as registers.

The following general rules apply to the assignment of point indexes by manufacturers:

- Point indexes within each object group begin at zero and are assigned in a continuous sequence
- There may be gaps in the sequence, but these should be small

The reason for these rules is that by having point indexes in sequence, higher efficiency is obtained in data transfers. This arises because data points can be identified in ranges rather than by requiring addresses for each point. Also, in many cases there will be less than 256 points in an object group, and if indexes start from zero then these will require only 8-bit range values.

It is noted that some manufacturers' devices may contain point indexes that are unique across object groups rather than just within object groups. For example, binary inputs may have the numbers 0–199, binary outputs 200–399 etc. This type of numbering is derived from the data map concepts associated with PLC devices and probably arose naturally from this in earlier implementations of DNP3. Although this type of numbering is in conformance with the original DNP documentation, subsequent clarification by the DNP3 Technical Committee requires numbering from zero within each object group.

5.8   Data object library

5.8.1   General

In DNP3 data and control information is formed at the application level into data objects. Each data object has a structure that is defined by the DNP3 documentation, so that DNP3 is interoperable across different manufacturers' equipment. The collection of data objects is called the object library.

There are 90 data objects described in the DNP3 Basic Four documentation. Additional data objects may be described in the future by the DNP3 Users Group.

Each object is denoted by a group number and a variation number. DNP3 represents the group and variation numbers each with 8-bit fields. There are a number of general types of objects, and these are organized into decade ranges. There are usually more than one specific group type within each range. For each group, there are usually a number of variations.

Table of Object Groups

Group Range	Object Group Description
0 - 9	Binary Input Objects
10 - 19	Binary Output Objects
20 - 29	Counter Objects
30 - 39	Analog Input Objects
40 - 49	Analog Output Objects
50 - 59	Time Objects
60 - 69	Class Objects
70 - 79	File Objects
80 - 89	Device Objects
90 - 99	Application Objects
100+	Alternate Numeric Objects

As can be seen from the table, the object groups are organized into ranges of similar source types, such as binary input objects (0–9), or file objects (70–79). It may also be noted that some data objects appear closely related to physical data monitoring and control points, and others (range 50 on) appear less so. In the latter case, the data object is often not representing physical things, for example file objects represent software, and class objects represent an attribute that may be assigned to other objects.

In a few cases, there are objects defined that have no data attached to them at all. Whilst these do not sound very useful, their function is performed merely by the transmission of the object identifier. For example, the class object is used in a request message only to identify the class attribute of objects that are being requested.

Within each object group there may be defined a number of variations. It is important to note that each variation is normally just a different representation of the same underlying data point. It may have more or less information than other variations, but the same point is being represented by the object.

For the objects that are related to physical points, the type of data is classified into four different types. These are shown in the following table. Each physical point will generally be able to be represented by each of the four types, which are defined as different variations for each object group.

The differences between these are illustrated further in the following paragraphs.

The static type is probably the simplest to understand. Static simply refers to the current value of any point at the time the information is transmitted. This might be the current value of a binary input or output, the most recently converted value of an analog input, the value of a register, or the value of a counter. Static values are associated directly with physical inputs and outputs, or with internal registers and counters. There is a one-to-one relationship between these devices and the static points, so therefore there are as many static points as there are physical devices, registers, or counters.

Event data is different to static data in that it is generated on the occurrence of a particular event, such as a change in state of a binary point. If a physical device such as a binary input has an event variation configured for it, then whenever it changes an event data object will be generated for that input-change. In the case of analog inputs, events are generated when the change in the value reaches a configured deadband value, such as 5% of scale. The event object generated would typically be buffered in an event buffer for subsequent transmission to the master station. It should be noted that any number of event objects can be created for the one input, one for each change. Normally changes would be held in the buffer until they have been transmitted successfully to the master station.

The typical use of event data in DNP3 is in a report-by-exception (RBE) operating mode. In this mode, the master station database is maintained by transmission of changes in field states rather than through transmission of static data. By transmitting only changes in field states, the amount of communication traffic can be significantly reduced. Another use of event data types is for reporting alarm events. These are events that may require the attention of the operator and so are presented to the operator on the screen at the master station.

The frozen data types are applicable to analog values and counters. A frozen static value is simply the value in a freeze buffer that is associated with an analog or counter. The buffer holds a copy of the analog or counter, taken at a previous time when a 'freeze' operation was performed. This might be in response to a master station command, or alternatively the freeze may be generated by local logic at the device or RTU. It may be noted that a physical point, such as a counter, will typically have only one freeze buffer associated with it, and there will be only one frozen static data object associated with that point.

The frozen event data type is, like the event data type, a data object that is created on the occurrence of a particular event. As for the event data type, there can be multiple frozen event data objects created and buffered for any one point. An example of where this type of object might be used is where snapshots of system power flows may be taken on specific trigger events. By defining these as frozen events, multiple time-tagged snapshots can be taken and stored for the point.

Summary

- DNP3 has defined data objects forming an object library
- Each data object has a defined structure
- Objects are organized into decade ranges by type of information source
- Different data types may be used to represent an information source, eg static (current value) and event (historical value)
- Each data object definition can have multiple variations

5.8.2   Data object listing

The following tables present each of the data object-variations for each type of information source. The structure of each data object is described in a short format. The description can be interpreted with the Key to Data Structure included in the Appendix. A sub-set of the key information is also included for convenience at the end of the data object listing.

Binary input objects

OBJECT GROUP RANGE 0 –9, BINARY INPUT OBJECTS

Group	Var	Type	Description	Structure
01	01	Static	Binary Input (single-bit)	Packed Binary
	02	Static	Binary Input with Status	Flag 1
02	01	Event	Binary Input Change without Time	Flag 1
	02	Event	Binary Input Change with Time	Flag 1; Time
	03	Event	Binary Input Change with Relative Time	Flag 1; Relative Time

- Binary input objects represent the state of a physical input or a software input, such as a flag.
- Single-bit binary objects are always packed into 8-bit bytes
- Unused bit positions are packed with zeros
- The event flag elements contain the same information as the static flag
- The only difference is the object group-variation reference
- Event objects may be used for recording events, or for updating databases using quiescent operation-reporting on change only
- Time-tagging uses local time at the device
- Relative time is preceded with a common time object in message and provides a means of transmitting a number of time stamps in an efficient manner

Binary output objects

OBJECT GROUP RANGE 10 – 19, BINARY OUTPUT OBJECTS

Group	Var	Type	Description	Structure
10	01	Static	Binary Output	Packed Binary
	02	Static	Binary Output Status	Flag 2
12	01	Static	Control Relay Output Block	Control Code; Count; On Time; Off Time; Status Code
	02	Static	Pattern Control Block	Control Code; Count; On Time; Off Time; Status Code
	03	Static	Pattern Mask	Packed Binary

- Binary outputs can be software (eg flags) or hardware (physical outputs)
- Binary outputs are controlled with OG 10 V01
- Binary output status is returned with OG 10 V02
- Control relay block provides a number of control options including, pulse on, pulse off, latch on, latch off
- Control relay block can also be used to provide control over select / trip / close relay combinations
- The pattern control block is similar to the control relay block except that it can apply the required control action to a number of points simultaneously. The individual points are selected from the available points using the pattern mask

Counter objects

OBJECT GROUP RANGE 20 – 29, COUNTER OBJECTS

Group	Var	Type	Description	Structure
20	01	Static	32-Bit Binary Counter	Flag 3; UI32
	02	Static	16-Bit Binary Counter	Flag 3; UI16
	03	Static	32-Bit Delta Counter	Flag 3; UI32
	04	Static	16-Bit Delta Counter	Flag 3; UI16
	05	Static	32-Bit Binary Counter without flag	UI32
	06	Static	16-Bit Binary Counter without flag	UI16
	07	Static	32-Bit Delta Counter without flag	UI32
	08	Static	16-Bit Delta Counter without flag	UI16

- On counter roll-over, the roll-over bit is set in the counter flag
- Once the roll-over is reported, the bit is cleared
- Delta counters reset their count to zero on reporting, and continue counting. Therefore they accumulate pulses from the last time their value is reported
- As for data objects, counter objects are information objects that reflect the state of registers within the outstation. The data objects are not the registers themselves

OBJECT GROUP RANGE 20 – 29, COUNTER OBJECTS - CONTINUED

Group	Var	Type	Description	Structure
21	01	Frozen Static	32-Bit Frozen Counter	Flag 3; UI32
	02	Frozen Static	16-Bit Frozen Counter	Flag 3; UI16
	03	Frozen Static	32-Bit Frozen Delta Counter	Flag 3; UI32
	04	Frozen Static	16-Bit Frozen Delta Counter	Flag 3; UI16
	05	Frozen Static	32-Bit Frozen Counter with Time Freeze	Flag 3; UI32; Time
	06	Frozen Static	16-Bit Frozen Counter with Time Freeze	Flag 3; UI16; Time
	07	Frozen Static	32-Bit Frozen Delta Counter with Time Freeze	Flag 3; UI32; Time
	08	Frozen Static	16-Bit Frozen Delta Counter with Time Freeze	Flag 3; UI16; Time
	09	Frozen Static	32-Bit Frozen Counter without flag	UI32
	10	Frozen Static	16-Bit Frozen Counter without flag	UI16
	11	Frozen Static	32-Bit Frozen Delta Counter without flag	UI32
	12	Frozen Static	16-Bit Frozen Delta Counter without flag	UI16

- A frozen counter data object returns the value of the count at the time of the last freeze command. Note that the counter itself continues to count after the freeze command
- A frozen delta counter data object returns the value of the count at the time of the last freeze. The counter is reset at the time of the freeze and continues to count from zero
- Counter with time freeze data objects record the local time when the data was frozen

OBJECT GROUP RANGE 20 – 29, COUNTER OBJECTS - CONTINUED

Group	Var	Type	Description	Structure
23	01	Frozen Event	32-Bit Frozen Counter Event without Time	Flag 3; UI32
	02	Frozen Event	16-Bit Frozen Counter Event without Time	Flag 3; UI16
	03	Frozen Event	32-Bit Frozen Delta Counter Event without Time	Flag 3; UI32
	04	Frozen Event	16-Bit Frozen Delta Counter Event without Time	Flag 3; UI16
	05	Frozen Event	32-Bit Frozen Counter Event with Time	Flag 3; UI32; Time
	06	Frozen Event	16-Bit Frozen Counter Event with Time Freeze	Flag 3; UI16; Time
	07	Frozen Event	32-Bit Frozen Delta Counter Event with Time Freeze	Flag 3; UI32; Time
	08	Frozen Event	16-Bit Frozen Delta Counter Event with Time Freeze	Flag 3; UI16; Time

- A counter change event occurs when a counter value exceeds a configured count. The change event data object reports the value of the counter when this occurs
- A delta counter change event occurs in the same manner. When the change event data object is generated, the delta counter is reset to zero and then continues counting from zero
- Event with time data objects include the time of the event

OBJECT GROUP RANGE 20 – 29, COUNTER OBJECTS - CONTINUED

Group	Var	Type	Description	Structure
23	01	Frozen Event	32-Bit Frozen Counter Event without Time	Flag 3; UI32
	02	Frozen Event	16-Bit Frozen Counter Event without Time	Flag 3; UI16
	03	Frozen Event	32-Bit Frozen Delta Counter Event without Time	Flag 3; UI32
	04	Frozen Event	16-Bit Frozen Delta Counter Event without Time	Flag 3; UI16
	05	Frozen Event	32-Bit Frozen Counter Event with Time	Flag 3; UI32; Time
	06	Frozen Event	16-Bit Frozen Counter Event with Time Freeze	Flag 3; UI16; Time
	07	Frozen Event	32-Bit Frozen Delta Counter Event with Time Freeze	Flag 3; UI32; Time
	08	Frozen Event	16-Bit Frozen Delta Counter Event with Time Freeze	Flag 3; UI16; Time

- A frozen counter event represents a counter freeze reported as an event
- This makes sense if the freeze is initiated other than by the master station, perhaps due to local logic

Analog input objects

OBJECT GROUP RANGE 30 – 39, ANALOG INPUT OBJECTS

Group	Var	Type	Description	Structure
30	01	Static	32-Bit Analog Input	Flag 4; I32
	02	Static	16-Bit Analog Input	Flag 4; I16
	03	Static	32-Bit Analog Input without Flag	I32
	04	Static	16-Bit Analog Input without Flag	I16
	05	Static	Short Floating Point Analog Input	Flag 4; FLT32
	06	Static	Long Floating Point Analog Input	Flag 4; FLT64
31	01	Frozen Static	32-Bit Frozen Analog Input	Flag 4; I32
	02	Frozen Static	16-Bit Frozen Analog Input	Flag 4; I16
	03	Frozen Static	32-Bit Frozen Analog Input with Time Freeze	Flag 4; I32; Time
	04	Frozen Static	16-Bit Frozen Analog Input with Time Freeze	Flag 4; I16; Time
	05	Frozen Static	32-Bit Frozen Analog Input without Flag	I32
	06	Frozen Static	16-Bit Frozen Analog Input without Flag	I16
	07	Frozen Static	Short Floating Point Frozen Analog Input	Flag 4; FLT32
	08	Frozen Static	Long Floating Point Frozen Analog Input	Flag 4; FLT64
32	01	Event	32-Bit Analog Change Event without Time	Flag 4; I32
	02	Event	16-Bit Analog Change Event without Time	Flag 4; I16
	03	Event	32-Bit Analog Change Event with Time	Flag 4; I32; Time
	04	Event	16-Bit Analog Change Event with Time	Flag 4; I16; Time
	05	Event	Short Floating Point Analog Change Event	Flag 4; FLT32
	06	Event	Long Floating Point Analog Change Event	Flag 4; FLT64
	07	Event	Short Floating Point Analog Change Event with Time	Flag 4; FLT32; Time
	08	Event	Long Floating Point Analog Change Event with Time	Flag 4; FLT64; Time
33	01	Frozen Event	32-Bit Frozen Analog Event without Time	Flag 4; I32
	02	Frozen Event	16-Bit Frozen Analog Event without Time	Flag 4; I16
	03	Frozen Event	32-Bit Frozen Analog Event with Time	Flag 4; I32; Time
	04	Frozen Event	16-Bit Frozen Analog Event with Time	Flag 4; I16; Time
	05	Frozen Event	Short Floating Point Frozen Analog Event	Flag 4; FLT32
	06	Frozen Event	Long Floating Point Frozen Analog Event	Flag 4; FLT64
	07	Frozen Event	Short Floating Point Frozen Analog Event with Time	Flag 4; I32; Time
	08	Frozen Event	Long Floating Point Frozen Analog Event with Time	Flag 4; I16; Time
34	01	Static*	16-Bit Analog Input Reporting Deadband Object	UI16
	02	Static*	32-Bit Analog Input Reporting Deadband Object	UI32
	03	Static*	Floating Point Analog Input Reporting Deadband Object	FLT32

* Note that although these are defined as static types, they are not returned in a read request for Class 0 data.

- The analog input data objects give the value of a hardware or software analog point
- Frozen analog input data objects represent the value of the point at the time of the freeze command
- Analog change data objects are generated when the current value changes from a previously reported value by more than a configurable deadband
- Frozen analog event data objects are used when a frozen value is reported as an event. This might be used when the freeze is initiated by conditions at an outstation and the information is to be reported to the master station when it happens
- Object group 34 variations are for reading or writing the deadband values associated with change event generation for analog points. Deadbands may be 'fixed' or 'integrating' depending on the process used to generate events.

Analog output objects

OBJECT GROUP RANGE 40 – 49, ANALOG OUTPUT OBJECTS

Group	Var	Type	Description	Structure
40	01	Static	32-Bit Analog Output Status	Flag 5; I32
	02	Static	16-Bit Analog Output Status	Flag 5; I16
	03	Static	Short Floating Point Analog Output Status	Flag 5; FLT32
	04	Static	Long Floating Point Analog Output Status	Flag 5; FLT64
41	01	Static	32-Bit Analog Output Block	I32; Status Code
	02	Static	16-Bit Analog Output Block	I16; Status Code
	03	Static	Short Floating Point Analog Output Block	FLT32; Status Code
	04	Static	Long Floating Point Analog Output Block	FLT64; Status Code

- Analog output status data objects represent the actual value of the output
- Analog output block data objects are used to control the value of analog outputs.The analog value they contain is termed the 'requested value'. This value may be scaled before being applied to the actual output. The actual output value is returned by the analog output status data object

Time objects

OBJECT GROUP RANGE 50 – 59, TIME OBJECTS

Group	Var	Type	Description	Structure
50	01	Not used	Time and Date	Time
	02		Time and Date with Interval	Time; T32
51	01		Time and Date CTO	Time
	02		Unsynchronised Time and Date CTO	Time
52	01		Time Delay Coarse	UI16
	02		Time Delay Fine	UI16

- The time and date object is a 48-bit unsigned integer representing the elapsed time in milliseconds since 00:00 hours on January 1, 1970. This and other information element definitions are included in the Appendix
- The time and date with interval data object can be used to provide a starting time and a repeat interval
- The time and date CTO (common time of occurrence) data object is used with other objects that contain relative time references. Together they may be used to efficiently determine absolute time
- Unsynchronized time is the time recorded at an outstation where the local time has not been synchronized with the master station
- Time delay coarse is a time setting in seconds (0 to 65 535 seconds, ie up to 18 hours)
- Time delay fine is a time setting in milliseconds (0 to 65 535 milliseconds, ie up to 65 seconds)

Class objects

OBJECT GROUP RANGE 60 – 69, CLASS OBJECTS

Group	Var	Type	Description	Structure
60	01	Not Used	Class 0 Data	No data structure applicable. Group and Variation number only.
	02		Class 1 Data	
	03		Class 2 Data	
	04		Class 3 Data	

Class objects are different to all of the previous objects in that they are used in request messages only, to call for objects of a specific class. The class objects themselves carry no data, and for this reason there is no information structure. They comprise of the group and variation numbers only. What is returned by the outstation is not class objects, but objects with that specific class attribute.

Class is an attribute that can be assigned to any information elements, including object types, specific variations, particular points only, or any combination of these. It can be used to implement a prioritization system. The prioritization levels indicated by the DNP3 documentation are shown below:

Class	Priority
1	Highest
2	Medium
3	Low
0	No priority, not assigned

File objects

OBJECT GROUP 70

Group	Var	Type	Description	Structure
70	01		File Identifier	Free format
80	01		Internal Indications	
81	01		Storage Object	
82	01		Device Profile	
83	01		Private Registration Object	
	02	Static	Private Registration Object Descriptor	

- The file identifier data object is a free format object that is sent in a request. The request may or may not include the file itself. This object is used for transferring large blocks of data that do not conform to any of the other defined data object formats. It is suitable for handling configuration files to remote devices. The DNP3 documentation presents a possible file header format, and identification system, however no particular format is required by the DNP3 standard
- The file identifier object was superseded in 2000 by group 70 Variations 2–7
- The file operations associated with these objects are reasonably complex. The reader is referred to *Technical Bulletin* 2000–2001 (20 pages) for details on these if required

Device objects

OBJECT GROUP RANGE 80 – 89, DEVICE OBJECTS

Group	Var	Type	Description	Structure
80	01		Internal Indications	Packed Binary
81	01		Storage Object	Status BS8; Group UI8; Variation UI8
82	01		Device Profile	Functions BS64; NumObjects N, UI16; ObjectHeader 1..N
83	01		Private Registration Object	
	02	Static	Private Registration Object Descriptor	

- Internal indications are device dependent flags used to convey the internal state of an outstation. The number of bits is device specific. Note that this is different to and should not be confused with the two-byte IIN field in the application message header for response messages
- The remaining objects are somewhat more complex and are described in greater detail following. Also, reference should be made to DNP3 documentation for greater detail on these objects if required

Storage object

The storage object provides the status of buffer(s), queues, or other storage areas within the outstation. The group and variation references are provided for the data object that represents the particular storage area. Interpretation of the status bits is device dependent, and is specified in the device profile.

Device profile

The device profile data object is intended to provide a means of dynamic configuration of a master station to accept a new device. The device profile is sent by an outstation when it receives a request message that it cannot interpret. Also, the outstation may be configured to send this at startup.

On receipt of this message a master station may be able to dynamically reconfigure its database for the outstation so that application communications can function correctly. Alternatively, a less sophisticated master station could simply flag the outstation as off-line.

The device profile data object provides the following information:

- Functions supported by device
- List of supported objects, by providing:
- Quantity of objects
- Sample object headers

The structure of the data object is:

- A 64-bit string representing function codes 0–63
- A16-bit unsigned binary number giving the number (N) of object headers to follow
- A sequence of N object header block data

Note that each of the object headers is a variable format object constructed in accordance with the defined object header structure rules. Thus, some headers will include range field elements, depending on the content of the qualifier field.

Example structure of device profile object:

(Bit positions)	7	0	7	0	7	0	7	0
Functions	31							0
	64							32
NumObjects					15			0
ObjectHeader 1		Quantity		Qualifier	Variation		Object	
ObjectHeader 2		Start		Qualifier	Variation		Object	
					Quantity		Stop	
ObjectHeader3	7	Start	0	Qualifier	Variation		Object	
		Quantity	15		Stop	0	15 Start	8

Private registration object

The private registration object (PRO) provides for proprietary vendor specific structures. It is intended to be used when other defined data objects are not suitable. No restrictions are placed on the content of the object's data objects field, which is entirely at the discretion of the vendor.

The structure is as shown in the following diagram:

31	VEN	0
15	PRN	0
15	LEN	0
	DATA OBJECTS	0

- Vendor is a four-byte ASCII vendor name code
- The PRN field is a unique object identification number
- The LEN field gives the length of data objects in bytes
- The DATA OBJECTS field contains the vendor's information
- Format of DATA OBJECTS field is described by the PROD object

Private registration object descriptor

The private registration object descriptor (PROD) provides a description of the contents of the PRO data objects. It specifies the quantities of each vendor specific object/variation type found within the PRO. The DNP3 documentation should be used to obtain further details of this object if required.

Application object definition

OBJECT GROUP 90, APPLICATION OBJECT DEFINITIONS

Group	Var	Type	Description	Structure
90	01		Application Identifier	No data structure applicable. Group and Variation number only.

The application identifier data object is used to represent an application or operating system within an outstation. There is no data attached to this object group, as instead the qualifier field is used for this purpose. For this object group/variation, the one-byte qualifier field may be used to identify the application, or the all object referencing mode (qualifier code = 6) may be used to specify all relevant applications.

Alternate numeric objects

OBJECT GROUP RANGE 100+, ALTERNATE NUMERIC OBJECTS

Group	Var	Type	Description	Structure
100	01		Short Floating Point	Flag 4; Units; Value as defined
	02		Long Floating Point	Flag 4; Units; Value as defined
	03		Extended Floating Point	Flag 4; Units; Value as defined
101	01		Small-Packed Binary Coded Decimal	4 x BCD
	02		Medium-Packed Binary Coded Decimal	8 x BCD
	03		Large-Packed Binary Coded Decimal	16 x BCD

The various alternate numeric data objects are used for transmitting the value of real or calculated numerical information. Each data object includes a one-byte flag, a one-byte units code, and the value in its defined format. The floating point numbers are compliant with IEEE-754 standard for floating-point number representation.

The structure of each data object is shown in the following diagrams, as presented in the DNP3 documentation. The flag structure is in the Appendix but is repeated following these for convenience.

In *Technical Bulletin* 9804-006 it was recommended that Group 100 objects no longer be used, and that the floating point extensions to object groups 30–41 be used instead. Information on object group 100 is included in case the reader encounters this object type in early implementations of DNP3.

Object 100, Variation 1: Short Floating Point

7	Units	0	7	Flag	0
		Value			
Sign	7 Exponent 0	22		Significant	0

$$\text{Value} = 1.\ s_0\ s_1\ s_2\ \dots\ s_{22} \times 2^{(\text{Exponent} - 127)}$$

Object 100, Variation 2: Long Floating Point

7	Units	0	7	Flag	0
		Value			
Sign	10 Exponent 0	51	Significant		0

$$\text{Value} = 1.\ s_0\ s_1\ s_2\ \dots\ s_{51} \times 2^{(\text{Exponent} - 1023)}$$

Object 100, Variation 3: Extended Floating Point

7	Units	0	7	Flag	0
		Value			
Sign	14 Exponent 0	63	Significant		0

$$\text{Value} = 1.\ s_0\ s_1\ s_2\ \dots\ s_{63} \times 2^{(\text{Exponent} - 1023)}$$

Each of these objects is comprised of a sequence of four-bit BCD digits. There are 4, 8 or 16 BCD digits respectively for variations 1, 2 and 3.

BCD N			BCD 2		BCD 1	
3 Digit 0		...	3 Digit 0		3 Digit 0	

The flag structure is as follows. This is the same as flag 4 shown in the Appendix.

7	6	5	4	3	2	1	0

Bit	Interpretation
0	On-line
1	Restart
2	Communication lost
3	Remote forced data
4	Local forced data
5	Over-range
6	Reference check
7	Reserved

The DNP3 Basic Four documentation provides the following units code assignments. As the code allows for up to 256 different codes, it is entirely possible that other codes may be added over time and as required by users.

Units Code Key

0	Volts peak-peak	10	Frequency Hz
1	Amperes peak-peak	11	Frequency rad/sec ϖ
2	Volts RMS	12	Temperature C
3	Amperes RMS	13	Temperature F
4	Real Power kW	14	Temperature K
5	Apparent Power kVA	15	Force in Newtons N
6	Reactive Power kVAR	16	Mass kg
7	Energy kWh	17	Acceleration meter/sec squared
8	Imaginary Power kVARh	18	Pressure N/square meter
9	Power Factor pf	19	Torque Newton-meters

5.8.3 Key to data structure

General

DNP3 data objects have been constructed from a number of basic data types. Understanding the shorthand notation for these data types assists in readily understanding the structure of the various data objects, particularly if using the DNP3 documentation for particular data objects.

Some key information has been included in the text at this point as a reference in interpreting some of the information element descriptions. This information also appears in the Appendix, with some additional details.

The following table of data types is repeated from the DNP3 documentation.

Some examples of usages of these symbols are:

BS8 [0..7]   This denotes a bit-string of 8-bit length

I16 [0..15] $<2^{15}-1..-2^{15}>$ This denotes a bit-string of 8-bit length. The defined range of the data element is shown in the angled brackets

UI32 [0..31] $<0..2^{32}-1>$ This denotes an unsigned integer of 32-bit length. The defined range shown in angle brackets.

Bit positions

Understanding the bit positions within data elements is important for interpreting binary flags, and for determining the significance of bits in a multi-octet data element. The positions are shown in the following diagram repeated from the DNP3 documentation:

Table of Bit Positions

Bits	7	6	5	4	3	2	1	0
Octets	Data Size i							
1	7	6	5	4	3	2	1	0
2	15	14	13	12	11	10	9	8
	.	.	.	.	.	.	.	.
j	8j-1	8j-2	8j-3	8j-4	8j-5	8j-6	8j-7	8j-8

The following rules apply to bit and byte orders, and apply generally except where stated otherwise. These rules are reflected in the above table.

- Multi-byte fields are transmitted least significant byte first
- Bit-strings are transmitted in least significant bit order. Thus bit 0 of the second byte will correspond to the ninth bit of the original bit sequence

Time formats

Time

7	6	5	4	3	2	1	0
15	14	13	12	11	10	9	8
23	22	21	20	19	18	17	16
31	30	29	28	27	26	25	24
39	38	37	36	35	34	33	32
47	46	45	44	43	42	41	40

Time is transmitted in six bytes in format UI48, which is unsigned 48-bit binary. The scaling is 0 to $2^{48} - 1$ milliseconds. Time is expressed as elapsed time since midnight of January 1, 1970, ie at 0 hours, minutes, seconds, and milliseconds on that date.

Relative time

7	6	5	4	3	2	1	0
15	14	13	12	11	10	9	8

Relative time is transmitted in two bytes, in format UI16, which is unsigned 16-bit binary. The scaling is 0 to $2^{16} - 1$ milliseconds. Relative time is the elapsed time since the time given in the last common time object (CTO). A CTO must have been transmitted within the same message prior to inclusion of objects using relative time fields.

T32

This is a code used to represent 32-bit time intervals. It is transmitted in four bytes, in format UI16, which is unsigned 32-bit binary. The scaling is 0 to $2^{32} - 1$ milliseconds.

6

Advanced considerations of distributed network protocol

Objectives

When you have completed study of this chapter you should be able to:

- Describe the DNP3 sub-set definitions
- Describe how interoperability between DNP3 devices is achieved
- Describe the DNP3 conformance testing procedures
- Describe DNP3 time synchronization
- Describe DNP3 operation over TCP/IP and UDP/IP

6.1 DNP3 sub-set definitions

6.1.1 Implementation levels

To obtain interoperability between different manufacturers' versions of a protocol, it is necessary to ensure that all manufacturers' implementations support the same data objects and functions. However, to require that all manufacturers support all data objects and functions would not be very efficient. For example, a small IED such as a pole mounted re-closer would only require a small sub-set of the available data object types, whereas an RTU interfacing to a number of devices could require more. In DNP3, these issues are addressed through the definition of sub-set levels.

There are presently three sub-set levels defined in DNP3. These are designated in the format 'DNP3 Application Layer Protocol Level x', or simply abbreviated as DNP3-L1, L2 or L3. The levels are described in the table below.

Level 1	Level 1 is the simplest level of DNP implementation. It is intended for use between a master station or intermediate device such as a data concentrator, and a small IED end device. This might be a relay, a meter, or a stand-alone controller of some type. Normally any inputs and outputs are local to the device. Examples of small end devices include meters, relays, auto-reclosers or capacitor bank controllers.
Level 2	Level 2 defines a larger subset of DNP features than Level 1. It is intended to be used between a master station or data concentrator, and an RTU or a large IED. Normally any inputs and outputs are local to the device.
Level 3	Level 3 defines the largest subset of DNP features. It does not require support of all the possible DNP features, but it does cover the majority of the most frequently required features. This is implemented typically between a master station and a larger or more advanced RTU. The inputs and outputs of Subset Level 3 devices would typically be remote as well as local.

6.1.2   Implementation tables

The sub-sets are defined by listing the specific data objects that must be handled, and the operations to be performed on them, for each level. These requirements are set out in a table showing for each data object type the function codes and qualifier field values that must be supported by the master and slave at that level. The table is referred to as an implementation table.

Implementation tables are provided in the DNP3 sub-set definition for each of level 1, level 2 and level 3. An example implementation table is shown below, with one entry to illustrate the meaning.

OBJECT			REQUEST (slave must parse)		RESPONSE (master must parse)	
Obj	Var	Description	Func Code (dec)	Qual Codes (hex)	Func Codes (dec)	Qual Codes (hex)
1	1	Binary Input	1	00, 01, 06	129, 130	00, 01

The example level-2 table entry shown indicates the following:

- Slave must understand and respond to a read request (function code 1)
- Slave must be able to respond to 8-bit or 16-bit indexes in the range field (Q-codes 0 and 1)
- Slave must be able to respond to all-object request (Q-code 6)
- Slave must be able to provide both responses (129) and unsolicited responses (130) as requested, using 8-bit or 16-bit indexes in the range field

Some other aspects worth noting about the table are:

- For each data object there can be request and a response column entry
- These correspond to messages from master and slave
- Request messages are issued by the master and parsed by the slave
- Response messages are issued by the slave and parsed by the master
- The function code is given in decimal
- The qualifier field codes are given in hexadecimal (this presents them directly as I-size, Q-code)

Interestingly the level-1 implementation table does not include the ability to read a binary input as shown by this example. The lack of this fairly basic function illustrates the underlying concept that interrogation by class rather than by calling for specific object types is intended to be used at the lowest implementation levels.

A full sub-set implementation table is included at the end of this section showing the requirements for each of levels 1, 2 and 3. For convenience these have been combined into a single table showing all three levels. In the DNP3 documentation separate tables are shown for each level.

6.1.3 Summary of implementation sub-sets

In this sub-section, the sub-sets are described in terms of the main functions defined for each level.

Level 1 sub-set definition

Level 1 slave functions:

- Reads of class data objects
- Reads of binary output and analog output data objects
- Control operations to binary output and analog output data objects
- Write to restart internal indication bit
- Cold restart
- Delay measurement
- Write time

Level 1 master functions:

- Accept the following data object types
- Binary inputs and events
- Counters and counter events
- Analog inputs and events
- Binary and analog output status

Although an L1 master must parse many objects, an L1 slave is not required to generate them. This is logical when it is considered that a master may communicate with a large number of different slaves, so it will need a larger array of functions.

A slave may be able to send unsolicited responses, but this must be configurable off.

Level 1 includes full support of class referencing of objects, which is perhaps the simplest way to request objects, and is required to be fully supported by all levels. The implementation table shows that class 0 objects may be referenced using qualifier 06, which is the all-object mode. Classes 1 to 3 may be referenced using qualifiers 06, 07 or 08. The latter two provide for calling for a limited quantity of events at a time.

Level 2 sub-set definition

Level 2 slave functions – additional to level 1:

- Accepts freeze requests on binary counter objects
- Parses read requests for variation 0 (all variations) for some objects
- Parses read requests for variations 1, 2, & 3 of binary change objects
- Parses and may respond to requests for frozen counter objects
- May send unsolicited responses containing static data

Level 2 master functions – no extensions to level 1

Level 3 sub-set definition

Level 3 functions – additional to levels 1 and 2:

- Slave will process read requests for many specific objects and variations
- Supports a larger range of requests and function codes
- Enabling and disabling of unsolicited responses on a class-by-class basis
- Eg, will process the following:
  - Class 1 (object 60, var 2, qualifier 6)
  - Class 2 (object 60, var 3, qualifier 6)
  - Class 3 (object 60, var 4, qualifier 6)
- Dynamic assignment of data objects to classes

Qualifier field quick reference

The meanings of the function qualifier field codes were presented in an earlier chapter, showing the index size and qualifier sub-fields separately. The reader will recall that these are structured as below:

Qualifier field

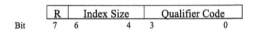

R	Index Size	Qualifier Code
Bit 7	6 4	3 0

In the implementation tables the qualifier field values are simply shown as a two-digit hexadecimal value, from which the I-size and Q-code values may be read directly. The reader will soon notice that only certain combinations of these appear in the implementation tables. It is convenient therefore to have a 'quick-reference' table for these combinations. This is shown below.

Qualifier Field (hex)	Meaning
00	Range-Index Mode with 8-bit range start and stop values.
01	Range-Index Mode with 16-bit range start and stop values.
06	All object mode.
07	Non-ranged mode with no indexes. 8-bit range value has quantity of data objects.
08	Non-ranged mode with no indexes. 16-bit range value has quantity of data objects.
17	Non-ranged mode with 8-bit indexes. 8-bit range value has quantity of data objects.
28	Non-ranged mode with 16-bit indexes. 16-bit range value has quantity of data objects.

This table shows that for the defined sub-sets, only a small number of methods of referencing data are actually used. These are:

- Range-index mode, where the range field has the start and stop index values
- Non-ranged mode with no indexes, where the range field has the number of data objects. In a response the data objects simply are appended

- Non-ranged mode with indexes. This is where the data objects are not in a consecutive order, and each require their own index reference
- All-object mode, which is used in a request only to refer to all the objects in the group

6.1.4   Function code quick reference

The function codes were provided in a previous chapter. Again, only a sub-set of the available functions are actually required by the defined implementation levels. These are summarized for reference below.

Function Code	Description	Meaning
0	Confirm	Used by both requests and responses.
1	Read	Respond with data objects requested.
2	Write	Store objects and respond with status.
3	Select	Pre-arm control point.
4	Operate	Carry out action on selected point. Respond with status.
5	Direct Operate	Select and operate control point. Respond with status.
6	Direct Operate, no Ack	Select and operate control point.
7	Immediate Freeze	Copy specified objects to freeze buffer. Respond with status.
8	Immediate Freeze, no Ack	Copy specified objects to freeze buffer.
9	Freeze and Clear	Copy specified objects to freeze buffer, then clear objects. Respond with status.
10	Freeze and Clear, no Ack	Copy specified objects to freeze buffer, then clear objects.
13	Cold Restart	Respond with time to availability, restart application.
20	Enable Unsolicited Messages	Enable unsolicited messages. Respond with status.
21	Disable Unsolicited Message	Disable unsolicited messages. Respond with status.
22	Assign Class	Assign specified data objects to class defined by class object headers preceding object identifiers. Respond with status.
23	Delay Measurement	Turnaround message. Include processing time in message so that master can calculate message travel time excluding outstation processing time.
129	Response	This indicates that the message is a response to a request.
130	Unsolicited Message.	This indicates that the message is an unsolicited response.

6.1.5   Sub-set implementation table

The following table shows the support requirements at each implementation level for all DNP3 data object groups and variations.

The table lists all defined object groups and variations. Where support of a particular object group is required, an 'X' is shown at the level at which support is required, and the function and qualifier codes are listed to the right of the table. Note that higher sub-set levels automatically include the requirements of lower levels.

OBJECT			LEVEL			REQUEST (slave must parse)		RESPONSE (master must parse)	
Obj	Var	Description	1	2	3	Function Code (dec)	Qualifier Code (hex)	Function Code (dec)	Qualifier Code (hex)
1	0	Binary Input - All Variations		X	X	1 22	06 00, 01		
1	1	Binary Input	X	X	X	1	00, 01, 06	129 130	00, 01
1	2	Binary Input with Status	X	X	X	1	00, 01, 06	129 130	00, 01
2	0	Binary Input Change - All Variations		X		1	06, 07, 08		
2	1	Binary Input Change without Time	X	X		1	06, 07, 08	129, 130	17, 28
2	2	Binary Input Change with Time	X	X		1	06, 07, 08	129, 130	17, 28
2	3	Binary Input Change with Relative Time	X	X		1	06, 07, 08	129, 130	17, 28
10	0	Binary Output - All Variations	X		X	1	06		
10	1	Binary Output				1	00, 01		
10	2	Binary Output Status	X	X		1	00, 01, 06	129 130	00, 01
12	0	Control Block - All Variations			X				
12	1	Control Relay Output Block	X			3, 4, 5, 6	17, 28	129	echo of request
12	2	Pattern Control Block			X	5, 6	17, 28	129	echo of request
12	3	Pattern Mask			X	5, 6	00, 01	129	echo of request
20	0	Binary Counter - All Variations		X	X	1, 7, 8, 9, 10 22	06 00, 01		
20	1	32-Bit Binary Counter	X	X				129 130	00, 01
20	2	16-Bit Binary Counter	X	X				129 130	00, 01

OBJECT			LEVEL			REQUEST (slave must parse)		RESPONSE (master must parse)	
Obj	Var	Description	1	2	3	Function Code (dec)	Qualifier Code (hex)	Function Code (dec)	Qualifier Code (hex)
20	3	32-Bit Delta Counter	X					129 130	00, 01
20	4	16-Bit Delta Counter	X	X				129 130	00, 01
20	5	32-Bit Binary Counter without Flag	X	X				129 130	00, 01
20	6	16-Bit Binary Counter without Flag	X	X				129 130	00, 01
20	7	32-Bit Delta Counter without Flag	X	X				129 130	00, 01
20	8	16-Bit Delta Counter without Flag	X	X				129 130	00,01
21	0	Frozen Counter - All Variations		X		1	06		
21	1	32-Bit Frozen Counter		X				129, 130	
21	2	16-Bit Frozen Counter		X				129, 130	
21	3	32-Bit Frozen Delta Counter							
21	4	16-Bit Frozen Delta Counter							
21	5	32-Bit Frozen Counter with Time of Freeze							
21	6	16-Bit Frozen Counter with Time of Freeze							
21	7	32-Bit Frozen Delta Counter with Time of Freeze							
21	8	16-Bit Frozen Delta Counter with Time of Freeze							
21	9	32-Bit Frozen Counter without Flag		X				129, 130	00, 01
21	10	16-Bit Frozen Counter without Flag		X				129, 130	00, 01
21	11	32-Bit Frozen Delta Counter without Flag							
21	12	16-Bit Frozen Delta Counter without Flag							
22	0	Counter Change Event - All Variations		X		1	06, 07, 08		
22	1	32-Bit Counter Change Event without Time	X					129, 130	17, 28
22	2	16-Bit Counter Change Event without Time	X					129, 130	17, 28
22	3	32-Bit Delta Counter Change Event without Time	X					129, 130	17, 28
22	4	16-Bit Delta Counter Change Event without Time	X					129, 130	17, 28
22	5	32-Bit Counter Change Event with Time							

OBJECT			LEVEL			REQUEST (slave must parse)		RESPONSE (master must parse)	
Obj	Var	Description	1	2	3	Function Code (dec)	Qualifier Code (hex)	Function Code (dec)	Qualifier Code (hex)
22	6	16-Bit Counter Change Event with Time							
22	7	32-Bit Delta Counter Change Event with Time							
22	8	16-Bit Delta Counter Change Event with Time							
23	0	Frozen Counter Event - All Variations							
23	1	32-Bit Frozen Counter Event without Time							
23	2	16-Bit Frozen Counter Event without Time							
23	3	32-Bit Frozen Delta Counter Event without Time							
23	4	16-Bit Frozen Delta Counter Event without Time							
23	5	32-Bit Frozen Counter Event with Time							
23	6	16-Bit Frozen Counter Event with Time							
23	7	32-Bit Frozen Delta Counter Event with Time							
23	8	16-Bit Frozen Delta Counter Event with Time							
30	0	Analog Input - All Variations		X		1	06		
30	1	32-Bit Analog Input	X					129 130	00,01
30	2	16-Bit Analog Input	X	X				129 130	00,01
30	3	32-Bit Analog Input without Flag	X					129 130	00,01
30	4	16-Bit Analog Input without Flag	X	X				129 130	00,01
31	0	Frozen Analog Input - All Variations							
31	1	32-Bit Frozen Analog Input							
31	2	16-Bit Frozen Analog Input							
31	3	32-Bit Frozen Analog Input with Time of Freeze							
31	4	16-Bit Frozen Analog Input with Time of Freeze							
31	5	32-Bit Frozen Analog Input without Flag							
31	6	16-Bit Frozen Analog Input without Flag							
32	0	Analog Change Event - All Variations		X		1	06, 07, 08		

OBJECT			LEVEL			REQUEST (slave must parse)		RESPONSE (master must parse)	
Obj	Var	Description	1	2	3	Function Code (dec)	Qualifier Code (hex)	Function Code (dec)	Qualifier Code (hex)
32	1	32-Bit Analog Change Event without Time	X			1	06, 07, 08	129,130	17,28
32	2	16-Bit Analog Change Event without Time		X		1	06, 07, 08	129,130	17,28
32	3	32-Bit Analog Change Event with Time							
32	4	16-Bit Analog Change Event with Time							
33	0	Frozen Analog Event - All Variations							
33	1	32-Bit Frozen Analog Event without Time							
33	2	16-Bit Frozen Analog Event without Time							
33	3	32-Bit Frozen Analog Event with Time							
33	4	16-Bit Frozen Analog Event with Time							
40	0	Analog Output Status - All Variations	X		X	1	06 00, 01		
40	1	32-Bit Analog Output Status			X		00, 01, 06	129,130	00, 01
40	2	16-Bit Analog Output Status	X	X				129 130	00, 01
41	0	Analog Output Block - All Variations			X		00, 01, 06		
41	1	32-Bit Analog Output Block	X		X	3, 4, 5, 6	17, 28	129	echo of request
41	2	16-Bit Analog Output Block	X			3, 4, 5, 6	17, 28	129	echo of request
50	0	Time and Date - All Variations							
50	1	Time and Date	X		X	2 1	07 quantity = 1	129	07, quantity=1
50	2	Time and Date with Interval							
51	0	Time and Date CTO - All Variations							
51	1	Time and Date CTO	X					129,130	07, quantity=1
51	2	Unsynchronized Time and Date CTO	X					129,130	07, quantity=1
52	0	Time Delay - All Variations							
52	1	Time Delay Coarse	X					129	07, quantity=1
52	2	Time Delay Fine	X					129	07, quantity=1
60	1	Class 0 Data	X			1	06		
60	2	Class 1 Data	X		X	1 20, 21, 22	06,07,08		

OBJECT			LEVEL			REQUEST (slave must parse)		RESPONSE (master must parse)	
Obj	Var	Description	1	2	3	Function Code (dec)	Qualifier Code (hex)	Function Code (dec)	Qualifier Code (hex)
60	3	Class 2 Data	X			1 20, 21, 22	06,07,08		
60	4	Class 3 Data	X		X	1 20, 21, 22	06,07,08		
70	1	File Identifier							
80	1	Internal Indications	X		X	2 1	00 index=7 01		
81	1	Storage Object							
82	1	Device Profile							
83	1	Private Registration Object							
83	2	Private Registration Object Descriptor							
90	1	Application Identifier							
100	1	Short Floating Point							
100	2	Long Floating Point							
100	3	Extended Floating Point							
101	1	Small Packed Binary-Coded Decimal							
101	2	Medium Packed Binary-Coded Decimal							
101	3	Large Packed Binary-Coded Decimal							
		No object				13			
		No object				23			

6.2 Interoperability between DNP3 devices

Interoperability between DNP3 devices is obtained from all of the following. These are in addition to the 'Basic Four' specification documents.

- Specification of minimum implementation sub-sets
- An active user group and technical committee
- Technical bulletins giving clarifications as required
- Device profile documents
- Implementation rules
- Conformance testing

6.2.1 Device profile document

The device profile document is a key tool of DNP3 in providing for interoperability between DNP3 devices and systems. It is a required document that must be provided by the manufacturer for any equipment conforming to the DNP3 standard. It addresses application level and data link level issues, but not physical layer issues.

The device profile document consists of these sections:

- Device profile
- Implementation table
- Point list (optional)

The device profile contains the following parts:

- Device and manufacturer identification
- Highest DNP3 level supported
- Device function
- Deviations (additional features) to sub-set definition requirements
- Configuration details

The implementation table is of the format shown in the example implementation table, and lists all the object groups and variations supported, and the function and qualifier codes for each.

A sample device profile document is included in the Appendix.

The DNP3 sub-set implementation document provides the following layout which may be used for the optional point list.

Description	Index	Default Static Variation			Default Event Variation				Point Name
		Obj	Var	Desc	Obj	Var	Desc	Desc	

6.2.2 Confirming interoperability of devices

To ensure that a DNP3 system will be interoperable with all its component parts, including master, RTUs and IEDs, it is necessary to examine the device profiles for each device.

The device profiles of slave devices will show the base DNP3 level as well as additional data objects and functions that are implemented. The DNP3 level for master devices interfacing to these must at minimum support the same DNP3 level, plus those of the additional features that are intended to be utilized.

The device profile document also lists many configuration details including default configurations for confirmations, retries and other details. All of these need to be checked for compatibility with the planned implementation.

Confirming interoperability:

- Determine DNP3 polling mode to be used
- Determine range of slave devices
- Assemble device profile documents for range of slave devices
- Determine minimum required DNP3 level
- Determine functions above this level that will require support
- Determine data objects above selected base level that will require support
- Examine device profiles for RTUs and establish compatibility with IEDs
- Examine device profiles for master station and establish compatibility with RTUs

6.3 Implementation rules and recommendations

The following sub-sections summarize rules and recommendations that appear in the sub-set definition document DNP3 Subset Definitions, Version 2, Nov 1995. These rules and recommendations provide information that extends and clarifies that contained in the Basic Four documents.

6.3.1 Error responses

Error responses are defined to cope with side-effects of having levels. These are the possibility that a device of one level will be polled for data objects that it cannot provide.

Types:

- Request not valid for its level
- Request not valid for the particular device

These are reported by the internal indications bits 0–2.

Bit	Description	Meaning
0	Function code not implemented	Implementation level does not support this function on specified data objects
1	Requested objects unknown	1. Implementation does not support this object group/variation 2. For static objects only: device has no objects of this group/variation Not to be used for event objects if the request is defined for this level
2	Parameters invalid	Some or all of the objects of this group/variation are out of the specified range. Objects within range may be sent with response.
Null	Bits 0-2 cleared and no objects returned	No objects available. Primarily used in response to event polls. Can also be used for static polls where no range was specified.

Event objects are also a special case, because although they are not tied to a physical device and they may not exist at a given time, because there may be no new events to report. In this case the device must provide a null response rather than a 'requested objects unknown' response.

6.3.2   Data classes and events

The simplest method of referencing data in requests in DNP3 is to call for objects by class. This in fact is a fundamental assumption behind the minimum implementation sub-sets, which at their lowest level depend on the use of calls by class to obtain many objects. This is provided for by requiring that all devices have their static data objects assigned to class 0, and all event objects assigned to one of the other classes.

The sub-set document defines a relationship between event type object variations and class. Event type object variations are required to be assigned by default as class 1, 2 or 3, but not class 0. Class 0 is to be assigned by default to static data points only.

Level 3 devices must allow a master to enable or disable event reporting for a point. To enable event reporting the master would assign the point to required data class 1, 2 or 3. To disable event reporting the master would assign the point to class 0.

Level 1 or 2 devices do not need to support enabling or disabling of event reporting by the master. For these devices, default assignments are required to be in-built.

Rules:

- All static objects are by definition class 0
- Event objects are by definition in class 1, 2 or 3 (may be configurable)
- All event objects must be assigned by default to class 1, 2 or 3
- Level 3 slave devices must allow disabling of event reporting

6.3.3   Default variation

If a master request does not specify a particular variation for a point, then the slave must send the default variation. This may be configurable. This occurs when the master requests by class, or uses object variation zero.

6.3.4   Order of responses

A slave must preserve the sequence of event order when responding requests for data by class. In particular, when a read request calls for multiple classes, the event data must not be returned in class groups, but rather in sequence of occurrence.

6.3.5   Actions on slave device startup

The following actions must occur on startup of a slave device:

- The device restart IIN bit must be set
- If configured for unsolicited responses, it must send one on startup
- This response must contain either no data, or all static data
- This response may also contain unreported event data. If provided, these must be included in the message prior to the static data

It is recommended that if a device does not report all of its static data on startup, the master should immediately poll for all static and event data.

6.3.6   Unsolicited responses

If unsolicited responses are supported, then:

- The slave device profile must state that unsolicited responses are supported
- It must identify which data objects and functions may use this mode
- The use of unsolicited responses must be able to be configured off
- The master must be able to dynamically disable them using a disable unsolicited request, function code 21
- A slave must send an unsolicited response on startup regardless of whether unsolicited responses have been previously disabled by a master station request

Slaves of level 2 or above may report static data objects in unsolicited responses under the following conditions:

- Upon startup of the device
- When the data object status flag bits change

Other rules:

- Master destination address for unsolicited responses must be configurable in the device
- All levels of master must support unsolicited responses

6.3.7   Operating binary outputs

- All slaves must be able to parse operations on control relay output blocks
- All slaves must be able to parse all output function codes and control types, eg select/operate, and pulse on. It cannot respond with function unknown, but may respond with operation not supported in the status of the control relay output block if it does not support the function

Recommendations:

- Using write requests to binary outputs is not recommended because there is no feedback of the success of the operation
- Recommended method is to use control relay output block
- If a direct write is used, then a separate feedback of binary status should be used

6.3.8   Fragments and frames

- Application layer fragments must not exceed 2048 bytes
- All devices must accept maximum sized data link layer frames (292 bytes)
- A master must not send multi-fragment requests
- A master must accept multi-fragment responses
- A slave must include all response data in a single response message. It must not reply with multiple responses

Recommendations:

- The maximum size of fragments should be configurable in master and slave devices
- Choice of qualifiers and objects by masters should be optimized to minimize bandwidth usage

6.3.9 Multiple objects

- All slave devices must be able to parse a master request containing any sub-set of all the objects supported by the device
- All master devices must be able to parse a single slave response, or unsolicited slave response, containing any sub-set of the objects the master device supports

6.3.10 Confirmation and retries

- All levels of master and slave devices may choose whether or not to require confirmation of data link frames
- A master or slave must transmit a data link confirm frame if requested by a send confirm expected request function code
- A master or slave must transmit an application layer confirmation response if requested by the confirm bit
- If a slave supports application layer retries, these must be configurable, and be disabled by default

If a slave is waiting for an application layer confirmation, and it receives a new request:

- It must assume the confirmation is not coming
- Retain any event data sent in the previous message
- Process the new request

Recommendations:

- Enabling of data link confirmations should be configurable in master and slave devices
- A slave should request only application layer confirmation responses as follows:
    - On event data. Slave clears sent events on receipt of confirmation
    - On large outgoing multi-fragment messages. This allows flow control by master
    - When a particular action is required in response to a slave state such as roll-over, or buffer overflow
- A slave should only use application layer retries for unsolicited messages

This is because:

- Data link layer may already have performed retries
- Data link layer retries only retransmit frames, not fragments

Masters should not request application layer confirmations because these are redundant where the request requires a response from the slave.

6.3.11 Flags in objects

Slave devices may ignore whether a master calls for data with or without flags, and may send the requested data with or without a flag at the choice of the slave.

The rules are:

- Slave may decide when to provide flag
- Slave may ignore whether master asks for flag or not
- If slave does not provide flag, point may be assumed to be normal, ie no fault bits set
- A master must be able to process object variations with or without flags

6.3.12 16- and 32-bit variations

- A slave must have a default configuration for object variation responses to non-specific requests
- These are class or variation 0 requests
- Slave responds with default variation
- Slave must respond with specific variation if requested

6.3.13 Over-range analog objects

- If a hardware device is over-range, over-range flag is set
- But hardware data is reported unaltered
- This could be +2047 or –2048 for a 12-bit DAC for example

If a hardware device is over-range:

- Over-range bit in flag field is set
- Data is reported as is from device

If a measured value is within range of the hardware, but exceeds that which can be represented by the data object variation requested, then a maximum positive or negative value is returned.

6.3.14 Counter roll-over

There is a problem in interpretation of the roll-over flag for counter objects. This arises from the flexibility provided by object variations which means a master will not know whether a counter rolled over at 16 bits or 32 bits.

- Slaves may choose not to set the roll-over flag
- Roll-over point must be specified in device profile
- A slave must have a default configuration for object variation responses to non-specific requests. This will specify the default counter object size
- A slave must provide at least 16 bits of a 32-bit counter if polled for 16-bit counter object
- Master must poll frequently enough to avoid roll-over in polled systems

It is recommended that roll-over flags are not set by slave devices and are ignored by masters.

6.3.15   Time-tagged binary input events

- Event sequence must be preserved
- Non-specific event object requests, ie for class or variation 0 data return:
- Time-tagged event object, or
- Non-time-tagged event object, or
- Both. In this case device must be configurable to limit reporting to one or the other

6.3.16   Freeze operations

- A master must request freeze operations on binary counter objects only (object 20), not on frozen counter objects (object 21)
- Level 2 or 3 devices must support freeze operations on binary counter objects, if they have them
- They are not required to support reads of frozen counter objects

6.3.17   Time synchronization

A slave device does not need to support delay measurement or write operations on time and date if it never sets the time synchronization required internal indication bit.

It is recommended that if relative time event objects are used, an unsynchronized CTO object should be used if the slave's time has not been set by the master.

6.4   Conformance testing

6.4.1   General

One of the recognized strengths of DNP3 is the existence of detailed compliance certification test procedures. These are produced and maintained by the DNP3 User Group. Currently the certification test procedures specify the test requirements and procedures for conformance testing of IEDs to DNP3 levels 1 and 2. The documents also contain some clarifications and extensions to Basic Four documents.

It is important to note that the certification procedures are focussed on the minimum requirements, as implemented in IEDs rather than at the level of SCADA master stations. This shows that although conformance and interoperability can be assured for systems featuring equipment certified to level 1 or level 2, there is no assurance for features and functions above these levels. Thus, if a system is to incorporate a diverse range of equipment with extended specifications (IEDs with many functions above the level 2 implementation sub-set), then specific assurance testing may be appropriate.

6.4.2   Specification

The protocol specification is clarified by the certification procedure as being made up of the following documents:

- Basic Four:
- DNP Version 3.00 Data Link Layer
- DNP Version 3.00 Transport Functions

- DNP Version 3.00 Application Layer
- DNP Version 3.00 Data Object Library Layer
- DNP Version 3.00 Sub-set Definitions Version 2.00
- Technical Notes published by the Technical Committee
- DNP3-2000 Intelligent Electronic Device Certification Procedure Level 1
- DNP3-2000 Intelligent Electronic Device Certification Procedure Level 2

This list demonstrates that to ensure compliance with DNP3 it is necessary to take into account all notes published by the Technical Committee, the sub-set definitions, and the certification procedures as well as the Basic Four documents.

6.4.3　Certification procedure requirements

There are three main parts to the certification procedure. These are:

- General information including an overview, notes, definitions and reference documents
- Pre-test review describing the desktop and bench-top pre-test review
- The test procedures, with each procedure having defined:
- Test subject
- Desired behavior
- Test procedure

The following table shows an overview of the content of the certification procedures, including the specific test subject titles. The actual certification procedure documents are separate for level 1 and level 2, however the main differences are in the application layer functions only. The level 2 document specifies a larger number of test subjects than for the level 1 document.

Section	Title	Description
1	Overview	Describes purpose of tests as to specifically ensure compliance with Level 1 of the Subset Definitions
2	Notes	General test requirements and assumptions.
3	Definitions	Includes • General definitions of terminology • Definitions of IIN bit meanings • Error responses shown by IIN2 bits • Definitions about change objects
4	Reference Documents	Defined to be: 1. Basic Four 2. Subset Definitions
5	Pretest Review • Device Profile Review • Equipment Review • Wiring Diagrams	This defines the pre-test desktop review requirements. These ensure the Device Profile documentation is conforming, it indicates conformance, and that the device is testable.
6	Link Layer • Reset Link and Passive Confirm support • Test Link • Request Link Status • Test Retries • DIR and FCV Bits • Data Link Rejects Invalid Frames	Tests link layer functionality. The section specifies for each function under test: • Desired behaviour • Test procedure
7	Transport Layer	Tests transport layer functionality. The section specifies: • Desired behaviour • Test procedure
8	Application Layer • Binary Output Status • Binary Outputs • Analog Output Status • Analog Outputs • Class Data • Indications • Time • Cold Restart • Application Layer Fragmentation • Multi-Drop Support • Unsolicited Responses • Collision Avoidance Additional sections for Level-2 • Binary Inputs • Binary Input Change • Common Time of Occurrence • Binary Counters • Binary Counters, Event • Analog Input • Analog Change Event • Multiple Read Requests	Tests application layer functionality. The section specifies for each function under test: • Desired behaviour • Test procedure

6.4.4 Certification authorities

The DNP3 Users Group has authorized three test houses to carry out conformance testing and issue conformance certificates for DNP3. Third party conformance testing is not a requirement to use DNP3, but if certification is required by an end user, this can only be obtained from one of these authorities.

Authorized Testing Authorities:

- Advanced Control Systems (Georgia, USA)
- Reltronics (Canada)
- Subnet Solutions (Calgary, Canada)

6.5 DNP3 polling and communications options

The designer of a SCADA system utilizing DNP3 needs to select an operational mode for the acquisition of data from the system. Whereas many older SCADA systems are based on purely polled data acquisition, DNP3 offers the choice of report-by-exception operation. The advantage that this operational mode gives is a substantial saving in bandwidth usage.

Instead of slave devices reporting the status of all of their points in response to master station polls, they report changes only. This method assumes, and requires, that the SCADA master can reliably retain its record of the present status of the slave and that any changes to that status will be reliably reported to the master. When the typical operation of SCADA systems is considered it is apparent that such a system can make considerable savings in the amount of data that is communicated. This reduction in communication requirements can translate to allowing a much larger number of slaves to be connected to a given communication path than might otherwise be the case.

In fact, the combination of polled versus non-polled operation, and report-by-exception combine to make four variations. The DNP3 documentation identifies the following four operating modes and identifies them in order of decreasing efficiency in use of communications bandwidth.

Operational Mode	Description
Quiescent	All communication is unsolicited report-by-exception Master never polls for data Master sends application layer confirmations
Unsolicited report-by-exception	As quiescent, plus Infrequent background polling for static data (integrity polls)
Polled report-by-exception	Master polls frequently for event data Master polls infrequently for static data
Polled static operation	Master polls regularly for static data or for data when and as required

A mode commonly used is unsolicited report-by-exception. This mode gives security against failure of communications systems, while still retaining the benefit of limited bandwidth usage. This addresses a problem that can occur with quiescent operation, which is undetected communication failures. In a fully quiescent system, if a link should fail there is no way to detect the failure because the master may not be attempting to initiate any communications over that link. In this case the failure would only be apparent if the master attempted to carry out a control action.

When implementing an unsolicited report-by-exception operating mode, the frequency of background polling and the amount of information sought by this can be adjusted to provide optimal system performance. For example, a periodic background poll might be used to return very limited data. This would consume only a small bandwidth, but would prove the continued operation of the communications system just as well as a larger data poll would.

Sometimes polled static operation will be used for particular critical tasks, combined with unsolicited report-by-exception for most data acquisition.

The minimum implementation mode supported is defined by the sub-set definition documents to be polled report-by-exception. However, the documents recommend that one of the reporting by exception modes should be available for any DNP3 implementation. To this effect, the following specific recommendations are made:

- All slave devices should report event data
- All master devices should support a report-by-exception mode of operation

6.6 Time synchronization

6.6.1 General method for time synchronization

One of the important SCADA features of DNP3 is that it provides for time-stamping of events. Time stamping in DNP3 provides resolution of events to one-millisecond. For events to match up correctly across a system, it is essential that the clocks in all outstations are synchronized with the master station clock.

Synchronizing of an outstation clock is done by sending a time and date object (object 50, variation 1) to the outstation. However, there is a finite delay in transmission from the master to the outstation, and if this is not accounted for when setting the clock, it would be set retarded by this transmission time. This delay time can be due to store-and-forward delays introduced by a variety of devices along the transmission path, including:

- Time in modem buffers
- Time in data radio buffers
- Time in intermediate repeater store-and-forward buffers

In addition to these, the reader might also add the possibility of processing delays between the application level and the lower levels, or 'stack delays' at both master and outstation. These would indeed be significant, except that the DNP3 specification accounts for these by requiring some of the time synchronization function to be performed at the data link layer. The data link is required to record the time of transmission or receipt of the first bit of any delay time message. When transmitting the message, the data link layer triggers a freeze of the master station clock, which is stored as *MasterSendTime*. Similarly, when a slave station receives a delay time message it must store a freeze of the local clock as *RtuReceiveTime*.

DNP3 provides for measurement of the round trip delay time by *Function Code 23 Delay Measurement*. The procedure is shown below.

Delay measurement procedure:

- Master sends *Function Code 23 Delay Measurement*
- Master records start of transmission time as *MasterSendTime*
- Outstation records the receipt time as *RtuReceiveTime*
- Outstation commences to send a response and records time as *RtuSendTime*
- Outstation calculates its internal processing turnaround time *RtuTurnAround* which is *RtuSendTime – RtuReceiveTime*

- Outstation includes in the response a *Time Delay* object (object 52, variation 1 or 2) having the value of the turnaround time *RtuTurnAround*
- Master freezes its clock as *MasterReceiveTime* on receiving the response

The master station now calculates the one-way propagation delay by taking the average of the forward and return trip times:

Delay = (MasterSendTime – MasterReceiveTime – RtuTurnAround)/2

The outstation time is now adjusted by the following procedure:

- Master sends a write request containing the time and date object (object group 50, variation 1). The time value is the master clock time at commencing sending this message MasterSend plus the calculated delay. This is the time that the master wants the outstation to be set to. If the delay estimate is correct, the message will be received at the outstation at real time = MasterSend + Delay.
- Outstation receives first bit of message at time RtuReceive.
- Outstation now sets the outstation time by the following calculation:
  Adjustment   = CurrentRtuTime – RtuReceive
  NewRtuTime   = Time in Time and Date Object + Adjustment

Note that the point in storing the RtuReceive time is that some delay can take place before actually writing the NewRtuTime, without causing any error. Any additional time delay is accounted for by determining the adjustment.

It should be observed that this method assumes the forward and return path travel times are equal, and that message travel times are repeatable. To the extent that these assumptions are not true, the time set will be in error.

It is also relevant to note that the DNP3 time synchronization functions have been provided to cover the situation of a relatively low-bandwidth communication path between master and slave. In this situation, the main delays are in the communication path itself. Where DNP3 is being carried over local or wide area networks (LANs or WANs) using DNP3 over TCP/IP or UDP/IP different considerations apply. These issues are discussed elsewhere in this text.

6.6.2   Global time synchronization

Time may be synchronized using a global request and the global address FFFF. This can only be used if the path delays to all outstations are similar enough to keep errors within acceptable limits.

6.7   DNP3 over TCP/IP and UDP/IP

6.7.1   General considerations

Inherent in the concept of a SCADA system is the presence of communications systems that link together one or more master devices with usually a number of remotely located slave devices. The scale of distances involved, and the nature of the data conveyed has dictated the technologies used to carry the communications. The systems used have often involved leased lines, or PSTN lines and analog (FSK) modems, and radio links using analog or data radios. The data rates involved are typically in the range of 2400 to 9600 baud.

As DNP3 was originally conceived, its physical layer was specified as using RS-232C bit-serial asynchronous communications. This is consistent with the historically typical communications system described above and was a natural choice.

However, DNP3 was developed in the electrical industry, which is characterized by short-range as well as long-range communications requirements. For example, in a substation environment, a large number of devices such as meters, relays and other IEDs may be utilized.

When DNP3 is used in a short-distance situation such as this, a multidrop configuration can be achieved by using RS-485. However, this is limited to half-duplex operation as only one device can drive the line at one time, and there is a limit of 32 devices on an RS-485 circuit. Regardless of the technical merit of this solution though, there are wider trends operating that are taking communications in a different direction.

Where the end devices are intelligent, that is they have on-board processing, they may be connected to the rest of the system via a data concentrator or control device such as an RTU. It is the fact that these are now intelligent devices that have changed the nature of communications requirements. Where in older systems, the SCADA system would stop at the RTU and then be hard-wired to the end devices, this is no longer true. Today, the need for communication of the protocol spans from the end device upwards.

At the other end of the scale, the requirements for communications have also become more extensive. Where once individual operating plants were largely islands, little connected with other locations, this is also no longer true. Today's operating environments have changed so that organizations can operate over larger geographic areas, and the communications systems have changed in parallel with this. A major component of this is the widespread adoption of local and wide area networks (LANs and WANs) to provide data connectivity across organizations. These technologies are being increasingly utilized in the electrical utility industry as in many other industries for the many benefits they bring.

Thus, coincidental with the growth of the open SCADA protocols of DNP3 and IEC60870-101 there has been a revolution to organization-wide connectivity, and this is based on the use of LANs and WANs. Within a substation or operating plant a LAN may be used to provide high-speed reliable communications between local equipment as well as via routers to nearby or remote LANs, or to an enterprise level WAN. Because of the benefits these technologies provide they have become ubiquitous, and are now found in control rooms, the plant floor, and the substation, all areas where not too many years ago they were rarely found.

It is hardly surprising then that pressure has emerged to carry DNP3 over a network environment, and this has resulted in extension of the DNP3 specification to include this. The DNP3 User Group Technical Committee has defined a method for carrying DNP3 involving the use of the Internet protocol suite for the transport and network layers, and the Ethernet physical layer. The technicalities of doing this are discussed in the following sections.

The following diagram shows the topology of a networked system using DNP3 and gives an idea how the control system may fit into the overall networked system.

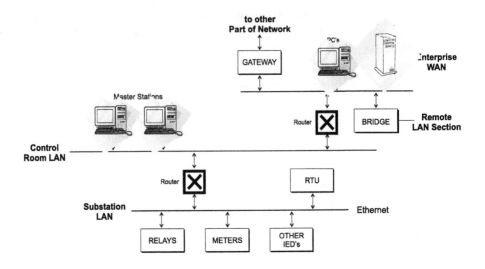

Figure 6.1
Typical network topology

The technical information in the following sub-sections is derived from the DNP3 document Transporting DNP3 over Local and Wide Area Networks, Version 1.0, December 1998. This document is available from the DNP3 User Group website and should be examined if more in depth information is required.

6.7.2 Internet protocol suite

The Internet protocol suite is the group of programs that provide the services of the Internet. These include Internet protocol (IP), transmission control protocol (TCP), user datagram protocol (UDP), file transfer protocol (FTP), and simple mail transfer protocol (SMTP). Of these we are concerned with those providing the transport and network services, TCP, UDP and IP. The relationship of these is shown in the following diagram.

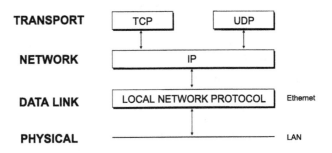

Figure 6.2
TCP/UDP/IP protocol relationships

The diagram shows that TCP and UDP each provide transport services, and each communicate with the network services provided by IP. This in turn communicates with the local network protocol, shown in this case as Ethernet (IEEE 802.3).

The functions of the three protocols are discussed in the following sub-sections.

Internet protocol

The Internet protocol provides what is termed a datagram service. It provides a means of sending individual packets of data, called datagrams from a source to a specified destination. The source and destination addresses are carried in the datagram header as 32-bit fields. IP provides no guarantee of delivery as there are no acknowledgments, and error checking is limited to a simple checksum of the header only. The responsibility for these functions is left to higher levels. IP also provides fragmentation of data into smaller packets as required by the network over which the datagram is passing, and for reassembly of the fragments into the original datagram at the destination end.

The Internet protocol service is also termed a connectionless service because no link establishment steps or monitoring of a link are involved. Each datagram is an independent single communication.

Internet protocol datagrams have a header of 20–24 bytes followed by their data. They can be in theory be up to 65 K bytes, but have a recommended maximum size of 576 bytes.

Transmission control protocol

Transmission control protocol (TCP) provides a reliable, connection-oriented means of transmitting data from one user to another. It is designed to make use of IP to transmit datagrams to provide an error-free transmission over the underlying layers to the destination TCP layer.

TCP establishes communication links between 'sockets' at each end. Following initialization of the link, communications may take place in both directions between each end. TCP breaks the data down into segments and passes these to IP, which in turn may fragment these into smaller datagrams.

TCP has a segment header of 20–24 bytes. The segment size is determined by the lowest 'maximum segment size' configured at each end of the link, or at 536 bytes for a non-local IP address.

User datagram protocol

User Datagram Protocol (UDP) is intended to provide a means of accessing the datagram service of IP more or less directly from the transport layer. One UDP datagram translates to one IP datagram being sent, with the additional information of source and destination ports, plus a checksum. UDP does not provide the reliable delivery feature of TCP, for example if an error is detected the packet will simply be discarded. Because UDP is packet based only, it is not connection oriented as is TCP. This allows it to utilize the broadcast addressing mode of IP to send to multiple destinations simultaneously.

6.7.3   Carrying DNP3 over a network

The idea of carrying DNP3 over a network environment involves encapsulation of the data frames from the DNP3 data link layer within the transport layer frames of the Internet protocol suite and allowing that protocol stack to deliver the DNP3 data link layer frames to the destination location in place of the original DNP3 physical layer.

The following method has been recommended by the Technical Committee:

- DNP3 shall use the Internet protocol suite to transport messages of LAN/WAN
- Recommended physical link is Ethernet (others may be used however)
- All devices shall support TCP and UDP
- TCP must be used for WANs
- TCP is strongly recommended for LANs
- UDP may be used for highly reliable single segment LANs
- UDP is necessary if broadcast messages are required
- The DNP3 protocol stack shall be retained in full
- Link layer confirmations shall be disabled

The resulting protocol stack is shown in the following diagram.

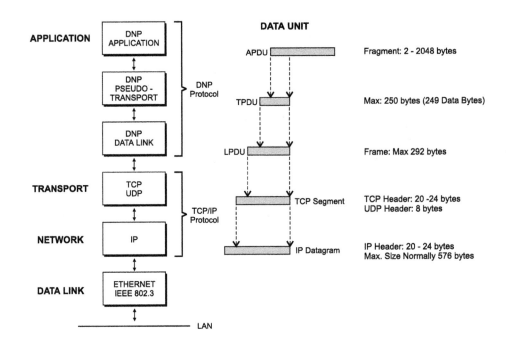

Figure 6.3
DNP3 over TCP/IP protocol stack

Referring to the diagram of the protocol stack, it is apparent that the pseudo-transport and data link layers of the DNP3 protocol remain in the stack and act over and above the transport, network, and data link layers provided by TCP, IP, and the Ethernet LAN protocol. It might be asked by the reader if the lower layers of the DNP3 protocol could have been eliminated. However, there are essential elements of the DNP3 protocol in the lower

DNP3 layers and these are required to operate together. These include addressing and error detection, which are in the data link frame.

To obtain the benefits of seamless integration with TCP/IP it is not possible to attempt to modify those protocols to allow for the features required by DNP3. Instead, the TCP/IP protocols are used as standard to provide transport of the DNP3 messages over the network.

6.7.4   Other issues

Link layer confirmations

Link layer confirmations are unnecessary when using DNP3 over TCP/IP and are specifically not allowed. TCP provides a reliable delivery mechanism, and is backed up at the application layer by confirmations when required.

Time synchronization

Use of the time synchronization delay measurement FC 23 is not appropriate for use over networks because all of:

- The propagation delay along the network is unmeasurably small (typical for LAN) or
- Collisions on the network cause variable delay (also on LAN)
- The propagation delay is unpredictable due to crossing routers
- The protocol stack causes a variable delay

Because of these limitations, the Technical Committee has defined a procedure for allowing time synchronization across a local LAN only. Synchronization is not defined at all for a WAN. The procedure requires that the master use a UDP datagram to broadcast record current time function (FC 24) to all slaves requiring it. The ethernet driver is required to have the ability to record the time of transmission, and receipt, of the last byte of the message. These times are to be the same due to small propagation delay of the LAN. The master then sends a time and date at last recorded time object (object group 50, variation 3) which allows the slaves to determine a time adjustment. Both the record current time function and the last recorded time object have been newly defined in DNP3 for this purpose.

7

Preview of IEC 60870-5

7.1   What is IEC 60870-5?

IEC 60870-5 refers to a collection of standards produced by the International Electrotechnical Commission, or IEC , to provide an open standard for the transmission of SCADA telemetry control and information.

The standard provides a detailed functional description for telecontrol equipment and systems for controlling geographically widespread processes, in other words for SCADA systems. The standard is intended for application in the electrical industries, and has data objects that are specifically intended for such applications, however it is not limited to such applications as it has data objects that are applicable to general SCADA applications in any industry. Nevertheless, the IEC 60870-5 protocol is primarily used in the electrical industries of European countries.

When the IEC 60870-5 set of standards was initially completed in 1995 with the publication of the IEC 870-5-101 profile, it covered only transmission over relatively low bandwidth bit-serial communication circuits. With the increasingly widespread use of network communications technology, IEC 60870-5 now also provides for communications over networks using the TCP/IP protocol suite. This same sequence of development occurred for DNP3.

In this preview, the main features of IEC 60870-5 are described under the headings listed below. These areas are all examined in greater detail in the subsequent chapters of Fundamentals and Advanced considerations of IEC 60870-5, in which the protocol will be described in detail by focussing on the protocol specification from the physical level through to the user application level.

- Standards
- System topology
- Message structure
- Addressing

- Message transport
- Application and user level functions
- Application data objects
- Interoperability

7.2 Standards

IEC 60870 refers to a standard produced in a number of parts between 1988 and 2000 by the International Electrotechnical Commission, or IEC. The IEC is an organization made up from national committees from around the world, and its role is to promote international cooperation on standardization in the electrical and electronic fields. This standard was originally referenced as IEC 870, but the prefix '60' has subsequently been added.

The IEC 60870 standard is structured in hierarchical manner, comprising six parts plus a number of companion standards. Each part is then made up of a number of sections, each of which has been published separately in a progressive manner. In addition to the main parts, there are four 'companion' standards that provide the fine details of the standard for a particular field of application. The companion standards extend the definition provided by the main parts of the standard by adding specific information objects for the field of application. The structure of the IEC 60870 standard is illustrated in Figure 7.1, following. This shows the main parts of the standard, plus the sections and companion standards concerned with transmission protocols.

Near the bottom of the figure, the companion standard IEC 60870-5-101 may be seen. This is titled 'Companion standard for basic telecontrol tasks'. It is in fact this document that is most often meant when IEC 870 or IEC 60870 is discussed in the context of SCADA systems. This is because it was only with the release of this document that a full definition for a complete SCADA transmission protocol was created, as it is this document that provides all of the application level data objects that are necessary for SCADA operation. Nevertheless, although IEC 60870-5-101 completes the definition for the transmission protocol, it includes many references to the details contained in Sections 1 to 5 of Part 5.

The fourth companion standard, IEC 60870-5-104 is also of particular importance in understanding the standard as it is used today, because it defines the transport of IEC 60870-5 application messages over networks. Its full title is 'Network Access using Standard Transport Profiles' which is referring to its use of TCP/IP for the transport and network protocols. This companion standard was published in December 2000, some six years after the IEC 60870-5-101 was published. It of course provides a very different physical and data transport mechanism to IEC 60870-101, but leaves most of the higher application level functions and data objects unaltered.

The standards are discussed in greater detail in a following section of this course. The key points to note from this preview are the hierarchical structure of the standard, the fact that it has been progressively developed and issued, and the fact that the two main describing documents are the profiles IEC 60870-5-101 and more recently IEC 60870-5-104.

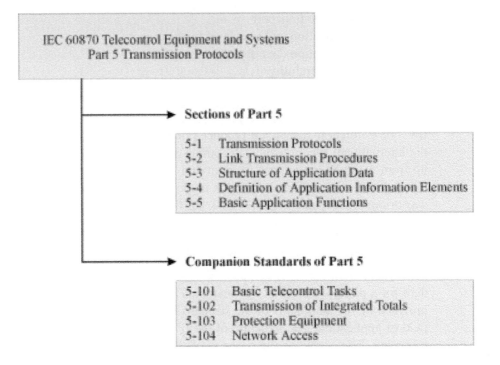

Figure 7.1
Structure of IEC 60870

7.3 System topology

IEC 60870-5-101, or T101, supports point-to-point and multidrop communication links carrying bit-serial low-bandwidth data communications. It provides the choice of using balanced or unbalanced communication at the link level. With unbalanced communication, only the master can initiate communications by transmitting primary frames. This simplifies system design because there is no need to support collision avoidance. All communications are initiated by master station requests, such as to request user data if available.

Balanced communication is available, but this is limited to point-to-point links only. Therefore whilst T101 can support unsolicited messages from a slave, it cannot do so for a multidrop topology and must employ a cyclic polling scheme to interrogate the secondary stations.

Balanced communication – limited to point-to-point links only:

- Either can initiate transaction
- Better efficiency of communications system usage
- Collision problems as two stations can transmit simultaneously. Collision avoidance and recovery required
- However, only for point-to-point links under T101

Unbalanced communication – suitable for multidrop:

- Only master can send primary frames
- Collision avoidance is not required
- Slave data link layer function is simpler

Under IEC 60870-5 there is an assumed hierarchical structure, so that for any two stations communicating with each other, one is the controlling station, and the other is the controlled station. There is also a defined 'monitor direction' and a 'control direction'. Thus monitored data such as analog values from the field are sent in the monitoring direction, and commands are sent in the control direction. If a station both sends monitored data and sends commands, it is acting both as a controlled and a controlling station. This is defined as dual-mode operation. It is accommodated by the protocol, but requires that use is made of originator addresses in the ASDU.

7.4 Message structure

The message structure under IEC 60870-5-101 is formed by a data link layer frame carrying link address and control information, a flag to indicate if Class 1 data is available, and optional application data. Each frame can carry a maximum of one application service data unit, or ASDU. Figure 7.2 shows the data link frame structure, and the structure of the application layer ASDU carried by it.

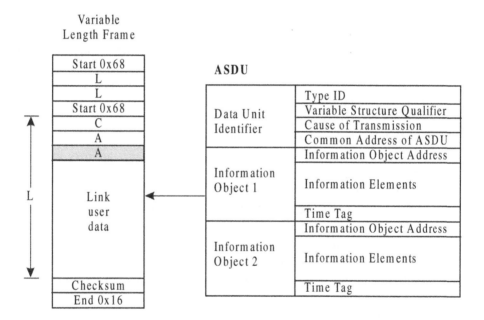

Figure 7.2
Message structure under IEC 60870-5-101

In the case where user data is not required in the frame, either a fixed length frame, or a single character acknowledgement may be used. These provide for efficient use of communications bandwidth.

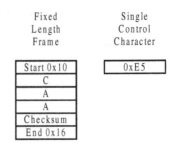

Figure 7.3
Fixed length frame and single control character

7.5   Addressing

Under IEC 60870-5-101 addressing is both at the link and at the application level. The link address field may be 1 or 2 octets for unbalanced, and 0, 1 or 2 octets for balanced communications. As balanced communications are point-to-point the link address is redundant, but may be included for security. The link address FF or FFFF is defined as a broadcast address, and may be used to address all stations at the link level.

At the application level, the ASDU contains a 1 or 2 octet common address. This is defined as the address of the controlling station in the 'control direction', and the address of the controlled station in the 'monitoring direction'. The common address of the ASDU combined with the information object address contained within the data itself combine to make the unique address for each data element.

As in DNP, there may be more than one logical or common address per device. As for the link level, the address FF or FFFF is defined as a broadcast address. Therefore to send a broadcast message it is necessary to include this address in both the data link and application address fields.

Optionally on a per-system basis, originator addresses can also be carried within the ASDU. This is not shown in Figure 7.2, but is an optional part of the cause of transmission field.

The information object address is 1 to 3 octets in length, and can be provided either just once within an ASDU, or for each separate information object within an ASDU. This allows for efficient transmission of blocks of sequential information.

7.6   Networked version

Under IEC 60870-5 there are two different methods of transporting messages. These are in effect two different, but closely related protocols. The first is IEC 60870-5-101, or T101, which provides for bit-serial communications over low-bandwidth communications channels. This method uses the data link frame shown in Figure 7.2 together with defined procedures to transport the data over the communications network.

The second method was defined much more recently with the release of the IEC 60870-5-104, or T104 profile. In this protocol the lower levels of the protocol have been completely replaced by the TCP and IP transport and network protocols. These protocols provide for transport of the application service data units (ASDUs) shown in Figure 7.2

over corporate local area networks and wide area networks using these standard protocols. The structure of the protocol, or 'protocol stack' is shown in Table 7.1.

Layer	Source	Selections
User Process	IEC 60870-5-101	Application functions
Application	IEC 60870-5-101	ASDUs and Application Information Elements.
Transport		
Network		TCP / IP Transport and network protocol suite
Link		
Physical		

Table 7.1
Protocol stack for IEC 60870-5-104

Whereas T101 provides full definition of the protocol stack right down to the physical level, this is not provided under T104 as existing and varied physical and link layer operations are employed.

In general, aside from the completely different operation of message transport, the operation of the protocol at the application and user level is unaltered. Some specific exceptions are in the area of time synchronization, and in broadcast messages.

7.7   Application data objects

IEC 60870-5 has information on a set of information objects that are suited to both general SCADA applications, and electrical system applications in particular. Each different type of data has a unique type identification number. Only one type of data is included in any one ASDU, and as illustrated in Figure 7.2 the type identification is the first field in the ASDU.

The information object types are grouped by direction and by type of information, as follows:

Group	Example in Monitor Direction	Example in Control Direction
Process information	A measured value, e.g. a bit, or an analog	A command, e.g. to set a bit, or a setpoint value
System information	End of initiation flag	Interrogation command, reset process command
Parameter		Set a filter time
File transfer	Read data file, write a configuration file.	

Table 7.2
Information object type groups

7.8   Interoperability

Interoperability under IEC 60870-5 is achieved by a ten-page interoperability statement. This identifies all of the different operating modes, configurable options, ASDUs, causes of transmission, and other information that is important in ensuring compatibility.

Because IEC 60870-5 has a simple structure in terms of its data types and data addressing options, this approach is relatively straightforward. It is necessary to check for compatibility of controlling station implementations with controlled station implementations and ensure that all required data types are supported.

8

Fundamentals of IEC 60870-5

8.1 The IEC 60870-5 standard

8.1.1 Overall structure of standard

The standard IEC 60870-5 was produced by the International Electrotechnical Commission Technical Committee 57, Working Group 03, and published progressively from 1988.

The structure of IEC 60870-5 was introduced in the Preview Section 7.1. This showed how the standard is structured in a hierarchical manner, and illustrated how the companion standards relate to the other sections making up Part 5. Table 8.1 extends the preview information by showing the full structure of IEC 60870, together with the years of publication of the component parts and sections.

The sections IEC 60870-5-1 to IEC 60870-5-5 are the core specification documents for Part 5, the Transmission Protocols part of the standard. The companion standard sections, or simply companion standards, IEC 60870-5-101 to IEC 60870-5-104, are each separate application protocols intended for specific purposes. They provide the definitions of application level data objects and functions to completely define a working protocol. They are also referred to as profiles, and may sometimes be given the shorthand references T101, T102, T103, and T104, the T standing for telecontrol.

As shown in the preview, IEC 60870-5-101 provided the first complete working SCADA protocol under IEC 60870-5. This defines all the necessary application level functions and data objects to provide for telecontrol applications operating over geographically wide areas, using low bandwidth bit-serial communications. It covers general communications with RTUs, including data types and services that are suitable for electrical and substation systems. The data types are generic and suitable for wider SCADA applications.

The IEC 60870-5-102 and IEC 60870-5-103 companion standards provide data types and functions to support electrical protection systems. These include distance protection, line differential protection, and transformer differential protection.

As explained in the preview, the IEC 60870-5-104 companion standard has special significance. This defines operation of the transmission protocol over networks using standard transport profiles specifying the TCP and IP protocols. This companion standard is not really independent of IEC 60870-5-101, but replaces the message transport sections with a network version, leaving the application level functions largely unaltered.

Main Parts

Reference	Description	Year
IEC 60870-1	General Considerations	1988
IEC 60870-2	Operating Conditions	1995
IEC 60870-3	Interfaces (electrical characteristics)	1989
IEC 60870-4	Performance Requirements	1990
IEC 60870-5	Transmission Protocols	1990
IEC 60870-6	Telecontrol Protocols Compatible with ISO and ITU-T Recommendations	1995

Sections of IEC 60870-5

Reference	Description	Year
IEC 60870-5-1	Transmission Frame Formats	1990
IEC 60870-5-2	Link Transmission Procedures	1992
IEC 60870-5-3	General Structure of Application Data	1992
IEC 60870-5-4	Definition and Coding of Application Information Elements	1993
IEC 60870-5-5	Basic Application Functions	1995

Companion Standards of IEC 60870-5

Reference	Description	Year
IEC 60870-5-101	Companion Standard for Basic Telecontrol Tasks	1995
IEC 60870-5-102	Companion Standard for Transmission of Integrated Totals	1996
IEC 60870-5-103	Companion Standard for Protection Communication	1997
IEC 60870-5-104	Network Access using Standard Transport Profiles	2000

Table 8.1
Full structure of IEC 60870 standard

8.1.2   Development of standards

IEC standards are subject to review and the issue of amendments from time to time, and since the publication of IEC 60870-5-101, this profile has had two amendments issued. The first amendment added a small number of information object definitions. The second amendment added a significant amount of clarifying detail, the purpose of which was to remove ambiguities and so better provide for interoperability. It is anticipated that during 2002 the standard will be reissued as one document including the two amendments.

With amendments the complete version of this profile is as shown in Table 8.2.

Reference	Description	Year-Month
IEC 60870-5-101	Companion Standard for Basic Telecontrol Tasks	1995-11
IEC 60870-5-101-am1	Companion Standard for Basic Telecontrol Tasks Amendment 1	2000-04
IEC 60870-5-101-am2	Companion Standard for Basic Telecontrol Tasks Amendment 2	2001-10

Table 8.2
IEC 60870-5-101 including amendments

8.1.3   Obtaining standards

Should access to the standards be required, they may be purchased online from the IEC (at www.iec.ch). As an alternative that may be less expensive, it is worth checking if they have been published as a national standard, as is often the case. In Australia, IEC 60870-5 sections 1 to 5 are available as AS 60870.5.1 to AS 60870.5.5 and are available online (at www.standards.com.au). However, the companion standards are not presently available and must be obtained from the IEC.

An alternative to purchase of the standards is to view them at a public or university library.

8.1.4   Description of contents

In this section the contents of each section of IEC 60870-5 are briefly described. This is intended to provide a guide to assist the reader should it be necessary to refer to them.

IEC 60870-5-1 1990

Transmission frame formats
This describes the operation of the physical and data link layers in terms of the services provided to higher layers. It provides a choice of four data link frame types identified as FT1.1, FT1.2, FT2 and FT3, each with a different level of security against data errors. Fixed and variable length versions of the frames are described, and a set of transmission rules is provided for each. Two single control character transmissions are provided as an efficient means of transmitting control information such as acknowledgments.

8.1.5   IEC 60870-5-1 1990

Link transmission procedures

This section represents the four frame formats from IEC 60870-5-1 and then describes the internal processes in terms of the service primitives and transmission procedures. The service primitives are the control indications passed between the link layer and its higher level user, and the transmission procedures describe the sequence of events occurring over the physical communications link. A control field is described that is transmitted over the link and is used by the link layer procedures of each side of the link in controlling the transmission process. The terms unbalanced and balanced transmission are presented and used to describe whether transmission can be initiated only by a master station, or by any station. Services and transmission procedures are presented in detail for both unbalanced and balanced transmissions.

8.1.6   IEC 60870-5-3 1992

General structure of application data

This section presents two models of the structure of data at the application level. The reference model 2 version shows how application user data, for example point information to be transmitted, is encapsulated within an application protocol data unit, with or without application protocol control information added, and then passed to the underlying link layer for transmission. It also describes a general structure for application data, and rules for forming application data units in general.

8.1.7   IEC 60870-5-4 1993

Definition and coding of application information elements

This section provides rules for the definition of information elements, and defines a common set of information elements that may be used for transmission of information in telecontrol applications. These include generic elements such as signed and unsigned integers, fixed and floating point numbers, bit-strings, and time elements. The intention of this section is to provide a set of information building blocks from which a companion standard, or profile can utilize selectively to build a complete set of application level information objects. No such set of information objects is selected by this section, however.

8.1.8   IEC 60870-5-5 1995

Basic application functions

This section describes the highest level functions of the transmission protocol, which are those application functions above layer 7 of the OSI model. Application service primitives are the request and response indications passed between the application layer and the application user. Application functions are described.

A set of basic application functions and associated service primitives, or requests and indications, are presented. These cover the highest level functions that would be required to carry out telecontrol operations. They include station initialization, methods of acquiring data, clock synchronization, transmission of commands, totalizer counts, and file transfer. Again, it is stated in this section that it would be the role of a specific companion standard to select from these functions and possibly add to them in defining a complete working protocol.

8.1.9   IEC 60870-5-101 1995

Companion standard for basic telecontrol tasks (including amendments 1 and 2).

The companion standard defines a complete telecontrol protocol by detailing selections from options described in sections 1 to 5 of IEC 60870 Part 5, and by defining a complete set of application service data units (ASDUs).

Its main sub-sections are listed below, and a short description of the contents of these follows this list:

- General rules
- Physical layer
- Link layer
- Application layer and user process
- Interoperability

General rules

This is really an introduction that states the main selections made for the physical layer, link layer, application layer, and user process. They in effect provide a brief overview of each of the following sections.

Physical layer

This describes the requirements for the interface with external data communication equipment using standard ITU-T V.24/V.28 (RS-232) or balanced X.24/X.27 (RS-485) signals. The types of fixed network configurations such as point-to-point, and multi-point, are described.

Link layer

Selections of the frame format F1.2, and the fixed and variable frame lengths are made. The detailed operation of the link layer is specified, making selections from IEC 60870-5-2. Operation of the link is described for both unbalanced and balanced operation, which corresponds to whether only the master station, or any station, may initiate message transmissions. Amendment 2 contains significant additional information clarifying the procedures with the use of state transition diagrams.

Application layer and user process

This defines the overall structure of the application level data, the application service data unit or ASDU, defines the set of ASDUs available, and makes selections of application functions from IEC 60870-5-5. The definition of ASDUs is carried out in two sub-sections. The first sub-section defines the available information elements. These are used in the second sub-section as building blocks in constructing the full set of ASDUs. The user process sub-section makes selections from IEC 60870-5-5 and includes additional detail for some of the functions.

Interoperability

This provides a check-box method for specifying the particular features supported by a specific product, under the following type headers:

- System or device
- Network configuration
- Physical layer
- Link layer
- Application layer

8.2 Protocol architecture

8.2.1 EPA and OSI reference models

As for DNP3, IEC 60870-5 is based on the three-layer enhanced performance architecture or EPA model for data communications. These models are described in detail later in this text, which shows how the EPA model is a simplified form of the OSI seven layer reference model to provide optimum performance for telecontrol applications.

In the Figure 8.1, the relationship between the OSI model and the EPA model is represented. This shows that the EPA model basically omits the presentation, session and transport layers of the OSI model.

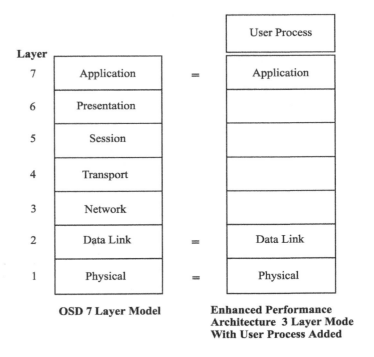

Figure 8.1
Relationship of EPA model to OSI 7 layer model

The structure of the EPA model is appropriate for a continuously operating system that operates over a single network. One layer is normally added to the top of the basic EPA model representation is identified as the user layer. This is included to represent the various functions or processes that must be defined to provide telecontrol system operations. These are required to be defined to provide for the interoperability between equipment that will result in a fully operable telecontrol system, rather than merely a data communication system.

For the first defined companion standard IEC 60870-5-101 or T101 profile, a four layer model as illustrated at the right-hand side of Figure 8.1 provides an accurate representation of the architecture of the protocol. In the case of the networked version IEC 60870-5-104, or the T104 profile, additional layers of the OSI model must be included to provide for transport of messages over networks using standard network protocols. These are the transport and network layers corresponding to the use of the TCP and IP protocols.

The two architectures are shown in Figure 8.2 below.

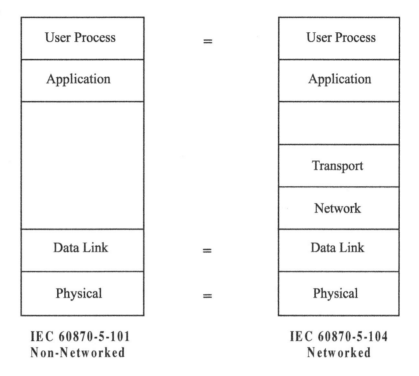

Figure 8.2
Architectures for T101 and T104

As is clear from Figure 8.2, the operation of the lower layers of the networked version, IEC 60870-5-104 is completely different from that of the non-networked version, IEC 60870-5-101. These layers correspond to all the layers below the application layer, which for these architectures are the layers concerned with message transport.

The remainder of this chapter will focus on the non-networked version only. The networked version will be returned to in Chapter 9.

8.2.2   Selections from standards

The benefit of the OSI reference model, and the EPA models derived from it and shown in Figure 8.2, is that they provide a framework for description of protocol operation. Describing the operation of the protocol is a matter of specifying the functions of each layer, and specifying the structure of information passing between the layers.

Under the IEC standard, it is the companion standard IEC 60870-5-101 that completely specifies the protocol. It does this by referring to the main sections of the IEC 60870-5 standard, and by making particular selections from options that may be available within those sections.

Table 8.3 shows how the different sections of the IEC 60870-5 set of standards correspond with the layers of the model.

Layer	Source	Selections
User Process	IEC 60870-5-5	Application functions
Application	IEC 60870-5-4	Application information elements
	IEC 60870-5-3	ASDUs
Link	IEC 60870-5-2	Transmission procedures
	IEC 60870-5-1	Frame formats
Physical	ITU-T	Interface specification

Table 8.3
Standards selections for IEC 60870-5-101

For comparison the corresponding information for the networked version IEC 60870-5-104 is shown in Table 8.4. This illustrates how the lower layers of the IEC 60870-5-101 companion standard have been completely replaced by the standard TCP/IP transport profiles.

Layer	Source	Selections
User Process	IEC 60870-5-101	Application functions
Application	IEC 60870-5-101	ASDUs and Application Information Elements.
Transport		
Network		TCP / IP Transport and network protocol suite
Link		
Physical		

Table 8.4
Standards selections for IEC 60870-5-104

8.3   Physical layer

The physical layer is concerned with the transmission and reception of data over the physical medium. This level is concerned with the transmission of bits and bytes, but not with the meaning of those bytes. The physical interface is defined in terms of the electrical characteristics, and individual signals passing over the interface.

The definition of the physical layer includes specification of the signal interface between the IEC 60870-5 and the communications devices to external world, and the network configurations that are attached to these. These are illustrated in Figure 8.3. This shows a SCADA master station server connected to a radio modem via a serial port operating at 9.6 kB/s. The radio modems form a multi-point-star configuration in which the master communicates with both outstations simultaneously, and either outstation can communicate back to the master.

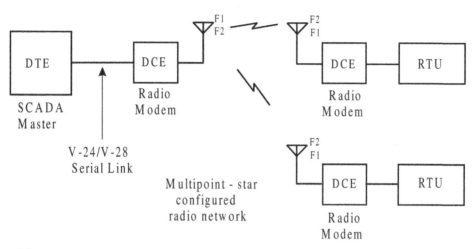

MASTER STATION　　　　　　　　　**OUTSTATIONS**

Figure 8.3
Interfacing to communications network

8.3.1　Communications interface

To allow the use of standard data communications equipment, the standard utilizes existing widely used standards covering the exchange between data terminal equipment (DTE) and data communication equipment (DCE). These communication interface standards are the ITU-T equivalents to the well known Electrical Industries Association RS-232 and RS-485 standards. These provide for unbalanced and balanced full-duplex serial data transmission between the data device and communications equipment such as a modem.

The use of this interface is illustrated in Figure 8.3, at the connection between the server of a SCADA master station, and a radio modem. The DTE-DCE interface is simply an RS-232 cable between a serial port of the computer, and a similar port on the radio modem. It is also used between the RTUs and their radio modems.

The data transmission speeds are defined as follows:

Interface Type	Transmission Speed (bits/sec)
V.24/V.28 FSK Interface	100, 200, 300, 600, 1200
V.24 / V.28 Modem Interface	300, 600, 1200, 2400, 4800, 9600
X.24 / X.27 Synchronous	2400, 4800, 9600, 19200, 38400, 56000, 64000

Table 8.5
DTE-DCE interface transmission speeds

In addition to interfaces using the specified standards, it should be noted that the T101 profile does allow the use of other physical interfaces by agreement between vendor and user.

8.3.2   Network configurations

The T101 profile specifies support for the following network configurations or topology:

- Point-to-point
- Multiple point-to-point
- Multi-point-star
- Multi-point-party line
- Multi-point-ring

These are defined by IEC 60870-1-1, and are depicted in Figure 8.4. In the drawing the square symbols represent controlling or master stations, and the triangles represent controlled, or outstations. The small circles at the points of connection are the ports.

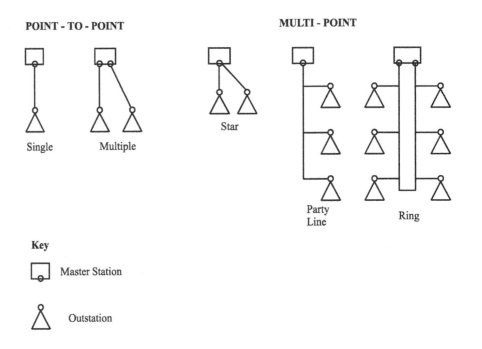

Figure 8.4
Network configurations

From the diagram it may be seen that these fall into two basic types; point-to-point and multi-point. A point-to-point link has one master station and one outstation. A multi-point network has a master station connected to a number of outstations. The ring configuration is only different in that it incorporates redundancy by providing a second port on the master station that can be used for communications should the ring be broken.

In the point-to-point configurations either the master or the outstation(s) can transmit messages, provided that a full-duplex channel is used. In the multi-point configurations the master communicates in parallel to all connected outstations. The outstations share a return communications channel, and therefore only one may transmit at a time.

Note that combinations of links may form a hierarchical network where intermediate RTUs may act as local master stations to RTUs connected to them. These are sometimes referred to as sub-master stations.

8.4   Data link layer

The data link layer is responsible for the passing of data across the communications channel, and ensuring that the data is received in full and uncorrupted by errors. It does this using a unit of data known as a frame, combined with procedures to govern its transmission and reception. The frame is made up of an amount of data that is large enough to carry control information such as a destination address, checking information used to detect errors, and a payload of data, if required. It is also an amount of data that is not too large, so that a transmission error will not cause the loss of too much data, or so that timing discrepancies between transmitter and receiver can lead to loss of synchronism.

IEC 60870-5-101, or T101, specifies the operation of the data link layer by referring to and making selections from the standards identified in Table 8.1, repeated in the following extract:

Link Layer	IEC 60870-5-2	Transmission procedures
	IEC 60870-5-1	Frame formats

In this section the operation of the data link layer is explained in detail, commencing with the data frame structure and then looking at the transmission procedures.

8.4.1   Frame format

The frame format used by T101 is referred to as the FT1.2 format. There are two forms of this, one of fixed length and the other of variable length. The fixed length frame is restricted to use for frames carrying no user data, and therefore is used only for data link control command and acknowledgment frames. In addition to the fixed and variable length frames, there is a 'single control character' frame which consists of a single byte. This may be used for acknowledgment only.

These frames are shown in Figures 8.5 and 8.6. Figure 8.5 shows the actual bit pattern that would be seen on the physical channel, interpreted from left to right. This representation includes the start and stop bits that are transmitted with every byte or octet of the frame. The overall frame construction is shown in Figure 8.6. This does not represent the bit pattern, but shows only the information content down to the octet level. For consistency with the applicable standards, these are presented vertically in octet order. Thus, the first octet is shown at the top, and following octets are shown below. Clarification of the order of bits and octets is included in the following section.

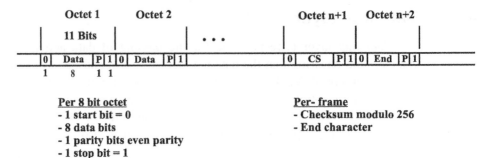

Per 8 bit octet
- 1 start bit = 0
- 8 data bits
- 1 parity bits even parity
- 1 stop bit = 1

Per- frame
- Checksum modulo 256
- End character

Figure 8.5
Bit-sequence representation of FT1.2 Frame

From the bit-sequence representation above, it is possible to see that the maximum data rate of the frame is approximately eight-elevenths of the bit transmission rate. This is reduced further when the frame overheads such as addressing, start and stop characters, checksum, and control information are accounted for. These overheads can be seen in Figure 8.6 which shows the overall frame structure.

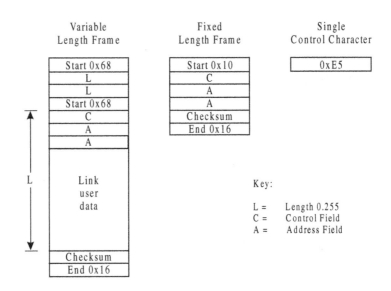

Figure 8.6
FT1.2 frame options under IEC 60870-5-101

The following points are noted about the data link frames:

- Only the variable length frame can carry user data
- The variable length frame can carry up to 253 octets of link user data
- The length L is repeated twice, and the two values of L must be equal for the frame to be accepted as valid
- The maximum frame length is 261 octets. However, a lower maximum frame length may be specified by a manufacturer or by the system user as a system parameter

- The fixed length frame is 5 or 6 octets long
- Address field A may be 1 or 2 octets, determined by a fixed system parameter
- A broadcast address is defined as 0xFF or 0xFFFF for 1 and 2 octet addresses respectively
- The checksum is the modulo 256 sum of the frame user data (not the link user data). This is the data between the last start character and the checksum, L octets for the variable frame
- Rules state that no more than one bit-time idle interval is allowed between characters within the frame, and that an idle interval of 33 bit-times must be allowed after detection of a frame error by the receiver

8.4.2 Order of information

One technical detail that can be difficult to find in the standards is the ordering of bits and bytes. Under IEC 60870-5, as for DNP3, the following ordering is standard.

Bits are transmitted starting with the least significant byte (LSB) and ending with the most significant byte (MSB). When a bit-sequence representation is given, the bits are shown in this order. However, when the structure of a message in terms of bytes or octets is depicted, the msb is at the left, and the lsb is at the right, which is consistent with the numerical weighting of the bits. A good way to mentally resolve this is to envisage the octet being right-shifted out of a UART register onto the communication channel.

Similarly for bytes, the least significant byte (LSB) is transmitted first, and the most significant byte (MSB) is transmitted last.

The ordering of bits and bytes is illustrated in Figure 8.7.

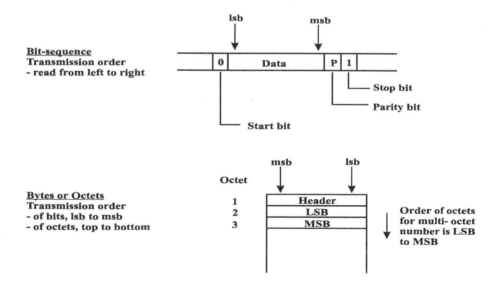

Figure 8.7
Order of information

8.4.3   Link layer concepts

This section presents some concepts that are important for understanding the operation of the link layer transmission procedures. The detailed operation of link layer is then discussed in terms of these concepts.

These are:

- Primary and secondary
- Unbalanced and balanced
- Service procedures
- Service primitives
- Transmission procedures

8.4.4   Primary and secondary

The terms primary and secondary refer to the ability of a station to initiate communications on a communication channel. Only a primary station can initiate communications. Secondary stations must wait until they are polled by the primary station before they can transmit data. More accurately these terms are applied to individual communications ports of stations, because in a hierarchical system, an intermediate station will be both a controlled and a controlling station. This is illustrated in Figure 8.8. This shows a hierarchical network configuration with primary and secondary ports marked P and S.

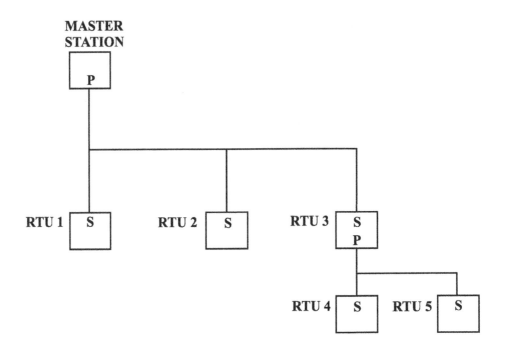

Figure 8.8
Primary and secondary stations

In Figure 8.8 RTU 3 is both a controlling and controlled station. Note that each of the two communications links has only one primary station.

8.4.5 Unbalanced and balanced transmission

The terms 'unbalanced transmission' and 'balanced transmission' are related to the terms 'primary' and 'secondary'. Unbalanced transmission refers to the configuration where the controlling station acts as a primary on the link, and one or more controlled stations act as secondary stations. The stations are not peer-to-peer at the link level, and so are unbalanced in their functionality.

This is the situation in Figure 8.8 for each of the two communications links. In this configuration the controlling station must acquire data from the controlled stations by polling each in turn for data. This is because they cannot initiate transmissions on their own. The advantage of unbalanced communication is that there is no possibility of collisions between controlled stations attempting to transmit information at the same time.

Balanced transmission refers to the configuration where any station on a link may act as a primary, which means it can initiate communications. This configuration is also known as peer-to-peer communications.

Under IEC 60870-5-101, only point-to-point (that is two station) links can be balanced. Multi-point links must be unbalanced. This is in contrast to DNP3, which uses balanced transmission only, and therefore has to have procedures to overcome collisions which can occur when more than one outstation commences communications simultaneously.

A balanced communications link is shown in Figure 8.9. In this case a master station is connected via a point-to-point link to a sub-master station. Note that each station can act as a primary and a secondary at the ports for this link. These may in fact be thought of as two separate processes within each station, which in fact is how they are logically within the stations. Station A has a primary process and a secondary process operating simultaneously for that link, and Station B has the same.

Figure 8.9
Balanced communications

Figure 8.10 shows the primary and secondary processes for unbalanced transmission. The processes are represented by circles identified as primary (P) or secondary (S). The primary station implements the primary process only, and the secondary stations each implement a secondary process only. Note that in effect there is a separate logical link for each secondary station and it is necessary for the primary to keep a record of the state of each link.

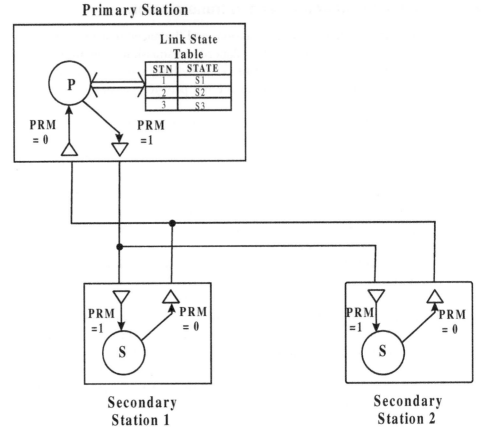

Figure 8.10
Unbalanced transmission processes

Figure 8.11 shows the processes for balanced transmission. In this case there is a primary and secondary process for each station.

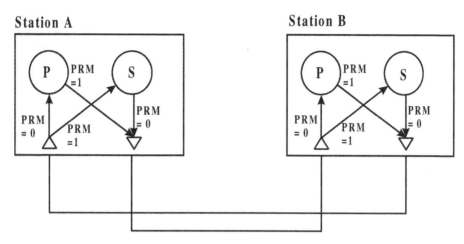

Figure 8.11
Unbalanced transmission processes

8.4.6   Service procedures

The term 'services' is descriptive of the function of the link layer, it provides specific services to the user, which is the application layer, to carry out the transmission of data.

There are three main types of services provided by the data link layer, which have the following names:

- Send/no reply
- Send/confirm
- Request/respond

The send/no reply service is used to send a message or command for which no reply is required from the addressed station. It is used for sending broadcast messages and for messages for which receipt confirmation is not important. The send/confirm service is used to send a command or data which must be reliably transmitted. For this service a confirmation response is required. The request/respond service is used to obtain data from the controlled station. In this case the controlled station responds not with a confirmation, but with the required data.

These services are illustrated in Figure 8.12. This shows the link layer of two stations on a communication channel, and a time-sequence diagram of the service interactions. At each side are shown the commands, data, and responses that are passed between the link layer and the service user, which is the application layer. These are termed the 'service primitives'. In the centre the message transmission is labelled with the transmission procedure name.

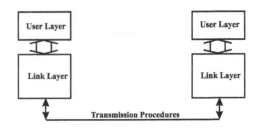

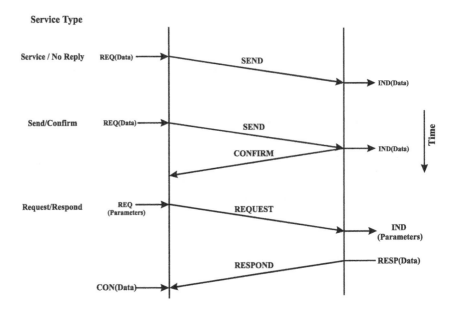

Figure 8.12
Link layer services

The transmission procedures are a set of rules that ensure that transmissions are successfully carried out in response to link user requests. They must be able to cope with errors on the transmission channel that may introduce errors, or cause information to be lost. The transmission procedures are different for unbalanced and balanced links, and described for each in the following sections.

8.4.7   Link initialization

Link initialization is a data link service carried out after a station has been off-line and first becomes available again. While the slave station is off-line the master periodically sends link status request functions until a status of link response is obtained. The sequences are shown following for both unbalanced and balanced modes.

Station / link initialization, unbalanced mode:

- Master sends link status request until status of link received
- Master sends link reset
- Link is active on receipt of ACK
- Slave generates station initialization complete event

Station/link initialization, balanced mode:

- Each station sends link status request until status of link received
- Each station sends link reset
- Link is active on receipt of ACK at each station
- One or both may generate station initialization complete event

8.4.8 Unbalanced transmission procedures

Unbalanced transmission procedures are required for links other than point-to-point, that is multi-point links. For these links the controlling station must control the data traffic by polling the outstations for data. Only when the controlling or primary station on a link polls a particular secondary station may that station respond.

8.4.9 The control field

The control field of the data frame is central to the operation of the transmission procedures. This field is almost identical to that used by the DNP3 protocol because it was derived from the same source document, IEC 60870-5-2 1992. The interpretation of the control field is dependent on whether the communication is a primary or secondary message. Figure 8.13 shows the control field for unbalanced transmission procedures, including the short descriptions of the meanings of the function codes for primary and secondary messages.

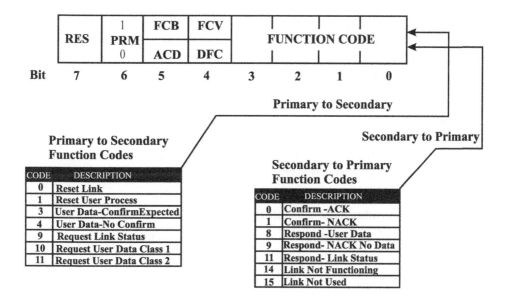

Figure 8.13
Control field – unbalanced transmission

Code	Meaning	Description
PRM	Primary Message	1 => Frame from primary or initiating station
FCB	Frame Count Bit	Alternates between 0 and 1 for sequential frames
FCV	Frame Count Valid	1 => FCB is valid 0 => ignore FCB
RES	Reserved	= 0
DFC	Data Flow Control Bit	Set to 1 by secondary station if further send of user data will cause buffer overflow
ACD	Access Demand Bit	Set to 1 if there is Class 1 data available

Table 8.6
Control field bit meanings – unbalanced transmission

The tables below show the detailed meanings for the function codes in the control field. The meanings are different depending on whether the message is a primary or a secondary transmission. The frame count bit is used in the primary direction only, and is only valid for certain functions. This is indicated by the state of the frame count valid bit.

Function codes from primary station

Function Codes	Frame Type	Service Function	FCV Bit
0	SEND – CONFIRM expected	Reset of remote link	0
1	SEND – CONFIRM expected	Reset of user process	0
2	SEND – CONFIRM expected	Reserved	–
3	SEND – CONFIRM expected	User data	1
4	SEND – NO REPLY expected	User data (unconfirmed)	0
8	REQUEST – RESPOND expected	Request for access demand	0
9	REQUEST – RESPOND expected	Request status of link	0
10	REQUEST – RESPOND expected	Request user data class 1	1
11	REQUEST – RESPOND expected	Request user data class 2	1

Codes 5–7, 12–15 are reserved.

Function codes from secondary station

Function Code*	Frame Type	Service Function
0	CONFIRM	ACK – positive acknowledgment**
1	CONFIRM	NACK – Message not accepted, link busy
8	RESPOND	User data
9	RESPOND	NACK – Requested data not available
11	RESPOND	Status of link (DFC = 0 or 1) or access demand
14		Link service not functioning
15		Link service not used or implemented

*Codes 2–7, 10, 12–13 are reserved **Note that control code 0xE5 may be used in place of the FC0 or FC9 frames.

Table 8.7
Function codes – unbalanced transmission

The functions of the control bits are explained in more detail in the following paragraphs.

Primary bits

The PRM bit is set if the frame is primary (initiating) or a secondary (responding). This is used directly by the link layer in interpreting the function code.

Frame count bits

These are the frame count bit (FCB) and the frame count valid bit (FCV). These bits are only used for primary messages. The frame count bit is used to detect losses or duplication of frames to a secondary station. The frame count valid bit enables the use of the FCB. When the FCV bit is true, the FCB is toggled for each successful SEND–CONFIRM transaction between the same primary and secondary stations.

How they work is like this:

- Following data link startup or a failed transaction, a secondary station will not accept any primary SEND–CONFIRM frames with FCV=1 until a reset transaction is completed. This means it will only accept either a RESET link or a RESET user process command
- After a secondary station receives a RESET link frame from a primary and it responds with a CONFIRM, that link will be operational until a frame transmission error occurs.
- The secondary station will expect the next frame to contain FCV=1 and FCB=1
- The next primary SEND–CONFIRM message will have FCV=1 and FCB=1. The secondary station will accept this as the FCB is valid and is set, as expected.
- Each subsequent primary SEND–CONFIRM message will have the FCB cleared or set in turn.

Data flow control bit

The data flow control bit (DFC) is included in secondary frames. The secondary station will set DFC = 1 if a further SEND of user data will cause its buffer to overflow. On receipt of a frame with DFC = 1 a primary station will cease to send data, but will request link status until DFC = 0.

Access demand bit

There are two classes of data defined, class 1 and class 2. Class 1 data has higher priority than class 2 data. The ACD bit is a means for the secondary station to indicate to the primary that there is class 1 data available.

Address field

The address field of the link layer frame is one or two octets in length, set as a fixed system parameter. This field contains the link address of the secondary station. A frame transmitted by the primary station on a link contains the link address of the secondary station to which the message is directed. A frame transmitted by a secondary station to the primary contains its own link address. By this means the primary station can identify which secondary station the message is from.

Transmission procedures

In this section the procedures are discussed briefly. The procedures are very similar to those used by the DNP3 protocol. This may be referred to for further illustration of the concepts presented.

Note that in the following procedures, no new procedure is commenced until the previous procedure is terminated. It is for this reason that a single-bit frame count bit is sufficient for protection against frame sequence number errors; there is a frame window of exactly one.

SEND/NO REPLY procedures

The frame is transmitted, and a minimum line-idle time of 33 bit-times is required before any further transmissions by the primary. On receipt of the message at the secondary, it is checked for error by comparison with the checksum octet, and if valid it is notified to the service user.

SEND/CONFIRM procedures

The primary station will transmit the message. If a confirmation is not received from the secondary station within a configured time-out period, it will re-transmit the message up until a configured number of retries.

If the secondary station receives the message, it will respond with either a positive or negative confirmation, function code 0 or 1. FC=0 means the message is correctly received and accepted, and in this case the procedure terminates. FC=1 means the secondary cannot accept the message, because its buffer is full or some other reason. In this case the primary will retry, up until a configured number of retries.

This procedure makes use of the frame count bit (FCB) to ensure that the message sequence is not disturbed. The FCB is toggled with each SEND/CONFIRM transmission from the primary station, and an expected FCB flag is maintained by the secondary station. If a message sent by the primary is not confirmed by the secondary, it is retransmitted with the FCB unchanged. Thus a message lost or corrupted in the primary to secondary transmission direction would when retransmitted still have the expected FCB value. Alternatively, if the problem was that the confirmation from the secondary station was lost or corrupted, the secondary station would be able to recognize receipt of a retransmitted message from the primary by the unchanged FCB bit. In this case it retransmits the original confirmation message.

As an alternative to sending a confirmation frame, which is a minimum of six octets in length (that is if single-octet address is used), the single control character response (hexadecimal 0xE5) is allowed. This option may be used to improve transmission efficiency when there is no need to transmit any other information back to the primary station.

REQUEST/RESPOND procedures

This procedure is similar to the SEND/CONFIRM except instead of receiving a confirmation back from the secondary station, a frame containing data is returned, or a negative response is returned indicating that no data is available. In the case of a negative response, either a frame with FC=9, or the single control character (0xE5) may be returned.

As for the SEND/CONFIRM procedures, the frame count bit is toggled at each end for each message transmission, and this is used to detect errors in the transmission in either direction. Basically, when both primary and secondary have incremented their frame count bits and they agree, the procedure is complete.

Philosophy of transmission

For unbalanced transmission only the controlling or primary station on a link can initiate transmissions. Because of this it is necessary that a polling system is implemented by the primary station in order to determine if there is change data available at each secondary station.

To accomplish this the controlling station will poll each secondary station on a cyclic basis for data. It will typically poll for class 2 user data using the request–respond function code 10. The secondary station will then return any class 2 data that it has available, and at the same time it will indicate if there is any class 1 data available by setting the access demand bit (ACD). Typically analog values will be assigned to class 2 and be updated during the cyclic scan, and all other data such as events will be assigned to class 1.

Note that although the polling operation is carried out by the link layer, the polling sequence itself is implemented by a higher level of the protocol, the user process level. The higher level generates services requests using service primitives to specify the polling actions to be carried out by the link layer.

8.4.10 Balanced transmission procedures

Balanced transmission procedures may only be used for point-to-point links equipped with duplex channel communication. Under balanced transmission each station can act as both a primary and a secondary station simultaneously. The control field and transmission procedures are modified slightly from the unbalanced case to accommodate this operation.

The control field

There are two modifications to the data link control field for balanced transmission. The first is that the access demand (ACD) bit is not required, because either station can initiate transmissions. The second is the inclusion of a direction bit (DIR). This indicates the direction of transmission of a message between the two stations. The control field for balanced transmission is shown in Figure 8.14.

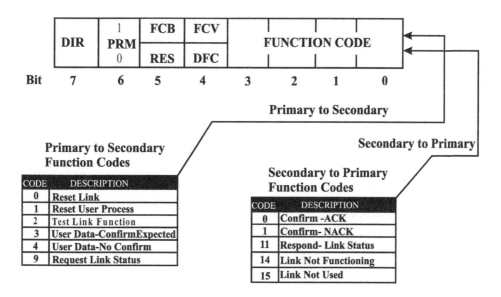

Figure 8.14
Control field – balanced transmission

Code	Meaning	Description
DIR	Direction of Message	1 => A to B 0 => B to A
PRM	Primary Message	1 => Frame from primary or initiating station
FCB	Frame Count Bit frames	Alternates between 0 and 1 for sequential
FCV	Frame Count Valid	1 => FCB is valid 0 => ignore FCB
RES	Reserved	= 0
DFC	Data Flow Control Bit	Set to 1 by secondary station if further send of user data will cause buffer overflow

Table 8.8
Control field bit meanings – balanced transmission

The tables below show the detailed meanings for the function codes in the control field. The changes from the codes for unbalanced transmission are shown in italics.

Function codes from primary station

Function Code	Frame Type	Service Function	FCV Bit
0	SEND – CONFIRM expected	Reset of remote link	0
1	SEND – CONFIRM expected	Reset of user process	0
2	SEND – CONFIRM expected	*Test for function of link*	1
3	SEND – CONFIRM expected	User data	1
4	SEND – NO REPLY expected	User data (unconfirmed)	0
8		*Used by unbalanced only*	–
9	REQUEST – RESPOND expected	Request status of link	0
10		*Used by unbalanced only*	1
11		*Used by unbalanced only*	1

Codes 5–7, 12–15 are reserved.

Function codes from secondary station

Function Code*	Frame Type	Service Function
0	CONFIRM	ACK – positive acknowledgment**
1	CONFIRM	NACK – Message not accepted, link busy
8		*Used by unbalanced only*
9		*Used by unbalanced only*
11	RESPOND	Status of link (DFC = 0 or 1)
14		Link service not functioning
15		Link service not used or implemented

*Codes 2–7, 10, 12–13 are reserved.

**Note that control code 0xE5 may be used in place of the FC0.

Table 8.9
Function codes – balanced transmission

The changes in functions from unbalanced transmission are:

- A test link primary function code FC=2 has been added
- Requests for access demand and for user data class 1 or 2 have been removed (primary function codes FC = 8, 10, 11)
- Secondary respond function codes FC = 8, 9 have been removed

These changes reflect the changes to the way data is transmitted. Under balanced transmission the request/respond service is not used for transmission of user data, but only for checking the status of the link. User data is transmitted directly by the link layer using the send service.

8.4.11 Address field

The address field for balanced communications may be zero, one or two octets. Thus there is the option of having no address field under balanced communications. This is the case because as there is only one station at each end of the link, there is no need for the secondary process at either end to verify the address.

In effect, for a balanced link, the direction (DIR) bit substitutes for the address, making the inclusion of the link address redundant.

Transmission procedures

The transmission procedures for balanced transmission are the same as those for unbalanced transmission. The only difference is that there are both primary and secondary processes operating simultaneously at each station. This is similar to two unbalanced links operating in parallel. These processes maintain a separate frame count bit sequence for each primary–secondary link and use these to detect and recover from errors in the same way as a single unbalanced primary–secondary link operates.

Philosophy of transmission

For balanced transmission either station on the link can initiate transmission. Therefore there is no need for a station to be polled for data as it can send it directly when it is available. This changes the services used at the link layer from the case for unbalanced transmission. Where unbalanced transmission makes use of the request/respond service to obtain user data from the secondary station, for balanced transmission the station with the data just uses the send/confirm service directly. Comparison of Figures 8.13 and 8.14 shows that the secondary codes for responding with user data FC8 and FC9 are not available for balanced transmission. Instead, primary function codes FC3 or FC4 are used to send the data directly.

8.4.12 Data link security

IEC 60870-5-101 and DNP3 utilize the FT1.2 and FT3 frame formats specified by IEC 60780-5-1 respectively. These formats differ in their security provisions as shown in Table 8.6. IEC 60870-5-101 uses an 8-bit checksum and a maximum frame size of 255 bytes. DNP uses a 16-bit cyclic redundancy code (CRC) for every 16 bytes of user data contained in the body of its frame.

Protocol	IEC 60870-5 Frame Type	Security Method	Hamming Distance Error Bits	Maximum Secured Length in Bytes
IEC 60870-5-101	FT1.2	8 bit checksum	4	255
DNP 3.0	FT3	16 Bit CRC	6	16

Table 8.10
Link layer error security

The effect of these differences in security is often quoted in terms of the 'Hamming distance'. This is equal to the minimum number of single bit errors that are required to allow an incorrect message to be mistakenly accepted as a good message, that is for the security system to fail. These are 4 and 6 for methods used by FT1.2 and FT3. However, these figures ignore the effect of the ratio of security code bits to message bits, which in the case of DNP is higher due to the inclusion of CRC codes within the body section of the FT3 frame format.

8.4.13 Link versus application data

There is a distinction between link data and application level data that is subtle and can be difficult to grasp at first sight. It derives from the fact that the application level messages are treated simply as data at the link layer level, and may be best illustrated by example.

Take the case where an unbalanced link is operating between primary station A and secondary station D. Suppose that the application level of station D requires some particular data from A. This is in the reverse direction to most data traffic, which is generally from the secondary station to the primary. In this case the application level request from D will generate a class 1 access demand at the link level. This will have to wait until that station is polled for data by the primary station A. At this point, if class 2 data has been polled for it will respond with any class 2 data, or with an FC9 'NACK – no data' frame, but in either case with the ACD (access demand) bit set. The primary station A will then poll for the class 1 data from station D, and at this point D will be able to transmit its class 1 data. This will contain the application level request by D, for the primary station to send the application level data that it requires.

The link layer frame that was requested by polling from primary A, carried an application level request from station D. This resulted in the application layer of A using the send service to return the requested data to station D. Note that a link layer request in direction A to D (the poll) has resulted in an application level request from D to A.

In the following sections dealing with the application layer and above, the operation of the link layer can be generally seen as a message transport mechanism that can be assumed to just transport the application level messages as required. However, awareness of the transport mechanism is important to understanding the response times, as these will depend on the transmission mode, and polling frequency for the unbalanced mode.

8.5   Application layer

The remaining sections of Chapter 8 describe the operation of the application layer and above of the IEC 60870-5 protocol. Most of this section is applicable to both the non-networked and networked versions of the protocol, IEC 60870-5-101 and IEC 60870-5-104. The areas that are different are discussed in the following chapter under Advanced considerations of IEC 60870-5.

This information is presented in the following sequence:

- Overall message structure
- ASDU structure
- Message addressing and routing
- Information elements
- Set of ASDUs

8.5.1   Overall message structure

In the preview, the overall message structure under IEC 60870-5 was presented. This is represented in Figure 8.15. This shows the application layer application service data unit or ASDU, and shows how this is carried as link user data by the data link layer under IEC 60870-5-101. For the networked version IEC 60870-5-104 the ASDU is carried by the TCP/IP protocols instead of the T101 link layer and so the link frame shown below does not apply to this case.

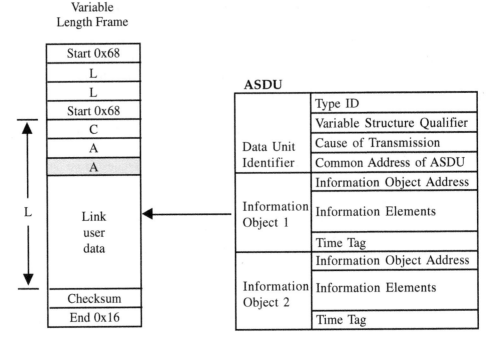

Figure 8.15
Message structure under IEC 60870-5-101

The only important point to note about the relationship between the ASDU and the link layer frame is that a maximum of just one ASDU is allowed per frame. This sets an upper limit for the size of the ASDU at 255 octets, minus 2-3 octets for the link control and address fields.

8.5.2 ASDU structure

The structure of the ASDU is in two main sections. These are the data unit identifier, and the data itself, made up of one or more information objects. The data unit identifier defines the specific type of data, provides addressing to identify the specific identity of the data, and it includes additional information in the cause of transmission field. The fields of the ASDU are now discussed in turn.

Type identification

The type identification field is a single-octet unsigned integer field. Its content is interpreted as a code in the ranges shown below.

Bit   7   0

Type Code

Code Range	Purpose
<1..127>	Standard type definitions
<128..135>	Reserved for message routing – private
<136..255>	For special use – private

Figure 8.16
Type identification field

The following notes apply to these codes:

- The value <0> is not used
- The range <128..255> is not defined by the standard, and may be used by particular vendors for system specific roles. However this has implications for interoperability

In the range of the standard type definitions, there are presently 58 specific types defined. These are grouped as shown in Table 8.11 which shows the overall groups and numbers of type identification codes that are defined.

Defined Type codes	Group
<1..40>	Process information in monitor direction
<45..51>	Process information in control direction
<70>	System information in monitor direction
<100..106>	System information in control direction
<110..113>	Parameter in control direction
<120..126>	File transfer

Table 8.11
Defined type code groups

It is important to note that the type identification applies to the whole ASDU, therefore if there are multiple information objects contained in the ASDU, they are all of the same type.

Table 8.13 provides a full list of the ASDU types. The table is broken into the code groups shown in Table 8.11. Full details of each individual ASDU type are given under 'Set of ASDUs' later in this text.

Table 8.13 also includes information code references which may be encountered. These references are defined by IEC 60870-5-5. They provide a hierarchical reference system using the following structure:

Level	Symbol	Description
1	M_	Monitored information
	C_	Control information
	P_	Parameter
	F_	File transfer
2	Various	see actual usages
3	_Nx	Not time tagged
	_Tx	Time tagged
	_xA	Type A: status and normalized, with quality
	_xB	Type B: scaled, with quality
	_xC	Type C: short floating point, with quality
	_xD	Type D: normalized without quality

Table 8.12
Reference information code structure

For example, M_ME_TA_1 is monitored information, a measured value, with time tag, and type A, which is a normalized value with quality.

Type No.	Description	Reference
<0>	not defined	
<1>	single-point information	M_SP_NA_1
<2>	single-point information with time tag	M_SP_TA_1
<3>	double-point information	M_DP_NA_1
<4>	double-point information with time tag	M_DP_TA_1
<5>	step position information	M_ST_NA_1
<6>	step position information with time tag	M_ST_TA_1
<7>	bitstring of 32 bit	M_BO_NA_1
<8>	bitstring of 32 bit with time tag	M_BO_TA_1
<9>	measured value, normalized value	M_ME_NA_1
<10>	measured value, normalized value with time tag	M_ME_TA_1
<11>	measured value, scaled value	M_ME_NB_1
<12>	measured value, scaled value with time tag	M_ME_TB_1
<13>	measured value, short floating point number	M_ME_NC_1
<14>	measured value, short floating point number with time tag	M_ME_TC_1
<15>	integrated totals	M_IT_NA_1
<16>	integrated totals with time tag	M_IT_TA_1
<17>	event of protection equipment with time tag	M_EP_TA_1
<18>	packed start events of protection equipment with time tag	M_EP_TB_1
<19>	packed output circuit information of protection equipment with time tag	M_EP_TC_1
<20>	packed single-point information with status change detection	M_PS_NA_1
<21>	measured value, normalized value without quality descriptor	M_ME_ND_1
<22..29>	reserved for further compatible definitions	

Table 8.13a
ASDU types – process information in monitoring direction

Table 8.13b shows types that were added to this category with amendment 2 of IEC 60870-5-101. These provide for a longer time tag format.

Type No.	Description	Reference
<30>	single-point information with time tag CP56Time2a	M_SP_TB_1
<31>	double-point information with time tag CP56Time2a	M_DP_TB_1
<32>	step position information with time tag CP56Time2a	M_ST_TB_1
<33>	bitstring of 32 bits with time tag CP56Time2a	M_BO_TB_1
<34>	measured value, normalized value with time tag CP56Time2a	M_ME_TD_1
<35>	measured value, scaled value with time tag CP56Time2a	M_ME_TE_1
<36>	measured value, short floating point number with time tag CP56Time2a	M_ME_TF_1
<37>	integrated totals with time tag CP56Time2a	M_IT_TB_1
<38>	event of protection equipment with time tag CP56Time2a	M_EP_TD_1
<39>	packed start events of protection equipment with time tag CP56Time2a	M_EP_TE_1
<40>	packed output circuit information of protection equipment with time tag CP56Time2a	M_EP_TF_1
<30>	single-point information with time tag CP56Time2a	M_SP_TB_1
<31>	double-point information with time tag CP56Time2a	M_DP_TB_1
<32>	step position information with time tag CP56Time2a	M_ST_TB_1
<33>	bitstring of 32 bits with time tag CP56Time2a	M_BO_TB_1
<34>	measured value, normalized value with time tag CP56Time2a	M_ME_TD_1
<35>	measured value, scaled value with time tag CP56Time2a	M_ME_TE_1
<36>	measured value, short floating point number with time tag CP56Time2a	M_ME_TF_1
<37>	integrated totals with time tag CP56Time2a	M_IT_TB_1
<38>	event of protection equipment with time tag CP56Time2a	M_EP_TD_1
<39>	packed start events of protection equipment with time tag CP56Time2a	M_EP_TE_1
<40>	packed output circuit information of protection equipment with time tag CP56Time2a	M_EP_TF_1
<41..44>	reserved for further compatible definitions	

Table 8.13b
ASDU types – process information in monitoring direction cont'd

Type No.	Description	Reference
<45>	single command	C_SC_NA_1
<46>	double command	C_DC_NA_1
<47>	regulating step command	C_RC_NA_1
<48>	set point command, normalized value	C_SE_NA_1
<49>	set point command, scaled value	C_SE_NB_1
<50>	set point command, short floating point number	C_SE_NC_1
<51>	bitstring of 32 bits	C_BO_NA_1

Table 8.13c
ASDU types – process information in control direction

Type No.	Description	Reference
<70>	end of initialization	M_EI_NA_1
<70..99>	reserved for further compatible definitions	

Table 8.13d
ASDU types – system information in monitor direction

Type No.	Description	Reference
<100>	interrogation command	C_IC_NA_1
<101>	counter interrogation command	C_CI_NA_1
<102>	read command	C_RD_NA_1
<103>	clock synchronization command	C_CS_NA_1
<104>	test command	C_TS_NA_1
<105>	reset process command	C_RP_NA_1
<106>	delay acquisition command	C_CD_NA_
<107..109>	reserved for further compatible definitions	

Table 8.13e
ASDU types – system information in control direction

Type No.	Description	Reference
<110>	parameter of measured value, normalized value	P_ME_NA_1
<111>	parameter of measured value, scaled value	P_ME_NB_1
<112>	parameter of measured value, short floating point number	P_ME_NC_1
<113>	parameter activation	P_AC_NA_1
<114..119>	reserved for further compatible definitions	

Table 8.13f
ASDU types – parameter in control direction

Type No.	Description	Reference
<120>	file ready	F_FR_NA_1
<121>	section ready	F_SR_NA_1
<122>	call directory, select File, call File, call section	F_SC_NA_1
<123>	last section, last segment	F_LS_NA_1
<124>	ack File, ack section	F_AF_NA_1
<125>	segment	F_SG_NA_1
<126>	directory	F_DR_TA_1
<127>	reserved for further compatible definitions	

Table 8.13g
ASDU types – file transfer

Variable structure qualifier

The variable structure qualifier is a single-octet that specifies the number of information objects or information elements, and how they are addressed. It contains a seven-bit binary number, and a 1-bit field that indicates which of two different possible information structures are used. Figure 8.17 shows the variable structure qualifier field, followed by a detail of the two information structures.

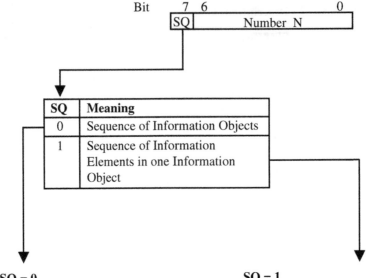

Figure 8.17
Variable structure qualifier and structures

It may be seen from Figure 8.17 that there are two different structures, depending on the state of the most significant bit of the variable structure qualifier. This is termed the SQ bit, which may be thought of as the structure qualifier bit.

When SQ = 0, the structure is a sequence of information objects. Each information object carries its own address, and therefore the information elements contained do not need to have sequential addresses. The number of information objects is given by the seven-bit value N. Therefore there can be up to 127 information objects in this ASDU.

When SQ = 1, the structure contains just one information object, but this may contain multiple information elements, all of the same format, such as a measured value. In this case there is only one information object address, and only one time tag (if used).

The effect of the SQ bit is that for each type identification number, there may effectively be two ASDUs. This is seen in the sub-section presenting the set of ASDUs, where it will be seen that some types have both variations (SQ=0 and SQ=1), and others have only one of these.

Cause of transmission

The cause of transmission (COT) field is used to control the routing of messages both on the communications network, and within a station, by directing the ASDU to the correct program or task for processing. This sub-section will initially look at the structure and meaning of the sub-fields within the COT, and then look at how these are used.

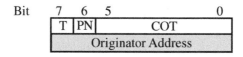

Key:

COT   Cause of Transmission <0..63>

PN   Positive / Negative Confirm bit

T   Test bit

OA   Originator Address <0..255>

Figure 8.18
Cause of transmission field

The cause of transmission or COT is a six-bit code which is used in interpreting the information at the destination station. The codes are shown in Table 8.14. Each defined ASDU type has a defined sub-set of the codes which are meaningful with it, and these are given in the section presenting the set of ASDUs.

The PN bit is the positive/negative confirmation bit. This is meaningful when used with control commands. This bit is used when the control command is mirrored in the monitor direction, and it provides indication of whether the command was executed or not. When the PN bit is not relevant it is cleared to zero.

The T or test bit is set when ASDUs are generated for test purposes and are not intended to control the process or change the system state. It is used for testing of transmission and equipment.

The originator address is optional on a system basis. It provides a means for a controlling station to explicitly identify itself. This is not necessary when there is only one controlling station in a system, but is required when there is more than one controlling station, or some stations are dual-mode stations. These are stations that act both as controlled and controlling stations. In these circumstances the originator address can be used to direct command confirmations back to the particular controlling station that issued the command, rather than to the whole system. The one exception to this is the originator address of zero <0>. This has the same effect as if there was no originator address. It is termed the default address and its effect is that the message is transmitted to all stations. The use of the originator address is discussed in greater detail under message addressing and routing.

COT code	Cause of Transmission
0	Not used
1	Periodic, cyclic
2	Background scan
3	Spontaneous
4	Initialized
5	Request or requested
6	Activation
7	Activation confirmation
8	Deactivation
9	Deactivation confirmation
10	Activation termination
11	Return information caused by a remote command
12	Return information caused by a local command
13	File transfer
14–19	Reserved for future definitions
20	Interrogated by station interrogation
21–36	Interrogated by group (1–16) interrogation
37	Requested by general counter request
38–41	Requested by group (1–4) counter request
42–43	Reserved for future definitions
44	Unknown type identification
45	Unknown cause of transmission
46	Unknown common address of ASDU
47	Unknown information object address

Table 8.14
Cause of transmission codes (COT)

8.5.3   Common address of ASDU

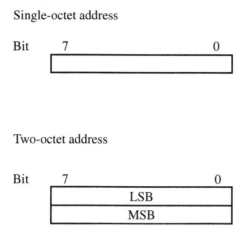

Figure 8.19
Common address of ASDU

The common address of the ASDU is either one or two octets in length, fixed on a per-system basis. The address is called a common address because it is in common to all of the data contained within the ASDU. This is normally interpreted as a station address, however it can be structured to form a station/sector address where individual stations are broken up into multiple logical units. The address <0> is not used.

The highest address 0xFF or 0xFFFF is global. This means that an ASDU with this address will be interpreted by all stations. Use of the global address is restricted to the ASDUs listed below. These are used when the same application function must be initiated simultaneously.

Type	Description	Purpose
100	Interrogation command	Reply with particular system data snapshot at common time
101	Counter interrogation command	Freeze totals at common time
103	Clock synchronization command	Synchronize clocks to common time
105	Reset process command	Simultaneous reset

Information object address

The information object address is the first field of the information object. It identifies the particular data within a defined station. The information object address may be one, two, or three octets in length. However, the case of three octets is provided only to allow for structured address systems, and one station is allowed only 65 536 different information object addresses, as for two-octet addressing. The information object address of zero is reserved for the case when the address is not relevant. The information object address is shown in Figure 8.20.

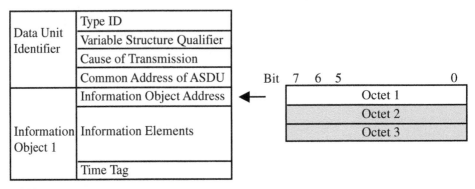

Figure 8.20
Information object address

On a system basis, specific data is uniquely identified by the combination of the common address and the information object address.

An example of how this might work in practice is where there are a number of identical intelligent electronic devices IEDs connected to a sub-master RTU, which is in turn connected to a master station. These could be re-closers on a distribution system. Each IED will have an identical data structure internally, as determined by the device manufacturer. Most likely this will be some tens of information elements or data points, which could be addressed by a one-octet information object address. However, as the system includes RTUs that have many more data points, two-octet addressing is used across the system. At a system configuration level, there will be a single model for that type of re-closer, and configuration of each device into the system database will be a matter of using the standard point-mapping for that device type and adding the station number to form unique point references.

8.5.4   Message addressing and routing

Control and monitor directions

An important concept in understanding addressing under IEC 60870-5 is the difference between control and monitor directions. It is an assumption that the overall system has a hierarchical structure involving centralized control. Under the protocol, every station is either a controlling station or a controlled station. The communications network structure will normally be aligned with this, and for unbalanced communications links the controlling stations will be primaries, and the controlled stations will be secondaries at the link level. This follows naturally from the fact that a hierarchical structure involves multiple controlled stations, controlled by one or at least few controlling stations.

In such a system, control messages such as commands or interrogations are transmitted by the controlling station, and these result in actions and return information transmitted by the controlled station.

Addressing of ASDUs

Messages are addressed in the control direction by the common address field of the ASDU. This address field is one or two octets, and defines the station (or logical station) to which the ASDU is being addressed. In the monitor direction, however, the common address field contains the address of the station returning the data. This is required so that the data can be uniquely identified and mapped to the right points in system data images.

In some cases a station that is generally a controlled station may itself act as a controlling station, perhaps to interrogate the master station for data, or to initiate an action in another controlled station. This is called reverse direction operation. A station that can act in both the forward and the reverse direction is called a dual-mode or combined station. When a dual-mode station issues a control ASDU to another station, it must set the controlled station's address as the common address of the ASDU. This is necessary, as for any control direction ASDU, so that the intended station can recognize the message as being directed at it. When the action is carried out, further communication will be necessary with the controlling station to send an action confirmation message, and possibly an execute message if two-phase operation is being used. But as monitor direction messages carry the address of the controlled station, this cannot be used to route the communications back to the controlling station. Instead, the originator address octet of the cause of transmission field is used for this purpose. Its operation is described in the following paragraphs and drawing.

When a control direction ASDU is transmitted by a dual-mode station that is not the system master station, that station must include a non-zero value in the originator address octet of the cause of transmission field. This has no effect in the control direction of the ASDU, but is used in the monitoring direction to route action confirmation and action termination messages back to the originator. When the controlled station returns an action confirmation or other message arising from this control ASDU, it includes the originator address from the control direction ASDU in the monitoring direction response. It is the responsibility of any intermediate routing devices to recognize a non-zero originator address in a monitor direction ASDU, and to route it back to that originator.

As the originator address sub-field is only one octet in length, and common addresses may be two octets, it is clear that either any dual-mode stations on a system must either be numbered within the range <1..256>, or a mapping must be used between originator addresses and common addresses if these are not in that range.

It should be noted that also arising from the control action may be some changes within the controlled station that need to be conveyed to the master station rather than the dual-mode station that initiated the control action. These would typically be to convey the changed system state, and might also include time-tagged events. The monitor direction ASDUs that carry this information need to be directed to the master station, and possibly to other areas of the network if required. These ASDUs are given an originator address value of zero. Thus, in a system which contains dual-mode stations, it is necessary to use the originator address sub-field, and all monitor direction messages going back to the master station will have this field set to zero.

These concepts are illustrated in Figure 8.21. This shows a system with intermediate RTUs acting as controllers and data concentrators, and multiple controlled stations linked to these. One of these issues a command to a peer station. Both action confirmation and change data messages are generated, and are routed to their correct destinations by the use of the originator address field.

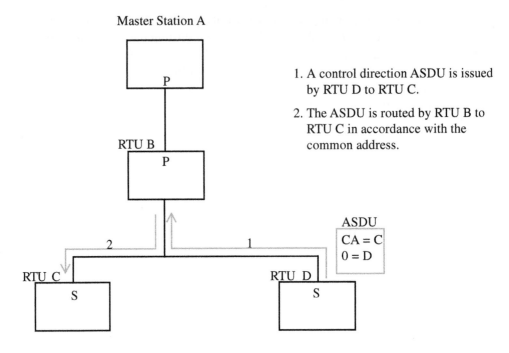

1. A control direction ASDU is issued by RTU D to RTU C.

2. The ASDU is routed by RTU B to RTU C in accordance with the common address.

Figure 8.21
Control command issued from dual-mode RTU

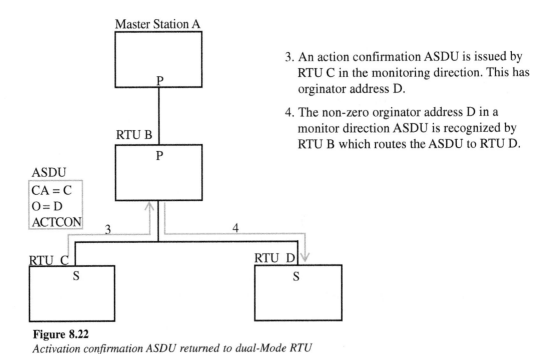

3. An action confirmation ASDU is issued by RTU C in the monitoring direction. This has orginator address D.

4. The non-zero orginator address D in a monitor direction ASDU is recognized by RTU B which routes the ASDU to RTU D.

Figure 8.22
Activation confirmation ASDU returned to dual-Mode RTU

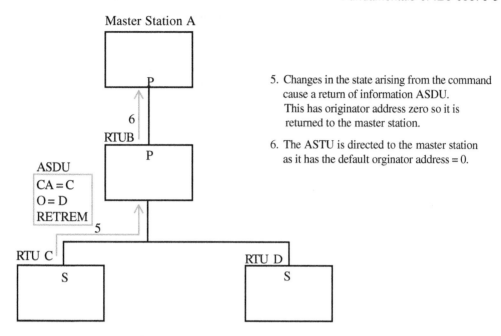

5. Changes in the state arising from the command cause a return of information ASDU. This has originator address zero so it is returned to the master station.

6. The ASTU is directed to the master station as it has the default orginator address = 0.

Figure 8.23
Monitoring information returned to SCADA master

8.6   Information elements

As has been shown in the preceding sections on ASDU structure, application data is carried within the ASDU within one or more information objects. Depending on the variable structure flag there may be multiple information objects each containing a defined set of one or more information elements, or there may be just one information object containing a number of identical information elements. In either case, the information element is the fundamental component used to convey information under the protocol. The information elements are used as building blocks in the definition of the set of ASDUs under the protocol.

In this section this set of information building blocks is presented. These are referred to in the following section when the set of ASDUs are defined.

In the following definitions, these interpretation rules should be noted:

- Key descriptions give the logical state for a set bit, i.e. bit = 1
- Blank bit positions are reserved and must be cleared, i.e. bit = 0
- Bit positions have been numbered <0..7> for consistency within this text and the powers of 2 the positions represent. Note that the IEC documents actually use <1..8>. This is a matter of definition only and does not change the meaning

The set of information elements is listed in Table 8.15. This is followed by representations of each of the data elements, grouped by general type.

General Type Symbol	Description
Process	
SIQ	Single-point information with quality descriptor
DIQ	Double-point information with quality descriptor
BSI	Binary state information
SCD	Status and change detection
QDS	Quality descriptor
VTI	Value with transient state indication
NVA	Normalized value
SVA	Scaled value
R32-IEEE STD 754	Short floating point number
BCR	Binary counter reading
Protection	
SEP	Single event of protection equipment
SPE	Start events of protection equipment
OCI	Output circuit information of protection equipment
QDP	Quality descriptor for events of protection equipment
Commands	
SCO	Single command
DCO	Double command
RCO	Regulating step command
Time	
CP56Time2a	Seven octet binary time
CP24Time2a	Three octet binary time
CP16Time2a	Two octet binary time
Qualifiers	
QOI	Qualifier of interrogation
QCC	Qualifier of counter interrogation command
QPM	Qualifier of parameter of measured values
QPA	Qualifier of parameter activation
QRP	Qualifier of reset process command
QOC	Qualifier of command
QOS	Qualifier of set-point command
File Transfer	
FRQ	File ready qualifier
SRQ	Section ready qualifier
SCQ	Select and call qualifier
LSQ	Last section or segment qualifier
AFQ	Acknowledge file or section qualifier
NOF	Name of file
NOS	Name of section
LOF	Length of file or section
LOS	Length of segment
CHS	Checksum
SOF	Status of file
Miscellaneous	
COI	Cause of initialization
FBP	Fixed test bit pattern, two octets

Table 8.15
Information elements

Quality bits

Quality bits are not information elements in themselves, but appear as individual bits within information elements. These are defined in this section.

Note that quality bits are set or cleared independently of each other. Examination of these shows that these may be used to differentiate between different types of situation or problem that may be affecting the data. Whether all are used will depend on the system. A simple approach would be to interpret any of the quality bits being set as 'bad value', whereas more sophisticated approaches may differentiate based on the actual bit(s) set. Their individual meanings are explained further below.

Blocked (BL)

This means that the value of the point is as it was prior to being blocked. Blocking prevents updating of the value of the point.

Substituted (SB)

This is where a value has been substituted or forced by manual entry or otherwise. It means that the value is not derived from the normal measurement.

Not topical (NT)

This means that the value was not updated successfully at the last time it was due to be updated.

Invalid (IV)

This indicates that the value cannot be used because it may be incorrect due to a fault or other abnormal condition.

Overflow bit (OV)

This means that a value is out of a defined range. It is used primarily with analog or counter values.

Elapsed time invalid (EI)

This is used with events of protection equipment. If set it means that the elapsed time interval value is invalid. This means that for some reason the elapsed time value cannot be relied upon and should be ignored.

8.6.1   Process related information elements

The following information elements from Table 8.15 are presented in this sub-section.

Symbol	Description
SIQ	Single-point information with quality descriptor
DIQ	Double-point information with quality descriptor
BSI	Binary state information
SCD	Status and change detection
QDS	Quality descriptor
VTI	Value with transient state indication
NVA	Normalized value
SVA	Scaled value
R32-IEEE STD 754	Short floating point number
BCR	Binary counter reading

Table 8.15 Extract A
Process related information elements

SIQ   Single point information

SIQ is single point information with quality descriptor. The status bit itself is bit 0. The 4 highest bits provide the quality information per the key below.

7	6	5	4	3	2	1	0
IV	NT	SB	BL				SPI

Key

SPI	Status ON
BL	Blocked
SB	Substituted
NT	Not topical
IV	Invalid

DIQ   Double-point information

The DIQ is double-point with quality. The quality bits are as previously defined, and the four states of the two status bits are given in the key following.

7	6	5	4	3	2	1	0
IV	NT	SB	BL			DPI	

Key – DPI Code

<0>	Indeterminate or intermediate state
<1>	OFF
<2>	ON
<3>	Indeterminate state

Key – Status Bits

BL	Blocked
SB	Substituted
NT	Not topical
IV	Invalid

BSI   Binary state information

This is a 4-octet, 32-bit set of independently assigned bits.

7	6	5	4	3	2	1	0	
7							0	
15							8	
23							16	
31							24	

SCD   Status change detection

This is a 4-octet information element containing the states of 16 independent bits, plus change status for each.

7	6	5	4	3	2	1	0	
7							0	Status bits
15							8	
23							16	Change bits
31							24	

Bits <0..15> are the status bits, and bits <16..31> are the corresponding change bits. A change bit is set if at least one change has occurred to the bit since last reported.

QDS   Quality descriptor

The quality descriptor may be used to provide the same quality information for analog and counter values as is included with the single or double-point with quality information elements. In addition it has an overflow bit OV.

7	6	5	4	3	2	1	0
IV	NT	SB	BL				OV

Key – Bit

OV	Overflow
BL	Blocked
SB	Substituted
NT	Not topical
IV	Invalid

VTI   Value with transient state indication

This information element may be used for step position for transformers and other devices with step positions.

7	6	5	4	3	2	1	0
T				Value I7			

Key

I7	Value I7[1..7] <−64..+63>
T	Transient state

NVA   Normalized value

A normalized value is a number in the range of −1.0 to 1.0, or as close as can be represented by the length of number used. If the resolution of the measuring device is less than that provided by the normalized value, then the lower significant bits are cleared to zero.

7	6	5	4	3	2	1	0
15			Value F16				0

Key

F16   Value F16[0..15] $<−1..+1−2^{-15}>$

SVA   Scaled value

This is used to transmit values where a fixed decimal point position is defined. Values are in the range −32 768 to +32 767. The range and the position of the decimal points are fixed parameters, set in the system database. For example, a value of 39.5 amps may be transmitted as 395 where the resolution is fixed at 0.1 amp.

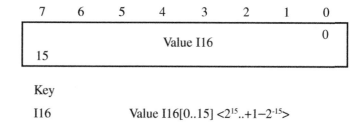

7	6	5	4	3	2	1	0
			Value I16				0
15							

Key

I16   Value I16[0..15] $<2^{15}..+1-2^{-15}>$

R32   short floating point number

The short floating point number is a 4-octet number defined by IEEE Standard 754. It is made up of a fraction, an exponent or power of 2, and a sign bit.

	7	6	5	4	3	2	1	
Octet 1	2^{-16}							2^{-23}
Octet 2	2^{-8}			Fraction				2^{-15}
Octet 3	2^{-0}	2^{-1}						2^{-7}
Octet 4	S	2^{7}		Exponent				2^{1}

Key

F	Fraction	UI23[0..22] $<0..1-2^{-23}>$
E	Exponent	UI[23..30] $<0..255>$
S	Sign	0= Positive, 1 = Negative

Interpretation

Case	Interpretation
F=<0>, E=<0>	Value = <0>
F non-zero, E=<0>	Non-normalized number
	Value = $(-1)^{S} \times 2^{E-126} \times (0.F)$
F non-zero, E <1..254>	Normalized number
	Value = $(-1)^{S} \times 2^{E-127} \times (1.F)$
F=<0>, E=<255>	Value = $(-1)^{S} \times$ infinity
F non-zero, E=<255>	Not a valid number

Note that a normalized number is one which has been scaled to the form 0.1xxxx so that it falls between 0.1 and 1.0, and then multiplied by 2 to give 1.xxxx. This removes the leading '1' to the right of the radix point, which is redundant because it is always a 1.

BCR   Binary counter reading

Key

I32	Counter value I32[0..31] $<-2^{31}..+2^{31}-1>$
SQ	Sequence number UI5[32..36] $<0..31>$
CY	Carry
CA	Counter adjusted
IV	Counter valid

Counter adjusted (CA): This means that the counter value has been adjusted since the last reading.

Sequence number (SQ): This number is incremented with each counter read operation.

Protection relay information elements

The following information elements from Table 8.15 are presented in this sub-section.

Symbol	Description
SEP	Single event of protection equipment
SPE	Start events of protection equipment
OCI	Output circuit information of protection equipment
QDP	Quality descriptor for events of protection equipment

Table 8.15 Extract B
Protection relay information elements

SEP   Single event of protection equipment

Key – Event state ES <0..3>

<0>	Indeterminate state
<1>	OFF
<2>	ON
<3>	Indeterminate state

Key

EI	Elapsed time invalid
BL	Blocked
SB	Substituted
NT	Not topical
IV	Invalid

SPE   Start events of protection equipment

7	6	5	4	3	2	1	0
		SRD	SIE	SL3	SL2	SL1	GS

Key

GS	General start of operation
SL1	Start of operation phase L1
SL2	Start of operation phase L2
SL3	Start of operation phase L3
SIE	Start of operation IE (earth current)
SRD	Start of operation in reverse direction

OCI   Output circuit information

7	6	5	4	3	2	1	0
				CL3	CL2	CL1	GC

Key

GC	General start of operation
CL1	Start of operation phase L1
CL2	Start of operation phase L2
CL3	Start of operation phase L3

QDP   Quality descriptor for events of protection equipment

7	6	5	4	3	2	1	0
IV	NT	SB	BL	EI			

Key

EI	Elapsed time invalid
BL	Blocked
SB	Substituted
NT	Not topical
IV	Invalid

8.6.2 Command information elements

The following information elements from Table 8.15 are presented in this sub-section.

Symbol	Description
SCO	Single command
DCO	Double command
RCO	Regulating step command

Table 8.15 Extract C
Command information elements

SCO   Single command

This is a command to operate a single output. Bits 2 to 7 are the Qualifier of Command sub-field. This is used for other commands also.

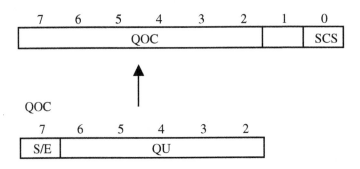

Key – Command

SCS   Single command state BS1[0] <0..1>

$\qquad$ <0> = Command OFF

$\qquad$ <1> = Command ON

Key – QOC Qualifier of command

$\qquad$ QU$\qquad$ Qualifier UI5[2..6] <0..31>

$\qquad$ <0>$\qquad$ = No additional definition

$\qquad$ <1>$\qquad$ = Short pulse duration

$\qquad$ <2>$\qquad$ = Long duration pulse

$\qquad$ <3>$\qquad$ = Persistent output

$\qquad$ <4..8>$\qquad$ = Reserved for further standard definitions

$\qquad$ <9..15>$\qquad$ = Reserved for selection of other predefined functions

$\qquad$ <16..31>$\qquad$ = Reserved for special use (private range)

$\qquad$ S/E$\qquad$ Select/Execute BS1[7] <0..1>

$\qquad\qquad$ <0>$\qquad$ = Execute

$\qquad\qquad$ <1>$\qquad$ = Select

An important feature of this command is that it has two forms depending on bit 7, the select and the execute form. The select form is used when select before execute operation is required. This is also known as two-phase command operation.

DCO   Double command

The double command state is used when two physical outputs are used to command operation. This is used to provide higher security against false operation due to equipment failure or transmission error. The qualifier of command sub-field is the same as for the single command.

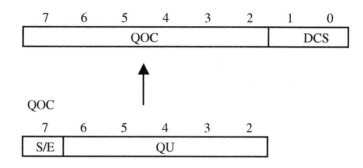

Key – Command

DCS   Double command state BS2[0..1] <0..3>

    <0>   = Not permitted

    <1>   = Command OFF

    <2>   = Command ON

    <3>   = Not permitted

RCO   Regulating step command

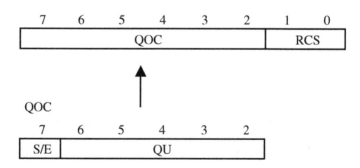

Key – Command

RCS   Single command state BS2[0..1] <0..3>

    <0>   = Not permitted

    <1>   = Next step LOWER

    <2>   = Next step HIGHER

    <3>   = Not permitted

8.6.3 Time information elements

The following information elements from Table 8.15 are presented in this sub-section.

Symbol	Description
CP56Time2a	Seven octet binary time
CP24Time2a	Three octet binary time
CP16Time2a	Two octet binary time

Table 8.15 Extract D
Command information elements

CP56Time2a – Seven-octet binary time

Seven-octet binary time is used for clock synchronization. Note that although days of the week are defined, these are not used and are set to zero.

7	6	5	4	3	2	1	0	Octet	Range
								1	0 .. 59 999 ms
								2	
		Minutes						3	0 .. 59 min
			Hours					4	0 .. 23 h
Day of week = 0			Day of month					5	0, 1 .. 31
				Month				6	1 .. 12
		Year						7	0 .. 99

CP24Time2a – Three-octet binary time

This is typically used for time tags of information objects. It is the first three octets of the seven-octet binary time element.

7	6	5	4	3	2	1	0	Octet	Range
		Milliseconds ms						1	0 .. 59 999 ms
								2	
		Minutes						3	0 .. 59 min

CP16Time2a – Two-octet binary time

This is used for elapsed times such as for relay operating time. It is the first two octets of the seven octet-binary time element.

7	6	5	4	3	2	1	0	Octet	Range
		Milliseconds ms						1	0 .. 59 999 ms
								2	

8.6.4 Qualifier information elements

The following information elements from Table 8.15 are presented in this sub-section.

Symbol	Description
QOI	Qualifier of interrogation
QCC	Qualifier of counter interrogation command
QPM	Qualifier of parameter of measured values
QPA	Qualifier of parameter activation
QOC	Qualifier of command
QRP	Qualifier of reset process command
QOS	Qualifier of set-point command

Table 8.15 Extract E
Command information elements

Qualifiers are information elements used in combination with other information elements in the definition of ASDUs.

QOI   Qualifier of interrogation

7	6	5	4	3	2	1	0
			QOI				

Key

QOI   Qualifier of command UI8[1..7] <0..255>

    <0>   = Not used

    <1..19> = Reserved for future standard definitions

    <20>   = Station interrogation – global

    <20+N> = Interrogation of group G, where G = <1..16>

    <37..63> = Reserved for future standard definitions

    <64..255>= Reserved for special use (private range)

QCC   Qualifier of counter interrogation command

7	6	5	4	3	2	1	0
FRZ		RQT					

Key

RQT   Request UI6[0..5] <0..63>

    <0>   = Not used

    <0+N>   = Request counter group G, where G = <1..4>

    <5>   = General request counter

    <6..31> = Reserved for future standard definitions

    <32..63> = Reserved for special use (private range)

FRZ   Freeze UI2[6..7] <0..3>

    <0>   = Read without freeze or reset

    <1>   = Freeze without reset

    <2>   = Freeze with reset

    <3>   = Reset

Note that the action specified by FRZ is applied to the group selected by the RQT code.

The four values of freeze code FRZ each specify a different operation immediately following the counter read. These are:

<0>	Continue to count from value. The read is just a snapshot
<1>	Stop counting and hold value as read
<2>	Clear the count to zero and stop counting
<3>	Clear the count and continue counting from zero

QPM   Qualifier of parameter of measured values

This information element is used in setting local parameters of measured values. The KPA code defines the type of parameter, and the other bits determine whether local changes are permitted, and whether the parameter is to be activated.

7	6	5	4	3	2	1	0
POP	LPC	KPA					

Key

KPA   Kind of Parameter UI6[0..5] <0..63>

<0>	= Not used
<1>	= Threshold value
<2>	= Smoothing factor (filter time constant)
<3>	= Low limit for transmission of measured values
<4>	= High limit for transmission of measured values
<5..31>	= Reserved for future standard definitions
<32..63>	= Reserved for special use (private range)

LPC   Local parameter change BS1 [6] <0..1>

<0>	= No change
<1>	= Change

POP   Parameter in operation BS1[7] <0..1>

<0>	= Operation
<1>	= Not in operation

QPA   Qualifier of parameter activation

7	6	5	4	3	2	1	0
QPA							

Key

QPA   UI8[0..7] <0..255>

<0..2>	= Not used
<3>	= Activation of cyclic transmission of object
<4..127>	= Reserved for future standard definitions
<128..255>	= Reserved for special use (private range)

QOC   Qualifier of command

7	6	5	4	3	2
S/E	QU				

Key – QOC Qualifier of command

QU   Qualifier UI5[2..6] <0..31>

        <0>   = No additional definition

        <1>   = Short pulse duration

        <2>   = Long duration pulse

        <3>   = Persistent output

        <4..8> = Reserved for further standard definitions

        <9..15> = Reserved for selection of other predefined functions

        <16..31> = Reserved for special use (private range)

S/E   Select/Execute BS1[7] <0..1>

<0>   = Execute

<1>   = Select

Note that code <0> may be used when the control function performance is fixed and not affected by the command qualifier.

QRP   Qualifier of reset process command

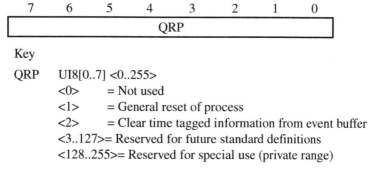

Key

QRP   UI8[0..7] <0..255>

        <0>   = Not used

        <1>   = General reset of process

        <2>   = Clear time tagged information from event buffer

        <3..127>= Reserved for future standard definitions

        <128..255>= Reserved for special use (private range)

QOS   Qualifier of set-point command

7	6	5	4	3	2	1	0
S/E	QL						

Key

QL   Qualifier UI7[0..6] <0..127>

        <0>   = Default

        <1..63> = Reserved for further standard definitions

        <64..127> = Reserved for special use (private range)

S/E   Select/Execute BS1[7] <0..1>

        <0>   = Execute

        <1>   = Select

8.6.5   File transfer information elements

The following information elements from Table 8.15 are presented in this sub-section.

Symbol	Description
FRQ	File ready qualifier
SRQ	Section ready qualifier
SCQ	Select and call qualifier
LSQ	Last section or segment qualifier
AFQ	Acknowledge file or section qualifier
NOF	Name of file
NOS	Name of section
LOF	Length of file or section
LOS	Length of segment
CHS	Checksum
SOF	Status of file

Table 8.15 Extract E
Command information elements

FRQ   File ready qualifier

7	6	5	4	3	2	1	0
BSI	U17						

Key

UI7   Qualifier Code UI7[0..6] <0..127>
    <0>   = Default
    <1..63> = Reserved for further standard definitions
    <64..127> = Reserved for special use (private range)

BS1   Non-confirmation BS1[7] <0..1>
    <0>   = Positive confirmation of select, request,
                deactivate or delete
    <1>   = Negative confirmation

SRQ   Section ready qualifier

7	6	5	4	3	2	1	0
BSI	U17						

Key

UI7   Qualifier Code UI7[0..6] <0..127>
    <0>   = Default
    <1..63> = Reserved for further standard definitions
    <64..127> = Reserved for special use (private range)

BS1   Not Ready BS1[7] <0..1>
    <0>   = Section ready to load
    <1>   = Section not ready to load

SCQ   Select and call qualifier

7	6	5	4	3	2	1	0
CODE2				CODE1			

Key

CODE1   Selection Code UI4[0..3] <0..15>
  <0>   = Default
  <1>   = Select file
  <2>   = Request file
  <3>   = Deactivate file
  <4>   = Delete file
  <5>   = Select section
  <6>   = Request section
  <7>   = Deactivate section
  <8..10> = Reserved for further standard definitions
  <11.15> = Reserved for special use (private range)

CODE2   Fault Code UI4[4..7] <0..15>
  <0>   = Default
  <1>   = Requested memory space not available
  <2>   = Checksum failed
  <3>   = Unexpected communication service
  <4>   = Unexpected name of file
  <5>   = Unexpected name of section
  <6..10> = Reserved for further standard definitions
  <11.15> = Reserved for special use (private range)

LSQ   Last section or segment qualifier

7	6	5	4	3	2	1	0
LSQ							

Key

LSQ   Selection Code UI8[0..7] <0..255>
  <0>   = Not used
  <1>   = File transfer without deactivation
  <2>   = File transfer with deactivation
  <3>   = Section transfer without deactivation
  <4>   = Section transfer with deactivation
  <5..127> = Reserved for further standard definitions
  <128.255> = Reserved for special use (private range)

AFQ   Acknowledge file or section qualifier

7	6	5	4	3	2	1	0
CODE2				CODE1			

Key

CODE1   Selection Code UI4[0..3] <0..15>
                <0>   = Not used
                <1>   = Positive acknowledge of file transfer
                <2>   = Negative acknowledge of file transfer
                <3>   = Positive acknowledge of section transfer
                <4>   = Negative acknowledge of section transfer
                <5..10> = Reserved for further standard definitions
                <11.15> = Reserved for special use (private range)

CODE2   Fault Code UI4[4..7] <0..15>
                <0>   = Default
                <1>   = Requested memory space not available
                <2>   = Checksum failed
                <3>   = Unexpected communication service
                <4>   = Unexpected name of file
                <5>   = Unexpected name of section
                <6..10> = Reserved for further standard definitions
                <11.15> = Reserved for special use (private range)

NOF   Name of file

	7	6	5	4	3	2	1	0
Octet 1	7				NOF			0
Octet 2	15							8

Key

NOF   Name of File UI16[0..15] <0..65535>
                <0>   = Default
                <1..65535> = Name of file

NOS   Name of section

	7	6	5	4	3	2	1	0
Octet 1	7				NOS			0
Octet 2	15							8

Key

NOS   Name of Section UI16[0..15] <0..65535>
                <0>   = Default
                <1..65535> = Name of section

LOF   Length of file

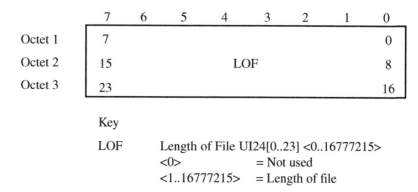

Key

LOF   Length of File UI24[0..23] <0..16777215>
           <0>   = Not used
           <1..16777215>   = Length of file

The length is that of the complete file or section in octets.

LOS   Length of segment

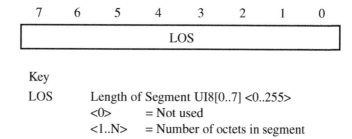

Key
LOS   Length of Segment UI8[0..7] <0..255>
           <0>   = Not used
           <1..N>   = Number of octets in segment

The length N ranges between 1 and a maximum number which is determined by the maximum length of the data link user data field, the data unit identifier and the information object address. The maximum value of N taking these into account is between 234 and 240.

CHS   Checksum

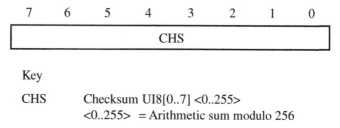

Key

CHS   Checksum UI8[0..7] <0..255>
           <0..255>   = Arithmetic sum modulo 256

When used in a last segment ASDU the checksum is the modulo 256 sum over all the octets of the section. When used in a last section ASDU, the checksum applies to the whole file. This allows verification on a per-section basis, and finally on the complete file.

SOF   Status of file

7	6	5	4	3	2	1	0
FA	FOR		STATUS				

Key

STATUS   Status of File UI5[0..4] <0..32>

                <0>   = Default

                <1..15> = Reserved for further standard definitions

                <16..32> = Reserved for special use (private range)

FOR   File Origin BS1[6] <0..1>

                <0>   = Name defines file

                <1>   = Name defines subdirectory

FA   File Active BS1[7] <0..1>

                <0>   = File waits for transfer

                <1>   = Transfer of this file is active

8.6.6   Miscellaneous information elements

The following information elements from Table 8.15 are presented in this sub-section.

Symbol	Description
COI	Cause of initialization
FBP	Fixed test bit pattern, two octets

Table 8.15 Extract F
Command information elements

COI   Cause Of initialization

7	6	5	4	3	2	1	0
BSI				U17			

Key

UI7   Qualifier UI7[0..6] <0..127>

                <0>   = Local power switch on

                <1>   = Local manual reset

                <2>   = Remote reset

                <3..31>   = Reserved for future standard definitions

                <32..127> = Reserved for special use (private range)

BS1   Select/Execute BS1[7] <0..1>

                <0>   = Initialization with unchanged local parameters

                <1>   = Initialization after changed local parameters

FBP   **Fixed test bit pattern, two octet**

7	6	5	4	3	2	1	0
1	0	1	0	1	0	1	0
0	1	0	1	0	1	0	1

Key

Pattern   Fixed Value UI16[1..16] <0x55AA>

8.7   Set of ASDUs

This section presents the set of application service data units or ASDUs defined under IEC 60870-5-101. ASDUs are the application level units of data that are used to convey SCADA information between controlling stations and controlled stations. Thus, there are ASDUs for each type of information carrying, such as sending control parameters, sending set-points, sending commands to set or clear particular status points, and for sending data such as measured analog values or counter values.

In Figure 9.17, the overall structure of the ASDUs was presented. This showed that each ASDU is made up of a data unit identifier followed by one or more information objects. The reader will recall that there are two types of structures that can be used, and these depend on the state of SQ bit of the variable structure qualifier field, which is in the data unit identifier. If the SQ bit is zero, then multiple information objects are allowed, between 1 and 127.

The two structures are shown in simplified form in Figures 8.24 and 8.25 following.

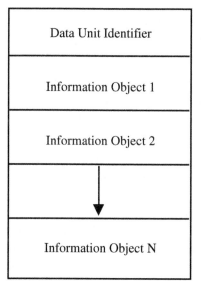

This is the structure with SQ = 0, which implies a sequence of information objects.

Each object has its own information object address.

Figure 8.24
Simplified structure of ASDU with SQ=0

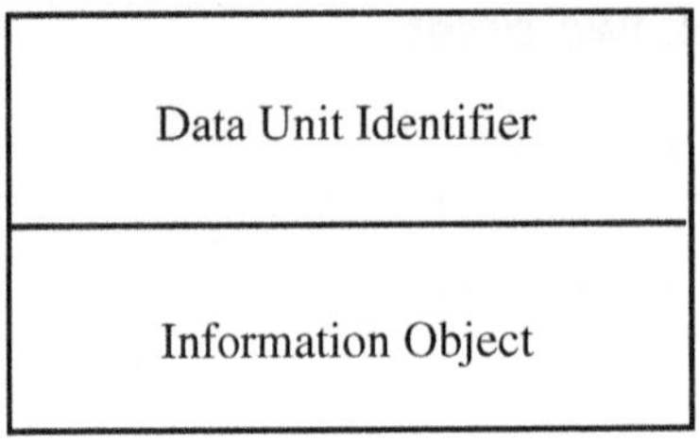

Data Unit Identifier
Information Object

This is the structure with SQ = 1, which implies a sequence of information elements within one information object.

There is just one information object address, which is the address for the first information element.

Figure 8.25
Simplified structure of ASDU with SQ=1

For each defined type identification, there are either one or two forms of the ASDU depending on whether one or both variable structure codes are allowed. The ASDUs are made of components that have all been introduced and described in the preceding sections. These are summarized below.

ASDU components:

- Data unit identifier
  - Type identification
  - Variable structure qualifier
  - Cause of transmission
  - Common address of ASDU

- Information object
  - Information object address
  - One or more information elements
  - Time tag if used

- Additional information objects (if SQ = 0)
  - Information object address
  - One or more information elements
  - Time tag if used

The following sub-sections show the ASDUs organized by type numbers and groups. To avoid unnecessary repetition, for each ASDU only the information objects are shown. The reader must remember that the complete ASDU has the data unit identifier prior to the information object or objects.

Also, note that only one information object is shown for each of SQ = 0 and SQ = 1. In the case of SQ = 0, which implies a sequence of information objects the reader must be aware that although only one information object is presented, multiple information objects may be used to form the ASDU.

In the case of SQ = 1, which implies a sequence of information elements within one information object, there is of course only the one information object. For these note that there is only one information object address and one time tag, if used. The information object addresses for sequential information elements within the ASDU are obtained by incrementing from the address of the first information element. Thus for the ith information element, the address is given by IOA + I − 1. The time tag therefore applies to all of the information elements within the ASDU.

8.7.1 Process information in monitor direction

Type 1 Single-point without time

INFORMATION OBJECT TYPE: 1
CODE: M_SP_NA_1
DESCRIPTION: Single point information without time tag
VALID WITH SQ: 0, 1

Information object for SQ = 0 (sequence of Information Objects)

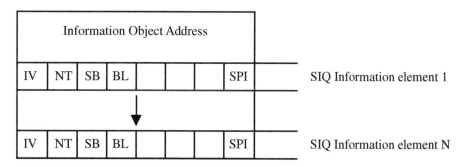

Information object for SQ = 1 (Sequence of Information Elements)

Valid cause of transmission codes

<2>	Background scan
<3>	Spontaneous
<5>	Requested
<11>	Return of information caused by remote command
<12>	Return of information caused by local command
<20>	Interrogated by station interrogation
<20 + G>	Interrogated by group G interrogation, G= <1..16>

Notes

SIQ is single point information with quality

Types 2, 30 Single-point with time

INFORMATION OBJECT TYPE: 2, 30
CODE: M_SP_TA_1, M_SP_TB_1
DESCRIPTION: Single-point information with time tag
VALID WITH SQ: 0

Information Object for SQ = 0 (Sequence of Information Objects)

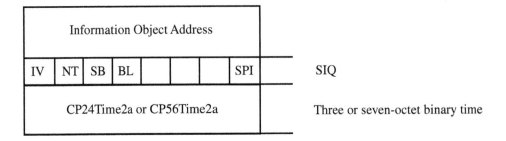

Valid cause of transmission codes

<3>	Spontaneous
<5>	Requested
<11>	Return of information caused by remote command
<12>	Return of information caused by local command

Notes

SIQ – Single-point information with quality descriptor
Type 2 has three-octet time. Type 30 has seven-octet time

Type 3 Double-point without time

INFORMATION OBJECT TYPE: 3
CODE: M_DP_NA_1
DESCRIPTION: Double-point information without time tag
VALID WITH SQ: 0, 1

Information Object for SQ = 0 (Sequence of Information Objects)

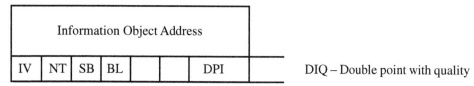

DIQ – Double point with quality

Information Object for SQ = 1 (Sequence of Information Elements)

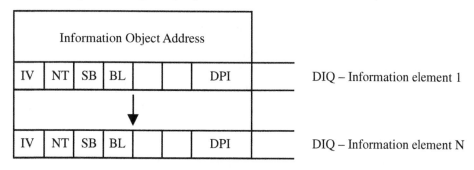

DIQ – Information element 1

DIQ – Information element N

Valid cause of transmission codes

<2>   Background scan
<3>   Spontaneous
<5>   Requested
<11>   Return of information caused by remote command
<12>   Return of information caused by local command
<20>   Interrogated by station interrogation
<20 + G>   Interrogated by group G interrogation, G= <1..16>

Notes

DIQ – Double-point information with quality descriptor

Types 4, 31 Double-point with time

INFORMATION OBJECT TYPE:	4, 31
CODE:	M_DP_TA_1, M_DP_TB_1
DESCRIPTION:	Double-point information with time tag
VALID WITH SQ:	0

Information Object for SQ = 0 (Sequence of Information Objects)

Information Object Address							
IV	NT	SB	BL			DPI	DIQ
CP24Time2a or CP56Time2a							

Three or seven-octet binary time

Valid cause of transmission codes

<3>	Spontaneous
<5>	Requested
<11>	Return of information caused by remote command
<12>	Return of information caused by local command

Notes

DIQ – Double-point information with quality descriptor
Type 4 has three-octet time. Type 31 has seven-octet time

Type 5, Step position information

INFORMATION OBJECT TYPE:	5
CODE:	M_ST_NA_1
DESCRIPTION:	Step position information
VALID WITH SQ:	0

Information Object for SQ = 0 (Sequence of Information Objects)
Single information object only.

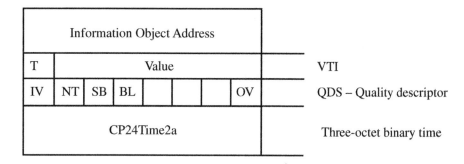

Valid cause of transmission codes

<2>	Background scan
<3>	Spontaneous
<5>	Requested
<11>	Return of information caused by remote command
<12>	Return of information caused by local command
<20>	Interrogated by station interrogation
<20 + G>	Interrogated by group G interrogation, G= <1..16>

Notes

VTI – Value with transient state indication

Type 6, 32 Step position with time

INFORMATION OBJECT TYPE:	6, 32
CODE:	M_ST_TA_1, M_ST_TB_1
DESCRIPTION:	Step position information with time tag
VALID WITH SQ:	0

Information Object for SQ = 0 (Sequence of Information Objects)
Single information object only.

Information Object Address								
T	Value							VTI
IV	NT	SB	BL				OV	QDS – Quality Descriptor
CP24Time2a or CP56 Time 2a								Three or Seven-octet binary time

Valid cause of transmission codes

<2>	Background scan
<3>	Spontaneous
<5>	Requested
<11>	Return of information caused by remote command
<12>	Return of information caused by local command

Notes

VTI – Value with transient state indication
Type 6 has three-octet time. Type 32 has seven-octet time

Type 7, Bit-string of 32 bits

INFORMATION OBJECT TYPE: 7
CODE: M_BO_NA_1
DESCRIPTION: Bit-string of 32 bits
VALID WITH SQ: 0

Information Object for SQ = 0 (Sequence of Information Objects)
Information Object Address

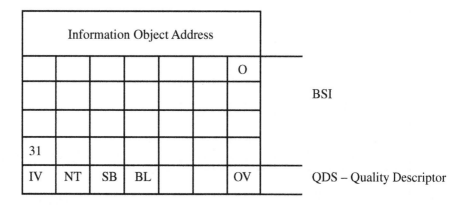

Valid cause of transmission codes

Code	Description
<2>	Background scan
<3>	Spontaneous
<5>	Requested
<11>	Return of information caused by remote command
<12>	Return of information caused by local command
<20>	Interrogated by station interrogation
<20 + G>	Interrogated by group G interrogation, G= <1..16>

Notes

BSI – Binary state information, 32-bit

Types 8, 33 Bit-string of 32 bits with time

INFORMATION OBJECT TYPE:	8, 33
CODE:	M_BO_TA_1, M_BO_TB_1
DESCRIPTION:	Bit-string of 32 bits with time tag
VALID WITH SQ:	0

Information Object for SQ = 0 (Sequence of Information Objects)

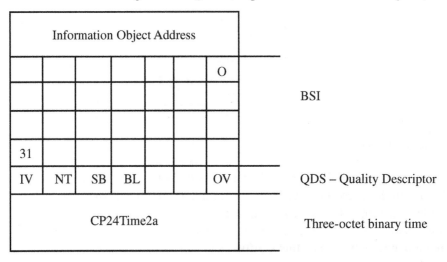

Information Object for SQ = 1 (Sequence of Information Elements)

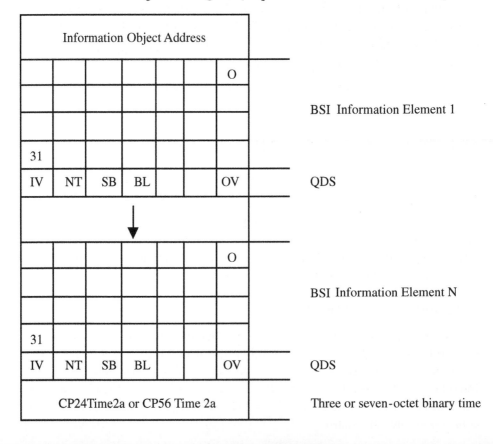

Valid cause of transmission codes

<3>   Spontaneous
<5>   Requested

Notes

BSI – Binary state information, 32-bit.
Type 8 has three-octet time. Type 33 has seven-octet time.

Type 9, Measured, normalized value

INFORMATION OBJECT TYPE: 9
CODE: M_ME_NA_1
DESCRIPTION: Measured value, normalized value
VALID WITH SQ: 0, 1

Information Object for SQ = 0 (Sequence of Information Objects)

Information Object for SQ = 1 (Sequence of Information Elements)

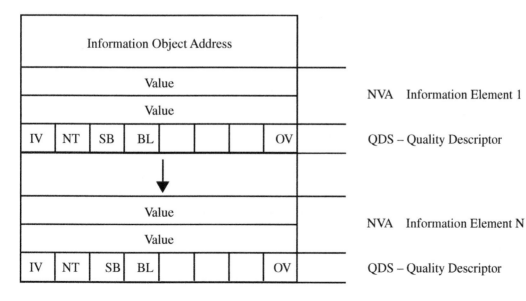

Valid cause of transmission codes

<2>	Background scan
<3>	Spontaneous
<5>	Requested
<11>	Return of information caused by remote command
<12>	Return of information caused by local command
<20>	Interrogated by station interrogation
<20 + G>	Interrogated by group G interrogation, G= <1..16>

Notes

NVA – Normalized value

Types 10, 34 Measured, normalized value with time

INFORMATION OBJECT TYPE:	10, 34
CODE:	M_ME_TA_1, M_ME_TD_1
DESCRIPTION:	Measured value, normalized value with time tag
VALID WITH SQ:	0

Information Object for SQ = 0 (Sequence of Information Objects)

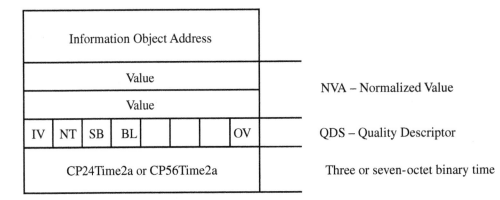

Valid cause of transmission codes

<3>	Spontaneous
<5>	Requested

Notes

NVA – Normalized value
Type 10 has three-octet time. Type 34 has seven-octet time

Type 11 Measured, scaled value

INFORMATION OBJECT TYPE:	11
CODE:	M_ME_NB_1
DESCRIPTION:	Measured value, scaled value
VALID WITH SQ:	0, 1

Information Object for SQ = 0 (Sequence of Information Objects)

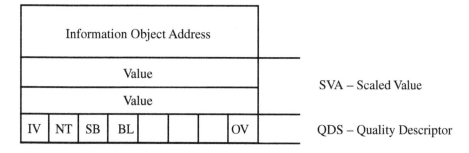

Information Object for SQ = 1 (Sequence of Information Elements)

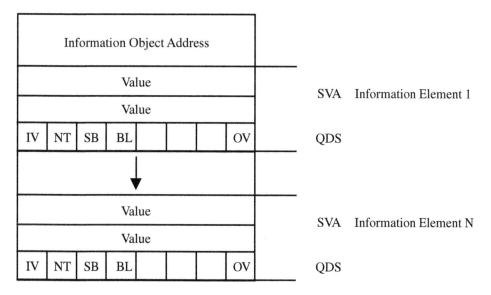

Valid cause of transmission codes

<2>	Background scan
<3>	Spontaneous
<5>	Requested
<11>	Return of information caused by remote command
<12>	Return of information caused by local command
<20>	Interrogated by station interrogation
<20 + G>	Interrogated by group G interrogation, G= <1..16>

Notes

SVA – Scaled value

Types 12, 35 Measured, scaled value with time

INFORMATION OBJECT TYPE:	12, 35
CODE:	M_ME_TB_1, M_ME_TE_1
DESCRIPTION:	Measured value, scaled value with time tag
VALID WITH SQ:	0

Information Object for SQ = 0 (Sequence of Information Objects)

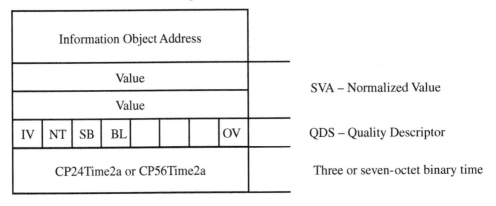

Valid cause of transmission codes

<3>	Spontaneous
<5>	Requested

Notes

SVA – Scaled value

Type 12 has three-octet time. Type 35 has seven-octet time

Type 13 Measured, short FP number

INFORMATION OBJECT TYPE: 13
CODE: M_ME_NC_1
DESCRIPTION: Measured value, short floating point number
VALID WITH SQ: 0, 1

Information Object for SQ = 0 (Sequence of Information Objects)

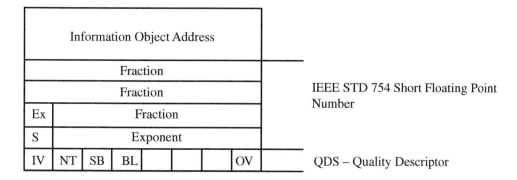

Information Object for SQ = 1 (Sequence of Information Elements)

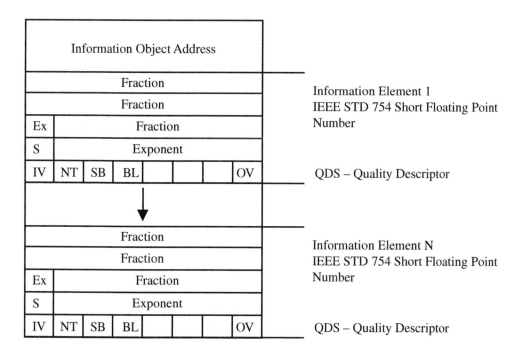

Valid cause of transmission codes

<2>	Background scan
<3>	Spontaneous
<5>	Requested
<11>	Return of information caused by remote command
<12>	Return of information caused by local command
<20>	Interrogated by station interrogation
<20 + G>	Interrogated by group G interrogation, G= <1..16>

Notes

IEEE STD 754 – Short floating point number

Types 14, 36 Measured short FP number with time

INFORMATION OBJECT TYPE:	14, 36
CODE:	M_ME_TC_1, M_ME_TF_1
DESCRIPTION:	Measured value, short floating point number with time tag
VALID WITH SQ:	0

Information Object for SQ = 0 (Sequence of Information Objects)

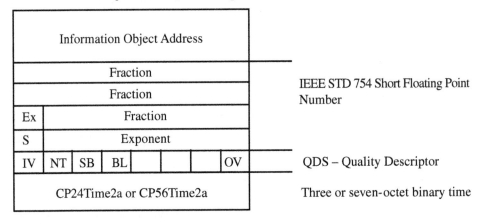

Valid cause of transmission codes

<2>	Background scan
<3>	Spontaneous
<5>	Requested
<11>	Return of information caused by remote command
<12>	Return of information caused by local command
<20>	Interrogated by station interrogation
<20 + G>	Interrogated by group G interrogation, G= <1..16>

Notes

IEEE STD 754 – Short floating point number
Type 14 has three-octet time. Type 36 has seven-octet time

Type 15 Integrated totals

INFORMATION OBJECT TYPE: 15
CODE: M_IT_NA_1
DESCRIPTION: Integrated totals
VALID WITH SQ: 0, 1

Information Object for SQ = 0 (Sequence of Information Objects)

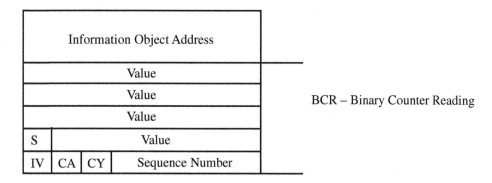

Information Object for SQ = 1 (Sequence of Information Elements)

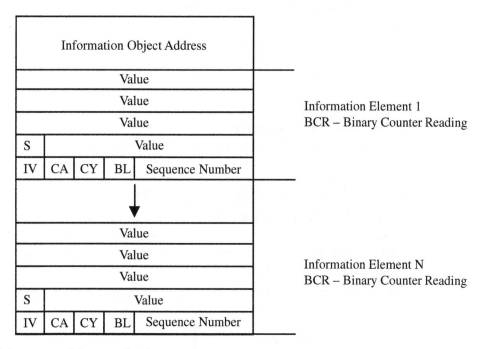

Valid cause of transmission codes

<2>	Background scan
<37>	Requested by general counter request
<37 + G>	Requested by group G counter request G = <1..4>

Notes

BCR – Binary counter reading

Types 16, 37 Integrated totals with time

INFORMATION OBJECT TYPE:	16,37
CODE:	M_IT_TA_1, M_IT_TB_1
DESCRIPTION:	Integrated totals with time tag
VALID WITH SQ:	0

Information Object for SQ = 0 (Sequence of Information Objects)

Information Object Address				
Value				
Value				
Value				
S	Value			
IV	CA	CY	Sequence Number	
CP24Time2a or CP56Time2a				

BCR – Binary Counter Reading (spanning Value rows)

Three or seven-octet binary time (for CP24Time2a or CP56Time2a)

Valid cause of transmission codes

<3>	Spontaneous
<37>	Requested by general counter request
<37 + G>	Requested by group G counter request G = <1..4>

Notes

BCR – Binary counter reading
Type 16 has three-octet time. Type 37 has seven-octet time

Types 17, 38 Event of protection with time

INFORMATION OBJECT TYPE:	17, 38
CODE:	M_EP_TA_1, M_EP_TD_1
DESCRIPTION:	Event of protection equipment with time tag
VALID WITH SQ:	0

Information Object for SQ = 0 (Sequence of Information Objects)

Information Object Address					
IV	NT	SB	BL	EI	ES
CP16Time2a					
CP24Time2a or CP56Time2a					

SEP (for IV NT SB BL EI ES row)

Two-octet binary time, elapsed time (for CP16Time2a)

Three or seven-octet binary time (for CP24Time2a or CP56Time2a)

Valid cause of transmission codes

<3>   Spontaneous

Notes

SEP – Single event of protection equipment
Type 17 has three-octet time
Type 38 has seven-octet time

Types 18, 39 Packed events of protection with time

INFORMATION OBJECT TYPE:	18, 39
CODE:	M_EP_TB_1, M_EP_TE_1
DESCRIPTION:	Packed start of events of protection equipment with time tag
VALID WITH SQ:	0

Information Object for SQ = 0 (Sequence of Information Objects)
Single information object only.

Information Object Address									
		SRD	SIE	SL3	SL2	SL1	GS		SEP
IV	NT	SB	BL	EI					QDP
CP16Time2a									Two-octet binary time, relay duration time
CP24Time2a or CP56Time2a									Three or seven-octet binary time

Valid cause of transmission codes

<3>   Spontaneous

Notes

SPE – Start event of protection equipment
QDP – Quality descriptor of protection equipment
Type 18 has three-octet time
Type 39 has seven-octet time

Types 19, 40 Packed output of protection with time

INFORMATION OBJECT TYPE:	19, 40
CODE:	M_EP_TC_1, M_EP_TF_1
DESCRIPTION:	Packed output circuit information of protection equipment with time-tag
VALID WITH SQ:	0

Information Object for SQ = 0 (Sequence of Information Objects)

Single information object only.

Information Object Address									
				CL3	CL2	CL1	GC		OCI
IV	NT	SB	BL	EI					QDP
CP16Time2a									Two-octet binary time, relay operating time
CP24Time2a or CP56Time2a									Three or seven-octet binary time

Valid cause of transmission codes

<3>   Spontaneous

Notes

OCI – Output circuit command of protection equipment
QDP – Quality descriptor of protection equipment
Type 19 has three-octet time
Type 40 has seven-octet time

Type 20 Packed single-point with status change detection

INFORMATION OBJECT TYPE:	20
CODE:	M_PS_NA_1
DESCRIPTION:	Packed single-point information with status change detection
VALID WITH SQ:	0

Information Object for SQ = 0 (Sequence of Information Objects)

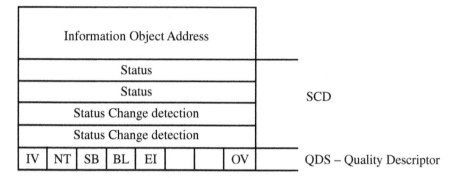

Valid cause of transmission codes

<2>	Background scan
<3>	Spontaneous
<5>	Requested
<11>	Return of information caused by remote command
<12>	Return of information caused by local command
<20>	Interrogated by station interrogation
<20 + G>	Interrogated by group G interrogation, G = <1..16>

Notes

SCD – Status + status change detection, 32 bits

Type 21 Measured, normalized value without quality

INFORMATION OBJECT TYPE: 21
CODE: M_ME_ND_1
DESCRIPTION: Measured value, normalized value
without quality descriptor
VALID WITH SQ: 0, 1

Information Object for SQ = 0 (Sequence of Information Objects)

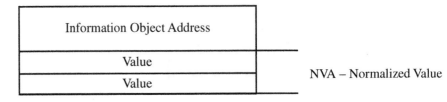

Information Object for SQ = 1 (Sequence of Information Elements)

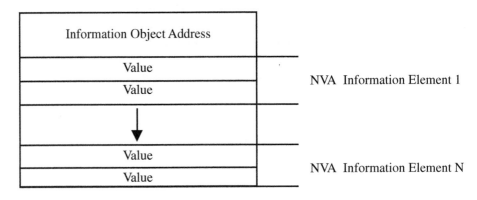

Valid cause of transmission codes

<1>	Periodic / cyclic
<2>	Background scan
<3>	Spontaneous
<5>	Requested
<11>	Return of information caused by remote command
<12>	Return of information caused by local command
<20>	Interrogated by station interrogation
<20 + G>	Interrogated by group G interrogation, G = <1..16>

Notes

NVA – Normalized value

Process Information in control direction

Type 45 single command

INFORMATION OBJECT TYPE:	45
CODE:	C_SC_NA_1
DESCRIPTION:	Single command
VALID WITH SQ:	0

Information Object for SQ = 0 (Sequence of Information Objects)

Single information object only.

Information Object Address			
S/E	QU	SCS	SCO – Single Command

Valid cause of transmission codes

In control direction
<6>	Activation
<8>	Deactivation

In monitor direction
<7>	Activation confirmation
<9>	Deactivation confirmation
<10>	Activation termination
<44>	Unknown type identification
<45>	Unknown cause of transmission
<46>	Unknown common address of ASDU
<47>	Unknown information object address

Notes

SCO – Single command

Type 46 Double command

INFORMATION OBJECT TYPE:	46
CODE:	C_DC_NA_1
DESCRIPTION:	Double command
VALID WITH SQ:	0, 1

Information Object for SQ = 0 (Sequence of Information Objects)
Single information object only.

Valid cause of transmission codes

In control direction
<6>   Activation
<8>   Deactivation

In monitor direction
<7>   Activation confirmation
<9>   Deactivation confirmation
<10>   Activation termination
<44>   Unknown type identification
<45>   Unknown cause of transmission
<46>   Unknown common address of ASDU
<47>   Unknown information object address

Notes

DCO – Double command

Type 47 Regulating step command

INFORMATION OBJECT TYPE:	47
CODE:	C_RC_NA_1
DESCRIPTION:	Regulating step command
VALID WITH SQ:	0

Information Object for SQ = 0 (Sequence of Information Objects)

Single information object only.

Information Object Address		
S/E	QU	RCS

RCO – Regulating Step Command

Valid cause of transmission codes

In control direction
<6>	Activation
<8>	Deactivation

In monitor direction
<7>	Activation confirmation
<9>	Deactivation confirmation
<10>	Activation termination
<44>	Unknown type identification
<45>	Unknown cause of transmission
<46>	Unknown common address of ASDU
<47>	Unknown information object address

Notes

RCO – Regulating step command

Type 48 Set-point command, normalized value

INFORMATION OBJECT TYPE: 48
CODE: C_SE_NA_1
DESCRIPTION: Set-point command, normalized value
VALID WITH SQ: 0

Information Object for SQ = 0 (Sequence of Information Objects)

Single information object only.

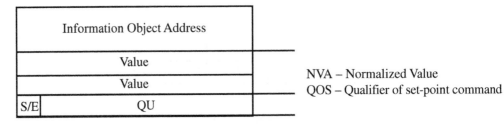

Valid cause of transmission codes

In control direction
<6>   Activation
<8>   Deactivation

In monitor direction
<7>   Activation confirmation
<9>   Deactivation confirmation
<10>   Activation termination
<44>   Unknown type identification
<45>   Unknown cause of transmission
<46>   Unknown common address of ASDU
<47>   Unknown information object address

Notes

NVA – Normalized value
QOS – Qualifier of set-point command

Type 49 Set-point command, scaled value

INFORMATION OBJECT TYPE: 49
CODE: C_SE_NB_1
DESCRIPTION: Set-point command, scaled value
VALID WITH SQ: 0

Information Object for SQ = 0 (Sequence of Information Objects)

Single information object only.

Information Object Address	
Value	
Value	SVA – Scaled Value
S/E QL	QOS – Qualifier of set-point command

Valid cause of transmission codes

In control direction
<6>   Activation
<8>   Deactivation

In monitor direction
<7>   Activation confirmation
<9>   Deactivation confirmation
<10>   Activation termination
<44>   Unknown type identification
<45>   Unknown cause of transmission
<46>   Unknown common address of ASDU
<47>   Unknown information object address

Notes

SVA – Normalized value
QOS – Qualifier of set-point command

Type 50 Set-point command, short FP number

INFORMATION OBJECT TYPE:	50
CODE:	C_SE_NC_1
DESCRIPTION:	Set-point command, short floating point number
VALID WITH SQ:	0

Information Object for SQ = 0 (Sequence of Information Objects)

Single information object only.

Information Object Address		
	Fraction	
	Fraction	
Ex	Fraction	
S	Exponent	
S/E	QL	

IEEE STD 754 Short Floating Point Number

QOS – Qualifier of set-point command

Valid cause of transmission codes

In control direction
<6>	Activation
<8>	Deactivation

In monitor direction
<7>	Activation confirmation
<9>	Deactivation confirmation
<10>	Activation termination
<44>	Unknown type identification
<45>	Unknown cause of transmission
<46>	Unknown common address of ASDU
<47>	Unknown information object address

Notes

IEEE STD 754 – Short floating-point number
QOS – Qualifier of set-point command

Type 51 Bit-string of 32 bits

INFORMATION OBJECT TYPE: 51
CODE: C_BO_NA_1
DESCRIPTION: Bit-string of 32 bits
VALID WITH SQ: 0

Information Object for SQ = 0 (Sequence of Information Objects)

Single information object only.

Information Object Address
Bit-strings
Bit-strings
Bit-strings
Bit-strings

BSI – Binary state information

Valid cause of transmission codes

In control direction
<6>   Activation
<8>   Deactivation

In monitor direction
<7>   Activation confirmation
<9>   Deactivation confirmation
<10>   Activation termination
<44>   Unknown type identification
<45>   Unknown cause of transmission
<46>   Unknown common address of ASDU
<47>   Unknown information object address

Notes

BSI – Binary state information

System information in monitor direction

Type 70 End of initialization

INFORMATION OBJECT TYPE: 70
CODE: M_EI_NA_1
DESCRIPTION: End of initialization
VALID WITH SQ: 0

Information Object for SQ = 0 (Sequence of Information Objects)

Single information object only.

Information Object Address	IOA = 0
CP8	COI – Cause of Initialization

Valid cause of transmission codes

<4>   Initialized

Notes

COI – Cause of Initialization

8.7.2　System information in control direction

Type 100 Interrogation command

INFORMATION OBJECT TYPE:　　100
CODE:　　C_IC_NA_1
DESCRIPTION:　　Interrogation command
VALID WITH SQ:　　0

Information Object for SQ = 0 (Sequence of Information Objects)

Single information object only.

Information Object Address	IOA = 0
UI8	QOI – Qualifier of Interrogation

Valid cause of transmission codes

In control direction
<6>　　　　　　Activation
<8>　　　　　　Deactivation

In monitor direction
<7>　　　　　　Activation confirmation
<9>　　　　　　Deactivation confirmation
<10>　　　　　Activation termination
<44>　　　　　Unknown type identification
<45>　　　　　Unknown cause of transmission
<46>　　　　　Unknown common address of ASDU
<47>　　　　　Unknown information object address

Notes

QOI – Qualifier of Interrogation

Type 101 Counter interrogation command

INFORMATION OBJECT TYPE:	101
CODE:	C_CI_NA_1
DESCRIPTION:	Counter interrogation command
VALID WITH SQ:	0

Information Object for SQ = 0 (Sequence of Information Objects)

Single information object only.

Information Object Address	IOA = 0
CP8	QCC – Qualifier of counter command

Valid cause of transmission codes

In control direction

<6>	Activation
<8>	Deactivation

In monitor direction

<7>	Activation confirmation
<9>	Deactivation confirmation
<10>	Activation termination
<44>	Unknown type identification
<45>	Unknown cause of transmission
<46>	Unknown common address of ASDU
<47>	Unknown information object address

Notes

QCC – Qualifier of counter command

Type 102 Read command

INFORMATION OBJECT TYPE: 102
CODE: C_RD_NA_1
DESCRIPTION: Read command
VALID WITH SQ: 0

Information Object for SQ = 0 (Sequence of Information Objects)

Single information object only.

Information Object Address

Valid cause of transmission codes

<5>   Request

Notes

There is only the information object address with the data unit identifier for this command.

Type 103 Clock synchronization command

INFORMATION OBJECT TYPE: 103
CODE: C_CS_NA_1
DESCRIPTION: Clock synchronization command
VALID WITH SQ: 0

Information Object for SQ = 0 (Sequence of Information Objects)

Single information object only.

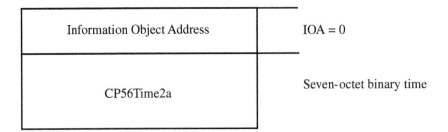

Information Object Address	IOA = 0
CP56Time2a	Seven-octet binary time

Valid cause of transmission codes

In control direction
<6>   Activation

In monitor direction
<3>   Spontaneous
<7>   Activation confirmation
<44>   Unknown type identification
<45>   Unknown cause of transmission
<46>   Unknown common address of ASDU
<47>   Unknown information object address

Notes

This command may be used in the monitor direction to transmit the outstation clock time. This enables messages stored at an outstation that span a change of hour to be interpreted without ambiguity. This arises because three-octet binary time provides only minutes and milliseconds up to one hour. Therefore, to interpret correctly time-tags from outstations, it is necessary to include outstation time hour changes within the messages. It is also necessary for the master station to keep a track of outstation hour whilst sequentially processing stored time-tagged data.

Type 104 Test command

> INFORMATION OBJECT TYPE: 104
> CODE: C_TS_NA_1
> DESCRIPTION: Test command
> VALID WITH SQ: 0

Information Object for SQ = 0 (Sequence of Information Objects)

Single information object only.

Information Object Address								IOA = 0
1	0	1	0	1	0	1	0	FBP – Fixed test pattern
0	1	0	1	0	1	0	1	

Valid cause of transmission codes

In control direction

<6>	Activation

In monitor direction

<7>	Activation confirmation
<44>	Unknown type identification
<45>	Unknown cause of transmission
<46>	Unknown common address of ASDU
<47>	Unknown information object address

Notes

FBP – Fixed test pattern

Type 105 Reset process command

INFORMATION OBJECT TYPE:	105
CODE:	C_RP_NA_1
DESCRIPTION:	Reset process command
VALID WITH SQ:	0

Information Object for SQ = 0 (Sequence of Information Objects)

Single information object only.

Information Object Address	IOA = 0
UI8	QRP – Qualifier of reset process cmd.

Valid cause of transmission codes

In control direction

<6>	Activation

In monitor direction

<7>	Activation confirmation
<44>	Unknown type identification
<45>	Unknown cause of transmission
<46>	Unknown common address of ASDU
<47>	Unknown information object address

Notes

QRP – Qualifier of reset process command

Type 106 Delay acquisition command

INFORMATION OBJECT TYPE:	106
CODE:	C_CD_NA_1
DESCRIPTION:	Delay acquisition command
VALID WITH SQ:	0

Information Object for SQ = 0 (Sequence of Information Objects)

Single information object only.

Information Object Address	IOA = 0
CP16Time2a	Two-octet binary time

Valid cause of transmission codes

In control direction

<6>	Activation

In monitor direction

<7>	Activation confirmation
<44>	Unknown type identification
<45>	Unknown cause of transmission
<46>	Unknown common address of ASDU
<47>	Unknown information object address

Notes

FBP – Fixed test pattern

8.7.3 Parameter in control direction

Type 110 Parameter of measured, normalized value

INFORMATION OBJECT TYPE: 110
CODE: PM_ME_NA_1
DESCRIPTION: Parameter of measured values, normalized value

VALID WITH SQ: 0

Information Object for SQ = 0 (Sequence of Information Objects)

Single information object only.

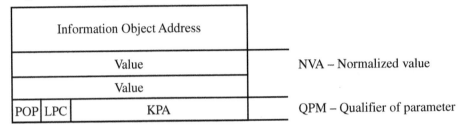

Valid cause of transmission codes

In control direction
<6>   Activation

In monitor direction
<7>   Activation confirmation
<9>   Deactivation confirmation
<20>   Interrogated by station interrogation
<20 + G>   Interrogated by group G interrogation, G= <1..16>
<10>   Activation termination
<44>   Unknown type identification
<45>   Unknown cause of transmission
<46>   Unknown common address of ASDU
<47>   Unknown information object address

Notes

QPM – Qualifier of parameter of measured values

Type 111 Parameter of measured, scaled value

INFORMATION OBJECT TYPE: 111
CODE: PM_ME_NB_1
DESCRIPTION: Parameter of measured values, scaled value
VALID WITH SQ: 0

Information Object for SQ = 0 (Sequence of Information Objects)

Single information object only.

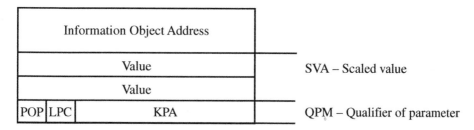

Valid cause of transmission codes

In control direction
<6>   Activation

In monitor direction
<7>   Activation confirmation
<20>   Interrogated by station interrogation
<20 + G>   Interrogated by group G interrogation, G = <1..16>
<44>   Unknown type identification
<45>   Unknown cause of transmission
<46>   Unknown common address of ASDU
<47>   Unknown information object address

Notes

QPM – Qualifier of parameter of measured values

Type 112 Parameter of measured, short floating point number

INFORMATION OBJECT TYPE:	112
CODE:	PM_ME_NC_1
DESCRIPTION:	Parameter of measured values, short floating point number
VALID WITH SQ:	0

Information Object for SQ = 0 (Sequence of Information Objects)

Single information object only.

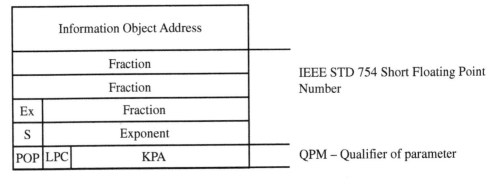

Valid cause of transmission codes

In control direction

<6>	Activation

In monitor direction

<7>	Activation confirmation
<20>	Interrogated by station interrogation
<20 + G>	Interrogated by group G interrogation, G= <1..16>
<44>	Unknown type identification
<45>	Unknown cause of transmission
<46>	Unknown common address of ASDU
<47>	Unknown information object address

Notes

QPM – Qualifier of parameter of measured values

Type 113 Parameter activation

INFORMATION OBJECT TYPE: 113
CODE: P_AC_NA_1
DESCRIPTION: Parameter activation
VALID WITH SQ: 0

Information Object for SQ = 0 (Sequence of Information Objects)

Single information object only.

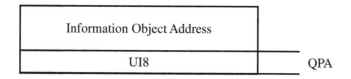

Valid cause of transmission codes

In control direction
<6>   Activation
<8>   Deactivation

In monitor direction
<7>   Activation confirmation
<9>   Deactivation confirmation
<44>   Unknown type identification
<45>   Unknown cause of transmission
<46>   Unknown common address of ASDU
<47>   Unknown information object address

Notes

QPA – Qualifier of parameter activation

8.7.4 File transfer

Type 120 File ready

INFORMATION OBJECT TYPE: 120
CODE: F_FR_NA_1
DESCRIPTION: File ready
VALID WITH SQ: 0

Information Object for SQ = 0 (Sequence of Information Objects)

Single information object only.

Information Object Address	
UI16	NOF – Name of file
UI24	LOF – Length of file
CP8	FRQ – File ready qualifier

Valid cause of transmission codes

<13>   File transfer

Notes

NOF – Name of file
LOF – Length of file
FRQ – File ready qualifier

Type 121 Section ready

INFORMATION OBJECT TYPE: 121
CODE: F_SR_NA_1
DESCRIPTION: Section ready
VALID WITH SQ: 0

Information Object for SQ = 0 (Sequence of Information Objects)

Single information object only.

Information Object Address	
UI16	NOF – Name of file
UI8	NOS – Name of section
UI24	LOF – Length of file
CP8	SRQ – Section ready qualifier

Valid cause of transmission codes

<13>   File transfer

Notes

NOF – Name of file
NOS – Name of section
LOF – Length of file

Type 122 Call directory

INFORMATION OBJECT TYPE:	122
CODE:	F_SC_NA_1
DESCRIPTION:	Call directory, select file, call file, call section
VALID WITH SQ:	0

Information Object for SQ = 0 (Sequence of Information Objects)

Single information object only.

Information Object Address	
UI16	NOF – Name of file
UI8	NOS – Name of section
CP8	SCQ – Select and call qualifier

Valid cause of transmission codes

<5>	Request (only for Call Directory)
<13>	File transfer (for all except Call Directory)

Notes

NOF – Name of file
NOF – Name of section
SCQ – Select and call qualifier

Type 123 Last section, last segment

INFORMATION OBJECT TYPE: 123
CODE: F_LS_NA_1
DESCRIPTION: Last section, last segment
VALID WITH SQ: 0

Information Object for SQ = 0 (Sequence of Information Objects)

Single information object only.

Information Object Address	
UI16	NOF – Name of file
UI8	NOS – Name of section
UI8	LSQ – Last section or segment qualifier
UI8	CHS – Checksum

Valid cause of transmission codes

<13>   File transfer

Notes

NOF – Name of file
NOF – Name of section
LSQ – Last section or segment qualifier
CHS – Checksum

Type 124 ACK file, ACK section

INFORMATION OBJECT TYPE:	124
CODE:	F_AF_NA_1
DESCRIPTION:	ACK File, ACK Section
VALID WITH SQ:	0

Information Object for SQ = 0 (Sequence of Information Objects)

Single information object only.

Information Object Address	
UI16	NOF – Name of file
UI8	NOS – Name of section
CP8	AFQ – ACK file or section qualifier

Valid cause of transmission codes

<13>   File transfer

Notes

NOF – Name of file
NOS – Name of section
AFQ – ACK file or section qualifier

Type 125 Segment

INFORMATION OBJECT TYPE: 125
CODE: F_SG_NA_1
DESCRIPTION: Segment
VALID WITH SQ: 0

Information Object for SQ = 0 (Sequence of Information Objects)

Single information object only.

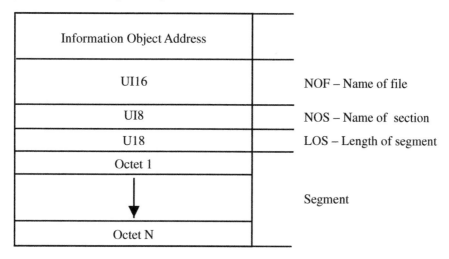

Valid cause of transmission codes

<13>   File transfer

Notes

NOF – Name of file
NOS – Name of section
LOS – Length of segment

Type 126 Directory

INFORMATION OBJECT TYPE: 126
CODE: F_DR_TA_1
DESCRIPTION: Directory
VALID WITH SQ: 1

Information Object for SQ = 1 (Sequence of Information Elements)

Information Object Address	
UI16	Information Element 1 NOF – Name of file or subdirectory
UI24	LOF – Length of file
FA | FOR | Status	SOF – Status of file
CP56Time2a	Seven-octet binary time Creation time of file
↓	
UI16	Information Element N NOF – Name of file or subdirectory
UI24	LOF – Length of file
FA | FOR | Status	SOF – Status of file
CP56Time2a	Seven-octet binary time Creation time of file

Valid cause of transmission codes

<3>	Spontaneous
<5>	Requested

Notes

NOF – Name of file or subdirectory
LOF – Length of file
SOF – Status of file

9

Advanced considerations of IEC 60870-5

Objectives

This chapter presents the following advanced considerations in the use of IEC 60870-5:

- Application level functions
- Interoperability
- Networked version IEC 60870-5-104

In this text the features of the IEC 60870-5 protocol are presented and described. The descriptions presented are intended to assist understanding by users of equipment implementing the protocol. Original equipment manufacturers for such systems, and anyone requiring a complete understanding of all aspects of the protocol should refer to the actual IEC standards for complete details, and for possible future amendments.

9.1 Application functions

Application functions are implemented by the user process layer of both controlling and controlled stations. Operating interactively and using the communications system including the link and physical communications layers, they make up an overall process that implements SCADA operations.

In the following sub-sections the main functions are described. These functions are specified in detail by IEC 60870-5-101, which largely refers to and makes selections from IEC 60870-5-5.

9.1.1 Station initialization

General procedure

Station initialization is required when a station is first powered up, or after a reset. Its purpose is to ensure the orderly commencement of monitoring and control operations. The procedure followed is basically to reset the link layer first, re-establish link communications, and then commence application level services. When the initialization process of a controlled station is completed, it will send an end of initialization ASDU to the controlling station so that control and monitoring functions can begin. The procedure involves both application and link level functions.

Initialization of controlling station:

- Link layer establishes links with controlled stations
- Controlling station sends C_EI (end of initialization) ASDU to the active controlled stations to tell them that they may commence sending process information
- Controlled stations may commence sending process data if available
- Controlling station performs a general interrogation
- Controlling station may perform clock synchronization

Initialization of controlled station:

- Link layer establishes communication with controlling station
- Once the application layer is ready, controlled station may send a M_EI (end of initialization) ASDU to the controlling station
- The controlled station now responds to general interrogation or other commands from the controlling station

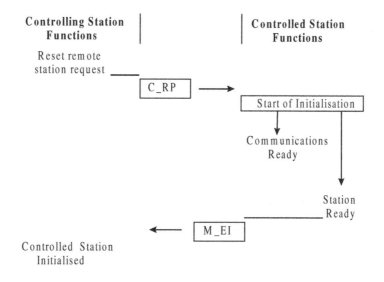

Figure 9.1
General sequence for controlling station initialization

Figure 9.1 shows the general sequence of initialization for the controlling station. After the start of initialization, the link layer communications services will become established by synchronizing across the link with controlled stations. This may occur before the application level functions are fully initialized. When all application level functions are available general interrogation and other functions are commenced. In the example the controlling station commences a general interrogation following initialization from 'cold'. In this case it has no controlled station data and so it must obtain the state of all process data.

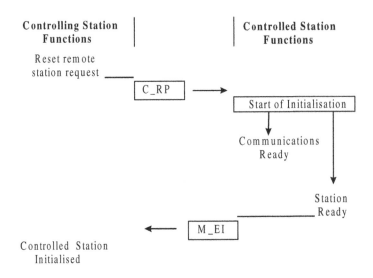

Figure 9.2
General sequence for controlled station initialization

Figure 9.2 shows the initialization sequence for a controlled station. In this case a reset process command ASDU is transmitted by the controlling station to the remote controlled station. This resets the local station. Only after the link communications and all application level functions are available is the end of initialization M_EI ASDU transmitted to the controlling station.

An end of initialization ASDU must be transmitted by each controlled station following its own initialization. In the case of multiple logical remote units in one physical device, each must transmit a separate end of initialization ASDU. In this case there is one link layer address, but more than one common address of ASDU for the device.

Link layer function

The link layer function has been presented elsewhere in this text and so only a brief review is noted here. The link layer services are responsible for establishing the link, and they proceed to do this immediately after being powered up or reset. On an unbalanced link, the primary station repeatedly sends 'request status of link' until it gets a 'status of link' response. It then sends a 'reset of remote link' which synchronizes the frame count bit (FCB) across the link. Once this sequence is completed the link is available for communication services to the application layer. Balanced communications are basically two unbalanced links operating in opposite directions, and so the synchronization process occurs independently for each direction.

9.1.2   Data acquisition

The following methods used for data acquisition are described by the IEC 60870-5 standard:

- By polling
- Cyclic data transmission
- Acquisition of events
- General interrogation

In attempting to explain, or to understand these processes, it is important to be clear about whether link layer or application level processes are being described. When unbalanced communications are used at the link layer level, then it is essential that a polling procedure operates at all times to sequentially interrogate each station so as to give it an opportunity to transmit. If this is not done, there is no way that a controlled station can communicate, because it must wait until it is polled before it can transmit anything.

It is important to recognize therefore, that when unbalanced communications are used, then a polling system must operate. This system operates in a way that is transparent to the application level processes. It is a function of the communications services, and resides in processes carried out at the link and application levels, but not the user process level.

Under IEC 60870-5-101 polling is a process that operates continually when unbalanced communications are used, and its function is to sequentially check for application level data from controlled stations, and to request its transmission when it exists at a station.

Such data can arise from any of the following application level processes, described in the following subsections:

- General interrogation
- Event data transmission
- Cyclic data transmission
- Background scan

The general usage of these means of data acquisition is as follows:

- Following initialization of a master station, or an intermediate or sub-master device, general interrogation is used to acquire current data on the system. This creates a current 'network image' of the state of the system. Once this is acquired then it requires only updating for subsequent changes to remain current
- Event data is created at controlled stations when status points change state, or when analog values change by greater than a defined increment. These are transmitted by the controlled stations, marked with the spontaneous cause of transmission code. These are recognized by the master station as events, and are used to update the network image for these points. The changes may also initiate other actions such as operator alarms configured at the master station. Optionally, some changes may be transmitted twice, firstly with high priority to update the change of state, and secondly with a lower priority to provide a time-stamped change of state. This is called double transmission, and is used for event logging
- Cyclic data transmission is used to slowly but continuously update process measurement values, that is analog values. This improves on the report on change event generation because if that alone was used, the majority of points

would be in error by up to the deviation amount that triggers an event. Cyclic data transmission is initiated by the controlled stations
- The background scan operates like cyclic data transmission in that it is a slow but continuously operating process. It provides a backup to event processing, and guards against the network image becoming incorrect due to the loss or corruption of a message. Background scans are initiated at the controlled stations, as for cyclic data. Generally the background scan is operated at a slower rate than cyclic data transmission, as its purpose is purely to provide security against undetected data loss

General interrogation

General interrogation is used for updating the controlling station following initialization, or following information loss or compromise. It is similar to cyclic data transmission by controlled stations in that it involves the transmission of all the static data. General interrogation occurs when the controlling station issues an interrogation command C_IC to the controlled station. On receiving the interrogation command the controlled station transmits its process information to the controlling station.

The particular data that is called for by a general interrogation can be defined as either all data, or by group. In the control direction, the group number is set as the value of the QOI or qualifier of interrogation. This can have the value <20> for global interrogation, or <21..36> corresponding to groups 1 to 16. When the information is returned in the monitor direction, the group is identified by the cause of transmission code of the same group number, that is in the range <20..36>. Note that only non-time-tagged data types are used for the returning information for a general interrogation. This may be seen by examining the set of ASDUs and noting the valid causes of transmission. This shows only the following ASDU types are used in response to a general interrogation: <1, 3, 5, 7, 9, 11, 13, 20, 21 and 100>.

An example of the general interrogation procedure is shown in Figure 9.3 and is described following the figure.

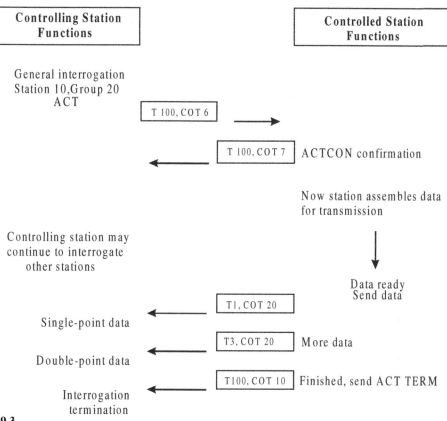

Figure 9.3
General interrogation procedure

The general interrogation procedure shown in Figure 9.3 is described below:

- The general interrogation commences with a type 100 ASDU transmitted by the controlling station. It has cause of transmission <6>, which means activation (ACT). The QOI or qualifier of interrogation code contained in this ASDU contains the interrogation group. In this case this is set to <20>, which means a general interrogation, that is all data is requested
- On receipt of this the controlled station first issues an activation confirmation in the monitoring direction. This is the same type 100 ASDU, but with cause of transmission <7>. It contains the same QOI data. The controlled station then assembles the requested data
- The controlling station may proceed to interrogate other stations without waiting for the returned data from this station
- When the station has the return data available, it will indicate that there is class 1 data available at the next link-layer poll, and will then send this data using ASDUs corresponding to the data types. These will carry the cause of transmission <20> indicating that they are being transmitted in response to a group 20 general interrogation command. When all of the station data is transmitted, it must send an action termination ACT TERM ASDU. This is a type 100 ASDU with cause of transmission <10>

Whilst Figure 9.3 shows a general interrogation directed at a particular station, there is no reason why a global general interrogation cannot be performed. A global general interrogation could be carried out using the global common address <0xFF or 0xFFFF>. This would call for data from all stations, which could either be all data or could be selected by group numbers, which might be used to implement a priority system.

Acquisition of events

In a modern SCADA system, efficient use of limited transmission bandwidth is achieved through the use of change-data processing. This approach involves sending just the changed data to master stations, rather than sending static data in every transmission to the master. When changes in data occur, these generate 'event' data. The event data contains the changed data items, and may also contain time-tags to indicate when the change occurred.

Events are generated at the application level of the controlled station, and are transmitted with the cause of transmission (COT) code '<3> spontaneous'. This indicates to the controlling station that they are change data.

Because of its efficiency in the use of communications bandwidth, event transmission is the normal means by which the controlling station database is kept current with the process state at controlled stations.

Cyclic data transmission

Cyclic data transmission is used to provide a periodic updating of process data to current values. This type of data is also referred to as 'static' data, which simply means current state data. Cyclic data transmission is normally used as a supplementary measure to change-data only processing, and it is normally executed at low priority.

Cyclic data is indicated by the cause of transmission COT code <1>. Examination of the set of ASDUs shows that only process information in the monitoring data without time tags, suitable for analog measurements have this COT. Cyclic data is intended for analog value updating only. Generally systems are also configured to report changes in analog values when they deviate from the previously sent value by a specified amount. This might typically be between 1% and 5% of span, depending on the importance of display accuracy. Cyclic data transmission augments this by ensuring that analog values are refreshed at regular intervals.

Cyclic data transmission is performed at the application function level of a controlled station. It periodically generates cyclic data and makes it available for transmission to the controlling station by the communications services.

Background scan

A background scan is very similar to the cyclic data transmission for analog values. It is for other non-time-tagged data types, such as digital status values. As for the cyclic scan, it is initiated by the controlled station rather than by the controlling or master station. The background scan operates on a low-priority continuous basis. Process values reported by cyclic data transmission are not sent with the background scan. The cause of transmission COT <2> is used in the monitor direction to identify ASDUs generated by a background scan.

Order of information transmission

When both event data and static data are transmitted from a station, it is important to ensure that processing occurs in the correct sequence. For example, if a change event for a point is generated after a static data read, but the receipt and processing of these at the controlling station occur in reverse order, then the resulting image for that point in the controlling station database will be incorrect. To prevent this occurring there is a defined priority order of transmission that a controlled station must follow when transmitting data to a controlling station.

This order is designed to ensure that the most topical data is delivered last. The specified order is shown in Table 9.1. This priority order does not prevent the controlling station from requesting data in any different order. For details of particular ASDU priorities the reader should refer directly to the standard, which lists specific type numbers for each priority.

Priority Sequence	Type of Information
1	End of initialisation
2	Commands
3	Event reporting Acquisition of transmission delay Clock synchronisation
4	Read command, Test procedure, reset process, parameter loading
5	Station interrogation, transmission of integrated totals
6	Cyclic data transmission and file transfer

Table 9.1
Order of transmission of information by controlled station

The reader may note an apparent conflict between the specified order of transmission, and the fact that the link layer operation causes transmission of class 2 data prior to commencing any class 1 data transmission from a controlled station. This is the case because it is only after a frame is transmitted with the ACD bit set that the controlling station becomes aware that there is class 1 data awaiting transmission.

It is probably for this reason that class 2 is generally used for cyclic analog data only, or not at all. With analog data an error in processing sequence is unlikely to cause any significant problem. All other data is typically treated as class 1, and is transmitted in the specified priority order, with current static data last.

Double transmission

Double transmission refers to the transmission of both non-time-tagged and time-tagged events arising from single status changes. This is allowed under IEC 60870-5 for all information types which may be transmitted spontaneously, that is with the cause of transmission COT code = <3>. This reflects the different usage of the time-tagged data from the untagged data. The time-tagged data is typically used to provide a sequence of event record which may be used for the display of trends, or directly by human operators to analyze event sequences. The non-time-tagged data however may be used directly in logical control of the system. These two types of data may be transmitted with different priority, with the non-time-tagged data being the higher priority.

9.1.3 Clock synchronization

Time synchronization is carried out in order to ensure that time-tagged data from outstations has accurate time information. All clocks are subject to time error, which will lead to a discrepancy between the master station time and the outstation time if synchronization is not carried out.

Synchronization is a simple process. The master station transmits a message containing the time according to its clock, to one or more outstations. This may be a broadcast message sent to all outstations. On receiving the new time, each outstation adjusts its own clock to the time in the message, plus a correction time to allow for the time the message would have taken to be transmitted and clocked into its own buffer.

Following this the outstation sends any previously buffered time-tagged data, and then sends a confirmation message containing its own clock time at the instant that the master station had transmitted the synchronization command. The master station may use this time to calculate the difference between outstation and master station times at the point of synchronizing.

The following two sub-sections describe the time synchronizing process in detail, and explain how the transmission delay, and from this the time correction, are determined.

Time synchronization process

Figure 9.4 illustrates how the time synchronization process is carried out. In the diagram the master station clock time is shown on the left side, transmission delay is shown horizontally over the communication path, and outstation time is shown at the right. Time also progresses from top to bottom in the diagram.

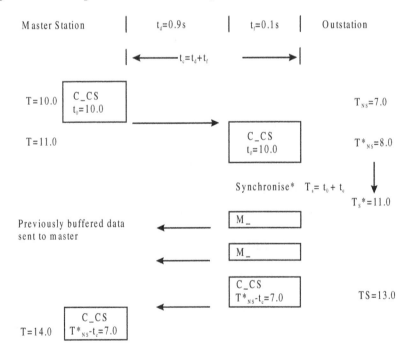

Figure 9.4
Time synchronization procedure

In Figure 9.4 the following time synchronization sequence occurs:

- At time T=10.0 the master station sends a synchronize command. The non-synchronized outstation time at this moment is T_{NS}=7.0
- The message arrives and is clocked into the outstation buffer at 1.0 second later, which is the sum of the transmission delay time plus the length of the message itself. This value is the correction time t_c
- The outstation now synchronizes its clock by setting it to the transmitted master station time plus its estimate of the correction time t_c. This point is marked by a star (*). Now the outstation time is synchronized T_S=11.0. This time is equal to the master station time provided that the estimate of the correction time t_c is good
- The master station sends an action confirmation ASDU back to the master station, but not before sending any time-tagged data accumulated prior to synchronization
- The action confirmation ASDU contains the unsynchronized outstation time at the instant of synchronization, minus the time correction t_c. This is therefore an estimate of the outstation time at the moment the master had issued the synchronization command. In this case it is $T^*_{NS} - t_c = 8.0 - 1.0 = 7.0$ s
- The master station receives this, and can calculate the time error that had accumulated at the outstation at the point of synchronization. In this case this value is $10.0 - 7.0 = 3.0$ s

It is clear that the accuracy of this process is dependent upon the accuracy with which the value of time correction can be made. This value is the sum of the message transmission delay time, and of the time length of the message. The latter is determined by the frame bit length in bits divided by the transmission speed in bits per second. The accuracy of this should be high. The transmission delay is a function of the communications network, and may be variable. It is the variability of the transmission delay that sets the limit on accuracy of clock synchronization. The process of measuring the transmission delay is discussed in the next section.

To ensure the reliability of time-tagged data, clock synchronization must be performed within an outstation configurable period. If this does not occur, the time-tagged data is sent with the invalid bit (IV) set in the time field.

One technical matter that is of interest primarily to system manufacturers is that this function is not purely an application level function. It requires components at the link layer level so that the time of transmission of the synchronization command can be correctly entered into the frame.

Acquisition of transmission delay

As is clear from the synchronizing procedure, the correct synchronization of an outstation's clock is dependent on the outstation knowing the delay time between the master station and itself. Measurement of this is carried out by the master station, and sent to the outstation for storing and use in subsequent time corrections. Clearly the delay time should be a function of the physical system, and should only require updating following system configuration changes.

The procedure uses the type 106 delay acquisition command C_CD. This is issued with COT = 6 (activation) by the master station, and then returned by the outstation. It carries the send time SDT in the control direction, and is sent back containing the return time SDT + t_R in the monitor direction. The value t_R is simply the time taken to turn around the message within the outstation. The master station records the time it is received back as RDT, the return delay time.

The master station then calculates the delay time as the average of the forward and reverse direction times, having subtracted the turnaround time within the outstation.

This average delay time is calculated by the following formula:

$t_D = [RDT - (SDT + t_R)] / 2$

The master station then sends the same type 106 delay acquisition command back to the outstation with the COT = 3 spontaneous. This is interpreted as 'load delay', and the outstation stores the value transmitted as the delay time. This may subsequently be used in clock synchronization.

As for the synchronizing process itself, the acquisition of delay time is a function with both application and link layer level components. In particular it is clear that the time that is returned from the outstation (SDT + t_R) must be the time at which the frame containing the ASDU is actually transmitted, not when it is buffered to await transmission. With an unbalanced link, of course this could be some time delay later, when the continuous link layer polling system polls that outstation for data.

9.1.4 Command transmission

Command transmission is described by the standard, and details are given for its operation. There are two standard command procedures:

- Direct command
- Select and execute command

Direct commands cause immediate changes, provided that there are no logical forces preventing operation of the particular outputs. Select and execute command sequences may be used for greater security against inadvertent error, both by human operators and by telecontrol system error.

Which type of command sequence is used is indicated in the QOC or qualifier of command field of the ASDU. The applicable ASDU types are those within the process information in control direction group.

These include:

- Type 45 Single Command C_SC
- Type 46 Double Command C_DC
- Type 47 Regulating Step Command C_RC
- Types 48–50 Set-point Commands C_SE

9.1.5 Other functions

The standards (IEC 60870-5-101 and IEC 60870-5-5) include details on the following application functions which are not covered in detail in this course. A brief summary is given for each of these following. The standards may be referred to for details if required.

- Transmission of integrated totals
- Parameter loading
- Test procedure
- File transfer

Transmission of integrated totals

This refers to the integration, or counting, of values in counters. The counting process is carried out over a specific and known time interval. If this interval is completed prior to the transmission of the counter values, then the terminology 'transmission of integrated totals' applies. Because of significant and indeterminate delays between acquisition and transmission that are typical of SCADA systems, these are invariably the type of totals that are transmitted. They are totals for time periods that have been completed.

There are two general forms of data transmission, totals and incremental values. If frozen copies of the counters at particular times are transmitted, then the incremental values in each period are calculated in the master station. If the outstation counters are reset after each freeze, then the frozen values transmitted are in fact incremental counts already.

Both types of count are accommodated by the standard. These are indicated within counter commands by the QCC qualifier of counter interrogation field.

Parameter loading

Parameters are values that change the way a system operates. The protocol provides for a two-phase procedure for parameter loading. This accommodates the common requirement to change a number of parameters simultaneously. After loading parameters, they are all activated simultaneously by a parameter activation command.

Test procedure

The test procedure is simply a loop-back test from the application level of one station to another, and then return. It causes no operational or state change. The test ASDU C_TS is transmitted to the controlled station and then returned by it.

File transfer

File transfer functions accommodate the fact that files may be larger than the maximum size of an ASDU, and therefore must be broken up for transmission. A file may be organized in sections and these into segments. The communications procedures are different for control and monitoring directions. Files generated in outstation devices are notified to the controlling station by sending a directory ASDU. When the controlling station uploads a file, the source file in the outstation is deleted, releasing buffer space for other files. Files transferred in the control direction are primarily used for downloading parameters or programs. This is controlled by the controlling station, and so directories are not used or transmitted in this direction.

9.2 Interoperability

9.2.1 General considerations

Interoperability under IEC 60870-5 refers to the ability of different systems to operate together to provide the telecontrol functions in accordance with the protocol. To ensure this will be the case, it is necessary to ensure that the various selections that can be made under the protocol are all compatible within a system.

Under the protocol there are a number of selections that can be made governing parameters such as address sizes, and selections of sub-sets of ASDUs for example. For any particular device, for example an intelligent electronic device, support of only certain

ASDU types may be provided. This makes sense as the device need only have the capabilities required to support its own functions. Other parameters such as communications speeds may be configurable items, that may be set to one of a number of possible values as required by the user.

To be able to check that a particular device is compatible with the specification chosen for a full system, a means of describing all of these parameters, and optional selections is required. IEC 60870-5-101 provides for this by including an interoperability section within the standard. This is section 8 of IEC 60870-5-101 Amendment 2. This is intended to be used by manufacturers to describe the specific functionality of their systems.

9.2.2 Interoperability document

The reader will benefit from examining either a blank interoperability statement by referring to the standard, or a completed one available for IEC 60870-5 compliant equipment. Due to copyright restriction this has not been included within this text.

The interoperability section has the following sections. These each have check boxes or list items that allow specification of the details for a particular device or system.

System or device selection:

- System definition
- Controlling station definition (master)
- Controlled station definition (slave)

Network configuration:

- Point-to-point
- Multiple point-to-point
- Multi-point-partyline
- Multi-point-star

Physical layer:

- Transmission speed (control direction)
- Transmission speed (monitor direction)

Link layer:

- Balanced or unbalanced
- Address field of link; octets, structure
- Maximum frame length
- Standard assignment of ASDUs to class 2 (types 9, 11, 13, 21)
- Special assignment of ASDUs to class 2 (list)

Application layer:

- Common address of ASDU; 1 or 2 octets
- Information object address; octets, structure
- Cause of transmission; 1 octet, or 2 with originator address
- Selection of ASDUs; full list, mark with X, R or B for using in standard, reverse or both directions
- Cause of transmission codes for each type (table with boxes)

Basic application functions:

- Station initialization
- Cyclic data transmission
- Read procedure
- Spontaneous transmission
- Double transmission; list of type numbers
- Station interrogation; checkbox list for groups 1–16 and global
- Clock synchronization
- Command transmission
- Transmission of integrated totals
- Parameter loading
- Parameter activation
- Test procedure

9.2.3 Certification and testing

Unlike for DNP3, there is no authority to provide certification of IEC 60870-5 compliance authorized directly by the IEC. However, there are commercial testing laboratories that do offer testing to this standard.

At website http://www.trianglemicroworks.com/iec60870-5 the 'Implementers of IEC 60870-5' page lists consultants including firms offering compliance testing to the standard. Also listed are firms that offer test sets that may be used for system testing. These include ASE, Cybertec, FGH, KEMA, PTI and Tele-Data.

9.3 Other information sources

IEC 60870-5 has no official user group, however there is a mail-list where a number of members of the IEC working group and other technical experts discuss and answer questions about the protocols.

This can be accessed from the trianglemicroworks website:

- http://www.trianglemicroworks.com/iec60870-5/index.htm

This site has a substantial list of implementers of the protocol, grouped by equipment type category in a similar manner to that available at the DNP3 website. It also provides access to technical papers and discussion records.

The following information about the mail-list is repeated from the website:

- The mail-list was established as a result of discussions at the IEC Technical Committee 57 Working Group 03 meeting in Lucerne (April 1998) concerning the likely interoperability of products claiming to conform to IEC 60870-5-101, the desire of users to obtain 'plug and play' products, and how best to help users and suppliers interpret the standard in a consistent way. The objective of the mail-list is to create a place implementers and users of IEC 60870-5 can discuss different interpretations of the specifications in an effort to establish a consensus opinion on each topic. The mail-list is open to anyone with an interest in IEC 60870-5 and there are no membership fees.

9.4 Network operation

9.4.1 General introduction

This sub-section covers the operation of the IEC 60870-5-101 (or T101) protocol over networks using standard transport profiles. This, in other words, is the operation over networks using the TCP/IP protocols. Since the early use of the T101 protocol there has been an increasing level of interest in being able to use standard network profiles to carry protocol messages. This has occurred no doubt with the ever increasing penetration and usage of local and wide area networks, which may offer a ready-made communications infrastructure that is attractive for SCADA due to savings that can be achieved over installing separate communications infrastructure.

The interest in doing this led to some attempts to encapsulate the T101 messages, including the link layer components, for transmission over networks. This is referred to briefly in the introduction to IEC 60870-5-104 which mentions the use of packet assembler disassembler (PAD) type stations to provide access for balanced communications. However, such an approach is not based on standardization and so could only be applied in limited circumstances.

The need for a standard for carrying the communications protocol over data networks was addressed with the release of IEC 60870-5-104 in 2000. This standardized the use of the application functions and data objects of the protocol with a different message transport mechanism, which completely replaced the link and physical layers specified by the T101 profile. The structure of this in terms of standards is shown in Table 9.2.

Layer	Source	Selections
User Process	IEC 60870-5-101	Application Functions
Application	IEC 60870-5-101	ASDUs and Application Information Elements
Transport		
Network	TCP/IP Transport and Network Protocol Suite	
Link		
Physical		

Table 9.2
Standards selection for IEC 60870-5-104

Table 9.2 shows that the user process functions and application level definitions of T101 have been retained, but that the levels below these have been replaced by the transport and network profiles of TCP/IP. The lower data link and physical layers are not specified at all as these are not implemented directly by users of T104. This is because the boundary of the protocol is at the network interface level.

Without imposing any limits on networks, the standard indicates the following examples of networks that might be used under TCP/IP:

- X.25
- FR (frame relay)
- ATM (asynchronous transfer mode)
- ISDN (integrated service data network)

9.4.2 Architecture

The general communications arrangement of T104 based equipment is a TCP/IP protocol stack interfacing to a local area network via an IEEE 802.3 compliant port. This is shown in Figure 9.5.

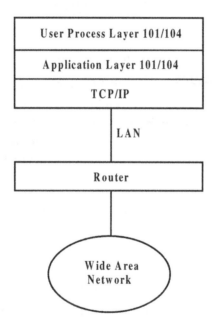

Figure 9.5
Architecture of IEC 60870-5-104

Figure 9.5 shows the T104 based device connecting to an IEEE 802.3 local area network (LAN). From the LAN messages can travel directly to other T104 devices on the LAN, or via routers to remotely located equipment such as a master station. Adaptation to the specific network beyond the router is a matter of selecting an appropriate router device.

If redundancy is required, this can be provided at the network level through multiple routers on the LAN. For a higher level of redundancy the equipment itself can be provided with more than one LAN network interface connection.

In addition to the LAN based interface, the protocol does allow for the use of a serial line interface in accordance with the TCP/IP protocol suite defined by RFC 2200 (refer to http://www.ietf.org for current RFCs). This protocol stack selections are shown in Figure 9.6 following, reproduced from IEC 60870-5-104.

Transport (layer 4)	RFC 793 (Transmission Control Protocol)	
Network (layer 3)	RFC 791 (Internet Protocol)	
Data Link (layer 2)	RFC 1661 (Point to Point Protocol PPP)	RFC 894 (Transmission of IP datagrams over ethernet networks)
	RFC 1662 (PPP /HDLC)	
Physical (layer 1)	X.21	IEEE 802.3
	Serial line	Ethernet

Figure 9.6
Protocol stack selections from RFC 2200

9.4.3 APDU structure

The application protocol data unit is the unit of information that is delivered by (or to) the application level to (or from) the underlying transport functions of the protocol for transmission. Under a general protocol definition, the APDU consists of a header containing control information, the APCI, plus data, termed the application service data unit or the ASDU. This is shown in Figure 9.7. For T101, however, the APCI header was not required and so the APDU was the same as the ASDU.

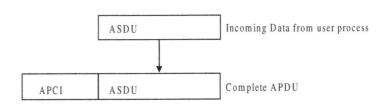

Figure 9.7
Formation of application protocol data unit

Under T104 the APCI is required and together with the ASDU as defined in T101 forms the APDU. The structure of the APDU including the APCI control field is shown in a vertical format in Figure 9.8.

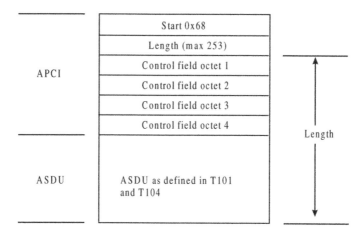

Figure 9.8
APDU including application protocol control information

In Figure 9.8 the ASDU structure is not detailed. The ASDUs are those of T010, with some additional ASDUs defined by T104.

9.4.4   Control field structure

There are three formats for the control field, designated the I, S, and U formats. Each version has the same length, which is four octets. The letters indicate the functions of the formats, which are information, supervisory, and unnumbered.

7	6	5	4	3	2	1	0	
		Send Sequence No.				1sb	0	Octet 1
msb		Send Sequence No.						Octet 2
		Receive Sequence No.				1sb	0	Octet 3
msb		Receive Sequence No.						Octet 4

Figure 9.9
Information (I) format control field

The I format control field is used for APDUs that contain an ASDU. That is, these control fields are used in APDUs that contain information. Note that this field is indicated by a zero in the first bit position.

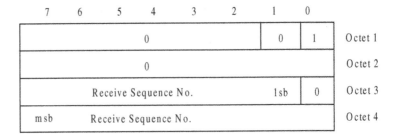

7	6	5	4	3	2	1	0	
0						0	1	Octet 1
0								Octet 2
Receive Sequence No.						1 sb	0	Octet 3
m sb	Receive Sequence No.							Octet 4

Figure 9.10
Supervisory (S) format control field

Figure 9.10 shows a supervisory format control field. This format is indicated by a 1 in the first bit position followed by a zero in the second bit position. There is only a receive sequence number in the field. This type is used for APDUs that contain only the APCI header. These do not have any information attached. It may be inferred therefore that the supervisory function is limited to controlling the transport of the APDUs.

7	6	5	4	3	2	1	0	
TESTFR		STOPDT		STARTDT		1	1	Octet 1
con	act	con	act	con	act			
0								Octet 2
0								Octet 3
0								Octet 4

Figure 9.11
Unnumbered control (U) format control field

Figure 9.11 shows the unnumbered control format control field. These are also used in APDUs that contain only the APCI. This control format is used as a start-stop mechanism for information flow. There are no sequence numbers. This control field may also be used where more than one connection is available between stations, and a changeover between connections is to be made without loss of data.

Where sequence numbers are used in these control fields, they are used to control the passage of APDUs over the network. Every APDU that is sent is given a sequence number. This occurs in both directions. The receiver of APDUs advises the sender of the highest sequence number received, and the sender uses this as a basis for re-sending ASDUs that may get lost. The receiver can use either an information transfer (I format) control field or a supervisory function (S format) control field to advise the sender of the sequence number. This will depend on whether the receiver is also sending information in the opposite direction.

The reader may recognize this system from elsewhere in this text. Very similar functionality is used in the HDLC protocol presented under Fundamentals of SCADA communications. Reviewing that material may assist understanding this process.

The reader may refer directly to the T104 standard (IEC 60870-5-104) for additional detail of the data transfer operations, however the information given here is sufficient for recognizing and understanding the structure of information that will be seen if packet analyzers are used to view the communications.

9.4.5   Port number and addresses

TCP/IP addresses are made up of a port number and an IP address. These are used at the transport (TCP) and network (IP) levels respectively. Each separate piece of equipment connected to a network has its own IP address, which is a special address assigned by the Internet Assigned Numbers Authority (IANA) to particular application process types. For IEC 60870-5-104 this number is 2404. This is the port number through which TCP/IP connections are established.

9.4.6   Set of ASDUs

The set of ASDUs defined under T104 is most of those under T101, plus a small set of additional ASDUs.

The changes from T101 set of ASDUs are:

- The time-tagged ASDUs with two-octet time-tags are not used. These are numbers <2, 4, 6, 8, 10, 12, 14, 16, 17, 18, 19>
- Type <104> test command is not used. A new Type <107> replaces this and includes a time-tag within the ASDU
- Command types <58, 59, 60, 61, 62, 63, and 64> are added. These are similar to the T101 commands <45 ..51>, but they each include a seven-octet time-tag

The reasons for the changes to the ASDU set derive from the fact that network communications can exhibit unpredictable delays, and can change the order of APDU delivery.

In the case of two-octet time-tags which have been deleted, it would be possible for an 'end of hour' transmission from an outstation to arrive out of order with respect to time-tagged data. This would mean that the hour for time-tagged data with only 2-octet times could be misinterpreted.

In the case of commands, the time-tagged command feature has been added, so that commands can be checked for currency. This reflects the possibility that a command APDU could be seriously delayed on the network, and subsequently cause an undesirable control action.

The additional command type numbers and descriptions are listed below. Their structure is not presented. It is identical to the T101 equivalent structure indicated, except that it has the seven-octet time appended. The ASDU label has a 'T' instead of an 'N', but is otherwise unchanged.

Type Number	T101 Equivalent* Type Number	Description
58	45	Single command with time tag CP56Time2a
59	46	Double command with time tag CP56Time2a
60	47	Regulating step command with time tag CP56Time2a
61	48	Set Point Commands, normalised value with time tag CP56Time2a
62	49	Set Point Commands, scaled value with time tag CP56Time2a
63	50	Set Point Commands, short floating-point number with time tag CP56Time2a
64	51	Single command with time tag CP56Time2a

*Same function without the time tag

Table 9.3
Command with time-tag ASDU types

9.4.7 Clock synchronization

Clock synchronization over networks is likely to be less reliable due to variable delays that occur due to queuing at network routing points. However, network service providers can specify worst case time delays, and provided that these are acceptable, then clock synchronization from the master station still makes sense. The clock synchronization function of T101 is largely retained, except that the link level functionality is removed.

10

Differences between DNP3 and IEC 60870

Objectives

When you have completed study of this chapter you should be able to:

- List the main differences between the DNP3 and the IEC 60870 standards
- List the main similarities between the DNP3 and the IEC 60870 standards

10.1   Comparing DNP3 and IEC 60870

10.1.1   General similarities

DNP3 and IEC 60870 have many similarities at a functional level, as well as in some technical details. These arise quite naturally from the common task that they provide a means of achieving. They also were developed out of the same basic framework and have some similarities in their message frames. It is probably useful, therefore, to begin by identifying their common features.

Common features of DNP3 and T101:

- High security data transmission (higher in DNP3)
- Polled and report-by-exception operation
- Unsolicited messages (limited in T101)
- Object based data definitions suitable for SCADA
- Time synchronization
- Time-stamped events
- Freeze and clear counters
- Select before operate control action
- Data groups or classes
- File download and upload

In functional terms at least, it is clear that the two protocols have many similarities.

10.1.2   Differences

In this section a number of areas are compared briefly to summarize the points of difference between T101 and DNP3.

10.1.3   Addressing

- T101 uses both link addresses and application addresses
- This gives greater flexibility in routing messages
- T101 has larger point address range, up to 3 bytes gives 16 777 216 addresses
- DNP3 uses link addresses only, no application layer addresses
- DNP3 link carries both source and destination addresses

Overall, T101 has greater flexibility in its addressing system, both by including data link and application level addresses, and through the use of variable address lengths. The benefit of variable lengths is that they allow savings on communications bandwidth when only small numbers of addresses are required.

Data link communications

- T101 uses unbalanced and balanced (limited to point–point only)
- T101 does not support unsolicited messages on multidrop communications
- DNP3 uses balanced communications only

Both DNP3 and IEC 60870-5-101 support balanced or peer–peer communications, however, IEC's balanced communications are limited to point-to-point configurations. This can be a significant limitation if a situation requiring a multidrop configuration is contemplated. An example would be where there are a large number of outstations connected to a limited bandwidth channel such as a VHF radio link. In such a case polling for data may require an unacceptable bandwidth, and DNP's support for multidrop balanced communications would be an advantage in implementing a reporting by exception system.

Frame format

- T101 uses FT1.2 frame; 8 bit checksum, length up to 255 byte
- T101 frames are fixed and variable length
- DNP3 uses FT3 frames; 16 bit CRC, length up to 255 byte
- DNP3 uses variable length only

When the fixed length frame option is used under T101, a very short and simple message is created in comparison to DNP's message. This reduces communications overheads substantially.

Application functions and data objects

Application functions:

- T101 allows only one control point per message
- T101 uses single character application acknowledgment
- DNP3 allows control over multiple points in one message

Data objects:

- T101 allows one type per message
- T101 combines function and data types in type code
- T101 data objects are oriented to substation communications
- DNP3 allows multiple data objects in one message
- DNP3 uses separate function codes
- DNP3 has one function code per message, applies to all data objects in message

There are considerable differences between T101 and DNP3 in the application functions and the data objects supported. The separation of functions and data objects in DNP3 provides perhaps greater flexibility, but also involves greater complexity.

Security

- T101 relies on data link confirm before clearing events
- DNP3 requires application confirms before clearing events
- Error checking is stronger in DNP3
- Both have select before operate

Whilst it is the case that DNP's error detection capability is stronger than for T101, whether or not this is significant would depend on the bit error rate on the communication lines as well as on the length of messages. Because T101 messages tend to be shorter than DNP3 messages, the overall effect may be not substantially different.

Interoperability

- T101 has no official certification procedures or authorities
- There are companies who provide testing to T101
- DNP3 has defined subset levels for IEDs
- DNP3 has defined conformance test procedures
- DNP3 has defined certification authorities in North America

The existence of testing procedures and authorities, combined with defined minimum implementation levels are recognized as strong features of DNP3. However, whilst DNP3 has established an early lead in this area, future developments may narrow this difference as use of the T101 standard evolves.

Complexity

In a number of respects T101 is a simpler protocol and may operate in a simpler manner. Some examples of this are:

- No separate application function codes
- Data objects are simpler, no variations as in DNP3
- Point addressing scheme is simpler than in DNP3
- Can be configured to have fixed length frames
- Can be configured to use unbalanced link layer transmissions
- This simplifies communications as collisions are avoided
- Uses single-byte ACK transmissions on data link layer
- FT1.2 format is simpler (but gives less error protection)
- No transport layer and only one data type per message simplifies parsing

On the other hand, it has been noted that T101 can have more low-level aspects that require configuration, which can increase difficulties during system integration. Also, although DNP3 is in a number of ways more complex, not all of the features have to be implemented. The minimum implementation sub-sets for DNP3 confine themselves to limited numbers of functions and addressing modes.

Efficiency

Some of the features of T101 such as the fixed frame length option, single character application acknowledgments, and less rigorous error checking can result in smaller messages. However, T101 may require a large number of messages to send information, so some of the benefit of reduced message overhead is lost. Without knowledge and analysis of the specific data to be predominantly carried on a system it is probably difficult to make any conclusions as to whether one or other protocol will operate more efficiently.

Where either protocol is to be carried over networks the message length will have a bearing on efficiency, because the message will be encapsulated within additional data. In this case the smaller messages of T101 could lead to a loss of efficiency in this situation.

Support for protocol

IEC 60870-5-101 is dominant in Europe compared to DNP3, but is confined to the electrical utility industry. DNP3 is at the same time becoming more recognized in Europe in the utility industry. An example of this is the use of IEEE Std 1379 'Recommended Practice for Data Communications Between Intelligent Electronic Devices and Remote Terminal Units in a Substation'. This recommended practice recognizes both DNP3 and T101 for use in this application. T101 and DNP3 are used to similar degrees in Asia, and DNP3 is dominant in Australia. T101 is supported by a number of major manufacturers as for DNP3.

In summary, it is clear that both protocols have substantial support, but that this varies with industry and geographic location.

Summary

Both IEC 60870-5-101 and DNP3 are open protocols that have been designed specifically for the telecontrol applications. They have been developed to meet common needs, have a common point of origin, and have emerged over a similar period of time. Both have also been developed to meet the needs of the electrical utility industry, although DNP3 has more data types that are weighted to general SCADA usage than for electrical utility usage particularly.

Comparison of the features of each has shown each has differences that may translate to benefits in some situations, and drawbacks in others. In a number of ways IEC appears to be a simpler protocol, but this will not necessarily translate to mean simpler implementation. DNP's implementation sub-set levels, defined test procedures and certification authorities together provide a sound basis for assuring interoperability of products from different manufacturers.

The choice between IEC 60870-5-101 or DNP3 for an organization will depend on many factors. In functional terms both achieve similar results. For the product developer, clearly the protocol supported will depend on the needs of customers, which will be derived from their industry and location. For many products support of both protocols will be essential.

10.2   Which one will win?

The choice between IEC or DNP3 for an organization will depend on many factors. In functional terms both achieve similar results. For the product developer, clearly the protocol supported will depend on the needs of customers, which will be derived from their industry and location. For many products, support of both protocols will be necessary. From the viewpoint of the user, this choice will be dictated by the existing installed system, or in the case of an entirely new system, from comparison of features of available equipment using one or the other protocol.

The fact is that both protocols are used on a world-wide scale and are here to stay for the foreseeable medium-term future.

In the longer term industry trends will have a significant bearing. The Utilities Communication Architecture (UCA) project has the potential to emerge as a major force to achieve interoperability and plug-and-play on a major scale. In this case, the extent to which the protocols adapt and integrate to this system may influence their ultimate longevity.

11

Intelligent electronic devices (IEDs)

Objectives

When you have completed study of this chapter you should be able to:

- Describe an IED
- Give typical examples of the functions expected of IEDs on the market

11.1 Definition

The term 'intelligent electronic device' (IED) is not a clear-cut definition, as for example the term 'protection relay' is. Broadly speaking, any electronic device that possesses some kind of local intelligence can be called an IED. In the protection and power system automation industry, the term really came into existence to describe a device that has versatile electrical protection functions, advanced local control intelligence, monitoring abilities and the capability of extensive communications directly to a SCADA system. That is the definition of an IED that will be applied throughout this chapter. The power system automation industry will be used as an example of an application of an IED in the following sections.

A multitude of relays from different manufacturers can perform the functions of protection, control, and monitoring (including measurement), but need the assistance of an RTU or communications processor, to which they are hardwired, to communicate with the SCADA supervisor. These devices may be called intelligent relays but are not included in the definition of an IED.

Similarly, some relays can communicate directly to a SCADA, but lack the control functionality. These relays are often used in conjunction with bay controllers, which provide the required control functions, to form a power system automation system. Again, these relays cannot be classified as IEDs.

The ability of an IED to perform all the functions of protection, control, monitoring, and upper level communications independently and without the aid of other devices like an RTU or communications processor (not including interface modules) is the identifying feature of an IED.

Note: The above definition refers to *ability*, and not to a specific application, where an IED may well communicate to an RTU, for example.

11.2 Functions

The functions of a typical IED can be classified into five main areas, namely protection, control, monitoring, metering and communications. Some IEDs may be more advanced than others, and some may emphasize certain functional aspects over others, but these main functionalities should be incorporated to a greater or lesser degree.

11.2.1 Protection

The protection functions of the IED evolved from the basic overcurrent and earth fault protection functions of the feeder protection relay (hence certain manufacturers named their IEDs 'feeder terminals'). This is due to the fact that a feeder protection relay is used on almost all cubicles of a typical distribution switchboard, and the fact that more demanding protection functions are not required enable the relay's microprocessor to be used for control functions. The IED is also meant to be as versatile as possible, and is not intended to be a specialized protection relay, for example generator protection. This also makes the IED affordable.

The following is a guideline of protection related functions that may be expected from the most advanced IEDs (the list is not all-inclusive, and some IEDs may not have all the functions). The protection functions are typically provided in discrete function blocks, which are activated and programmed independently.

- Non-directional three-phase overcurrent [low set, high set and instantaneous function blocks, with low set selectable as long time-, normal-, very-, or extremely inverse, or definite time]
- Non-directional earth fault protection [low set, high set and instantaneous function blocks]
- Directional three-phase overcurrent [low set, high set and instantaneous function blocks, with low set selectable as long time-, normal-, very-, or extremely inverse, or definite time]
- Directional earth fault protection [low set, high set and instantaneous function blocks]
- Phase discontinuity protection
- Three-phase overvoltage protection
- Residual overvoltage protection
- Three-phase undervoltage protection
- Three-phase transformer inrush/motor startup current detector
- Auto-reclosure function
- Underfrequency protection
- Overfrequency protection
- Synchro-check function
- Three-phase thermal overload protection

11.2.2   Control

Control functions include local and remote control, and are fully programmable:

- Local and remote control of up to twelve switching objects (open/close commands for circuit-breakers, isolators, etc)
- Control sequencing
- Bay level interlocking[1] of the controlled devices
- Status information[2]
- Information of alarm channels[2]
- HMI panel on device

Notes:

[1] Secure station level (interbay) interlocking demands peer-to-peer communications of <10 ms. This is not supported by all manufacturers' systems

[2] Status and alarm information is part of the control function blocks as they have a direct bearing on secure control functions

11.2.3   Monitoring

Monitoring includes the following functions:

- Circuit-breaker condition monitoring, including operation time counter, electric wear, breaker travel time, scheduled maintenance
- Trip circuit supervision
- Internal self-supervision
- Gas density monitoring (for SF6 switchgear)
- Event recording
- Other monitoring functions, like auxiliary power, relay temperature, etc

11.2.4   Metering

Metering functions include:

- Three-phase currents
- Neutral current
- Three-phase voltages
- Residual voltage
- Frequency
- Active power
- Reactive power
- Power factor
- Energy
- Harmonics
- Transient disturbance recorder (up to 16 analog channels)
- Up to twelve analog channels

11.2.5 Communications

Communication capability of an IED is one of the most important aspects of power system automation and is also the one aspect that clearly separates the different manufacturers' devices from one another regarding their level of functionality.

By definition, IEDs are able to communicate directly to a SCADA system, ie upper level communications. Different manufacturers use different communication protocols, although the most popular are DNP3 and Modbus.

An IED will, in addition to upper level communications, also have a serial port or optical interface to communicate directly to a substation PC or Laptop for configuration and data downloading purposes, should the SCADA link not be available or desirable in that instance.

12

Ethernet and TCP/IP networks

Objectives

When you have completed study of this chapter you should be able to:

- Describe the major hardware components of an IEEE 802.3 CSMA/CD network;
- Explain the method of connection of 10Base5, 10Base2 and 10BaseT networks;
- Explain the operation of the CSMA/CD protocol;
- List the fields in the Ethernet data frame;
- Describe the causes of Ethernet collisions and how to reduce them;
- Demonstrate how to apply the Ethernet design rules;
- Describe how the TCP/IP protocols fit into an Ethernet frame;
- Describe the structure and operation of the Internet protocol (IP);
- Describe the structure and operation of the transmission control protocol (TCP);
- Describe the structure and operation of the user datagram protocol (UDP);
- Describe the TCP/IP application level protocols

12.1   IEEE 802.3 CSMA/CD ('Ethernet')

The Ethernet network concept was developed by Xerox Corporation at its Palo Alto Research Center (PARC) in the mid-seventies. It was based on the work done by researchers at the University of Hawaii where there were campus sites on the various islands. Its ALOHA network was set up using radio broadcasts to connect the various sites. This was colloquially known as their 'Ethernet' since it used the 'ether' as the transmission medium and created a network 'net' between the sites. The philosophy was quite straightforward. Any station that wanted to broadcast to another station would do so immediately. The receiving stations then had a responsibility to acknowledge the message; thus advising the original transmitting station of a successful reception of the original message. This primitive system did not rely on any detection of collisions (two radio stations transmitting at the same time) but rather waited for an acknowledgment back within a predefined time.

The initial system installed by Xerox was so successful that they soon applied the system to their other sites typically connecting office equipment to shared resources such as printers and large computers acting as repositories of large databases, for example.

In 1980, the Ethernet Consortium consisting of Xerox, Digital Equipment Corporation and Intel (sometimes called the DIX consortium) issued a joint specification based on the Ethernet concepts and known as the Ethernet Blue Book 1 specification. This was later superseded by the Ethernet Blue Book 2 specification, which was offered to the IEEE as a standard. In 1983, the IEEE issued the 802-3 standard for Carrier Sense; Multiple Access; Collision Detect LANs based on the Ethernet standard which gave this networking standard even more credibility.

As a result of this, there are three standards in existence. The first – often termed Ethernet Version 1 – can be disregarded as very little equipment based on this standard is still in use. Ethernet Version 2 or 'Blue Book Ethernet' is, however, still in use and there is a potential for incompatibility with the IEEE 802.3 standard. Despite the generic term 'Ethernet' being applied to all CSMA/CD networks, it should be reserved for the original DIX standard. This manual will continue with popular use and refer to all the LANs of this type as Ethernet, unless it is important to distinguish between them.

Ethernet uses the CSMA/CD access method. This gives a system that can operate with little delay, if lightly loaded, but the access mechanism can fail completely if too heavily loaded. Ethernet is widely used commercially, and the network interface cards (NICs) are relatively cheap and produced in vast quantities. Because of its probabilistic access mechanism, there is no guarantee of message transfer and messages cannot be prioritized. It is becoming more widely used industrially despite these disadvantages.

12.2   Physical layer

The 802.3 standard defines a range of cable types that can be used for a network based on this standard. They include coaxial cable, twisted pair cable and fiber optic cable. In addition, there are different signaling standards and transmission speeds that can be utilized. These include both baseband and broadband signaling, and speeds of 1 Mbps and 10 Mbps. The standard is continuing to evolve, and this manual will look at 100 Mbps and gigabit Ethernet systems later.

The IEEE 802.3 standard documents (ISO 8802.3) support various cable media and transmission rates up to 10 Mb/s as follows:

- **10Base2**
  Ethernet and TCP/IP networks thin wire coaxial cable (0.25 inch diameter), 10 Mbps, single cable bus

- **10Base5**
  Thick wire coaxial cable (0.5 inch diameter), 10 Mbps, single cable bus

- **10BaseT**
  Unscreened twisted pair cable (0.4 to 0.6 mm conductor diameter), 10 Mbps, twin cable bus

- **10BaseF**
  Optical fiber cables, 10 Mbps, twin fiber bus

- **1Base5**

  Unscreened twisted pair cables, 1 Mbps, twin cable bus

- **10Broad36**

  Cable television (CATV) type cable, 10 Mbps, broadband

12.2.1   10Base5 systems

This is a coaxial cable system and uses the original cable for Ethernet systems – generically called 'Thicknet'. It is a coaxial cable, of 50 ohm characteristic impedance, and yellow or orange in color. The naming convention for 10Base5: means 10 Mbps; baseband signaling on a cable that will support 500 meter segment lengths. It is difficult to work with, and so cannot normally be taken to the node directly. Instead, it is laid in a cabling tray etc and the transceiver electronics (medium attachment unit, MAU) is installed directly on the cable. From there an intermediate cable, known as an attachment unit interface (AUI) cable is used to connect to the NIC. This cable can be a maximum of 50 meters long, compensating for the lack of flexibility of placement of the segment cable. The AUI cable consists of 5 individually shielded pairs - two each (control and data) for both transmit and receive; plus one for power.

Cutting the cable and inserting an N-connector and a coaxial Tee or more commonly by using a 'bee sting' or 'vampire' tap can make the MAU connection to the cable. This is a mechanical connection that clamps directly over the cable. Electrical connection is made via a probe that connects to the center conductor and sharp teeth which physically puncture the cable sheath to connect to the braid. These hardware components are shown in Figure 12.1.

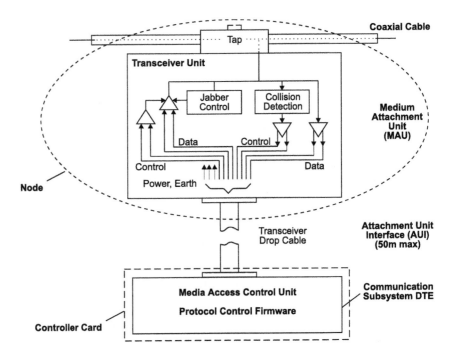

Figure 12.1
10Base5 hardware components

The location of the connection is important to avoid multiple electrical reflections on the cable, and the Thicknet cable is marked every 2.5 meters with a black or brown ring to indicate where a tap should be placed. Fan out boxes can be used if there are a number of nodes for connection, allowing a single tap to feed each node as though it was individually connected. The connection at either end of the AUI cable is made through a 25-pin D-connector, with a slide latch, often called a DIX connector after the original consortium.

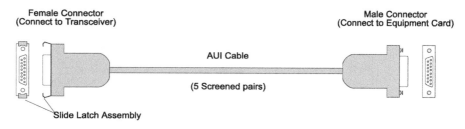

Figure 12.2
AUI cable connectors

There are certain requirements if this cable architecture is used in a network. These include:

- Segments must be less than 500 meters in length to avoid signal attenuation problems
- No more than 100 taps on each segment ie not every potential connection point can support a tap
- Taps must be placed at integer multiples of 2.5 meters
- The cable must be terminated with a 50 ohm terminator at each end
- It must not be bent at a radius exceeding 24.4 cm or 10 inches
- One end of the cable must be earthed

The physical layout of a 10Base5 Ethernet segment is shown in Figure 12.3.

The Thicknet cable was extensively used as a backbone cable until recently but 10BaseT and fiber is now far more popular. Note that when a MAU (tap) and AUI cable are used, the on board transceiver on the NIC is not used. Rather, there is a transceiver in the MAU and this is fed with power from the NIC via the AUI cable. Since the transceiver is remote from the NIC, the node needs to be aware that the termination can detect collisions if they occur. This confirmation is performed by a signal quality error (SQE), or heartbeat, test function in the MAU. The SQE signal is sent from the MAU to the node on detecting a collision on the bus. However, on completion of every frame transmission by the MAU, the SQE signal is asserted to ensure that the circuitry remains active, and that collisions can be detected. You should be aware that not all components support SQE test and mixing those that do with those that don't could cause problems. Specifically, if an NIC was to receive a SQE signal after a frame had been sent, and it was not expecting it, the NIC could think it was seeing a collision. In turn, as you will see later in the manual, the NIC will then transmit a jam signal.

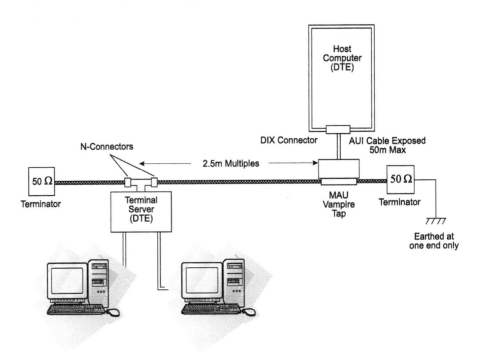

Figure 12.3
10Base5 ethernet segment

12.2.2   10Base2 systems

The other type of coaxial cable Ethernet networks is 10Base2 and is often referred to as 'Thinnet' or sometimes 'thinwire Ethernet'. It uses type RG-58 A/U or C/U with a 50 ohm characteristic impedance and of 5 mm diameter. The cable is normally connected to the NICs in the nodes by means of a BNC T-piece connector, and represents a daisy chain approach to cabling.

Connectivity requirements include:

- It must be terminated at each end with a 50 ohm terminator
- The maximum length of a cable segment is 185 meters and NOT 200 meters
- No more than 30 transceivers can be connected to any one segment
- There must be a minimum spacing of 0.5 meters between nodes
- It may not be used as a link segment between two 'Thicknet' segments
- The minimum bend radius is 5 cm

The physical layout of a 10Base2 Ethernet segment is shown in Figure 12.4.

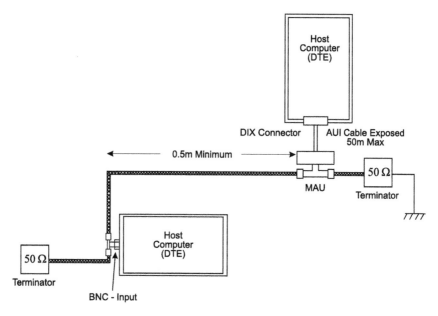

Figure 12.4
10Base2 ethernet segment

The use of Thinnet cable was, and remains, very popular as a cheap and relatively easy way to set up a network. However, there are disadvantages with this approach. A cable fault can bring the whole system down very quickly. To avoid such a problem, the cable is often taken to wall connectors with a make–break connector incorporated. The connection to the node can then be made by 'fly leads' of the same cable type. It is important to take the length of these fly leads into consideration in any calculation on cable length! There is also provision for remote MAUs in this system, with AUI cables making the node connection, in a similar manner to the Thicknet connection.

12.2.3   10BaseT

The 10BaseT standard for Ethernet networks uses AWG24 unshielded twisted pair (UTP) cable for connection to the node. The physical topology of the standard is a star, with nodes connected to a wiring hub, or concentrator. Concentrators can then be connected to a backbone cable that may be coax or fiber optic. The node cable can be category 3, although you would be well advised to consider category 5 for all new installations. This will allow an upgrade path as higher speed networks become more common, and given the small proportion of cable cost to total cabling cost, will be a worthwhile investment. The node cable has a maximum length of 100 meters; consists of two pairs for receive and transmit and is connected via RJ45 plugs. The wiring hub can be considered as a local bus internally, and so the topology is still considered as a logical bus topology. Figure 12.5 shows schematically how the 10BaseT nodes are interconnected by the hub.

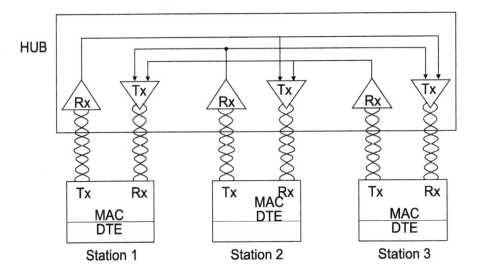

Figure 12.5
Schematic 10BaseT system

Collisions are detected by the NIC and so an input signal must be retransmitted by the hub on all output pairs. The electronics in the hub must ensure that the stronger retransmitted signal does not interfere with the weaker input signal. The effect is known as far end crosstalk (FEXT), and is handled by special adaptive crosstalk echo cancellation circuits.

The standard has become increasingly popular for new networks, although there are some disadvantages that should be recognized:

- The cable is not very resistant to electrostatic electrical noise, and may not be suitable for some industrial environments
- Whilst the cable is inexpensive, there is the additional cost of the associated wiring hubs to be considered
- The node cable is limited to 100 m

Advantages of the system include:

- Intelligent hubs are available that can determine which spurs from the hub receive information. This improves on the security of the network – a feature that has often been lacking in a broadcast, common media network such as Ethernet
- Flood wiring can be installed in a new building, providing many more wiring points than are initially needed, but giving great flexibility for future expansion. When this is done, patch panels – or punch down blocks – are often installed for even greater flexibility

12.2.4   10BaseF

This standard, like the 10BaseT standard, is based on a star topology using wiring hubs. It consists of three architectures. These are:

- **10BaseFL**
  The fiber link segment standard that is basically a 2 km upgrade to the existing fiber optic inter repeater link (FOIRL) standard. The original FOIRL

as specified in the 802.3 standard was limited to a 1 km fiber link between two repeaters, with a maximum length of 2.5 km if there are 5 segments in the link. Note that this is a link between two repeaters in a network, and cannot have any nodes connected to it

- **10BaseFP**
  A star topology network based on the use of a passive fiber optic star coupler. Up to 33 ports are available per star, and each segment has a maximum length of 500 m. The passive hub is completely immune to external noise and is an excellent choice for noisy industrial environments

- **10BaseFB**
  A fiber backbone link segment in which data is transmitted synchronously. It is designed only for connecting repeaters, and for repeaters to use this standard, they must include a built in transceiver. This reduces the time taken to transfer a frame across the repeater hub. The maximum link length is 2 km, although up to 15 repeaters can be cascaded, giving great flexibility in network design

12.2.5   10Broad36

This architecture, whilst included in the 802.3 standard, is no longer installed as a new system. This is a broadband version of Ethernet, and uses a 75 ohm coaxial cable for transmission. Each transceiver transmits on one frequency and receives on a separate one. The Tx/Rx streams require a 14 MHz bandwidth and an additional 4 MHz is required for collision detection and reporting. The total bandwidth requirement is thus 36 MHz. The cable is limited to 1800 meters because each signal must traverse the cable twice, so the worst case distance is 3600 m. It is this figure that gives the system its nomenclature.

12.2.6   1Base5

This architecture, whilst included in the 802.3 standard, is no longer installed as a new system. It is hub based and uses UTP as a transmission medium over a 500 meter maximum length. However, signaling is 1 Mbps, and this means special provision must be made if it is to be incorporated in a 10 Mbps network. It has been superseded by 10BaseT.

12.3   Signaling methods

Ethernet signals are encoded using the Manchester encoding scheme. This method allows a clock to be extracted at the receiver end to synchronize the transmission/reception process. The encoding is performed by an exclusive or between a 20 MHz clock signal and the data stream. In the resulting signal, a 0 is represented by a high to low change at the center of the bit cell, whilst a 1 is represented by a low to high change at the center of the bit cell. There may or may not be transitions at the beginning of a cell as well, but these are ignored at the receiver. The transitions in every cell allow the clock to be extracted, and synchronized with the transmitter.

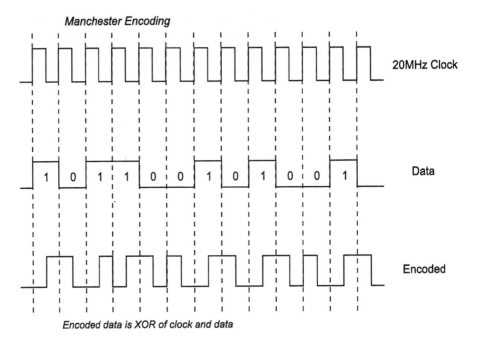

Figure 12.6
Manchester encoding

The voltage swings were from –0.225 to –1.825 volts in the original Ethernet specification. In the 802.3 standard, voltages on coax cables are specified to swing between 0 and –2.05 volts with a rise and fall time of 25 ns at 10 Mbps.

12.4 Medium access control

Essentially, the method for access control used is one of contention. As was described in the first section on this architecture, each node has a connection via a transceiver to the common bus. As a transceiver, it can both transmit and receive at the same time. Each node can be in any one of three states at any time.

These states are:

- Idle, or listen
- Transmit
- Contention

In the idle state, the node merely listens to the bus, monitoring all traffic that passes. If a node then wishes to transmit information, it will defer whilst there is any activity on the bus, since this is the 'carrier sense' component of the architecture. At some stage, the bus will become silent, and the node, sensing this, will then commence its transmission. It is now in the transmit mode, and will both transmit and listen at the same time. This is because there is no guarantee that another node at some other point on the bus has not also started transmitting having recognized the absence of traffic.

If this other node has indeed started transmitting, there will be a short delay as the two signals propagate towards each other on the cable, and then there will be a collision of signals. Quite obviously, the two transmissions cannot coexist on the common bus, since there is no mechanism for the mixed analog signals to be 'unscrambled'. The transceiver quickly detects this collision, since it is monitoring both its input and output and recognizes the difference. The node now goes into the third state of contention. The node will continue to transmit for a short time – the jam signal – to ensure the other transmitting node detects the contention, and then performs a back-off algorithm to determine when it should again attempt to transmit its waiting frames.

12.5   Frame transmission

When a frame is to be transmitted, the medium access control monitors the bus and defers to any passing traffic. After a period of 96 bit times, known as the interframe gap, to allow the passing frame to be received and processed by the destination node, the transmission process commences. Since there is a finite time for this transmission to propagate to the ends of the bus cable, and thus ensure that all nodes recognize that the medium is busy, the transceiver turns on a collision detect circuit whilst the transmission takes place. In fact, once a certain number of bits (576 bits in a 10 Mbps system) have been transmitted, provided that the network cable segment specifications have been complied with, the collision detection circuitry can be disabled. If a collision should take place after this, it will be the responsibility of higher protocols to request retransmission – a far slower process than the hardware collision detection process.

Here is a good reason to comply with cable segment specifications! This initial 'danger' period is known as the collision window, and is effectively twice the time interval for the first bit of a transmission to propagate to all parts of the network. The slot time for the network is then defined as the worst case time delay that a node must wait before it can reliably know that a collision has occurred.

It is defined as:

Slot time = 2 * (transmission path delay) + safety margin

For a 10 Mbps system, the slot time is FIXED as 512 bits or 64 octets.

12.6   Frame reception

The transceiver of each node is constantly monitoring the bus for a transmission signal. As soon as one is recognized, the NIC activates a carrier sense signal to indicate that transmissions cannot be made. The first bits of the MAC frame are a preamble and consist of 56 bits of 1010 etc. On recognizing these, the receiver synchronizes its clock, and converts the Manchester encoded signal back into binary form. The eighth octet is a start of frame delimiter, and this is used to indicate to the receiver that it should strip off the first eight octets and commence determining whether this frame is for its node by reading the destination address. If the address is recognized, the data is loaded into a frame buffer within the NIC.

Further processing then takes place, including the calculation and comparison of the frame CRC, checking with the transmitted CRC, checking that the frame contains an integral number of octets and is either too short or too long. Provided all is correct, the frame is passed to the logical link control (LLC) layer for further processing.

12.7   Collisions

You should recognize that collisions are a normal part of a CSMA/CD network. The monitoring and detection of collisions is the method by which a node ensures unique access to the shared medium. It is only a problem when there are excessive collisions. This reduces the available bandwidth of the cable and slows the system down while retransmission attempts occur. There are many reasons for excessive collisions and you will investigate these shortly.

The principle of collision cause and detection is shown in the following diagram.

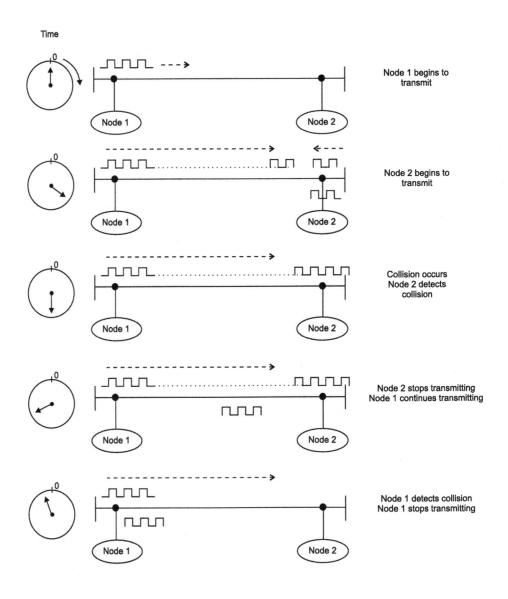

Figure 12.7
CSMA/CD collisions

Assume that both node 1 and node 2 are in listen mode and node 1 has frames queued to transmit. All previous traffic on the medium has ceased ie there is no carrier, and the interframe gap from the last transmission has timed out. Node 1 now commences to transmit its preamble signal, which immediately commences to propagate both left and right on the cable. At the left end, the termination resistance absorbs the transmission, but the signal continues to propagate to the right. However, the MAC sublayer in node 2 has also been given a frame to transmit from the LLC sublayer, and since the node 'sees' a free cable, it too commences to transmit its preamble. Again, the signals propagate on to the cable, and some short time later they 'collide'. Almost immediately, node 2's transceiver recognizes that the signals on the cable are corrupted, and the logic incorporated on the NIC asserts a collision detect signal. This causes node 2 to send a jam signal of 32 bits of random data, and then stop transmitting. In fact, the standard allows any data to be sent as long as, by design, it is not the value of the CRC field of the frame. It appears that most nodes will send the next 32 bits of the data frame as a jam, since that is instantly available.

This jam signal continues to propagate along the cable, as a contention signal since it is 'mixed' with the signal still being transmitted from node 1. Eventually, node 1 recognizes the collision, and goes through the same jam process as node 2. You can see from this that the frame from node 1 must be at least twice the end-to-end propagation delay of the network, or else the collision detection will not work correctly. The jam signal from node 1 will continue to propagate across the network until absorbed at the far end terminator, meaning that the system vulnerable period is three times the end-to-end propagation delay.

After the jam sequence has been sent, the transmission is halted. The node then schedules a retransmission attempt after a random delay controlled by a process known as the truncated binary exponential backoff algorithm. The length of the delay is chosen so that it is a compromise between reducing the probability of another collision and delaying the retransmission for an unacceptable length of time. The delay is always an integer multiple of the slot time. In the first attempt, the node will choose, at random, either one or zero slot times delay. If another collision occurs, the delay will be chosen at random from 0, 1, 2 or 3 slot times, thus reducing the probability that a further collision will occur. This process can continue for up to 10 attempts, with a doubling of the range of slot times available for the node to delay transmission at each attempt. After ten attempts, the node will attempt 6 more retries, but the slot times available for the delay period will remain as they were at the tenth attempt. After 16 attempts, it is likely that there is a problem on the network and the node will cease attempting to retransmit.

12.8   MAC frame format

The basic frame format for an 802.3 network is shown below. There are eight fields in each frame, and they will be described in detail.

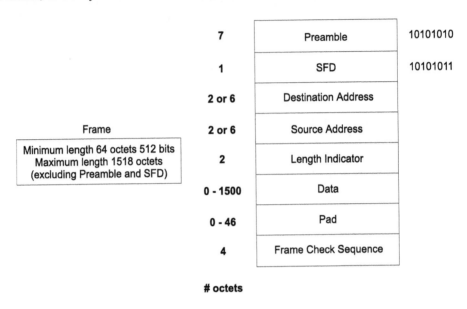

Figure 12.8
MAC frame format

12.8.1   Preamble

This field consists of 7 octets of the data pattern 10101010. The preamble is used by the receiver to synchronize its clock to the transmitter.

12.8.2   Start frame delimiter

This single octet field consists of the data 10101011. It enables the receiver to recognize the commencement of the address fields.

12.8.3   Source and destination address

These are the physical addresses of both the source and destination nodes. The fields can be 2 or 6 octets long, although the six octet standard is the most common. The six octet field is split into two three octet blocks. The first three octets describe the block number to which all NICs of this type belong. This number is the license number and all cards made by this company have the same number. The second block refers to the device identifier, and each card will have a unique address under the terms of the license to manufacture. This means there are 2^{48} unique addresses for Ethernet cards.

There are three addressing modes that are available. These are:

- **Broadcast**
  The destination address is set to all 1s or FFFFFFFFFFFF

- **Multicast**
  The first bit of the destination address is set to a 1. It provides group restricted communications

- **Individual, or point-to-point**
  First bit of the address set to 0, and the rest set according to the target destination node

12.8.4 Length

A two octet field that contains the length of the data field. This is necessary since there is no end delimiter in the frame.

12.8.5 Information

The information that has been handed down from the LLC sub layer.

12.8.6 Pad

Since there is a minimum length of the frame of 64 octets (512 bits or 576 bits if the preamble is included) that must be transmitted to ensure that the collision mechanism works, the pad field will pad out any frame that does not meet this minimum specification.

This pad, if incorporated, is normally random data. The CRC is calculated over the data in the pad field. Once the CRC checks OK, the receiving node discards the pad data, which it recognizes by the value in the length field.

12.8.7 FCS

A 32-bit CRC value that is computed in hardware at the transmitter and appended to the frame. It is the same algorithm used in the 802.4 and 802.5 standard.

12.9 Difference between 802.3 and Ethernet

As has already been discussed, there is a difference between an 802.3 network and a Blue Book Ethernet network. These differences are primarily in the frame structure and are tabulated below.

802.3 Network	Ethernet Network
Star topology supported using UTP, fiber etc	Only supports bus topology
Baseband and broadband signaling	Baseband only
Data link layer divided into LLC and MAC	No subdivision of DLL
7 octets of preamble plus SFD	8 bytes of preamble with no separate SFD
Length field in data frame	Field used to indicate the higher level protocol using the data link service
SQE can be used as network management device	SQE can only be used in version 2.0

Table 12.1
Differences between IEEE 802.3 and Blue Book Ethernet (V2)

The significant difference in the frame is the length field in 802.3 is interpreted as the higher protocol field in Ethernet. Since an 802.3 frame cannot be longer than 1500 bytes, the values in the protocol type field of the Ethernet V2 frame commence at 1500. This allows protocol analyzers to recognize one type of frame as opposed to the other.

12.10   Reducing collisions

The main reasons for collision rates on an Ethernet network are:

- The number of packets per second;
- The signal propagation delay between transmitting nodes;
- The number of stations initiating packets;
- The bandwidth utilization.

A few suggestions on reducing collisions in an Ethernet network are:

- Keep all cables as short as possible;
- Keep all high activity sources and their destinations as close as possible. Possibly isolate these nodes from the main network backbone with switches/ bridges/routers to reduce backbone traffic;
- Use buffered repeaters rather than bit repeaters;
- Check for unnecessary broadcast packets that are aimed at non-existent nodes;
- Remember that the monitoring equipment to check out network traffic can contribute to the traffic (and the collision rate).

12.11   Ethernet design rules

The following design rules on length of cable segment, node placement and hardware usage should be strictly observed.

12.11.1   Length of the cable segment

It is important to maintain the overall Ethernet requirements as far as the length of the cable is concerned. Each segment has a particular maximum length allowable. For example, 10Base2 allows 200 m maximum length. The recommended maximum length is 80% of this figure. Some manufacturers advise that you can disregard this limit with their equipment. This can be a risky strategy and should be carefully considered.

System	Maximum	Recommended
10Base5	500m	400m
10Base2	185m	150m
10BaseT	100m	80m
1Base5	500m	400m

Table 12.2
Maximum of recommended cable lengths

Cable segments need not be made from a single homogenous length of cable, and may comprise multiple lengths joined by coaxial connectors (two male plugs and a connector barrel). Although ThickNet (10Base5) and ThinNet (10Base2) cables have the same nominal 50 ohm impedance they can only be mixed within the same 10Base2 cable segment to achieve greater segment length.

To achieve maximum performance on 10Base5 cable segments, it is preferable that the total segment be made from one length of cable or from sections off the same drum of cable. If multiple sections of cable from different manufacturers are used, then these should be standard lengths of 23.4 m, 70.2 m or 117 m ($\pm$ 0.5 m), which are odd multiples of 23.4 m (half wavelength in the cable at 5 MHz). These lengths ensure that reflections from the cable-to-cable impedance discontinuities are unlikely to add in phase. Using these lengths exclusively a mix of cable sections should be able to be made up to the full 500 m segment length.

If the cable is from different manufacturers and you suspect potential mismatch problems, you should check that signal reflections due to impedance mismatches do not exceed 7% of the incident wave.

12.11.2 Maximum transceiver cable length

In 10Base5 systems the maximum length of the transceiver cables is 50 m but it should be noted that this only applies to specified IEEE 802.3 compliant cables. Other AUI cables using ribbon or office grade cables can only be used for short distances (less than 12.5 m) so check the manufacturer specifications for these!

12.11.3 Node placement rules

Connection of the transceiver media access units (MAU) to the cable causes signal reflections due to their bridging impedance. Placement of the MAUs must therefore be controlled to ensure that reflections from them do not significantly add in phase.

In 10Base5 systems the MAUs are spaced at 2.5 m multiples, coinciding with the cable markings.

In 10Base2 systems the minimum MAU spacing is 0.5 m.

12.11.4 Maximum transmission path

The maximum transmission path is made of five segments connected by four repeaters. The total number of segments can be made up of a maximum of three coax segments containing station nodes and two link segments, having no intermediate nodes. This is summarized as the 5-4-3-2 rule. These link segments are 10BaseFL fiber links as specified in IEEE 802.3.

5 segments 4 repeaters 3 coax segments 2 link segments	OR	5 segments 4 repeaters 3 link segments 2 coax segments

Table 12.3
5-4-3-2 rule

It is important to verify that the above transmission rules are met by all paths between any two nodes on the network.

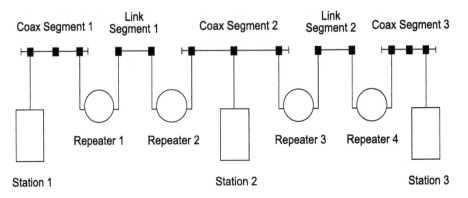

Figure 12.9
Maximum transmission path

Note that the maximum sized network of four repeaters supported by IEEE 802.3 can be susceptible to timing problems. The maximum configuration is limited by propagation delay.

Note that 10Base2 segments should not be used to link 10Base5 segments.

12.11.5   Maximum network size

10Base5	=	2800 m node to node
		(5 @ 500 m segments + 4 repeater cables + 2 AUI)
10Base2	=	925 m node to node (5 @ 185 m segments)
10BaseT	=	100 m node to hub

12.11.6   Repeater rules

Repeaters are connected to transceivers that count as one node on the segments.

Special transceivers are used to connect repeaters and these do not implement the signal quality error test (SQE).

Fiber optic repeaters are available giving up to 3000 m links at 10 Mbps. Check the vendor's specifications for adherence with IEEE 802.3 repeater performance and compliance with the fiber optic inter repeater link (FOIRL) standard.

12.11.7   Cable system grounding

Grounding has safety and noise connotations. IEEE 802.3 states that the shield conductor of each coaxial cable shall make electrical contact with an effective earth reference at one point only.

The single point earth reference for an Ethernet system is usually located at one of the terminators. Most terminators for Ethernet have a screw terminal to which a ground lug can be attached using a braided cable preferably to ensure good earthing.

Ensure that all other splices, taps or terminators are jacketed so that no contact can be made with any metal objects. Insulating boots or sleeves should be used on all inline coaxial connectors to avoid unintended earth contacts.

12.11.8   Fast Ethernet

Fast Ethernet provides a transmission speed of 100 Mbps, ten times faster than that of 'ordinary' Ethernet. It does, however, retain the same frame format. It is described by two standards, namely IEEE 802.3u and IEEE 802.3y.

IEEE 802.3u defines three different versions based on the physical media namely 100Base-TX (which uses two pairs of category 5 UTP or STP), 100Base-T4 (which uses four pairs of wires of category 3, 4 or 5 UTP) and 100Base-FX (which uses multimode or single-mode fiber optic cable).

IEEE 802.3y, on the other hand, defines 100Base-T2 which uses two pairs of wires of category 3, 4 or 5 UTP.

One of the limitations of the 100Base-T systems is the size of the collision domain, which is 250 m. This is the maximum sized network in which collisions can be detected, being one tenth of the size of the maximum 10 Mbps network. This limits the distance between our workstation and hub to 100 m, the same as for 10Base-T, but usually only one hub is allowed in a collision domain. This means that networks larger than 200 m must be logically connected together by store and forward type devices such as bridges, routers or switches. However, this is not a bad thing, since it segregates the traffic within each collision domain, reducing the number of collisions on the network. The use of bridges and routers for traffic segregation, in this manner, is often done on industrial CSMA/CD networks.

The dominant 100Base-T system is 100Base-TX which accounts for about 95% of all fast Ethernet shipments. The 100Base-T4 systems were developed to use four pairs of category 3 cable; however few users had the spare pairs available and T4 systems are not capable of full-duplex operation, so this system has not been widely used. With category 3 cable diminishing in importance, it is not expected that the 100Base-T2 systems will become significant.

12.11.9   Gigabit Ethernet

Gigabit Ethernet uses the same 802.3 frame format as 10 Mbps and 100 Mbps Ethernet systems. It operates at ten times the clock speed of fast Ethernet at 1 Gbps. By retaining the same frame format as the earlier versions of Ethernet, backward compatibility is assured with earlier versions, increasing its attractiveness by offering a high bandwidth connectivity system to the Ethernet family of devices.

Gigabit Ethernet is defined by the IEEE 802.3z standard. This defines three different physical layers: 1000Base-LX and 1000Base-SX using fiber and 1000Base-CX using copper. These physical layers were originally developed by IBM for the ANSI fiber channel systems to reduce the bandwidth required to send high speed signals. The IEEE merged the fiber channel to the Ethernet MAC using a gigabit media independent interface (GMII) which defines an electrical interface enabling existing fiber channel PHY chips to be used and enabling future physical layers to be easily added.

1000Base-T is being developed to provide service over four pairs of category 5 or better copper cable. As discussed earlier this uses the same technology as 100Base-T2. This development is defined by the IEEE 802.3ab standard.

Gigabit Ethernet retains the standard 802.3 frame format, however the CSMA/CD algorithm has had to undergo a small change to enable it to function effectively at 1 Gbps. The slot time (the time needed to transmit a minimum-sized frame) of 64 bytes used with both 10 Mbps and 100 Mbps systems has been increased to 512 bytes. Without this increased slot time the network would have been impractically small at one tenth of the size of fast Ethernet – only 20 meters!

The slot time defines the time during which the transmitting node retains control of the medium, and in particular is responsible for collision detection. With gigabit Ethernet it was necessary to increase this time by a factor of eight to 4.096 ms to compensate for the tenfold speed increase. This then gives a collision domain of about 200 m.

If the transmitted frame is less than 512 bytes the transmitter continues transmitting to fill the 512 byte window. A carrier extension symbol is used to mark frames which are shorter than 512 bytes and to fill the remainder of the frame. This is shown in Figure 12.10.

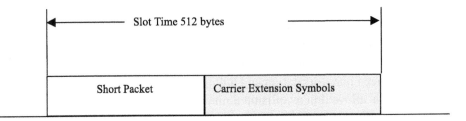

Figure 12.10
Carrier extension

While this is a simple technique to overcome the network size problem, it could cause problems with very low utilization if we send a lot of short frames, typical of some industrial control systems. For example, a 64 byte frame would have 448 carrier extension symbols attached and result in a utilization of less than 10%. This is unavoidable, but its effect can be minimized if we are sending a lot of small frames by a technique called packet bursting. Once the first frame in a burst has successfully passed through the 512 byte collision window, using carrier extension if necessary, transmission continues with additional frames being added to the burst until the burst limit of 1500 bytes is reached. This process averages the time wasted sending carrier extension symbols over a number of frames. The size of the burst varies depending on how many frames are being sent and their size. Frames are added to the burst in real-time with carrier extension symbols filling the interpacket gap. The total number of bytes sent in the burst is totaled after each frame and transmission continues until at least 1500 bytes have been transmitted. This is shown in Figure 12.11.

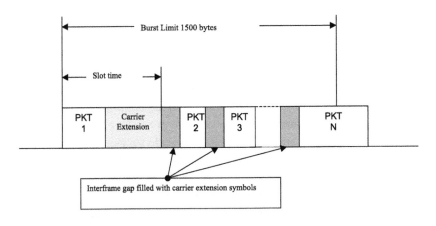

Figure 12.11
Packet bursting

12.12 TCP/IP

12.12.1 Introduction

TCP/IP is the *de facto* global standard for the network and transport layer implementation of internetwork applications because of the popularity of the Internet. The Internet (in its early years known as ARPANet), was part of a military project commissioned by the Advanced Research Projects Agency (ARPA), later known as the Defence Advanced Research Agency or DARPA. The communications model used to construct the system is known as the ARPA model. Although technically of questionable value for SCADA systems due to the large overhead, it is important for the DNP3 protocol.

Whereas the OSI model was developed in Europe by the International Standards Organization (ISO), the ARPA model (also known as the DoD model) was developed in the USA by ARPA. Although they were developed by different bodies and at different points in time, both serve as models for a communications infrastructure and hence provide 'abstractions' of the same reality. The remarkable degree of similarity is therefore not surprising.

Whereas the OSI model has 7 layers, the ARPA model has 4 layers. The OSI layers map onto the ARPA model as follows:

- The OSI session, presentation and applications layers are contained in the ARPA process and application layer
- The OSI transport layer maps onto the ARPA host-to-host layer (sometimes referred to as the service layer)
- The OSI network layer maps onto the ARPA Internet layer
- The OSI physical and data link layers map onto the ARPA network interface layer

The relationship between the two models is depicted in the following figure.

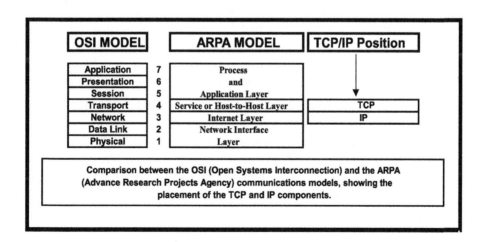

Comparison between the OSI (Open Systems Interconnection) and the ARPA (Advance Research Projects Agency) communications models, showing the placement of the TCP and IP components.

Figure 12.12
OSI vs ARPA models

TCP/IP, or rather – the TCP/IP protocol suite - is not limited to the TCP and IP protocols, but consists of a multitude of interrelated protocols that occupy the upper three layers of the ARPA model. TCP/IP does NOT include the bottom network interface layer, but depends on it for access to the medium.

As depicted in the following figure ('Internet frame'), an Internet transmission frame originating on a specific host (computer) would contain the local network (e.g. Ethernet) header and trailer applicable to that host. As the message proceeds along the Internet, this header and trailer could be replaced depending on the type of network on which the packet finds itself – be that X.25, frame relay or ATM. The IP datagram itself would remain untouched, unless it has to be fragmented and reassembled along the way.

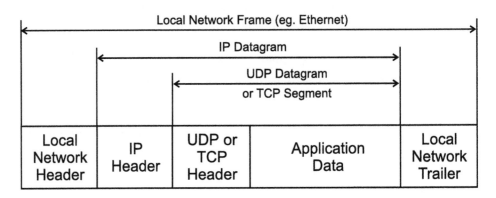

Figure 12.13
Internet frame

Note: Any Internet-related specification is referenced as a request for comments or RFC. RFCs can be obtained from various sources on the Internet such as www.rfc-editor.org.

The Internet layer

This layer is primarily responsible for the routing of packets from one host to another. Each packet contains the address information needed for its routing through the internetwork to the destination host. The dominant protocol at this level is the Internet protocol (IP).

There are, however, several other additional protocols required at this level such as:

- Address resolution protocol (ARP), RFC 826. This is used for the translation of an IP address to a hardware (MAC) address, such as required by Ethernet
- Reverse address resolution protocol (RARP), RFC 903. This is the complement of ARP and translates a hardware address to an IP address
- Internet control message protocol (ICMP), RFC 792. This is a protocol used for exchanging control or error messages between routers or hosts

The host-to-host layer

This layer is primarily responsible for data integrity between the sender host and receiver host regardless of the path or distance used to convey the message. It has two protocols associated with it, namely:

- User data protocol (UDP), a connectionless (unreliable) protocol used for higher layer port addressing with minimal protocol overhead (RFC 768)

- Transmission control protocol (TCP), a connection-oriented protocol that offers a very reliable method of transferring a stream of data in byte format between applications (RFC 793)

The process and application layer

This layer provides the user or application programs with interfaces to the TCP/IP stack. Protocols at this level include (but are not limited to) file transfer protocol (FTP), trivial file transfer protocol (TFTP), simple mail transfer protocol (SMTP), telecommunications network (TELNET), post office protocol (POP3), remote procedure calls (RPC), remote login (RLOGIN), hypertext transfer protocol (HTTP) and network time protocol (NTP).

12.12.2 Internet layer protocols (packet transport)

This section will deal with the Internet protocol (IP) and the Internet control message protocol (ICMP).

IP version 4 (IPv4)

IP (RFC 791) is responsible for the delivery of packets ('datagrams') between hosts. It is analogous to the postal system, in that it forwards (routes) and delivers datagrams on the basis of IP addresses attached to the datagrams, in the same way the postal service would process a letter based on the postal address. The IP address is a 32-bit entity containing both the network address (the 'zip code') and the host address (the 'street address').

IP also breaks up (fragments) datagrams that are too large. This is often necessary because the LANs and WANs that a datagram may have to traverse on its way to its destination may have different frame size limitations. For example, Ethernet can handle 1500 bytes but X.25 can handle only 576 bytes. IP on the sending side will fragment a datagram if necessary, attach an IP header to each fragment, and send them off consecutively. On the receiving side, IP will again rebuild the original datagram.

The IPv4 header

The IP header is appended to the information that IP accepts from higher-level protocols, before passing it around the network. This information could, within itself, contain the headers appended by higher level protocols such as TCP. The header consists of at least five 32-bit (4 byte) 'long words' i.e. 20 bytes total and is made up as follows.

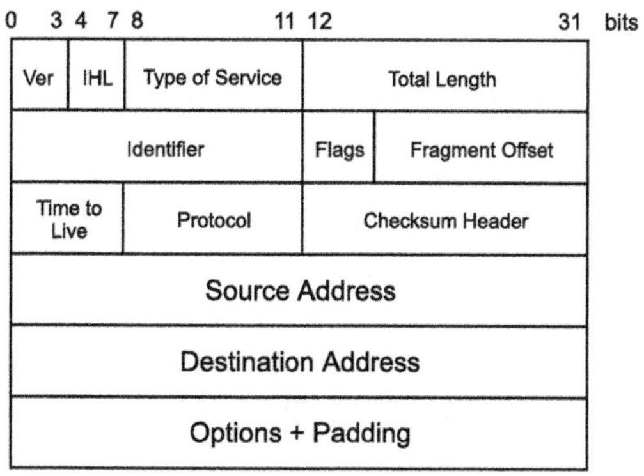

Figure 12.14
IPv4 header

The Ver (version) field is 4 bits long and indicates the version of the IP protocol in use. For IPv4 it is 4.

This is followed by the 4-bit IHL (Internet header length) field that indicates the length of the IP Header in 32-bit 'long words'. This is necessary since the IP header can contain options and therefore does not have a fixed length.

The 8-bit type of service (ToS) field informs the network about the quality of service required for this datagram. The ToS field is composed of a 3-bit precedence field (which is often ignored) and an unused (LSB) bit that must be 0.

The remaining 4 bits may only be turned on (set =1) one at a time, and are allocated as follows:

Bit 3:   Minimize delay
Bit 4:   Maximize throughput
Bit 5:   Maximize reliability
Bit 6:   Minimize monetary cost

Total Length (16 bits) is the length of the entire datagram, measured in bytes. Using this field and the IHL length, it can be determined where the data starts and ends. This field allows the length of a datagram to be up to $2^{16} = 65\ 536$ bytes, although such long datagrams are impractical. All hosts must at least be prepared to accept datagrams of up to 576 octets.

The 16-bit identifier uniquely identifies each datagram sent by a host. It is normally incremented by one for each successive datagram sent. In the case of fragmentation, it is appended to all fragments of the same datagram for the sake of reconstructing the datagram at the receiving end. It can be compared to the 'tracking' number of an item delivered by registered mail or UPS.

The 3-bit flag field contains 2 flags, used in the fragmentation process, viz. DF and MF. The DF (don't fragment) flag is set (=1) by the higher-level protocol (e.g. TCP) if IP is NOT allowed to fragment a datagram. If such a situation occurs, IP will not fragment and forward the datagram, but simply return an appropriate ICMP error message to the sending host. If fragmentation does occur, MF=1 will indicate that there are more fragments to follow, whilst MF=0 indicates that it is the last fragment to be sent.

The 13-bit fragment offset field indicates where in the original datagram a particular fragment belongs i.e. how far the beginning of the fragment is removed from the end of the header. The first fragment has offset zero. The fragment offset is measured in units of 8 bytes (64 bits); i.e. the transmitted offset is equal to the actual offset divided by eight.

The TTL (time to live) field ensures that undeliverable datagrams are eventually discarded. Every router that processes a datagram must decrease the TTL by one and if this field contains the value zero, then the datagram must be destroyed. Typically a datagram can be delivered anywhere in the world by traversing fewer than 15 routers.

The 8-bit protocol field indicates the next (higher) level protocol header present in the data portion of the IP datagram, in other words the protocol that resides above IP in the protocol stack and which has passed the datagram down to IP. Typical values are 1 for ICMP, 6 for TCP and 17 for UDP. A more detailed listing is contained in RFC 1700.

The checksum is a 16-bit mathematical checksum on the header only. Since some header fields change all the time (e.g. TTL), this checksum is recomputed and verified at each point that the IP header is processed. It is not necessary to cover the data portion of the datagram, as the protocols making use of IP, such as ICMP, IGMP, UDP and TCP, all have a checksum in their headers to cover their own header and data.

Finally, the source and destination addresses are the 32-bit IP addresses of the origin and the destination hosts of the datagram.

IPv4 addressing

The ultimate responsibility for the issuing of IP addresses is vested in the Internet Assigned Numbers Authority (IANA). This responsibility is, in turn, delegated to the three Regional Internet Registries (RIRs) viz. APNIC (Asia-Pacific Network=Information Centre), ARIN (American Registry for Internet Numbers), and RIPE NCC (Reseau IP Europeans). RIRs allocate blocks of IP addresses to Internet service providers (ISPs) under their jurisdiction, for subsequent issuing to users or sub-ISPs.

The IPv4 address consists of 32 bits, e.g. 11000000011001000110010000000001. Since this number is fine for computers but a little difficult for human beings, it is divided into four octets w, x, y and z. Each octet is converted to its decimal equivalent. The result of the conversion is written in the format 192.100.100.1. This is known as the 'dotted decimal' or 'dotted quad' notation. As mentioned earlier, one part of the IP address is known as the network ID or 'NetID' while the rest is known as the 'HostID'.

Originally, IP addresses were allocated in so-called address classes. Although the system proved to be problematic, and IP addresses are currently issued 'classless', the legacy of IP address classes remains and has to be understood. To provide for flexibility in assigning addresses to networks, the interpretation of the address field was coded to specify either a small number of networks with a large number of hosts (class A), or a moderate number of networks with a moderate number of hosts (class B), or a large number of networks with a small number of hosts (class C). There was also provision for extended addressing modes: class D was intended for multicasting whilst E was reserved for future use.

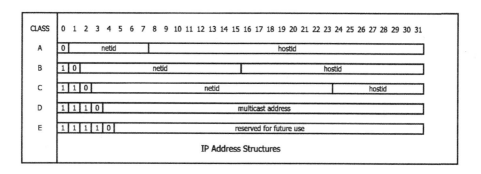

Figure 12.15
Address structure for IPv4

For class A, the first bit is fixed at 0. The values for 'w' can therefore only vary between 0 and 127_{10}. 0 is not allowed and 127 is a reserved number used for testing. This allows for 126 class A NetIDs. The number of HostIDs is determined by octets 'x', 'y' and 'z'. From these 24 bits, $2^{24} = 16\ 777\ 218$ combinations are available. All zeros and all ones are not permissible, which leaves 16 777 216 usable combinations.

For class B, the first two bits are fixed at 10. The binary values for 'w' can therefore only vary between 128_{10} and 191_{10}. The number of NetIDs is determined by octets 'w' and 'x'. The first 2 bits are used to indicate class B and hence cannot be used. This leaves fourteen usable bits. Fourteen bits allow $2^{14} = 16\ 384$ NetIDs. The number of HostIDs is determined by octets 'y' and 'z'. From these 16 bits, $2^{16} = 65\ 536$ combinations are available. All zeros and all ones are not permissible, which leaves 65 534 usable combinations.

For class C, the first three bits are fixed at 110. The binary values for 'w' can therefore only vary between 192_{10} and 223_{10}. The number of NetIDs is determined by octets 'w', 'x' and 'y'. The first three bits (110) are used to indicate class C and hence cannot be used. This leaves twenty-two usable bits. Twenty-two bits allow $2^{22} = 2\ 097\ 152$ combinations for NetIDs. The number of HostIDs is determined by octet 'z'. From these 8 bits, $2^8 = 256$ combinations are available. Once again, all zeros and all ones are not permissible which leaves 254 usable combinations.

In order to determine where the NetID ends and the HostID begins, each IP address is associated with a subnet mask, or, technically more correct, a netmask. This mask starts with a row of contiguous 1s from the left; one for each bit that forms part of the NetID. This is followed by 0s, one for each bit comprising the HostID.

IP version 6 (IPv6)

IPv4 has several shortcomings, the major one being the 32-bit IP address that (only!) allows for 2^{32} different IP addresses. As early as 1993 it was realized that the world was running out of IP addresses and the Internet Engineering Task Force (IETF) chartered the Internet Protocol Next Generation (IPng) working group. IPv6 (IPng) differs from IPv4 in several respects.

The 128-bit network address allows for 2^{96} times more IP addresses – in reality several thousand IP addresses for each square meter of the earth!

- The IP header is more efficient. Despite 12 bytes needed for each IP address instead of 4, the overall header is only twice the length of the IPv4 header
- The header allows extensions for applications and options
- There is no header checksum
- A flow label allows for quality of service requirements
- It has built-in security for authentication and encryption

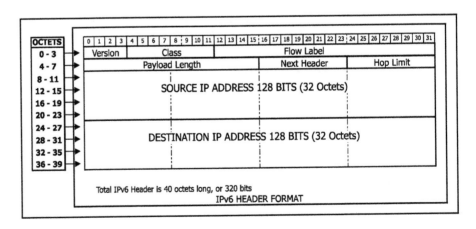

Figure 12.16
IPv6 header

Here follows a brief description of the header fields:

- The 4-bit version number in the IP header holds the IP version number (6 for IPv6)
- The 8-bit traffic class field holds a value indicating the datagram's delivery criteria
- The flow label field is 24 bits in length and a host may use it to specify special handling for certain packages
- The 16-bit payload length field contains an unsigned integer to specify the total length of the IP datagram in bytes. Payloads bigger than 65 535 are allowed, and are called jumbo payloads
- The next header field, similar to the protocol field in IPv4, is 1 byte in length and identifies the header immediately following the IPv6 header. This is the same as the IPv4 protocol field. Some examples are shown in the table below: If there is no extension header, it points to the protocol 'above' IP e.g. TCP or UDP

Destination options

The hop limit field, similar to the TTL field in IPv4, is 1 byte in length and determines the number of hops the datagram can travel. It is decremented at each node, and an error message sent back if it becomes zero.

The source and destination IP addresses in 128-bit format are placed in the header. The destination address is for the recipient of the package and may NOT be the ultimate recipient if a routing header is present.

Extension headers

In order to reduce the size of the header and to reduce the time needed to process it, options have been removed from the main header and are only appended when needed. The hop-by-hop extension header, when added, is processed by all intermediate routers and therefore has to follow directly after the main header.

The other extension headers are only processed at the final destination and are added individually, if needed, in the following sequence:

- Hop-by-hop options header
- Destination options header (for options processed by the first destination that appears in the Ipv6 destination address field, plus any subsequent destinations listed in the routing header)
- Routing header
- Fragment header
- Authentication header
- Encapsulating security payload header
- Destination options header (for options to be processed by the final destination only)

The following figure illustrates the IPv6 and optional headers, in their suggested order.

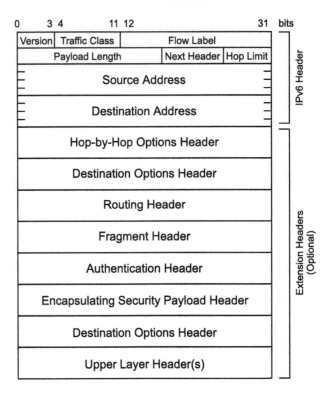

Figure 12.17
IPv6 extension headers

IPv6 addresses

IPv6 addresses are 128 bits long and are identifiers for individual interfaces or sets of interfaces. All IPv6 addresses are assigned to interfaces (i.e. network interface cards) and NOT to nodes i.e. hosts. Since each interface belongs to a single node, any of that node's interfaces' unicast addresses may be used as an identifier for the node.

A single interface may be assigned multiple IPv6 addresses of any type:

- There are three types of IPv6 addresses. These are unicast, anycast, and multicast
- Unicast addresses identify a single interface
- Anycast addresses identify a set of interfaces such that a packet sent to an anycast address will be delivered to one member of the set
- Multicast addresses identify a group of interfaces, such that a packet sent to a multicast address is delivered to all of the interfaces in the group. There are no broadcast addresses in IPv6, their function being superseded by multicast addresses. Addresses are written in the format x:x:x:x:x:x:x:x where each x represents 16 bits in hexadecimal format, for example 1432:FEDA:AABB:1234:5678:9ABC:1111:9999. Four 0s (:0000: can be abbreviated as :0:. A series of leading and trailing 0s can be written as :: (double colon)

The leading bits in the address indicate the specific type of IPv6 address. The variable-length field comprising these leading bits is called the format prefix (FP).

Unicast addresses

There are several forms of unicast address assignment in IPv6. These are:

- Aggregatable global unicast addresses
- Unspecified addresses
- Loopback addresses
- IPv4-based addresses
- Site local addresses and
- Link local addresses

Aggregatable global unicast addresses are used for global communication. The first 3 bits (010) identify the address as an aggregatable global unicast address. The remainder of the bits is subdivided into fields in order to provide a hierarchical identification of the network providers, networks, subnetworks and end-user devices. Unspecified addresses can be written as 0:0:0:0:0:0:0:0, or simply '::'. These can be used as source addresses by stations that have not yet been configured with IP addresses. They can never be used as destination addresses. This is similar to 0.0.0.0 in IPv4. A loopback addresses (0:0:0:0:0:0:0:1) can be used by a node to send a datagram to itself. It is similar to the 127.0.0.1 of IPv4.

An IPv4-based IPv6 address can be constructed out of an existing IPv4 address. This is done by prepending 96 zero bits to a 32-bit IPv4 address. The result is written as 0:0:0:0:0:0:192.100.100.3, or simply ::192.100.100.3.

Site local addresses are partially equivalent of the IPv4 private addresses (i.e. addresses for private use that cannot be used on the Internet). A typical site local address will consist of the relevant prefix, a set of 38 zeros, a subnet ID, and the interface identifier. Site local addresses cannot be routed in the Internet, but only between two stations on a single site.

Link local addresses are used by stations that are not yet configured with either a provider-based address or a site local address may use link local addresses. Theses are composed of the link local prefix, 1111 1110 10, a set of 0s, and an interface identifier. These addresses can only be used by stations connected to the same local network and packets addressed in this way cannot traverse a router.

ICMP

When nodes fail, or become temporarily unavailable, or when certain routes become overloaded with traffic, a message mechanism called the Internet control message protocol (ICMP) reports errors and other useful information about the performance and operation of the network.

ICMP communicates between the Internet layers on two nodes and is used by routers as well as individual hosts. Although ICMP is viewed as residing within the Internet layer, its messages travel across the network encapsulated in IP datagrams in the same way as higher layer protocol (such as TCP or UDP) datagrams. The ICMP message, consisting of an ICMP header and ICMP data, is encapsulated as 'data' within an IP datagram that is, in turn, carried as 'payload' by the lower network interface layer (for example, Ethernet).

There are a variety of ICMP messages, each with a different format, yet the first 3 fields as contained in the first 4 bytes or 'long word' is the same for all.

The various ICMP messages are shown in the Figure 12.18.

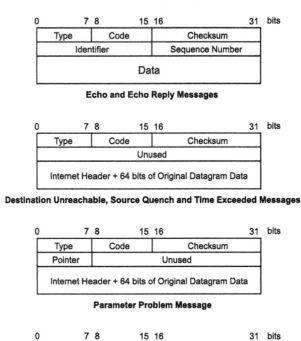

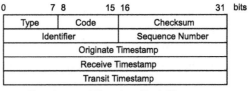

Figure 12.18
ICMP message formats

The three common fields are:

- An ICMP message type (4 bits) which is a code that identifies the type of ICMP message
- Code (4 bits) in which interpretation depends on the type of ICMP message
- A checksum (16 bits) that is calculated on the entire ICMP datagram

ICMP messages can be further subdivided into two broad groups viz. ICMP error messages (destination unreachable, time exceeded, invalid parameters, source quench or redirect) and ICMP query messages (echo request and reply messages, timestamp request and reply messages, and subnet mask request and reply messages).

Here follows a few examples of ICMP error messages

Source quench

If a gateway (router) receives a high rate of datagrams from a particular source it will issue a source quench ICMP message for every datagram it discards. The source node will then slow down its rate of transmission until the source quench messages stop, at which stage it will gradually increase the rate again.

Redirection

When a gateway (router) detects that a source node is not using the best route in which to transmit its datagram, it sends a message to the node advising it of the better route.

Time exceeded

If a datagram has traversed too many routers, its TTL counter will eventually reach a count of zero. The ICMP time exceeded message is then sent back to the source node. The time-exceeded message will also be generated if one of the fragments of a fragmented datagram fails to arrive at the destination node.

Parameter problem messages

When there are problems with a particular datagram's contents, a parameter problem message is sent to the original source. The pointer field points to the problem bytes.

Unreachable destination

When a gateway is unable to deliver a datagram, it responds with this message. The datagram is then 'dropped' (deleted).

In addition to the reports on errors and exceptional conditions, there is a set of ICMP messages to request information, and to reply to such request.

Echo request and reply

An echo request message is sent to the destination node. This message essentially inquires: 'Are you alive?' A reply indicates that the pathway (i.e. the network(s) in between, the gateways (routers) and the destination node are all operating correctly.

Timestamp request and replies

This can be used to estimate to synchronize the clock of a host with that of a timeserver.

Subnet mask request and reply

This can be used by a host to obtain the correct subnet mask. Where implemented, one or more hosts in the internetwork are designated as subnet mask servers and run a process that replies to subnet mask request messages.

12.12.3 Host-to-host layer: end-to-end reliability

TCP

Transmission control protocol (TCP) is a connection-oriented protocol and is said to be 'reliable', although this word is used in a data communications context. TCP establishes a session between two machines before data is transmitted. Because a connection is setup beforehand, it is possible to verify that all packets are received on the other end and to arrange re-transmission in case of lost packets. Because of all these built-in functions, TCP involves significant additional overhead in terms of processing time and header size.

TCP fragments large chunks of data into smaller segments if necessary, reconstructs the data stream from packets received, issues acknowledgment of data received, provides socket services for multiple connections to ports on remote hosts, performs packet verification and error control, and flow control.

The TCP header is structured as follows:

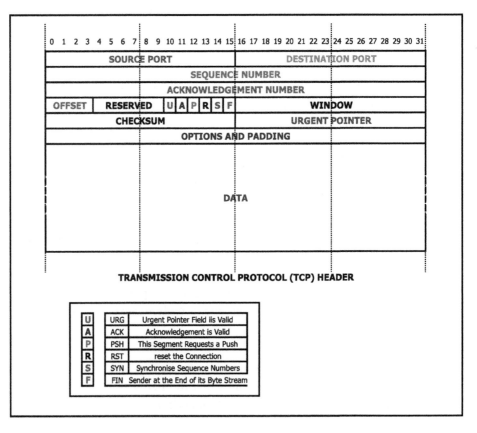

Figure 12.19
TCP header format

The source and destination ports (16 bits each) identify the host processes at each side of the connection. Examples are post office protocol (POP3) at port 110 and simple mail transfer protocol (SMTP) at port 25. Whereas a destination host is identified by its IP address, the process on that host is identified by its port number. A combination of port number and IP address is called a socket.

The sequence number (32 bits) ensures the sequentiality of the data stream. TCP by implication associates a 32-bit number with every byte it transmits. The sequence number is the number of the first byte in every segment (or 'chunk') of data sent by TCP. If the SYN flag is set, however, it indicates that the sender wants to establish a connection and the number in the sequence number field becomes the initial sequence number or ISN. The receiver acknowledges this, and the sender then labels the first byte of the transmitted data with a sequence number of ISN+1. The ISN is a pseudo-random number with values between 0 and 232.

The acknowledgment number (32 bits) is used to verify correct receipt of the transmitted data. The receiver checks the incoming data and if the verification is positive, acknowledges it by placing the number of the next byte expected in the acknowledgment number field and setting the ACK flag. The sender, when transmitting, sets a timer and if acknowledgment is not received within a specific time, an error is assumed and the data is retransmitted.

Data offset (4 bits) is the number of 32-bit words in the TCP header. This indicates where the data begins. It is necessary since the header can contain options and thus does not have a fixed length.

Six flags control the connection and data transfer. They are:

- URG: Urgent pointer field significant
- ACK: Acknowledgment field significant
- PSH: Push function
- RST: Reset the connection
- SYN: Synchronize sequence numbers
- FIN: No more data from sender

The window field (16 bits) provides flow control. Whenever a host sends an acknowledgment to the other party in the bi-directional communication, it also sends a window advertisement by placing a number in the window field. The window size indicates the number of bytes, starting with the one in the acknowledgment field, that the host is able to accept.

The checksum field (16 bits) is used for error control.

The urgent pointer field (16 bits) is used in conjunction with the URG flag and allows for the insertion of a block of 'urgent' data in the beginning of a particular segment.

The pointer points to the first byte of the non-urgent data following the urgent data.

UDP

User datagram protocol (UDP) is a 'connectionless' protocol and does not require a connection to be established between two machines prior to data transmission. It is therefore said to be 'unreliable' – the word 'unreliable' is used here as opposed to 'reliable' in the case of TCP and should not be interpreted in its everyday context.

Sending a UDP datagram involves very little overhead in that there are no synchronization parameters, no priority options, no sequence numbers, no timers, and no retransmission of packets. The header is small, the protocol is streamlined functionally. The only major drawback is that delivery is not guaranteed. UDP is therefore used for communications that involve broadcasts, for general network announcements, or for real-time data.

The UDP header

The UDP header is significantly smaller than the TCP header and only contains four fields.

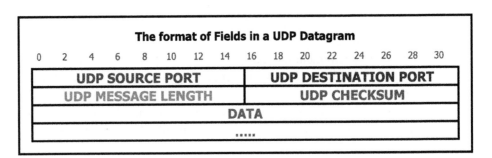

Figure 12.20
UDP header format

UDP source port (16 bits) is an optional field. When meaningful, it indicates the port of the sending process, and may be assumed to be the port to which a reply should be addressed in the absence of any other information. If not used, a value of zero is inserted.

UDP destination port has the same meaning as for the TCP header, and indicates the process on the destination host to which the data is to be sent. UDP message length is the length in bytes of the datagram including the header and the data.

The 16-bit UDP checksum is used for validation purposes.

13

Fieldbus and SCADA communications systems

Objectives

When you have completed study of this chapter you should be able to:

- List the main features of Profibus DP, PA and FMS
- List the features of Foundations
- Give 4 main differences betweeen Foundation Fieldbus and Profibus

13.1 Introduction

The two main Fieldbus standards that may impact on SCADA systems are discussed below. These are:

- Profibus
- Foundation Fieldbus

13.2 Profibus

13.2.1 Introduction to Profibus

Profibus is an open standard fieldbus defined by the German DIN 19245 Parts 1 and 2. It is based on a token bus/floating master system. There are three different types of Profibus – FMS, DP and PA. The fieldbus message specification (FMS) is used for general data acquisition systems. DP is used when fast communications is needed. PA is used in areas when intrinsically safe devices and intrinsically safe communications are needed.

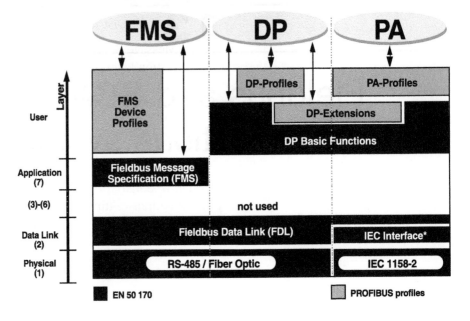

Figure 13.1
Profibus protocol architecture (courtesy of Profibus)

13.2.2   The physical layer

The physical layer specifies the type of Profibus transmission medium. The EIA-485 voltage standard is defined for the FMS and DP versions of Profibus.

The IEC 1158-2 is used in the PA version:

- FMS (RS-485):   187.5 Kbps   General use
- DP (RS-485):   500 Kbps/1.5 Mbps/12 Mbps   Fast devices
- PA (IEC 1158-2):   31.25 Kbps   Intrinsically safe

Basic properties of the RS-485 voltage standard for Profibus

Topology:	Linear bus, terminated at both ends
Medium:	Twisted pair shielded cable
Wire size:	18 AWG (0.8 mm)
Attenuation:	3 dB/km at 39 kHz
Number of stations:	32 stations without repeaters extendible to 127
Bus length:	max. 1200 meters extendible to 4800 meters at slow rates
Speed:	up to 12 Mbps
Connector:	Phoenix-type screw or 9-pin D-sub connector

IEC 1158-2 is a standardized current standard used in special areas of a factory or plant that require intrinsically safe devices. IEC 1158-2 modulates a Manchester encoded bipolar NRZ +/–10 mA signal on top of a 9 to 32 V DC voltage. This 10 mA creates a +/– 1-volt signal that is read by each of the devices on the bus.

It is very easy to connect Profibus FMS, DP and PA versions together on the same system, as the main difference between them is only the physical layer. This allows deployment of lower cost devices in most of the plant (FMS) and fast devices (DP) in parts of the plant that need the speed. Intrinsically safe devices (PA) are used in the areas of the plant where intrinsic safety is required.

13.2.3   The data link layer

The data link layer is defined by Profibus as the fieldbus data link layer (FDL).

The medium access control (MAC) part of the FDL defines when a station may transmit data. The MAC ensures that only one station transmits data at any given time.

Profibus communication is termed hybrid medium access. It uses two methods of operation, namely token passing and master/slave operation.

The token passing method ensures the assignment of the bus access right within a precisely defined time interval. The token is circulated between all masters with a maximum (and configurable) token rotation time. Token passing is especially useful for communication between complex automation masters that require equal rights on the bus. The token is passed in a defined sequence (in order of increasing addresses).

The master/slave method allows the master that currently has the token to communicate with the associated slave devices. The master can then read from or write data to the slave devices.

A typical configuration is shown below.

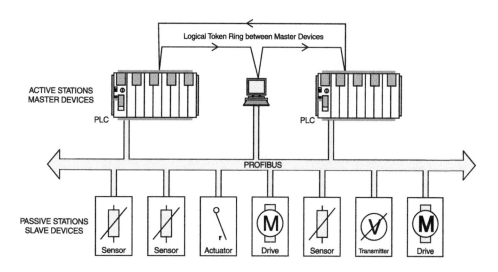

Figure 13.2
Typical architecture of a Profibus system

During the bus system startup phase, the task of the active station's media access control layer (MAC) is to detect logical assignment and establish the token ring. The MAC also handles adding or deleting stations (which have become inactive), deleting multiple nodes with the same address or deleting multiple or lost tokens.

13.2.4   The application layer

This consists of two sections, namely the fieldbus message specification (FMS) and the lower layer interface (LLI). The application layer is defined in DIN 19245 Part 2.

13.2.5   The Profibus communication model

The part of the application process in a field device that is readable for communication purposes is called the virtual field device (VFD). The VFD contains the communication objects that may be manipulated by the services of the application layers. The objects of a real device that are readable for the communication (variables, programs, data domains) are called communication objects.

All communication objects of a Profibus station are entered into its local object dictionary (source OD) and can be classified as either static or dynamic communication objects.

Static communication objects are defined in the static object dictionary. They may be predefined by the manufacturer of the device, or defined during the configuration of the bus system. Static communication objects are used mainly for communication in the field area.

Profibus recognizes the following static communication objects:

- Simple variable
- Array – sequence of simple variables of the same type
- Record – sequence of simple variables, not necessarily of the same type
- Domain – data range
- Event

Dynamic communication objects are entered into the dynamic part of the OD (list of variable lists of program invocations). They may be predefined or defined, deleted or changed by the application services in the operational phase.

Profibus supports the following dynamic communication objects:

- Program invocation
- Variable list (sequence of simple variables, arrays or records)

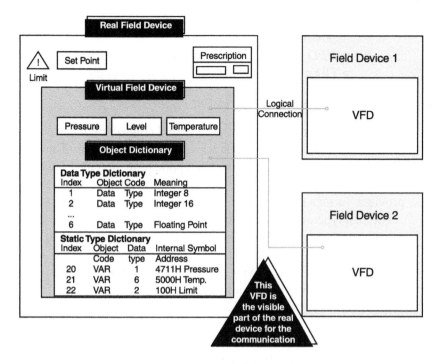

Figure 13.3
Virtual field device (VFFD) with object dictionary (OD)

There are two methods for accessing the variables, either addressing by name (using a symbolic name) or physical addressing (to access a physical location in memory). Profibus defines logical addressing (by symbolic name) as the preferred method as this increases the speed of access.

Application services

From the point of view of an application process, the communication system is a service provider offering various application services – the FMS services. The FMS describes the communication objects, the application services and the resulting models from the viewpoint of the communication partner. Services can be classified as confirmed services, only permitted on connection-oriented communication relationships, or unconfirmed services used on connectionless communication relationships such as broadcast and multicast.

Service primitives in the Profibus standard describe the execution of the services. The services can be divided into the following groups:

- Context management services allow establishment and release of logical connections
- Variable access services permit access to simple variables, records, arrays and variable lists
- Domain management services enable the transmission of contiguous memory areas
- Program invocation management services allow the control of program execution

- Event management services make the transmission of alarm messages possible
- VFD support services permit device identification and status report
- OD management services permit object dictionaries to be read and written

Lower layer interface (LLI)

The LLI conducts the data flow control and connection monitoring as well as the mapping of the FMS services onto the layer 2 with consideration of the various types of devices. The user communicates with other application processes over the logic channels, the communication relationships. For the execution of the FMS and FMA7 services the LLI provides various types of communication relationships.

The first type of communication relationship is a connection-oriented relationship. This requires a connection establishment phase (or initiate service) before the connection can be used for data transmission. When the connection is no longer required it may be released with the abort service (or connection release phase).

The second type of communication relationship is a connectionless-oriented relationship. In this type of relationship data can be transferred cyclic, i.e. exactly one variable is permanently read or written over a connection. A typical application for cyclic data transfer is the periodic update of the remove inputs and outputs of a PLC. Alternatively, data can be transferred acyclic i.e. an application sporadically accesses various communication objects over a connection.

Communication relationship list (CRL)

The CRL contains the description of all communication relationships of a device independent of the time of their usage.

Network management

In addition to the application services and FMS models, Profibus includes specifications for network management (fieldbus management layer 7, FMA7).

FMA7 functions are defined in three groups:

- Context management allows the establishment and release of management connections
- Configuration management allows the CRL to be loaded and read, access to variables, statistic counters and parameters of the layers 1 and 2, identification of communication components of the stations and registration of stations
- Fault management allows the indication of faults and events and the reset of stations

Profibus profiles

For the various application fields it is necessary to adopt the functionality actually needed for the real world. A profile includes application specific definitions of the meanings of the communication functions, as well as the interpretation of status and error indications.

Profiles for the following application fields are available:

- Building automation
- Drive control
- Sensors and actuators

- Programmable logic controllers
- Textile machines

These enable different manufacturers, which use the same profile, to have full inter-operability with the different devices on a common interconnecting Profibus.

13.3   Foundation fieldbus

13.3.1   Introduction to Foundation fieldbus

The concept behind Foundation fieldbus (FF) is to preserve the desirable features of the present 4–20 mA standard (such as a standardized interface to the communications link, bus power derived from the link and intrinsic safety options) while taking advantage of the new digital technologies.

To understand how this standard works, it is helpful to look at Foundation fieldbus in terms of the OSI Model. The FF consists of three parts that correspond to OSI layers 1, 2, 7 and 8. Layer 8 of the OSI model corresponds to the 'user' layer.

13.3.2   The physical layer and wiring rules

The physical layer standard has been approved and is detailed in the IEC 1158-2 and the ISA standard S50.02-1992. It supports communication rates of 31.25 Kbps. All of these use the Manchester bi-phase L encoding scheme with four encoding states. Devices can be optionally powered from the bus under certain conditions as detailed below for the various configurations. The 31.25 Kbps (or H1, or low-speed bus) can support from 2 to 32 devices that are not bus powered, two to twelve devices that are bus powered or two to six devices that are bus powered in an intrinsically safe area. Repeaters are allowed and will increase the length and number of devices that can be put on the bus.

The low speed bus was intended to utilize existing plant wiring and is referred to as type B wiring (shielded twisted pair) and with #22 AWG can be used for segments up to 1200 m. The higher speeds require higher grade cabling and are referred to as type A. For type A cable (shielded twisted pair) for H1 – #18 AWG can be used up to 1900 m. Two additional types of cabling are specified and are referred to as type C (multi-pair twisted without shield) and type D (called multi-core, no shield). Type C using #26 AWG cable is limited to 400 m per segment and type D with #16 AWG is restricted to segments less than 200 m.

- Type A #18 AWG   1900 m
- Type B #22 AWG   1200 m
- Type C #26 AWG   400 m
- Type D #16 AWG multi-core   200 m

The Foundation fieldbus wiring method is floating balanced and equipped with a termination resistor combination connected across each end of the transmission line. Neither of the wires should ever be connected to ground. The terminator consists of a 100-ohm quarter watt resistor and a capacitor sized to pass 31.25 kHz. As an option one of the terminators can be center tapped and grounded to prevent voltage buildup on the fieldbus. Power supplies must be impedance matched for FF. Off the shelf power supplies must be conditioned. If a 'normal' power supply is placed across the line it will load down the line due to its low impedance. This will cause the transmitters to stop transmitting.

Fast response times for the bus are one of the FF goals. For example, at 31.25 Kbps on the H1 bus response times as low as 32 microseconds are expected (this will vary based on the loading of the system but will average between 32 microseconds and 2.2 milliseconds with an average approximately 1 msec).

Spurs can be connected to the 'home run'. The length of the spurs depends on the type of wire used and the number of spurs connected. The maximum length is the total length of the spurs and the home run.

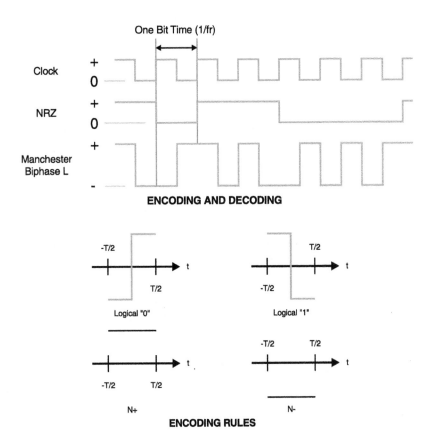

Symbols		Encoding
1	(ONE)	Hi-Lo transition (mid-bit)
0	(ZERO)	Lo-Hi transition (mid-bit)
N+	(NON-DATA PLUS)	Hi (No transition)
N-	(NON-DATA MINUS)	Lo (No transition)

ENCODING RULES

Figure 13.4
Foundation fieldbus physical layer

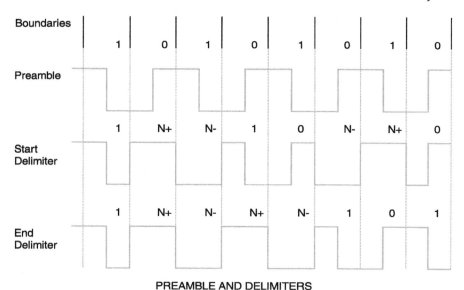

Figure 13.5
Use of N+ and N– encoding states

The physical layer standard has been out for some time. As indicated in Figure 13.6, there are three other layers that need to be discussed. These are the data link, the application and the user layers.

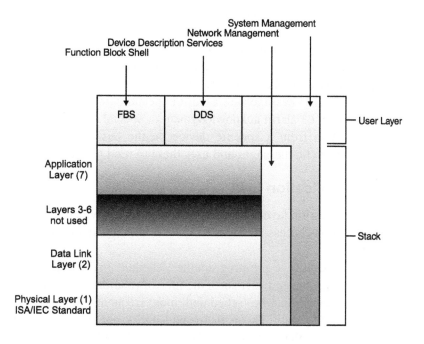

Figure 13.6
The OSI model of the FF protocol stack

13.3.3   The data link layer

The communications stack as defined by the FF corresponds to OSI layers two and seven, the data link and applications layers. The DLL (data link layer) controls access to the bus through a centralized bus scheduler called the link active scheduler (LAS). (Note: The DLL has been formalized as a standard under the ISA SP50 and the IEC SC65C/WG6.)

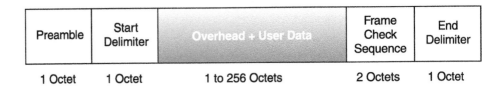

Preamble	Start Delimiter	Overhead + User Data	Frame Check Sequence	End Delimiter
1 Octet	1 Octet	1 to 256 Octets	2 Octets	1 Octet

Figure 13.7
Data link layer packet format

The LAS controls access to the bus by granting permission to each device according to pre-defined 'schedules'. No device may access the bus without LAS permission. There are two types of schedules implemented cyclic (scheduled) and acyclic (unscheduled). It may seem odd that one could have an unscheduled 'schedule', but these terms actually refer to messages that have a periodic or non-periodic routine, or 'schedule'.

The cyclic messages are used for information (process and control variables) that requires regular, periodic updating between devices on the bus. The technique used for information transfer on the bus is known as the publisher–subscriber method. Based on the user pre-defined (programmed) schedule the LAS grants permission for each device in turn access to the bus. Once the device receives permission to access the bus it 'publishes' its available information. All other devices can then listen to the 'published' information and read it into memory (subscribe) if it requires it for its own use. Devices not requiring specific data simply ignore the 'published' information.

The acyclic messages are used for special cases that may not occur on a regular basis. These may be alarm acknowledgment or special commands such as retrieving diagnostic information from a specific device on the bus. The LAS detects time slots available between cyclic messages and uses these to send the acyclic messages.

13.3.4   The application layer

The application layer in the FF specification is divided into two sub-layers – the Foundation fieldbus access sublayer (FAS) and the Foundation fieldbus messaging specification (FMS).

The capability to pre-program the 'schedule' in the LAS provides a powerful configuration tool for the end user since the time of rotation between devices can be established and critical devices can be 'scheduled' more frequently to provide a form of prioritization of specific I/O points. This is the responsibility and capability of the FAS. Programming the schedule via the FAS allows the option of implementing (actually, simulating) various 'services' between the LAS and the devices on the bus.

Three such 'services' are readily apparent such as:

- Client/server – with a dedicated client (the LAS) and several servers (the bus devices)
- Publisher/subscriber – as described above, and
- Event distribution – with devices reporting only in response to a 'trigger' event, or by exception, or other pre-defined criteria

These variations, of course, depend on the actual application and one scheme would not necessarily be 'right' for all applications, but the flexibility of the Foundation fieldbus is easily understood from this example.

The second sub-layer, the Foundation fieldbus messaging specification (FMS), contains an 'object dictionary' which is a type of database that allows access to Foundation fieldbus data by tag name or an index number. The object dictionary contains complete listings of all data types, data type descriptions, and communication objects used by the application. The services allow the object dictionary (application database) to be accessed and manipulated. Information can be read from or written to the object dictionary allowing manipulation of the application and the services provided.

13.3.5   The user layer

The FF specifies an eighth layer called the user layer that resides 'above' the application layer of the OSI model; this layer is usually referred to as layer 8. In the Foundation fieldbus this layer is responsible for three main tasks – network management, system management and function block/device description services.

The network management service provides access to the other layers for performance monitoring and managing communications between the layers and between remote objects (objects on the bus). The system management takes care of device address assignment, application clock synchronization, and function block scheduling. This is essentially the time co-ordination between devices and the software, and ensures correct time stamping of events throughout the bus.

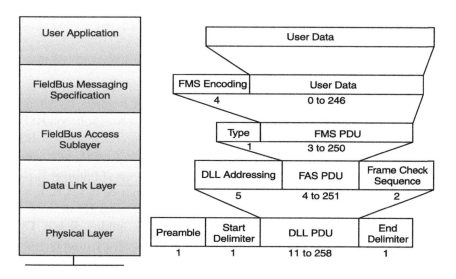

Figure 13.8
The passage of information packets to the physical layer

Function blocks and device descriptions services provide pre-programmed 'blocks' which can be used by the end user to eliminate redundant and time-consuming configuration. The block concept allows selection of generic functions, algorithms, and even generic devices from a library of objects during system configuration and programming. This process can dramatically reduce configuration time since large 'blocks' are already configured and simply need to be selected. The goal is to provide an open system that supports interoperability and a device description language (DDL), which will enable multiple vendors, and devices to be described as 'blocks' or 'symbols'. The user would select generic devices then refine this selection by selecting a DDL object to specify a specific vendor's product. Entering a control loop 'block' with the appropriate parameters would nearly complete the initial configuration for the loop. Advanced control functions and mathematics 'blocks' are also available for more advanced control applications.

13.3.6 Error detection and diagnostics

FF has been developed as a purely digital communications bus for the process industry and incorporates error detection and diagnostic information. It uses multiple vendors' components and has extensive diagnostics across the stack from the physical link up through the network and system management layers by design.

The signal method used by the physical layer timing and synchronization is monitored constantly as part of the communications. Repeated messages and the reason for the repeat can be logged and displayed for interpretation.

In the upper layer, network and system management is an integral feature of the diagnostic routines. This allows the system manager to analyze the network 'online' and maintain traffic loading information. As devices are added and removed optimization of the link active scheduler (LAS) routine allows communications optimization dynamically without requiring complete network shutdown. This ensures optimal timing and device reporting, giving more time to higher priority devices and removing, or minimizing, redundant or low priority messaging.

With the device description (DD) library for each device stored in the host controller (a requirement for true interoperability between vendors) all the diagnostic capability of each vendors' products can be accurately reported and logged and/or alarmed to provide continuous monitoring of each device.

13.3.7 High speed Ethernet

High speed Ethernet (HSE) is the Foundation fieldbus backbone network running at 100 Mbps. HSE field devices are connected to the backbone via HSE linking devices, field devices running function blocks (FBs), and host computers. An HSE linking device is a device used to interconnect H1 fieldbus segments to HSE to create a larger network. An HSE switch is an Ethernet device used to interconnect multiple HSE devices such as HSE linking devices and HSE field devices to form an even larger HSE network. HSE hosts are used to configure and monitor the linking devices and H1 devices. Each H1 segment has its own link active scheduler (LAS) located in a linking device. This feature enables the H1 segments to continue operating even if the hosts are disconnected from the HSE backbone. Multiple H1 (31.25 Kbps) fieldbus segments can be connected to the HSE backbone via linking devices.

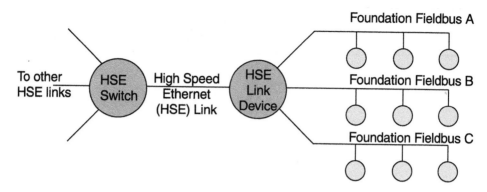

Figure 13.9
High speed Ethernet and Foundation fieldbus

14

UCA protocol

Objectives

When you have completed study of this chapter you should be able to:

- Describe the overall structure of UCA
- Describe the uniform application interface

14.1 Introduction

The electric industry – through the Electric Power Research Institute (EPRI) – began developing the Utility Communications Architecture (UCATM) in 1988. The result is a complete set of standards allowing UCA compliant monitoring and control devices to interoperate with utility applications (not just SCADA) in a multi-vendor environment.

UCA is more than a communications protocol. It is a comprehensive system intended to allow utilities to purchase 'off-the-shelf' UCA compliant devices (such as pole top reclosures, transformers, pumps, valves, flow meters etc) and to have these devices automatically integrated into the SCADA and information technology systems. The industry agreed data relevant to that device will be automatically transferred to SCADA and IT systems identifying themselves as requiring it.

The 'plug and play' concepts, ease of configuration and integration, and predefined data models mean UCA will reduce the costs within the various utility industries, and ensure the success of UCA. UCA is already a fact of life for the electricity industry with many vendors offering UCA compliant products and a large installed base of systems, particularly in the US. Within the water and gas industries it will take a number of years before the data models are agreed and trialled.

Outside the utilities there is little push for UCA, although the concepts are likely to become routine in the SCADA industry.

In 1999, the Institute of Electrical and Electronic Engineers (IEEE) published the UCA Version 2 as an IEEE standard.

14.2   UCA development

Figure 14.1 is a timeline showing key milestones in UCA's development.

The electric industry-through EPRI-began UCA's development in 1988, and published UCA Version 1 in 1991. Following publication of UCA Version 1, EPRI enlisted the support of the water and gas industries through the AWWA Research Foundation (AWWARF) and Gas Research Institute (GRI).

The electric industry developed and tested UCA technology during the years 1992 through 1997. EPRI commissioned and completed a number of successful demonstration projects at electric utilities and combined electric/gas/water utilities. This period also solidified the UCA device object model and common application services model concepts, which provide the most powerful aspects of UCA as an application standard.

UCA's development period culminated in 1996 and 1997, when EPRI published draft UCA Version 2. The Water UCA effort also achieved major milestones in 1996 and 1997 with completion of the Water UCA Functional Definition and Standards Assessment.

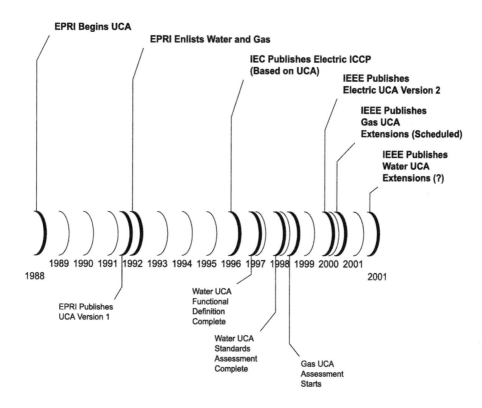

Figure 14.1
UCA timeline (Figure courtesy American Water Works Association)

EPRI began a successful campaign to have the IEEE oversee UCA's continued development. As a result, the IEEE published UCA Version 2 as an IEEE standard in 1999. UCA-2 addressed the issues that were identified in field testing of the original specification, and it embraced the Internet suite of protocols which had become widely accepted since the early days of UCA-1.

In 1998, EPRI and GRI re-vitalized their joint evaluation of UCA for Gas. The project showed that UCA is an excellent fit for the gas industry and will end in the first quarter of 2000.

Throughout the rest of 2000 and 2001, the UCA community will focus their efforts on establishing the commercial market for UCA. Focus areas include the gas and water industries. (AWWA has established a standards committee to evaluate the UCA.)

14.3   UCA technology

There are three basic building blocks of the UCA as shown in Figure 14.2. These are:

- A uniform communications infrastructure
- A uniform data model
- A uniform application interface

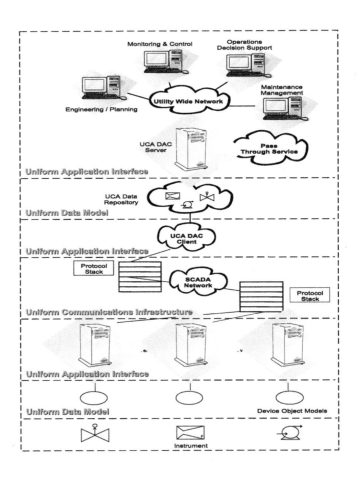

Figure 14.2
UCA technology components

14.3.1 Uniform communications infrastructure

The next few paragraphs explain the UCA uniform communications infrastructure.

14.3.2 UCA version 2 options

Figure 14.3 shows the UCA Version 2 profile options. The UCA categorizes their profile stack as the L, T and A-Profiles. The L-Profile corresponds to the OSI physical and data link layers. The T-Profile corresponds to the OSI network and transport layers. Finally, the A-Profile corresponds to the OSI session, presentation and application layers.

At the L-Profile level, the UCA allows all current LAN and WAN technology. The UCA also specifies asynchronous data link control (ADLC) technology for multidrop serial phone and radio links commonly used with SCADA monitoring and control systems.

(ADLC was developed to allow UCA to be deployed over slow speed serial links. It is likely to become an important industry standard in the future as current digital radio networks use proprietary data link layers. The use of proprietary data link layers means there is no interoperability between radios from different manufacturers eg a TRIO data radio will not communicate with an MDS radio.)

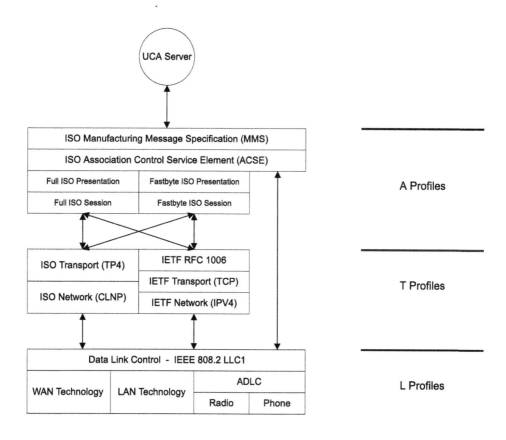

Figure 14.3
UCA Version 2 profiles (Figure courtesy American Water Works Association)

The UCA provides for two options at the T-Profile level. Utilities can use ISO network and transport standards or IETF (Internet) network and transport standards.

At the application level (A-Profile), the UCA uses the ISO session and presentation layers. It uses the association control service element (ACSE) to establish and release a communications connection between applications.

Finally, UCA uses the manufacturing message specification (MMS) standard. MMS provides the message structure, message syntax, and message dialog procedures for monitoring and control information communications.

There has been interest expressed within the DNP3 technical standards committee to extending DNP3 to include additional capability to allow DNP3 to be used instead of MMS. This is likely to be a long term objective (2008?), rather than something that will be available in the near future. The idea that UCA could be used in conjunction with communications protocols other than MMS is an integral part of the philosophy of UCA, although the protocol must have sufficient functionality to support the requirements of UCA. For this reason IEC 870 is a potential candidate to support UCA, whereas Modbus probably isn't.

The UCA A-Profiles also allow ISO 'Fastbyte' session and presentation layers as an option to the complete ISO session and presentation layers. This is intended to reduce protocol overheads.

14.3.3   Recommended water/gas industry UCA profiles

The gas industry, through the Gas Research Institute (GRI), has explored the UCA in several projects. One project, UCA/RAPS, has already evaluated UCA Version 2 and recommended specific UCA profiles for gas applications. Figure 14.4 shows the recommended water and gas industry profiles.

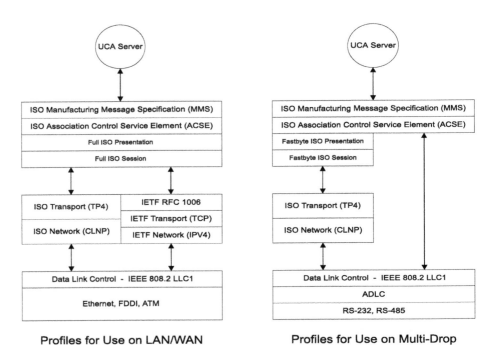

Figure 14.4
Water/gas UCA profile recommendations (Figure courtesy American Water Works Association)

14.3.4   Uniform application interface

The uniform applications interface comprises of:

- Common applications services model
- UCA DAC client
- UCA data repository
- UCA DAC server

Common application service model

Figure 14.5 is an overview of the common applications services model (CASM). The CASM standard is a key development that allows UCA compliant devices and applications to be truly compatible. CASM defines a standard set of communications functions and other data handling functions for monitoring and control of utility field devices. Some of these functions include data read, data write, equipment control, data logging, alarm and event detection, and unsolicited data reporting. CASM also provides multi-cast transmission services, time synchronization services, security services, and services for transmitting large binary data objects.

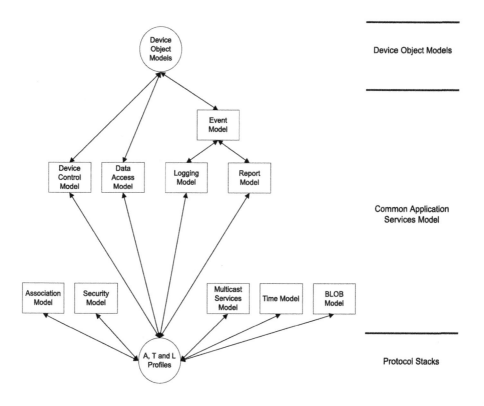

Figure 14.5
Common application services model overview (Figure courtesy American Water Works Association)

CASM also defines how to map its services to standard MMS services, which gives vendors specific instructions on how to implement CASM in UCA V2. However, the CASM functional definition is independent of any underlying application layer message standard. This provides a path for the UCA to evolve to other application layer standards when new technology becomes available.

The UCA also defines components to implement a UCA data-concentrator function. These components are the UCA data acquisition and control (DAC) client, the UCA data repository, and the UCA DAC server. Figure 14.2 shows how these three components fit into the UCA.

The UCA DAC client

The UCA DAC client manages communications with remote devices via the CASM services.

It also provides functions for:

- Browsing the remote device server object directory
- For automatically integrating new field devices into the UCA system
- Program downloads to remote devices
- Management of remote device program execution

The UCA data repository

- Acts as a data concentration point for device object models from the remote devices
- Acts as a proxy for the remote device objects and handles applications requests to read and write data and browse the remote device object libraries
- Includes functions for database maintenance and editing
- Supports UCA self-configuration functions

The UCA DAC server

- Manages communications with the various utility applications
- Interacts with the UCA data repository to handle application requests to read data, and transmit control commands, browse the remote device object libraries, etc
- Enforces security procedures on all application service requests
- Provides interfaces to server non-UCA applications. It provides data mapping services to interact with proprietary database applications, and standard interfaces for office applications
- Provides a pass-through service. This allows UCA applications to interact directly with the remote devices when the need arises

14.3.5   Uniform data model

The UCA defines a uniform data model for utility devices and equipment via the device object modeling concepts. Device object models are UCA's most powerful tool as a standard for utility data integration. Figure 14.6 illustrates the resulting UCA device object modeling concepts using a typical water utility pressure reducing valve (PRV) as an example.

14.3.6   Logical devices

UCA device object modeling describes utility equipment through four levels of abstraction. The highest level is the logical device. In a SCADA application, each individual site is usually modeled as a logical device, and the site RTU (or similar IED) implements the device object models. The site RTU contains a UCA server to provide device object information to the rest of the utility. In our example, the logical device is the PRV site.

14.3.7   Bricks

Logical devices are made up of a collection of bricks, which are the second layer of abstraction in the UCA. Bricks usually represent an individual equipment component within the site. In our example, the PRV logical device has five bricks: two pressure monitor bricks, a main PRV valve brick, a motorized pilot valve brick, and a flow monitor brick.

Note that the bricks in our example are re-usable at many sites throughout a utility. This is particularly true of the pressure monitor and flow monitor bricks.

14.3.8   Component data classes

Bricks are made up of a collection of component data classes, which reside at the third level within the UCA object hierarchy. Component data classes define the various types of information available about a device.

In our example, the pressure monitor brick contains information about the pressure input, which is the measured pressure signal.

It also contains:

- Statistical information about the input. For example, the daily highest value and time stamp and the daily lowest value and time stamp
- The pressure monitor contains a group of alarm status flags indicating low alarm, high alarm, high-high alarm, etc
- Pressure monitors also contain an associated set of alarm setpoints
- Finally, pressure monitors contain standard CASM report control blocks to regulate when and how the pressure monitor reports information about its measurement value and alarm status flags

Component data classes are used over and over in many different types of bricks. They are in simple terms the processing rules related to particular inputs or outputs.

14.3.9 Data attributes

The component data classes are made up of collections of data attributes, which reside at the fourth and lowest-level within the UCA object hierarchy. Data attributes represent the specific, concrete pieces of information provided by UCA devices. Again, the UCA data attribute definitions are common across all utilities. They define the attribute name and data format.

In our pressure monitor example, the pressure input (i.e., the MV) has four specific pieces of information (i.e., data attributes) associated with it. Inputs have an integer representation of the measured value (in 16-bit integer format) plus a floating point representation (in 32-bit IEEE single precision format). They also have data quality flags (16-bit wide bit string), and the measured value time stamp (in a 6-octet time format).

14.3.10 Device object use in actual practice

Do not be alarmed if the preceding description of UCA device objects seems complicated and confusing.

In most cases end users will simply purchase UCA compliant devices.

System designers and application developers will work mostly at the brick level. Consider again our example of the PRV sites. The site designers will decide what physical equipment has to go at a site, and go about their normal process of sizing the equipment and determining the installation details. In the UCA world, this determines the bricks that must reside in the site's logical device. All of the lower level information is standard.

The instrumentation and control engineer would specify instrumentation with the correct bricks.

14.3.11 Current status

Within the electricity industry in the US UCA is widely accepted by both utilities and vendors. For example the following is a list of utilities and vendors participating in the UCA effort.

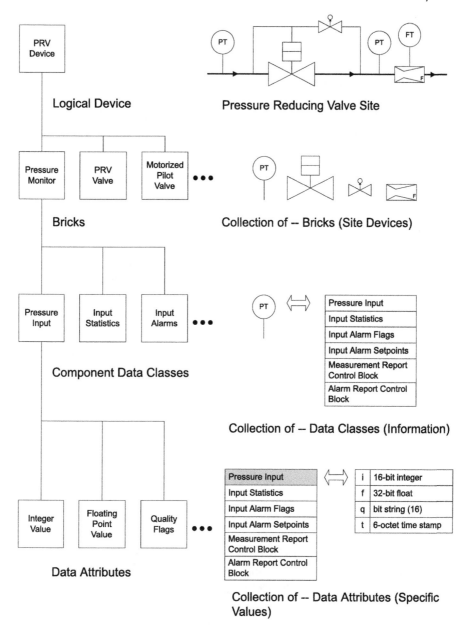

Figure 14.6
Device object model overview (Figure courtesy American Water Works Association)

14.3.12   Utilities

American Electric Power, Ameren, Arizona Electric Power, Baltimore Gas and Electric, Bonneville Power Authority, Boston Edison, Cinergy, City Public Service San Antonio, Commonwealth Edison, Duke, Duquesne Light, Florida Power Corp, GPU Energy, Indianapolis Power and Light, National Grid (England), Northern States Power, NUON/TB (Netherlands), Ontario Power (Canada), Potomac Electric Power, Pennslyvania Power and Light, Southern California Edison, Tampa Electric, Texas Utilities, Tennessee Valley Authority, United Power Association, ENEL (Italy), Entergy, VEW (Germany).

14.3.13   Vendors

ABB, Alligator Communications, Alstom (GEC), Basler, Beckwith, Bitronics, Cooper, Cycle Software, Dascan/G&W Electric, Doble, Dranetz/BMI, GE/Multilin, Harris/GE, Modicon/Square D, Power System Engineering, Process Systems, QEI/Kearney Switch, Rochester Instrument Systems, SEL, Siemens Energy & Automation, Siemens Power Transmission & Dist., Sisco, Inc, Tamarack, Inc, Tasnet, Telegyr (now a division of Siemens), US West Communications Services, Valmet (now Neles Automation).

(This list is 2–3 years old).

Within the water industry, the American Water Works Association UCA technical committee will meet in June, 2001 to formally approve a recommendation for the adoption of UCA within the water industry in the US. It will be several years however before the device object models are developed and agreed and we see UCA systems becoming routine in the industry.

The gas industry has approved UCA and work is advanced on approving several device object models.

14.3.14   Security

Security is an important issue for UCA.

Traditional SCADA systems with proprietary protocols largely relied on 'security by obscurity'. As the industry has evolved towards 'open' protocols, the degree of security has reduced. UCA with its open standards, and auto configuration has made this problem worse. The plug and play nature of this allows potential attackers to simply ask devices to describe themselves. The UCA standard specifies security services that are required to be supported.

The IEEE are sponsoring a consultant (Herb Falk of Sisco Inc) to define the amendments to the IEC 870 and DNP3 standards necessary to implement security in these protocols. They have taken the unusual step of including a non IEEE standard (DNP3) within the scope of this work because DNP3 is sufficiently widespread that 'otherwise we would have failed to secure the (electricity) industry'.

However security of SCADA data communications is probably a relatively small part of the security issues relating to SCADA. Recent studies by Major Barry Ezell of the US Army identified (by surveying a large number of water utilities world-wide) that the biggest threat came through attacks on the SCADA master system, and that the disgruntled ex-employee was the most likely source of threat. It also identified that many simple measures essential to secure a system such as enforced rotation of passwords, and removing USERIDs of staff who left the company were not routinely practised in SCADA installations although they are commonplace in the IT world.

An excellent reference for security issues (not specific to SCADA) can be found in 'Practices for securing Critical Information Assets', published by the Critical Infrastructure Assurance Office. (http://www.iwar.org.uk/cip/resources/prac.pdf) contains useful reference material including security audit procedures.

14.4   Summary

The preceding discussion introduces the three foundations of UCA technology: a uniform communications infrastructure, a uniform application interface, and a uniform data model. These three elements combine to accomplish UCA's goal of vendor and platform independence.

UCA technology has self-configuration functions built in. This is a key advantage of UCA over other integration options. New UCA devices automatically integrate themselves into the UCA system when they are connected to the network.

The end result of implementing UCA is to eliminate much of the effort currently required to integrate utility systems. This results in a true productivity increase for all parties, and equally benefits utilities, vendors, integrators and consultants. Eliminating effort leads to much more open access to information, reduces costs for everyone, and allows everyone to focus on adding value to the information.

Reference

'UCATM: From Inception to International Standard' a paper presented at IMTECH 2000, Seattle, April 2000, by Eric Von Sacken, Manager of Systems Development, Colorado Springs Utilities, Colorado Springs, CO and W. Fredrick Riddle, Senior Consultant, EMA Inc. St. Paul, MN.

15

Applications of DNP3 and SCADA protocols

Objectives

When you have completed study of this chapter you should be able to:

- Detail the practical issues in installing a SCADA system based on DNP3
- List the steps to follow in configuring an operational system

15.1 Water industry application

15.1.1 General description

This section presents the details of a recent SCADA system installed in the water industry in Australia. The Port Hedland Town Water Supply SCADA System was constructed in 1999 for the Water Corporation of Western Australia by Hunter Watertech Pty Ltd. It is a state of the art SCADA system that provides monitoring and control over the borefields, pumping stations and reservoirs and main distribution system supplying fresh water to the town of Port Hedland, Western Australia.

This section provides an overview of the system, and then focuses on how the DNP3 protocol is used in the project.

15.1.2 System overview

The Port Hedland TWS System is supplied by two borefields, the DeGrey River borefield and the Yule River borefield which are approximately 60 km to the east and 50 km to the west of the town respectively. There are 7 boresites equipped at Yule River and 11 at DeGrey River. Each boresite is equipped with submersible bore pump and an electrical switchboard including control gear, RTU, and radio. Measurements of level, salinity, water temperature and pressure and electrical power are taken at each site and telemetered along with other control information.

The boresites join to a collector main, which feeds into a collection reservoir situated within each borefield. Pumping stations including water chlorination facilities are located beside the collection reservoirs. Water mains then carry the water between the borefield pumping stations and town. Within town there is a large main reservoir, and three satellite reservoirs, including two elevated towers.

The system includes a 5 MVA 66 kV/22 kV substation at DeGrey, and 22 kV electrical distribution throughout the borefields. Backup electrical generation plant at both Yule and DeGrey pumping stations provide for reliability of general power and lighting, water treatment and control systems.

The system is shown in the overview diagram following.

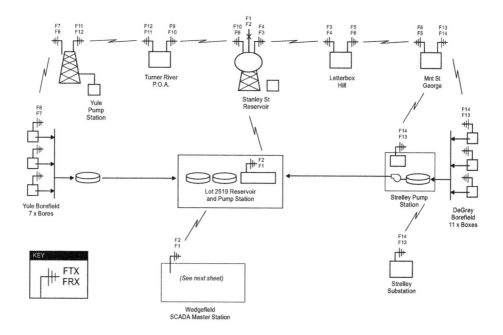

Figure 15.1
Port Hedland town water system overview

15.1.3   Description of control system

The Port Hedland TWS System is controlled from an operations and maintenance centre located in Wedgefield, which is a central location near the main in-town reservoir. A Citect based HMI system provides the operator interface at this location. Two personal computers are configured as main and standby servers, and these maintain the system database. Another two personal computers act as the operator interfaces and are located within the work environment. An Ethernet 10baseT LAN interconnects these.

The communications system is based on 900 MHz radios. A short link from the Wedgefield control connects to the Stanley Street elevated reservoir. This location provides an excellent position for directional antennae for links to each borefield, and an omnidirectional antenna provides links to other sites around the town. The radio path to DeGrey Borefield has an intermediate repeater and a final repeater located on Mt St George, which overlooks the DeGrey borefield area. The link to Yule is achieved in a single hop to the Yule borefield pumping station. Essential communication paths are backed up by PSTN phone links.

The system has been designed to not require continuous supervision by operations. Reservoir level schedules and borefield pumping mode sequence tables are used to specify the desired system control parameters in advance, and effectively allow the system to run itself. Continuous control of systems is actually distributed to 'control zones'. These are self-contained control areas that include water pumping and destination reservoirs. Each borefield and its reservoir are a control zone, for example. For each zone, the control parameter tables are maintained within the local PLC, and updated from the central SCADA control when changed. The use of distributed control provides security against interruption if communications are lost with the control zone, as in this case it will continue to operate in accordance with the control schedule. The system includes an automatic telephone dial-out system for out-of-hours priority alarms, and remote laptop dial-up access.

The overall communication system and control system arrangement is shown below.

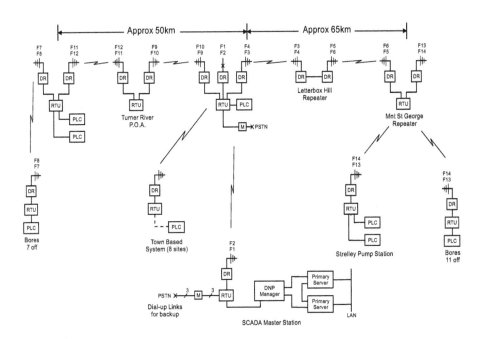

Figure 15.2
System block diagram

15.1.4 RTUs

In this and the following sub-sections, aspects of the control system that relate to DNP3 are discussed. Information shown enclosed in panels is from the Port Hedland Technical Training Course Notes produced by Hunter Watertech Pty Ltd and is included with their kind permission.

The following describes the Hunter Watertech (HWT) PDS range of RTU types used in the project. These devices are highly adaptable, being able to support a range of communications protocols and carry out roles including RTU, data concentrator, store and forward device, and as a bridge to convert between protocols.

Introduction to PDS RTUs

The Hunter Watertech (HWT) PDS500, PDS Compact 500, PDS Compact 550 and PDS 104 are intelligent microprocessor based telemetry units. They may be used as stand-alone devices, or in conjunction with small PLC systems, for data acquisition and telemetry applications. They are powerful and flexible in the roles they can perform. The primary functions of the PDS family of devices are described below.

Telemetry unit

The basic role of a PDS is to operate as a telemetry unit that forms part of a network based on the DNP3 protocol. They have the capacity to use a wide range of alternate protocols allowing the PDS to act as a communications interface for PLC installations and other devices. Their medium of communication can include voice and digital radio, landline, modem and RS-232/422/485 serial connections. Comprehensive network features allow for inter-device communications including store and forward for RTUs in locations beyond normal range.

Programmable logic controller

The PDS500 and PDS Compact RTUs provide varying numbers of digital and analog lines to service sites with minimal I/O to those with vast requirements. The PDS Compact 500 has 16 DIs, 8 DOs, 4 AIs and 1 AO. The PDS Compact 550 has exactly double the I/O of the PDS Compact 500. The PDS500 on its own has 2 DOs, 2 DIs and 1 AI, but is expandable with up to 15 plug in modules that each support up to 16 digital or 8 analog I/O lines. The PDS 104 is used as a communications device having 5 communication channels, and one DI (typically used for AC phase failure alarms). Other products are available in HWT's PDS range of RTUs.

The communications philosophy in this example system uses DNP3 protocol between the HWT RTUs in the field and the master station, based on CI Technologies' Citect HMI system.

Communication philosophy

Some SCADA systems collect data by continuously polling. On fast networks, such as PLC or Ethernet networks, the poll times for data can be set in terms of milliseconds. When a SCADA master is communicating with remote sites via collision based radio networks, dial-up networks, etc, transmission rates can be as low as 1200 bps. Polling may occur at anything from 5 minutes to a number of hours, depending on how many sites are on the network and the required data update rates. Control and monitoring at this rate of data polling may not be acceptable for many conventional systems, and may lead to errors when real time trending or remote control is attempted.

To avoid these problems, data is collected using DNP3 protocol at a lower network rate while allowing access to the communication network for other purposes such as DNP3 peer-to-peer communications and RTU maintenance, remotely. PDS RTUs can be configured to pre-empt the polling system, so that if specified, digital and/or analog points change in value the RTU will immediately time-tag the changes and report them to the master station. This utilizes DNP3 protocol's unsolicited response facilities.

The panels below show an RTU from a reservoir. In this situation there are only a few signals coming into the RTU and there is no PCL used. In other installations such as borefield switchboards or pump stations, the RTU is mounted within a larger switchboard and interfaces to a PLC.

Site components

The devices that can make up an RTU installation are:

- Sealed box (eg IP65)
- Main switch and circuit breakers
- Power supply
- Batteries
- PDS RTU
- Instruments or similar devices
- Radio and aerial
- Cables and ducting
- Communication device (eg PSTN modem)

The following panel shows how PDS communication ports are used in this installation. Various ports on the PDS telemetry processors are provided for RTU communications.

PORT	PDS500	PDS Compact	PDS104
General purpose serial communication ports	Port 0, 1 & DIAG	Port 0 & Port 1 (expansion port optional)	Port 0, 1, 2, 3 & DIAG
Model 50 PLC port	Yes	No	No
Bus I/O port	Yes	No	No
FSK modem port (radio / landline)	Yes	Yes	No
Expansion port (for optional boards)	No	Yes	No

The PDS serial ports, DIAG and Ports 0 and 1 (plus 2 & 3 on the PDS104), may be used for any of the following purposes. Configuration settings need to be appropriate for these modes to be used and not all combinations of these functions are possible as each port can only perform one operation at a time.

- **Connection to a PSTN data modem or data radio**
  The PDS RTU Radio port handles low speed data communications on standard voice radio channels, but data radio and PSTN data modems require a serial connection

- **Connection to a MODBUS device or other brand of PLC**
  PLCs and other similar devices must be connected through a serial port eg RS-232, RS-422 or RS-485 communications to PLC devices (eg using MODBUS protocol)

- **Other connections**
  There are a number of varied applications that also use serial ports:
  eg Point-to-point communication between RTUs

Network-to-network bridges
ASCII communications to LCD or hand-held display units
ASCII communications to smart instruments

PDS to computer connections are :

- **DNP3 configuration software**
  Utility for setting up and diagnostics, it uses either the DIAG port or other RS-232 serial ports using DNP3 protocol

- **Terminal diagnostics**
  Terminals or PCs with terminal emulation software, such as HyperTerminal, can intercept the ASCII characters being sent on the network through either the DIAG port on a PDS500 or port 0 on a PDS Compact 500. This facility is also used by the PDS firmware to interact in the process of I/O calibration

- **ISaGRAF software**
  IEC 61131-3 PLC programs can be downloaded to an RTU or debugged on site with a laptop and a serial cable usually connected to port 1 or port 0 as configured

- **PDS to computer network**
  The PDS104 Gateway or PDS Compact eNET RTU support TCP/IP allowing connectivity of PDS RTU networks to Internet or intranet wide area networks, or local area computer networks

15.1.5   DNP3 configuration aspects

The implementation of DNP3 protocol is described briefly here by the manufacturer. Note that the RTU devices provide support for networked transmission of DNP3 frames as well as standard direct asynchronous transmission.

Introduction to DNP3

DNP3 (distributed network protocol) is an industry standard SCADA communications protocol. It originated in the electricity industry in the USA and was based on drafts of the IEC870-5 SCADA protocol standards (now known as IEC 60870-5). DNP3 is now in widespread use in many industries across the world and is managed by the DNP3 User Group.

DNP3 describes standards for SCADA protocol facilities such as data requests, polling, controls, and report by exception (RBE). Master–slave and peer-to-peer communication architectures are supported by DNP3.

Inter-operability is one of the key aspects of DNP3. It is enforced by way of minimum implementation sub-sets to which vendors must adhere. Currently, the DNP3 standard is supplemented by a sub-set definitions document describing 3 minimum sub-set levels. In addition, a vendor's DNP3 implementation must be provided with a device profile document describing information required by the DNP3 User Group, including details of the implementation of one of the three minimum sub-set levels, and other protocol information.

The DNP3 protocol also caters for expansion & evolution of the standard without detracting from the strengths of inter-operability that it promotes. This is achieved by an object-oriented approach to the data. Data objects can be added to the DNP3 standard without affecting the way that devices inter-operate.

The PDS RTU supports DNP3 to sub-set level 2 implementation with a range of additional features from the DNP3 standard.

In summary the PDS RTU provides the following facilities for use of DNP3:

- SCADA data configuration
- DNP3 operation on multiple ports
- Networking DNP3 frames
- Peer-to-peer communication
- Individual point range queries

15.1.6　Data mapping in RTUs

This section describes the data mapping, or indexing used by the RTUs.

PDS software architecture

The PDS processor has many tasks running concurrently. Various RTU facilities are accessible, external to the PDS RTU, in three ways:

- Direct mapping of physical input and output points
- Mapping of processed or derived data for SCADA master or peer-to-peer for other RTUs
- Configuration and status information

PDS RTU data is arranged into two basic types, binary and analog data. Each element of these two types is identified with a point index that ranges from 0 to 65 535. A single binary point is one bit of information and may be accessed using DNP3 binary input and binary output objects. Analog points are generally 16-bit, but 32-bit points are included that can be used to represent either 32-bit integers or 32-bit floating point quantities via DNP3 objects. DNP3 counter objects are also supported.

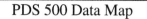

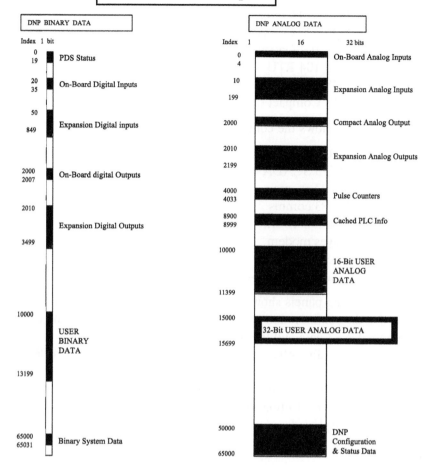

15.1.7 DNP3 configuration

Configuration of the RTUs is carried out with proprietary configuration software supplied by the RTU manufacturer.

The PDS DNP3 configuration software is the primary method of establishing and diagnosing RTUs in the workshop and on site. It is a simple, user friendly method of configuring a PDS RTU. It can be used to read and write configuration and real-time data, and to load and save data to and from a file into a PDS RTU.

DNP3Config is used for the configuration of HWT RTUs implementing the DNP3 protocol.

These HWT RTUs are:

- PDS 550 Compact
- PDS 500 Compact
- PDS 104 Gateway
- PDS 104 RTU
- PDS 500
- PDS Compact eNET RTU

DNPConfig allows the configuration of the following HWT RTU functions:

- RTU ports configuration and function
- DNP3 SCADA tables
- DNP3 events
- DNP3 comms
- DNP3 network
- Hayes modem
- PDS status
- Load IEC 61131-3 ISaGRAF application

The following panels show the setting up of a PC to perform configuration of an RTU. Note that the configuration is being carried out over the operating communication network using the DNP3 data and file transfer capabilities.

The DNP3Config software connects and communicates to an RTU via the PC's serial Com port.

The communication setup between your PC and the network can be edited by selecting the icon below, or selecting View Options from the menu bar. The 'DNP3 Options' popup will then be displayed.

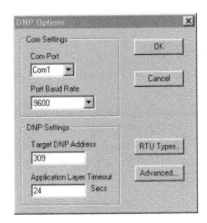

The *Com Port* refers to the computer's serial port that is connected to the PDS. The default *Port Baud Rate* for connection from a PDS to DNP3Config is 9600 bps.

Target DNP3 Address is the software DNP3 address of the RTU you are to communicate with. This address must be known in order to communicate with the RTU.

The *Application Layer Timeout* is the number of seconds DNP3Config will wait for a reply to any command it sends out before signaling a 'message timed out' error. This has a default setting of 24 seconds which is usually sufficient for communicating with a local device. If DNP3Config will be talking to a device via a radio or landline network, then the timeout can be increased to allow the PDS to retry communications if the first attempt is unsuccessful due to the network being busy.

Local DNP3 Address is set in the Advanced Settings. It is the address of your PC running DNP3Config, and is usually a unique number allocated to each person/PC.

RTU type

The particular RTU type may be selected to allow RTU specific characteristics to be configured. This popup menu is accessed by the 'RTU Types' button on the 'DNP3 Options' popup.

You will notice all the HWT RTUs that can be configured. To minimize confusion and error, select the required RTU type to be configured. Note that only the tabs for the configuration windows relevant to the selected RTU will be available.

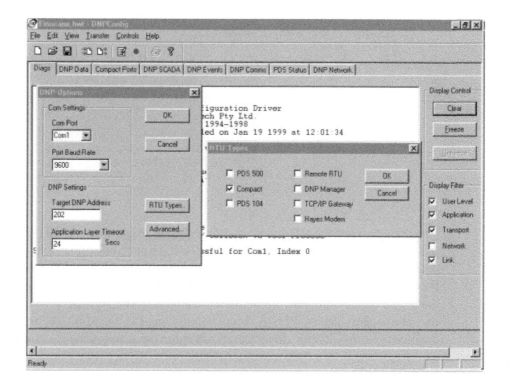

The communication ports are setup as required.

RTU ports and modes

Multi-port RTUs have the ability to interface to different devices. These devices may be radios, PLCs, modems or other HWT RTUs.

The Port Function allows the RTU ports to be configured for the following functions:

- DNP3   (DNP3 communications I/O e.g. radio, RTU)
- ISaGRAF   (Uploading and monitoring of ISaGRAF program)
- PLC Device   (PLC Port e.g. Modbus, Direct, Koyo)
- ISaGRAF-User (ISaGRAF serial comms special function)

The *Port Baud* rate setting must be set to match the port speed of the interconnecting device. The *Port Mode* selection determines the method of data transmission from the RTU serial port (e.g. RS-232, Data Radio, Hayes Modem, etc).

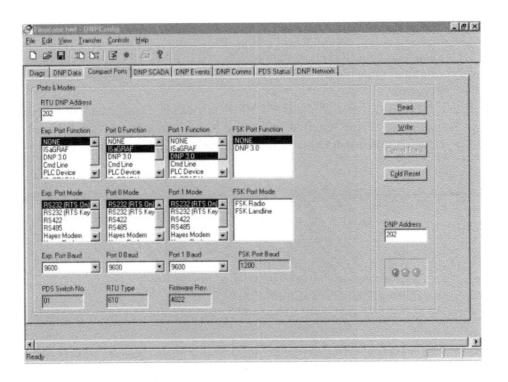

In the next part, the RTU local data is assigned in groups to DNP3 classes. Note from the configuration screen the additional 'Buff Event' and 'Trig Event' options. These determine the behavior of the reporting of events from the RTU. The difference between these is that the buffered events are stored for periodic transfer to the master, whereas the trigger events are sent immediately using a DNP3 unsolicited response. This is a mechanism provided by PDS RTUs for optimizing the use of limited bandwidth communications systems. Its function is described in the panel following the configuration screen.

SCADA table

The RTU uses a DNP3 SCADA interface, which requires configuration of the local RTU binary, analog and floating-point data. In DNP3 this RTU I/O is described as an object type with an index (address) belonging to a class. How and when I/O data is exchanged between the SCADA master and the RTU is determined by this configuration.

Objects The choice of objects can be summarized as inputs to SCADA master or outputs from SCADA master.

Index	The first DNP3 index in the group.
Class	Class 0 or class 1, 2, 3 triggered or buffered event.
Count	The count field defines the size of the group of points.
Deviation	The amount by which the point has to change value before an event is recognized.

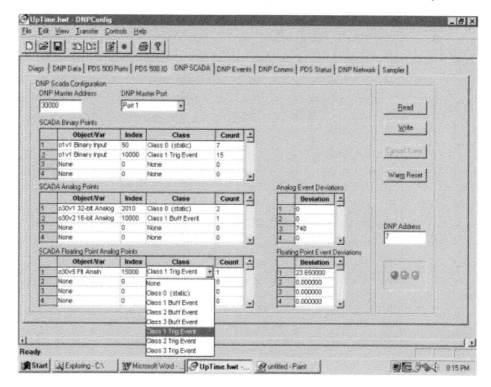

DNP3 events

In order to minimize network congestion, consecutive messages are inhibited for a set time to allow other devices to use the network (Min Unsol Event Tx Delay). When an event happens at a site, this will often trigger a series of other events, so a short time delay can also be set to allow all changes to be included in the one transmission (Notification Event Delay).

The event object type that will be used by the RTU in RBE messages to the DNP3 master can be defined for each data type.

Some DNP3 masters can process multiple analog events for the same point, however analog event buffer mode can be set to single if the master station does not permit this.

If no triggered events occur and the buffered events accumulate, they will eventually cause an unsolicited message to the master when the number of events reaches Class x Min Events.

Each class can be individually enabled or disabled by the DNP3 master station.

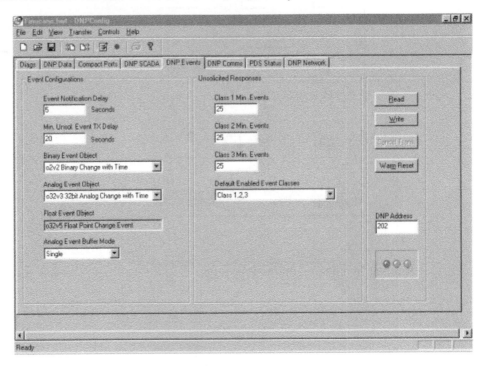

Confirmations and retries are set up via the following screen.

When a message is sent from a DNP3 device, the device will wait for a confirmation message sent back from the destination device. Data to be transmitted is broken down into fragments (application layer) and then again down into frames (data link layer). At both of these layers timeout and number of retries applies, so that the RTU can determine if the message was received and recover if not.

Data link layer has these parameters for each port, called *DL Retries* and *DL Confirm Timeout* (in seconds). The *Data Link Confirm Mode* is usually set to *Sometimes*, which means to only apply link confirmation (with retries) to the data link layer when the original message has more than one frame in a fragment. If a message is small and takes no more than one frame, then the timeouts at the data link layer are not necessary because the application layer timeout will be checking on the same data. It can also be set to *Never* and *Always*.

The application layer can have different types of messages and are allowed individual timeouts, but still use the one *Appl. Layer Attempts* value. *Complete Fragment Timeout* is applied to each application layer fragment, except event messages (RBE) which use *Appl. Layer (Event) Confirm Timeout*.

Select Arm Timeout is used in select–operate two-phase communications (common in electricity systems).

Time Update Request Rate is the preferred rate for RTU time synchronization from the master station.

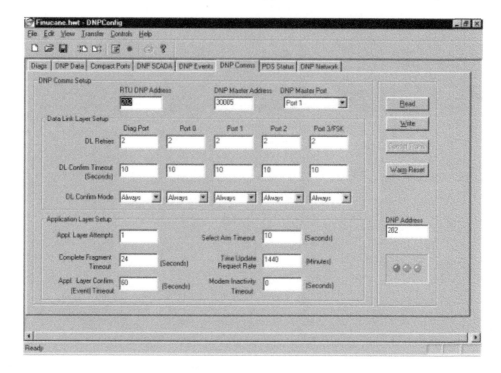

Note that although data link confirms have been set here to 'Always', a more usual setting is 'Sometimes' or 'Never' depending upon the characteristics of the communications network. The choice of 'Sometimes' or 'Never' allows the device to not double up on link layer and application layer confirmations. When in 'Always' mode, link layer and application layer confirmations can occur once each per fragment for small requests or responses. As many messages are small, they will fit in one DNP3 data link frame so there may be no point in confirming the data at both data link and application levels.

Routing of DNP3 messages defines their passage from source to destination via device ports. DNP3 frame routing is transparent to both master station and outstation RTU. In the screen below, two ports are being used for routing messages. One of these is connected to a PSTN modem, and the other to the radio communications network. Note how messages are filtered by source port and by source and destination addresses.

DNP3 network table

The PDS RTU determines how to route DNP3 data link frames by using a network routing table. Each PDS RTU can be configured with a network routing table and route DNP3 packets. Typically, though, only a small number of nodes in a DNP3 network are required to route frames. These nodes usually have two or more DNP3 communication ports, and a unique routing table. The PDS DNP3 network routing table is organized in rows. Each row contains one route table entry and describes one scenario for routing of DNP3 frames received at this node. Static and dynamic routing can be configured.

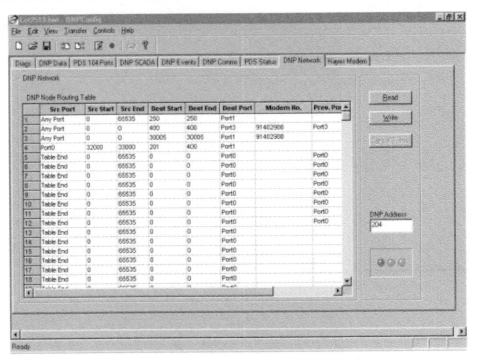

Diagnostics are provided for observing DNP3 messages. Two means of accessing messages are provided. One may be used while carrying out configuration of an RTU. This looks at the DNP3 messages between the configuration PC and the RTU. A more general tool is also provided which is called the command line diagnostics. This operates at the RTU as DNP3 protocol analyzer by displaying all DNP3 message traffic. This is a software function built into the RTU, which is accessed by connecting a PC with terminal emulation software to one of the RTU ports.

Some of the RTU diagnostics commands available and the general functionality can be seen in the following section.

DNP3 diags

This window displays communications between DNP3Config and the RTU that it is connected to. All protocol layers are available and can be selected for viewing. It does not display any communications from other RTUs. This tool is useful to diagnose DNP3 communications between the attached RTU and remote RTU.

Command line diagnostics allows direct observation of network messages and an alternate means of observing system and PDS information.

When command line diagnostics is active, this data is sent as ASCII characters to a configured serial port. Terminal emulation software, such as HyperTerminal, NTTY, WINTTY, PROCOM or TELIX running on a PC will display the data.

Here is the appearance of the DNP3Config window. The command line diagnostics operates as a terminal mode, so it will look a little different to this.

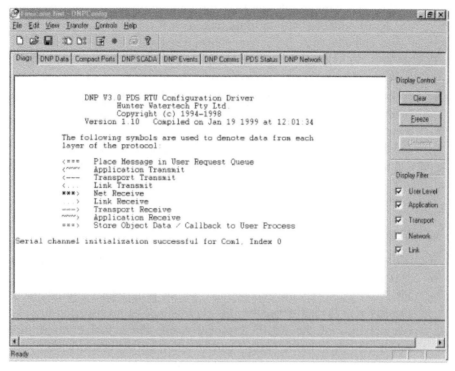

Some of the commands available and the general functionality can be seen in the following section.

Diagnostics display mode

This command is used to filter diagnostics displays when in diagnostic display mode. The format of DNPDIAG command is :

DNPDIAG mode filter [filter ....]

Where:

  mode = ENABLE or DISABLE

  filter = * 0 1 2 3 4 LINK NET TRANS APPL USER SOE COV

The following filters can be individually enabled or disabled, and are retained in non-volatile memory :

  0–4   Comms on DNP communication channels
             (0–3 = PORT 0–3, 4 = DIAG)
  LINK   DNP link layer packets including bytes
  NET   PDS DNP network layer results
  TRANS DNP transport layer information
  APPL   DNP application layer information
  USER   PDS User application request & response information
  SOE   PDS DNP sequence of events binary event information
  COV   PDS DNP change of value analog & floating point event info

Messages coming into the PDS through the protocol layers typically look like

...> ch# addr:src	data link layer Rx
—> ch# addr:src	transport layer Rx
~~> ch# addr:src	application layer Rx
===> addr:src	user Rx

Outbound (Tx) messages have arrows going the other way. Generally, the upper layers are enough to indicate trends in network messages and all others are disabled with a command such as:

dnpdiag disable *	disable all
dnpdiag enable 4 appl	show only application and user layers on DIAG port

This filter will allow the recognition of most network aberrations (eg one RTU constantly sending report-by-exception events).

Summary

This section has provided a view of the DNP3 configuration aspects of a modern SCADA system in the water industry. These have provided a demonstration of how features such as DNP3 objects may be represented within proprietary equipment, and how routing of messages is carried out using routing tables. The information has shown that despite the complexities of the DNP3 protocol itself, the actual configuration of devices when integrating them into a system can be relatively straightforward.

16

Future developments

Objectives

When you have completed study of this chapter you will be able to:

- Give an indication of where the SCADA industry is heading with DNP3

This section attempts to take a brief look at the future for DNP3 and other SCADA protocols. Of course, attempting to make predictions about the future is always going to be a risky business. However, it is reasonable to review the past and present and look for trends and change drivers.

DNP3 and IEC 60870-5-101 emerged as 'open' protocols from a long period during which proprietary protocols were the norm. This period extended from the early days of SCADA, from the 1950s through to the 1980s. This period was an expansionary period for process control systems world-wide generally, during which many systems have been developed and installed. In the latter part of this period the need for standardization and interoperability became apparent and more widely recognized. Standards bodies began to address the standardization of communications for telecontrol applications.

Why has this been the case? What factors have driven this? Economics and cost factors have. In the 1990s industrial growth has slowed world-wide. As growth has slowed, business has become more competitive and sought savings to costs at all levels of organizations. As organizations have become leaner the need for organization-wide information flow through communications systems and computers has increased.

In prior decades SCADA systems were typically islands, isolated from management and other systems. In the present, this is no longer the case. SCADA systems typically are required to interface to management information systems. Systems are being interconnected on a wider scale also. Where a water utility in the past may have operated separate SCADA systems in separate operating areas, they are becoming integrated. In the electrical utility industry deregulation has brought about increasing inter-utility communications. The high costs of interconnecting and maintaining systems on a wide scale have been behind the emergence of the Utilities Communications Architecture (UCA) project.

The UCA concepts represent a significant step forward in the application of standards to provide benefits of interoperability between systems. Through the use of uniform data models the concept of plug-and-play will allow UCA compliant systems to configure themselves when equipment is added. Although UCA has been slow in developing, and has originated in the North American utility industry, there are signs that it will emerge to become a strong force in the next decade. DNP3 and IEC 60870-5-101 are not presently incorporated into UCA, but there is no fundamental reason that they cannot be incorporated in future.

The spread of LAN/WAN technology and broadband data services generally is a trend that has been in place for some decades. However, it is probably fair to say that future growth in broadband connectivity is going to exceed past growth substantially. Again, whereas SCADA systems have had their own communications infrastructure in the past, this will change. The availability of broadband data access on an increasing widespread basis will mean that more often control systems will be interconnected through common data services. Routing of control system data over networks will become the norm, and security considerations will become an increasingly important issue.

Appendix A

Glossary

3GPP	Third Generation Partnership Project for mobile telephony.
10Base2	IEEE 802.3 (or Ethernet) implementation on thin coaxial cable (RG58/Au).
10Base5	IEEE 802.3 (or Ethernet) implementation on thick coaxial cable.
10BaseT	IEEE 802.3 (or Ethernet) implementation on unshielded 22AWG twisted pair cable.
A1-Net	Austrian name for GSM 900 networks.
Access control mechanism	The way in which the access to the physical transmission medium is managed by the LAN.
ACD	Automatic Call Distribution.
ADDRESS	A normally unique designator for location of data or the identity of a peripheral device, which allows each device on a single communications line to respond to its own message.
ARP	Address Resolution Protocol. A TCP/IP process used by a router or a source host to translate the IP address into the physical hardware address, for delivery of the message to a destination on the same physical network.
ADSL	Asymmetric Digital Subscriber Line.
AIOD	Automatic Identification of Outward Dialed calls.
Alias frequency	A false lower frequency component that appears in data reconstructed from original data acquired at an insufficient sampling rate (less than twice the maximum frequency of the original data).

AM Amplitude Modulation. A modulation technique whereby the amplitude of a high frequency sinusoidal carrier is modulated by the signal (eg audio) to be transmitted.

ASK Amplitude Shift Keying. A variation of AM used for transmitting data across an analog network, such as a switched telephone network. The amplitude of a single (carrier) frequency is varied or modulated between two levels, one for binary 0 and one for binary 1.

AMPS Advanced Mobile Phone System. A first generation mobile phone system primarily used in the USA. Uses Frequency Division Multiple Access (FDMA).

Analog A continuous real time phenomena where the information values are represented in a variable and continuous waveform.

ANSI American National Standards Institute. The national standards development body in the USA.

AP Access Point for wireless LANs (in effect a wireless hub connected to the system backbone).

API Application Programming Interface.

Application layer The highest layer of the seven layer ISO/OSI Reference Model structure, which acts as an interface between user applications and the lower layers of the stack.

ARP Address Resolution Protocol.

Arpanet The packet switching network, funded by the DARPA, that has evolved into the world-wide Internet.

Arp cache A table of recent mappings of IP addresses to the physical addresses, maintained in each host and router.

AS (1) Australian Standard. (2) Autonomous System.

ASCII American Standard Code for Information Interchange. A universal standard for encoding alphanumeric characters into 7 or 8 binary bits.

ASIC Application Specific Integrated Circuit.

ASN.1 Abstract Syntax Notation One. An abstract syntax used to define the structure of the protocol data units associated with a particular protocol entity.

Asynchronous Communications where characters can be transmitted at an arbitrary, unsynchronized point in time and where the time intervals between transmitted characters may be of varying lengths. Communication is controlled by start and stop bits at the beginning and end of each character.

ATM	Asynchronous Transfer Mode. A fast cellular switching system which uses 53-byte cells for transmission of data over wide and local area networks.
Attenuation	The decrease in the magnitude of strength (or power) of a signal. In cables, generally expressed in dB per unit length.
Attenuator	A passive network that decreases the amplitude of a signal (without introducing any undesirable characteristics to the signals such as distortion).
AUI cable	Attachment Unit Interface Cable for 10Base5. Sometimes called the drop cable. Attaches hosts to transceiver unit (MAU).
AWG	American Wire Gauge.
Balanced circuit	A circuit so arranged that the impressed voltages on each conductor of the pair are equal in magnitude but opposite in polarity with respect to ground.
Bandwidth	The range of frequencies available expressed as the difference between the highest and lowest frequencies is expressed in Hertz (or cycles per second). Also used as an indication of capacity of the communications link.
Base address	A memory address that serves as the reference point. All other points are located by offsetting in relation to the base address.
Baseband	Baseband operation is the direct transmission of a signal (eg eg voice or data) over a transmission medium without the prior modulation on a high frequency carrier band.
Baud	Unit of signaling speed derived from the number of events per second (normally bits per second). However if each event has more than one bit associated with it the baud rate and bits per second are not equal.
BCC	Block Check Character. Error checking scheme with one check character; a good example being Block sum check.
BCD	Binary Coded Decimal. A code used for representing decimal digits in a binary code.
B-CDMA	Broadband CDMA, now known as W-CDMA.
BERT/BLERT	Bit Error Rate/Block Error Rate Testing. An error checking technique that compares a received data pattern with a known transmitted data pattern to determine transmission line quality.
BGP-4	Border Gateway Patrol-4. An exterior gateway protocol, developed by Cisco, and currently the *de facto* standard for routing between autonomous systems.

BIOS	Basic Input/Output System.
Bipolar	A signal range that includes both positive and negative values.
Bit (binary digit)	Derived from 'BInary digiT', a one or zero condition in the binary system.
Bits per sec (BPS)	Unit of data transmission rate.
Block sum check	This is used for the detection of errors when data is being transmitted. It comprises a set of binary digits (bits) which are the modulo 2 sum of the individual characters or octets in a frame (block) or message.
Bluetooth	Short distance wireless access technology (2.4 GHz band).
BNC	Bayonet Nut Connector. Bayonet type coaxial cable connector.
Bridge	A device to connect similar sub-networks without its own network address. A store-and-forward device used mostly to segment networks.
Broadband	Opposite of baseband. In broadband operation the data to be transmitted is first modulated on a high frequency carrier signal. It can then be simultaneously transmitted with other data modulated on different carrier signals on the same transmission medium.
Broadcast	A message on a bus intended for all devices which requires no reply.
BS	British Standard. Basic Service Set (IEEE 802.11 Wireless LANs).
BSC	Bisynchronous Transmission. A byte or character oriented communication protocol that has become the industry standard (created by IBM). It uses a defined set of control characters for synchronized transmission of binary coded data between stations in a data communications system.
Buffer	An intermediate temporary storage device used to compensate for a difference in data rate and data flow between two devices (also called a spooler for interfacing a computer and a printer).
Burst mode	A high-speed data transfer in which the address of the data is sent followed by back to back data words while a physical signal is asserted.
Bus	A data path shared by many devices with one or more conductors for transmitting signals, data or power.
Byte	A term referring to eight associated bits of information; sometimes called a 'character' or 'octet'.

Capacitance (mutual)	The capacitance between two conductors with all other conductors, including shield, short-circuited to the ground.
Capacitance	Storage of electrically separated charges between two plates having different potentials. The value is proportional to the surface area of the plates and inversely proportional to the distance between them.
Cascade	Two or more electrical circuits in which the output of one is fed into the input of the next one.
CCITT (see ITU-T)	Consultative Committee International Telegraph and Telephone. An international organization that sets world-wide telecommunications standards (eg V.21, V.22, V.22 bis).
CDMA	Code Division Multiple Access (IS-95). A cellular technology based on spread-spectrum techniques.
cdma2000	New second-generation CDMA specification.
CDPD	Cellular Digital Packet Data.
Centrex	Central Office Exchange Server.
Character	Letter, numeral, punctuation, control figure or any other symbol contained in a message.
Characteristic impedance	The impedance that, when connected to the output terminals of a transmission line of any length, makes the line appear infinitely long. The ratio of voltage to current at every point along a transmission line on which there are no standing waves.
Clock	The source(s) of timing signals for sequencing electronic events eg synchronous data transfer.
CMRR	Common Mode Rejection Ratio.
CMV	Common Mode Voltage.
CNR	Carrier to Noise Ratio. An indication of the quality of the modulated signal.
CODEC	Coder and Decoder. Used to convert analog speech into digital signal and vice versa.
Collision	The situation when two or more LAN nodes attempt to transmit at the same time.
Common mode signal	The common voltage to the two parts of a differential signal applied to a balanced circuit.
Common carrier	A private data communications utility company that furnishes communications services to the general public.
Conditioned lines	Leased circuits with equalization to improve data transmission performance.

Contention	The facility provided by the dial network or a data PABX which allows multiple terminals to compete on a first come, first served basis for a smaller number of computer posts. Also used as a medium access method by Ethernet/IEEE 802.3 networks where multiple network interface cards contend for access to the bus.
CRC	Cyclic Redundancy Check. An error-checking mechanism using a polynomial algorithm based on the content of a message frame at the transmitter and included in a field appended to the frame. At the receiver, it is then compared with the result of the calculation that is performed by the receiver.
Crosstalk	A situation where a signal from a communications channel interferes with an associated channel's signals.
CSMA/CD	Carrier Sense Multiple Access/Collision Detection. When two stations transmit at the same time on a local area network, they both cease transmission and signal that a collision has occurred. Each then tries again after waiting for a predetermined time period. This contention-based mechanism forms the basis of the ethernet/IEEE 802.3 specifications.
CSC	Circuit Switched Cellular.
CSD	Circuit Switched Data.
CT-2	Second-generation digital cordless standard.
CT-3	Third generation cordless standard, similar to DECT.
CTI	Computer Telephony Integration.
CTS	Cordless Telephone System for GSM phone systems.
D-AMPS	Digital AMPS (IS-54), a.k.a. North American TDMA.
DASK	Differential Amplitude Shift Keying.
Data link layer	This corresponds to layer 2 of the ISO Reference Model for open systems interconnection. It is concerned with the reliable transfer of data (no residual transmission errors) across the data link being used.
Datagram	A type of service offered on a packet-switched data network. A datagram is a self-contained packet of information that is sent through the network with minimum protocol overheads.
DCS-1800	A different version of GSM, operating in the 1800 MHz band.
DDS	Digital Data Service. Leased digital circuits supplied by Telecom service provider.

Decibel (dB)	A logarithmic measure of the ratio of two signal levels where $dB = 20\log 10 V1/V2$ or where $dB = 10\log 10 P1/P2$ and where V refers to Voltage or P refers to Power. Note that it has no units of measure.
Decoder	A device that converts a combination of signals into a single signal representing that combination.
DECT	Digital European Cordless Telephone Standard.
Default	A value or setup condition assigned, which is automatically assumed for the system unless otherwise explicitly specified.
Delay distortion	Distortion of a signal caused by the frequency components making up the signal having different propagation velocities across a transmission medium.
DES	Data Encryption Standard.
DFSK	Differential Phase Shift Keying.
DID	Direct Inward Dialing.
Dielectric constant (E)	The ratio of the capacitance using the material in question as the dielectric, to the capacitance resulting when the material is replaced by air.
Digital	A signal which has definite states (normally two).
DIN	Deutsches Institut Für Normierung. German National standards agency.
DIP	Acronym for dual in line package referring to integrated circuits and switches.
DMA	Direct Memory Access. A technique of transferring data between the computer memory and a device on the computer bus without the intervention of the microprocessor. Also abbreviated to DMA.
DOD	Direct Outward Dialing.
DPSK	Differential Phase Shift Keying.
Driver software	A program that acts as the interface between a higher level coding structure and the lower level hardware/firmware component of a computer.
DTMF	Dual Tone Multi-Frequency. Audio signaling technique used with touch-tone telephones.
Duplex	The ability to send and receive data simultaneously over the same communications line.
DWDM	Dense Wavelength Division Multiplexing.
Dynamic range	The difference in decibels between the overload or maximum and minimum discernible signal level in a system.

E-1	Digital circuit operating at 2048 Mbps. Corresponds to 30-channels in the European digital hierarchy.
EBCDIC	Extended Binary Coded Decimal Interchange Code. An eight-bit character code used primarily in IBM equipment. The code allows for 256 different bit patterns.
EDAC	Error Detection and Correction.
EEPROM	Electrically Erasable Programmable Read Only Memory. Non-volatile memory in which individual locations can be erased and re-programmed.
EIA	Electronic Industries Association. A standards organization in the USA specializing in the electrical and functional characteristics of interface equipment.
EIA-232-C	Interface between DTE and DCE, employing serial binary data exchange. Typical maximum specifications are 15 m at 19200 baud.
EIA-422	Interface between DTE and DCE employing the electrical characteristics of balanced voltage interface circuits.
EIA-423	Interface between DTE and DCE, employing the electrical characteristics of unbalanced voltage digital interface circuits.
EIA-449	General-purpose 37-pin and 9-pin interface for DCE and DTE employing serial binary interchange.
EIA-485	The recommended standard of the EIA that specifies the electrical characteristics of drivers and receivers for use in balanced digital multi-point systems.
EISA	Enhanced Industry Standard Architecture.
EMI/RFI	Electromagnetic Interference/Radio Frequency Interference. 'Background noise' that could modify or destroy data transmission.
EMS	Expanded Memory Specification.
	The activation of a function of a device by a defined signal.
Encoder	A circuit which changes a given signal into a coded combination for purposes of optimum transmission of the signal.
EPROM	Erasable Programmable Read Only Memory. Non-volatile semiconductor memory that is erasable in ultra violet light and re-programmable.
Equalizer	The device that compensates for the unequal gain characteristic of the signal received.
Error rate	The ratio of the average number of bits that will be corrupted to the total number of bits that are transmitted for a data link or system.

ESS	Extended Service Set (IEEE 802.3 Wireless LANs).
Etherloop	Ethernet over the local loop. High-speed customer access technology.
Ethernet	Name of a widely used LAN, based on the CSMA/CD medium access method (IEEE 802.3).
ETSI	European Telecommunications Standardization Institute.
Farad	Unit of capacitance whereby a charge of one coulomb produces a one volt potential difference.
FCC	Federal Communications Commission.
FCS	Frame Check Sequence. A general term given to the additional bits appended to atransmitted frame or message by the source to enable the receiver to detect possible transmission errors.
FDDI	Fiber Distributed Data Interface.
FDM	Frequency Division Multiplexing.
FIFO	First in, First Out.
Filled cable	A cable construction in which the cable core is filled with a material that will prevent moisture from entering or passing along the cable.
FIP	Factory Instrumentation Protocol.
Firmware	A computer program or software stored permanently in PROM or ROM or semi-permanently in EPROM.
Flame retardancy	The ability of a material not to propagate flame once the flame source is removed.
Floating	An electrical circuit that is above the earth potential.
Flow control	The procedure for regulating the flow of data between two devices preventing the loss of data once a device's buffer has reached its capacity.
FM	Frequency Modulation.
Frame	The unit of information transferred across a data link. Typically, there are control frames for link management and information frames for the transfer of message data.
Frequency	Refers to the number of cycles per second.
FSK	Frequency Shift Keying.
FTTC	Fiber to the Curb.
FTTH	Fiber to the Home.
Full-duplex	Simultaneous 2 way independent transmission in both directions. See Duplex.

G	Giga (metric system prefix – 109).
Gateway	A device to connect two different networks which translates the different protocols.
G.Lite	Most common ADSL standard based on ITU-T G.992.1
GMSS	Geostationary Mobile Satellite Standard, a satellite air interface developed from GSM.
GPRS	General Packet Radio Service.
Ground	An electrically neutral circuit having the same potential as the earth. A reference point for an electrical system also intended for safety purposes.
GSM	Global System for Mobile communications, a.k.a. Groupe Speciale Mobile. Mobile system that operates in the 900 or 1800 MHz band.
H.323	The UTU-T standard for Packet Based Multimedia Communication Systems (VoIP).
Half-duplex	Transmissions in either direction, but not simultaneously.
Hamming distance	A measure of the effectiveness of error checking. The higher the Hamming Distance (HD) index, the safer is the data transmission.
Handshaking	Exchange of predetermined signals between two devices establishing a connection.
HDLC	High Level Data Link Control. The international standard communication protocol defined by ISO to control the exchange of data across either a point-to-point data link or a multidrop data link.
HDR	High Data Rate a.k.a. 1xEV. A wireless Internet access technology based on CDMA.
HDS	High-speed Digital Subscriber Line.
Hertz (Hz)	A term replacing cycles per second as a unit of frequency.
Hex	Hexadecimal. Numbering system to Base 16. 4-bit binary numbers are represented by digits 0–9, A–F.
HFC	Hybrid Fiber Coax.
HLR	Home Location Register.
Host	This is normally a computer belonging to a user that contains (hosts) the communication hardware and software necessary to connect the computer to a data communications network.
HUMAN	High speed Unlicensed Metropolitan Network.

I/O address	A method that allows the CPU to distinguish between different hardware components in a system.
ICMP	Internet Control Message Protocol.
IEC	International Electrotechnical Commission.
IEE	Institution of Electrical Engineers.
IEEE	Institute of Electrical and Electronic Engineers. An American based international professional society that issues its own standards and is a member of ANSI and ISO.
IFC	International FieldBus Consortium.
Impedance	The total opposition that a circuit offers to the flow of alternating current or any other varying current at a particular frequency. It is a combination of resistance R and reactance X, measured in ohms.
Inductance	The property of a circuit or circuit element that opposes a change in current flow, thus causing current changes to lag behind voltage changes. It is measured in henrys.
Insulation Resistance (IR)	That resistance offered by an insulation to an impressed DC voltage, tending to produce a leakage current though the insulation.
Interface	A shared boundary defined by common physical interconnection characteristics, signal characteristics and measurement of interchanged signals.
Interrupt handler	The section of the program that performs the necessary operation to service an interrupt when it occurs.
Interrupt	An external event indicating that the CPU should suspend its current task to service a designated activity.
IP	Internet Protocol.
IR	Infrared.
ISA	Industry Standard Architecture (for IBM Personal Computers).
ISDN	Integrated Services Digital Network. Telecommunications network that utilizes digital techniques for both transmission and switching. It supports both voice and data communications.
ISO	International Standardization Organization.
ITU	International Telecommunications Union.
IVR	Integrated Voice Recognition.

Jabber	Garbage that is transmitted when a LAN node fails and then continuously transmits.
JTAPI	Java Telephony Application Programming Interface.
Jumper	(1) A wire connecting one or more pins on the one end of a cable only. (2) A connection between two pins on a circuit board to select an operating function.
k (kilo)	This is 210 or 1024 in computer terminology, e.g. 1 kb = 1024 bytes.
LAN	Local Area Network. A data communications system confined to a limited geographic area typically about 3 km with high data rates (4 Mbps to 155 Mbps).
LCD	Liquid Crystal Display. A low power display system used on many laptops and other digital equipment.
Leased (or private) line	A private telephone line without inter-exchange switching arrangements.
LED	Light Emitting Diode. A semi-conductor light source that emits visible light or infrared radiation.
Line driver	A signal converter that conditions a signal to ensure reliable transmission over an extended distance.
Linearity	A relationship where the output is directly proportional to the input.
Link layer	Layer Two of the ISO/OSI Reference Model. Also known as the data link layer.
LMDS	Local Multi-point Distribution System.
LLC	Logical Link Control (IEEE 802.2).
Loop resistance	The measured resistance of two conductors forming a circuit.
Loopback	Type of diagnostic test in which the transmitted signal is returned on the sending device after passing through all, or a portion of, a data communication link or network. A loop-back test permits the comparison of a returned signal with the transmitted signal.
m	Meter. Metric system unit for length.
M	Mega. Metric system prefix for 10^6.
MAC	Media Access Control (IEEE 802).
MAN	Metropolitan Area Network.

Manchester encoding	Digital technique (specified for the IEEE 802.3 Ethernet baseband network standard) in which each bit period is divided into two complementary halves; a negative to positive voltage transition in the middle of the bit period designates a binary '1', whilst a positive to negative transition represents a '0'. The encoding technique also allows the receiving device to recover the transmitted clock from the incoming data stream (self-clocking).
Mark	This is equivalent to a binary 1.
MAU	(1) Media Access Unit (Ethernet 10Base5).
	(2) Multistation Access Unit (IBM Token Ring).
MCU	H.323 Multi-point Control Unit.
MDF	Main Distribution Frame.
MFC	Multi-Frequency Compelled. Inter-exchange signaling system using 2 out of 5 audible tones.
Microwave	AC signals having frequencies of 1 GHz or more.
MMDS	Multi-point Microwave Distribution Service.
MMS	Manufacturing Message Services. A protocol entity forming part of the application layer. It is intended for use specifically in the manufacturing or process control industry. It enables a supervisory computer to control the operation of a distributed community of computer based devices.
MNP	Microcom Networking Protocol. An error-correction and data compression protocol used by modems.
Modem	MODulator–DEModulator. A device used to convert serial digital data from a transmitting terminal to a signal suitable for transmission over a telephone channel or to reconvert the transmitted signal to serial digital data for the receiving terminal.
MOS	Metal Oxide Semiconductor.
MOV	Metal Oxide Varistor.
MSU	Mobile Subscriber Unit e.g. a mobile (cell) phone.
MSC	Mobile Switching Center.
MTBF	Mean Time Between Failures.
MTSO	Mobile Telephone Switching Office.
MTTR	Mean Time To Repair.
Multidrop	A single communication line or bus used to connect three or more points.

Multiplexer (MUX)	A device used for division of a communication link into two or more channels either by using frequency division or time division.
NAMPS	Narrowband AMPS. An enhancement of the AMPS system to increase its call capacity.
Narrowband	Typically frequencies below 1.5 Mbps.
Network architecture	A set of design principles including the organization of functions and the description of data formats and procedures used as the basis for the design and implementation of a network (ISO).
Network layer	Layer 3 in the ISO/OSI Reference Model, the logical network entity that services the transport layer responsible for ensuring that data passed to it from the transport layer is routed and delivered throughout the network.
Network topology	The physical and logical relationship of nodes in a network; the schematic arrangement of the links and nodes of a network typically in the form of a star, ring, tree or bus topology.
Network	An interconnected group of nodes or stations.
Node	A point of interconnection to a network.
Noise	A term given to the extraneous electrical signals that may be generated or picked up in a transmission line. If the noise signal is large compared with the data carrying signal, the latter may be corrupted resulting in transmission errors.
Non-linearity	A type of error in which the output from a device does not relate to the input in a linear manner.
NRZ	Non Return to Zero. Pulses in alternating directions for successive 1 bits but no change from existing signal voltage for 0 bits.
NRZI	Non Return to Zero Inverted.
OC-1	Optical Carrier Level 1. 51.84 Mbps. The lowest optical rate in the SONET standard.
OFDMA	Orthogonal Frequency Division Multiple Access.
OHM (W)	Unit of resistance such that a constant current of one ampere produces a potential difference of one volt across a conductor.
Optical isolation	Two networks with no electrical continuity in their connection because an optoelectronic transmitter and receiver has been used.
OSI	Open Systems Interconnection.
OSPF	Open Shortest Past First. An interior gateway (i.e. routing) protocol.

Packet	A group of bits (including data and call control signals) transmitted as a whole on a packet switching network. Usually smaller than a transmission block.
PAD	Packet Assembler/Disassembler. An interface between a terminal or computer and a packet switching network.
Parallel transmission	The transmission method where data is sent simultaneously over separate parallel lines. Usually unidirectional such as the Centronics interface for a printer.
PBX	Private Branch Exchange.
PCF	Point Control Function. A polling type of medium access control used by IEEE 802.11 Wireless LANs for real-time data.
PCM	Pulse Code Modulation. The sampling of a signal and encoding the amplitude of each sample into a series of uniform pulses.
PCMCIA	Personal Computer Memory Card Industries Association. Standard interface for peripherals for laptop computers.
PCS	Personal Communication Service (IS-136) based on D-AMPS (IS-54).
PDH	Plesiochronous Digital Hierarchy.
PDU	Protocol Data Unit.
Peripherals	The input/output and data storage devices attached to a computer e.g. disk drives, printers, keyboards, display, communication boards, etc.
Physical layer	Layer one of the ISO/OSI Reference Model, concerned with the electrical and mechanical specifications of the network termination equipment.
PLC	(1) Programmable Logic Controller. (2) Power Line Carrier.
PLL	Phase Locked Loop.
Point-to-point	A connection between only two items of equipment.
Polyethylene	A family of insulators derived from the polymerization of ethylene gas and characterized by outstanding electrical properties, including high IR, low dielectric constant, and low dielectric loss across the frequency spectrum.
PVC	Polyvinyl chloride. A general purpose family of insulation materials whose basic constituent is polyvinyl chloride or its copolymer with vinyl acetate. Plasticizers, stabilizers, pigments and fillers are added to improve mechanical and/or electrical properties of this material.

Port	(1) A place of access to a device or network, used for input/output of digital and analog signals. (2) A number used by the transmission control protocol to identify individual processes (programs) running on a computer.
Presentation layer	Layer 6 of the ISO/OSI Reference Model, concerned with negotiation of a suitable transfer syntax for use during an application, for example the translation of EBCDIC to ASCII. Encryption is also handled at this level.
Protocol	A formal set of conventions governing the formatting, control procedures and relative timing of message exchange between two communicating systems.
PM	Phase Modulation.
PSDN	Public Switched Data Network. Any switching data communications system, such as Telex and public telephone networks, which provides circuit switching to many customers.
PSTN	Public Switched Telephone Network. This is the term used to describe the (analog) public telephone network.
PSK	Phase Shift Keying a.k.a. Binary Phase Shift Keying (BPSK).
PTT	Post, Telephone and Telecommunications Authority.
PVC	(1) Polyvinyl chloride. (2) Permanent Virtual Circuit.
QAM	Quadrature Amplitude Modulation.
QoS	Quality of Service.
R/W	Read/Write.
RAM	Random Access Memory. Semiconductor read/write volatile memory. Data is lost if the power is turned off.
RAS	(1) Remote Access Server. (2) H.323 Registration, Admission and Status.
Reactance	The opposition offered to the flow of alternating current by inductance or capacitance of a component or circuit.
Repeater	An amplifier which regenerates the signal and thus expands the network.
Resistance	The ratio of voltage to electrical current for a given circuit measured in ohms.
Response time	The elapsed time between the generation of the last character of a message at a terminal and the receipt of the first character of the reply. It includes terminal delay and network delay.
RF	Radio Frequency.

RFI	Radio Frequency Interference.
Ring	Network topology commonly used for interconnection of communities of digital devices distributed over a localized area, eg a factory or office block. Each device is connected to its nearest neighbors until all the devices are connected in a closed loop or ring. Data are transmitted in one direction only. As each message circulates around the ring, it is read by each device connected in the ring.
RIP	Routing Information Protocol. One of the older Interior Gateway (routing) protocols.
Rise time	The time required for a waveform to reach a specified value from some smaller value.
RMS	Root Mean Square.
ROM	Read Only Memory. Computer memory in which data can be routinely read but written to only once using special means when the ROM is manufactured. A ROM is used for storing data or programs on a permanent basis.
Router	A linking device between network segments which operates at Layer 3 of the ISO/OSI Reference Model.
RSVP	Resource reSerVation setup Protocol.
RTP	Real Time Protocol.
RTCP	Real Time Control Protocol.
RTSP	Real Time Streaming Protocol.
SAA	Standards Association of Australia.
SAP	Service Access Point.
SDH	Synchronous Digital Hierarchy.
SDLC	Synchronous Data Link Control. IBM standard protocol superseding the Bisynchronous standard.
SDM	Space Division Multiplexing.
SDP	Session Description Protocol.
SDSL	Symmetrical Digital Subscriber Line.
Serial transmission	The most common transmission mode in which information bits are sent sequentially on a single data channel.
Session layer	Layer 5 of the ISO/OSI Reference Model, concerned with the establishment of a logical connection between two application entities and with controlling the dialog (message exchange) between them.

Simplex transmissions	Data transmission in one direction only.
Slew rate	This is defined as the rate at which the voltage changes from one value to another.
SMDS	Switched Multimegabit Data Service.
SMS	Short Message Service.
SNA	Systems Network Architecture.
SONET	Synchronous Optical Network. Allows low order bit-rate signals to be dropped and inserted without needing electrical demultiplexing.
Standing wave radio	The ratio of the maximum to minimum voltage (or current) on a transmission line at least a quarter-wavelength long.
Star	A type of network topology in which there is a central node that performs all switching (and hence routing) functions.
STM-1	Synchronous Transport Module Level 1. 155.52 Mbps. Lowest level of SDH Hierarchy, corresponds to SONET OC-3.
STP	Shielded Twisted Pair.
STS-1	Synchronous Transport Signal level 1. 51.84 Mbps electrical format of the OC-1 SONET signal.
SVC	Switched Virtual Circuit.
Switch	(1) A device such as a telephone exchange for connecting one circuit to another. (2) A linking device between network segments which operates at layer 2 or 3 of the ISO/OSI Reference Model. In a layer 2 switch, each port functions as a bridge.
Switched line	A communication link for which the physical path may vary with each usage, such as the public telephone network.
Synchronization	The co-ordination of the activities of several circuit elements.
Synchronous transmission	Transmission in which data bits are sent at a fixed rate, with the transmitter and receiver synchronized. Synchronized transmission eliminates the need for start and stop bits.
T-1	Digital circuit operating at 1.544 Mbps. Corresponds to 24-channels in the North American digital hierarchy.
TAPI	Telephony Application Programming Interface (Microsoft).
TCM	Trellis Coded Modulation.
TCP	Transmission Control Protocol.
TDM	Time Division Multiplexing.

TDMA	Time Division Multiple Access.
TDR	Time Domain Reflectometer. This testing device enables the reflections user to determine cable quality with providing information and distance to cable defects.
Telegram	In general a data block which is transmitted on the network. Usually comprises address, information and check characters.
Temperature rating	The maximum, and minimum temperature at which an insulating material may be used in continuous operation without loss of its basic properties.
TETRA	Terrestrial Trunked Radio.
TIA	Telecommunications Industry Association.
Time sharing	A method of computer operation that allows several interactive terminals to use one computer.
Token ring	Collision free, deterministic bus access method as per IEEE 802.5 ring topology.
Topology	Physical configuration of network nodes, eg bus, ring, star, tree.
Transceiver	(1) Transmitter/Receiver. (2) Network access point for IEEE 803.2 networks.
Transient	An abrupt change in voltage of short duration.
Transmission line	One or more conductors used to convey electrical energy from one point to another.
Transport layer	Layer 4 of the ISO/OSI Reference Model, concerned with providing a network independent reliable message interchange service to the application oriented layers (layers 5 through 7).
TSAPI	Telephone Services Application Programming Interface (Novell).
Twisted pair	A data transmission medium, consisting of two insulated copper wires twisted together. This improves its immunity to interference from nearby electrical sources that may corrupt the transmitted signal.
UDP	User Datagram Protocol.
UMS	Unified Messaging System.
UMTS	Universal Mobile Telephone Standard. The new Third Generation global mobile communications standard.
Unbalanced circuit	A transmission line in which voltages on the two conductors are unequal with respect to ground e.g. a coaxial cable.
UTP	Unshielded Twisted Pair.

VDSL	Very High Speed DSL. Customer access technology providing up to 55 Mbps over 100 m of copper loop.
Velocity of propogation	The speed of an electrical signal down a length of cable compared to speed in free space expressed as a percentage.
VFD	Virtual Field Device. A software image of a field device describing the objects supplied by it (e.g. measured data, events, status etc) and which can be accessed by another network.
VHF	Very High Frequency.
VLAN	Virtual Local Area Network. Uses 802.1p/Q protocol with switches to associate nodes in different areas into one virtual network.
VLR	Visitor Location Register.
Volatile Memory	A electronic storage medium that loses all data when power is removed.
Voltage rating	The highest voltage that may be continuously applied to a wire in conformance with standards of specifications.
VPN	Virtual Private Network.
VSD	Variable Speed Drive.
VSWR	Voltage Standing Wave Ratio.
VT	Virtual Terminal.
WAN	Wide Area Network.
WAP	Wireless Application Protocol.
WDM	Wavelength Division Multiplexing.
Wideband	Typically frequencies above 1.5 Mpbs.
WLAN	Wireless LAN.
WLL	Wireless Local Loop.
Word	The standard number of bits that a processor or memory manipulates at one time. Typically, a word has 16 bits.
xDSL	A generic name for a Digital Subscriber Line, a high-speed customer access system operating over existing twisted pair telephone cable.
X.21	CCITT standard governing interface between DTE and DCE devices for synchronous operation on public data networks.

X.25   CCITT standard governing interface between DTE and DCE device for terminals operating in the packet mode on public data networks.

X.25 PAD   A device that permits communication between non-X.25 devices and the devices in an X.25 network.

X.3/X.28/X.29   A set of internationally agreed standard protocols defined to allow a character oriented device, such as a visual display terminal, to be connected to a packet switched data network.

Appendix B

Implementers of DNP3

A listing of businesses that manufacture products or provide services supporting DNP3 is provided on the DNP3 User Group web site. The list is organized by type. The following table has been compiled using some of the information available on that web site as at April 2001. It is a subset showing those providing SCADA master or RTU systems.

Table of manufacturers for SCADA and RTUs supporting DNP3

Company	Product
ABB Power T&D	ABB Power RICH system
	ABB DPU2000 relay
ABB Inc.	MicroSCADA DNP3 slave & master, WinNT
	RANGER
	RTU211& RTU560 DNP3 slave, small to medium RTU, scalable
ABB Systems Control	S.P.I.D.E.R. BECOS-32X64
Advanced Control Systems	HPM 9000/ SCADA master, EMS, DMS
	MPR-7575 pole-top RTU
	MPR-7010 substation RTU
Applied System Engineering	RTU test set
ATI Systems	Pole-top RTU
C3-ilex	EOScada communication front end sub-set: level 3
	9300 & 9310 pole-top & substation RTU
CAE Electronics Ltd	Master station
CI Technologies Inc.	PC based SCADA systems
Control Microsystems	SCADAPack RTUs/PLCs
Cybectec Inc.	RTU, SMP, PAC

DAQ Electronics, Inc.	Callisto line of intelligent remotes for distribution
Demand Side Solutions Inc.	Driver for factory link
DigitaLogic Inc.	SCADA/RTU Pole-top RTUs
Dynatrol Systems Inc.	RTUs – substation, implementation
Elipse Software	Elipse-SCADA
Energy Innovations	Mini-SCADA systems
EnergyLine	WinMon IED interface software 5800 series switch control
Foxboro	C50 pole-top RTU
GE Harris **Energy Control Systems**	Powerlink PC-master, Enmac DMS, XA/21 EMS Dart, SCD
GE Fanuc Automation, **CIMPLICITY Systems**	CIMPLICITY software D20, D25 multi-function IED
GE Harris **Energy Control Systems**	PowerLink PC-base SCADA master, DNP3 over UDP/IP for LAN applications
Hathaway Automation Tech.	RMS-900 SR8550, IR8660 substation RTUs
Hinz Automation Inc.	Intellution FIX232 slave
Horton Automation	Micrapac RTU product family
Hunter Watertech Pty. Ltd.	PDS telemetry products PDS 500, PDS compact, multipurpose RTUs
Industrial Systems Inc.	PC-based SCADA software
Intellution	FIX software for WIN 95/98/NT
IST Energy	Pole-mounted RTUs Substation RTUs
IOServer Pty Limited	OPC server
Landis & Gyr Energy Mgt, Inc.	Telegyr/5700
Locamation Control Systems B.V.	SAS2000 full scalable substation automation & RTUs, integration with IEDs
MIKRONIKA	SYNDIS
MITS (a unit of Logica)	MOSAIC SCADA/DMS MD1000 and MD3311 RTU's
Mitsubishi Electric Corporation	MELSCADA MELRTU
Motorola	MOSCAD RTUs NARI SCADA
National Instruments Corporation	SCADA master

Neles Automation	OASyS SCADA/DMS Sage 2100 & Micro/1C substation RTU PoleCAT RTU
NovaTech, LLC	RTU concentrator
Nu-Lec Power	Pole-top control cubicle
Panorama Software Limited	Panorama SCADA master
PC Soft International	Wizcon SCADA/HMI and Wizcon for Internet
Reliatronics Inc.	RTU-1000
Remsdaq Limited	RTUs for pole mount and substation applications
Philippine Industrial Automation	Substation automation
Rockwell Software	RSView32 SCADA master
Romteck P/L	Delta range
SANION	RTU, DMS, SCADA total distribution automation system
Schneider Electric	Talus 100 RTU and Talus 200 RTU Talus 2000 RTU
Sensa/Mexico	Smart Control/SCADA/D.B. Pole RTU/SW, Control/DRAC
ShenZhen PCsoft TECH. CO.	SCADA, EMS, DMS system software
Siemens Power & Transmission Distribution	SICAM SCADA – NT based SCADA SICAM SAS Pole-top RTU
SNC Lavalin Energy Control	Master station
Standard Automation	OPC/DDE server
SUBNET Solution Inc.	SUBSTATION EXPLORER, Windows based substation HMI
Telegyr Systems, Inc.	Telegyr NMS on NT SCADA system Telegyr 8000 SCADA system The feeder controller pole-top RTU
Teletrol C.A.	DNP 2.0 I/O driver for Realflex 4
TesserNet Systems Inc.	DNP3 scan task for RTAP/Plus
The Flood Group	Master station
Transdyn Control	DYNAC SCADA
Transmitton Ltd	Fastflex RTUs for use in a wide range of SCADA applications
Trihedral Engineering Limited	VTS visual tag system

Wescon Technology, Inc.   PowerWare PC base SCADA master
Supports DNP3 over UDP/IP for LAN
applications

QEI Inc   Quics 4 master station
Substation RTUs

Quindar Products Ltd   QUICS IV master station
XPPB, XPAC, XPDC, XPPQ RTUs

Appendix C

Sample device profile document

A device profile document is provided with any DNP3 compliant device. The document format and content is specified by the DNP3 documentation, and provides full information on the device including the DNP3 level, additional features, data objects supported, and configuration details.

The device profile document format is specified as:

- Device profile
- Implementation table
- Point list (optional)

The following device profile document has been reproduced with the kind permission of Nu-Lec Pty Ltd. The content remains the property of Nu-Lec. This device profile is for a Nu-Lec recloser.

The Nu-Lec Pty Ltd device profile document includes the point list for the device. However, due to space limitations this cannot be included within this manual. A small part of the point list titled 'ACR – Counter Point' has been included as a sample. For reference, the full content of the document is listed below.

Content of Nu-Lec Pty Ltd CAPM-4 controller device profile document:

DNP3 Device Profile
DNP3 Implementation Table
Point List

    ACR – Binary Input Points (Status)
    ACR – Analogue Input Points (Status – Small Set)
    ACR – Analogue Input Points (Status – Full Set)
    ACR – Counter Point
    ACR – Binary Output Points
    ACR – Analogue Output Points
    LBS – Binary Points Data (Status)
    LBS – Analogue Input Points (Status – Small Set)
    LBS – Analogue Input Points (Status – Full Set)
    LBS – Counter Points
    LBS – Binary Output Points
    LBS – Analogue Output Points

DNP3 device profile

DNP V3.00 Device Profile	
Vendor Name: Nu-Lec Industries P/L, Brisbane, Australia	Device Name: CAPM-4 Controller
Highest DNP Level Supported For Requests: 2 For Responses: 2	Device Function: Slave

Conforms to DNP V3.00 level 2 subset definition requirements with many additional level 3 features built in.

These extra features include the parsing of read requests (FC 1) for the following objects and/or qualifiers:

    Binary Input (Object 1 Variations 0 Qualifiers 00, 01,07,08,17,28)
    Binary Input (Object 1 Variation 1 Qualifiers 00, 01, 06,07,08,17,28)
    Binary Output (Object 10 Variation 0 Qualifiers 00, 01, 07, 08, 17, 28)
    Binary Output (Object 10 Variation 2, Qualifiers 00, 01, 06, 07, 08, 17, 28)
    Binary Counter (Object 20 Variation 6 Qualifiers 00, 01, 06, 07, 08, 17, 28)
    Frozen Counter (Object 21 Variation 10 Qualifiers 00, 01, 06, 07, 08, 17, 28)
    Analogue Input (Object 30 Variation 0, Qualifiers 00, 01, 07, 08, 17, 28)
    Analogue Input (Object 30 Variations 1, 2, 3, 4 Qualifiers 00, 01, 06,07,08,17,28)
    Analogue Change Event (Object 32 Variations 1, 2, 3, 4 Qualifiers 06, 07, 08)
    Analogue Input Deadband (Object 34 Variations 1, 2, Qualifiers 00, 01, 06,07,08,17,28)
    Analogue Output Status (Object 40 Variation 1, 2 Qualifiers 00, 01,07,08,17,28)
    Analogue Output Block (Object 41 Variation 1, 2 Qualifiers 00, 01, 07, 08, 17, 28)

Also, the following functions are included:

    Function codes 7, 8, 9, 10 for Binary Counters (Object 20 Variation 6)
    Function code 14 - Warm Restart
    Function code 20 - Enable Unsolicited Messages
    Function code 21 - Disable Unsolicited Messages
    Function code 22 - Assign Data Classes

Maximum Data Link Frame Size (octets):
    Transmitted: 292
    Received: 292
	Maximum Application Fragment Size (octets):
	    Transmitted: 2048
	    Received: 249

Maximum Data Link Retries:
    Configurable   0..255
	Maximum Application Layer Retries:
	    None

Requires Data Link Layer Confirmation: Configurable, 3 settings Never, Always, Sometimes (on multi frame fragments only)	
Requires Application Layer Confirmation: Sometimes (only when reporting event data or when sending multifragment responses)	

DNP3 implementation table

CAPM DNP V3.00 Implementation Table

OBJECT			REQUEST (slave must parse)				RESPONSE (master must parse)	
Obj	Var	Description	Func Codes (dec)		Qual Codes (hex)		Func Codes	Qual Codes (hex)
1	0	Binary Input - All Variations	1	22	00, 01	06	N/A	N/A
					07, 08, 17, 28			
1	1	Binary Input	1		00, 01, 06, 07, 08, 17, 28		129	00, 01 / 17, 28 / Note 4
1	2	Binary Input With Status	1		00, 01, 06, 07, 08, 17, 28		129	00, 01 / 17, 28 / Note 4
2	0	Binary Input Change - All Variations	1		06, 07, 08		N/A	N/A
2	1	Binary Input Change without Time	1		06, 07, 08		129, 130	17, 28
2	2	Binary Input Change with Time	1		06, 07, 08		129, 130	17, 28
2	3	Binary Input Change with Relative Time	1		06, 07, 08		N/A	N/A
10	0	Binary Output - All Variations	1		00, 01	06	N/A	N/A
					07, 08, 17, 28			
10	2	Binary Output Status	1		00, 01, 06, 07, 08, 17, 28		129	00, 01 / 17, 28 / Note 4
12	1	Control Relay Output Block	3, 4, 5, 6		00, 01, 07, 08 17, 28		129	Echo of request
20	0	Binary counter ñ All Variations	1, 7, 8, 9, 10		00, 01	06	N/A	N/A
					07, 08, 17, 28			
20	1	32 Bit Binary Counter with flag	1		00, 01, 06, 07, 08, 17, 28		129	00, 01 / 17, 28 / Note 4
20	2	16 Bit Binary Counter with flag	1		00, 01, 06, 07, 08, 17, 28		129	00, 01 / 17, 28 / Note 4
20	5	32 Bit Binary Counter without flag	1		00, 01, 06, 07, 08, 17, 28		129	00, 01 / 17, 28 / Note 4
20	6	16 Bit Binary Counter without flag	1		00, 01, 06, 07, 08, 17, 28		129	00, 01 / 17, 28 / Note 4
21	0	Frozen Counter ñ All variations	1	22	00, 01	06	N/A	N/A

OBJECT			REQUEST (slave must parse)		RESPONSE (master must parse)	
Obj	Var	Description	Func Codes (dec)	Qual Codes (hex)	Func Codes	Qual Codes (hex)
				07, 08, 17, 28		
21	1	32 Bit Frozen Counter with flag	1	00, 01, 06, 07, 08, 17, 28	129	00, 01
						17, 28 Note 4
21	2	16 Bit Frozen Counter with flag	1	00, 01, 06. 07, 08, 17, 28	129	00, 01
						17, 28 Note 4
21	9	32 Bit Frozen Counter without flag	1	00, 01, 06. 07, 08, 17, 28	129	00, 01
						17, 28 Note 4
21	10	16 Bit Frozen Counter without flag	1	00, 01, 06. 07, 08, 17, 28	129	00, 01
						17, 28 Note 4
30	0	Analogue Input - All Variations	1 22	00, 01 06 07, 08, 17, 28	N/A	N/A
30	1	32 Bit Analogue Input	1	00, 01, 06, 07, 08, 17, 28	129	00, 01
						17, 28 Note 4
30	2	16 Bit Analogue Input	1	00, 01, 06, 07, 08, 17, 28	129	00, 01
						17, 28 Note 4
30	3	32 Bit Analogue Input without Flag	1	00, 01, 06, 07, 08, 17, 28	129	00, 01
						17, 28 Note 4
30	4	16 Bit Analogue Input without Flag	1	00, 01, 06, 07, 08, 17, 28	129	00, 01
						17, 28 Note 4
32	0	Analogue Change Event - All Variations	1	06, 07, 08	N/A	N/A
32	1	32 Bit Analogue Change Event without Time	1	06, 07, 08	129, 130	17, 28
32	2	16 Bit Analogue Change Event without Time	1	06, 07, 08	129, 130	17, 28
32	3	32 Bit Analogue Change Event with Time	1	06, 07, 08	129, 130	17, 28
32	4	16 Bit Analogue Change Event with Time	1	06, 07, 08	129, 130	17, 28
34	0	Analogue Input Reporting Deadband ñ All Variations Note 6	1	00, 01, 06, 07, 08, 17, 28	N/A	N/A

OBJECT			REQUEST (slave must parse)		RESPONSE (master must parse)	
Obj	Var	Description	Func Codes (dec)	Qual Codes (hex)	Func Codes	Qual Codes (hex)
34	1	16 bit Analogue Input Deadband reporting Note 6	1, 2	00, 01, 06, 07, 08, 17, 28	129, 130	17, 28
34	2	32 bit Analogue Input Deadband reporting Note 6	1, 2	00, 01, 06, 07, 08, 17, 28	129, 130	17, 28
40	0	Analogue Output Status - All Variations	1	00, 01　06 07, 08, 17, 28	N/A	N/A
40	1	32 Bit Analogue Output Status	1	00, 01, 06, 07, 08, 17, 28	129	00, 01 17, 28 Note 4
40	2	16 Bit Analogue Output Status	1	00, 01, 06, 07, 08, 17, 28	129	00, 01 17, 28 Note 4
41	1	32 Bit Analogue Output Block	3, 4, 5, 6	00, 01, 07, 08, 17, 28	129	Echo of request
41	2	16 Bit Analogue OutputBlock	3, 4, 5, 6	00, 01, 07, 08, 17, 28	129	Echo of request
50	0	Time and Date	1	00, 01, 06 07, 08, 17, 28,	129	00, 01 17, 28 Note 4
50	1	Time and Date	2	00, 01, 06 08, 17, 28 07 (quantity = 1)	129	00, 01 17, 28 Note 4
			1	00, 01, 06 08, 17, 28, 07 (quantity = 1)	129	00, 01 17, 28 Note 4
52	2	Time Delay Fine	N/A	N/A	129	07, (quantity 1)
60	1	Class 0 Data	1 20,,21	06	N/A	N/A
60	2	Class 1 Data	1 20,,21, 22	06, 07, 08	N/A	N/A
60	3	Class 2 Data	1 20, 21, 22	06, 07, 08	N/A	N/A
60	4	Class 3 Data	1 20, 21, 22	06, 07, 08	N/A	N/A
80	1	Internal Indications	2	00 index = 7	N/A	N/A
112		Virtual Terminal Output Block Note 5	2	00, 01, 06, 08, 17, 28	N/A	N/A
113		Virtual Terminal Event Data	1	06, 07, 08	129	17, 28

Note

1. All shaded areas are the additional level 3 or above function, objects, variations and/or qualifiers supported by CAPM.
2. Bold italics response function codes represent CAPM default objects. These are the object variations that the CAPM will issue as in its response to an event (class 1, 2, 3) poll, an integrity (class 1, 2, 3, 0) poll, in a response to a variation 0 read request, or in an unsolicited response message. Where more than one data object variation is highlighted then default object can be configured. Selection of default objects is explained in manual.
3. All request and response options marked N/A are not applicable.
4. For static (non-change-event) objects, qualifiers 17 or 28 are only responded when a request is sent with qualifiers 17 or 28, respectively. Otherwise, static object requests sent with qualifiers 00, 01, 06, 07, or 08, will be responded with qualifiers 00 or 01. (For change-event objects, qualifiers 17 or 28 are always responded.)
5. The virtual terminal objects (112 and 113) are used to transport SOS data between WSOS and the CAPM. No other data is supported.
6. A write with an analog input deadband value of zero will be rejected. The response will have the 'parameter in qualifier, range or data field not valid or out of range' internal indicator bit (IIN2-2) set.

DNP3 function codes

Request				Response	
Function Code	Description	Function Code	Description	Function Code	Description
1	Read	9	Freeze and Clear	129	Response
2	Write	10	Freeze and Clear, No Ack	130	Unsolicited Response
3	Select	13	Cold Restart (Note 1)		
4	Operate	14	Warm Restart (Note 1)		
5	Direct Operate	20	Enable Unsolicited Msgs		
6	Direct Operate, No Ack	21	Disable Unsolicited Msgs		
7	Immediate Freeze	22	Assign Class		
8	Immediate Freeze, No Ack	23	Delay Measurement		

Note

1. When a cold or warm restart command is received by the CAPM it will restart the DNP3 protocol handler only. The CAPM itself does not restart.

It is recommended by the DNP3 User Group that master stations do not ask for a data link acknowledgment nor an application confirm on restart commands (refer to 'Cold/Warm Restart Sequence', Technical Bulletin 9701-003).

The CAPM reports a time object of 500 ms for both restart types. The master station should not initiate any message sequences for this period. However, if the CAPM has unsolicited messages configured ON then it will automatically establish communications on restart. This may be within the 500 ms period.

DNP3 qualifiers

Q

Qualifier (Hex)	Use in a Request	Use in a Response
00, 01	A range of static points, or a single point with a point number. Object headers use either 8 bit (Q=00) or 16 bit (Q=01) start and stop range indices.	Static Objects
06	All points. Object headers and data sizes are determined by CAPM configured parameters.	Not valid
07, 08	A limited quantity of events or a single point with no number (eg Time and Date). Object headers have either 8 bit quantity fields (Q=07) or 16 bit quantity fields (Q=08).	A single point with no number (eg Time and Date)
17, 28	Controls (usually one or more unrelated points) Object headers have either 8 bit quantity field with 8 bit indices (Q=17) or 16 bit quantity field with 16 bit indices (Q=28)	Event objects (usually one or more unrelated points)

DNP3 internal indication bits

The following DNP3 response internal indication bits are not supported.

- IIN1-6 Device trouble. For system health status refer to the abnormal operator conditions' binary input point that is described in **Error! Reference source not found.**.

- IIN2-4 Request already executing
- IIN2-5 Corrupt configuration

DNP3 object status flags

Binary inputs

Only the on-line and status bits are supported. This means that, depending upon the point's status, the reported flag will always be either 0x01 or 0x81 since the CAPM always regards its points as on-line.

Binary outputs

Only the on-line and status bits are supported. Refer to the relevant binary output appendix for on/offline condition information.

Analog inputs

Only the on-line and over-range bits are supported. Since the CAPM always regards its points as on-line, the flag will always be reported as either 0x01 or 0x21.

DNP3 control operation

The success or failure of control operation is returned in the control response message. The CAPM support for control success is shown below.

Response Status Value	CAPM Control Response Description
0	Control request accepted
1	Control request denied. Select/Operate timed out. The time out parameter is configurable.
2	Control request denied. Operate without select message.
3	Control request denied. Formatting error
4	Control request denied. Control operation not supported Examples: 1. Trip control sent to a point that supports only Pulse or Latch operations. The supported operations are indicated on a per point basis in manual. 2. The binary output (or analogue output) point number is out of range. 3. The analogue output value is out of range.
5	Control request denied. Already Active
6	Control request denied. Control rejected by CAPM because of an underlying condition preventing the action. These conditions are indicated on a per point basis in the manual.

All binary output points have a matching binary input status point. The master station must always use the corresp*onding binary status for the control to verify the success of the action.

DNP3 technical bulletins

Technical Bulletin	Description	Nulec Manual Version	Comment
2000-004	Application Layer Confirmation Messages	N00-324R20	
2000-003	Change Management	-	Note 1
2000-002	Control Retries	N00-324R28	
2000-001	Sequential File Transfer Objects	-	Not Applicable. Note 2
9912-003	Broadcast Message Confirmation and Address Reservation		
9912-002	Unsolicited Event Reporting; Retry Configuration	N00-324R28	
9905-001	Qualifier Code 11	-	Not Applicable. Note 2
9809-001	Analogue Input Reporting Deadband	N00-324R28	
9804-008	Unissued Object and Variation Numbers	N00-324R20	
9804-007	Clarification of Collision Avoidance Procedure	N00-324R28	
9804-006	Analogue Object Floating Point Variations	-	Not Applicable. Note 2
9804-005	8 Bit Unsigned Integer Object 102	-	Not Applicable. Note 2
9804-004	Virtual Terminal Objects 112 and 113	N00-324R27	
9804-003	Recommended Layer Terminology	N00-324R20	
9804-002	DNP Confirmation and Retry Guidelines	N00-324R20	
9804-001	Rules for Synchronising Application Sequence Numbers	N00-324R20	
9704-007	Implementation for Reset Link Frames	N00-324R20	
9701-006	Extension of Engineering Units for Floating Point Objects	-	Not Applicable. Note 2
9701-004	Octet String Objects 110 and 111	-	Not Applicable. Note 2
9701-003	Cold/Warm Restart Sequence	N00-324R20	
9701-002	Control Relay Output Block Minimum Implementation	N00-324R20	
9701-001	Datalink Restart Recovery	N00-324R20	

Note

1) It is Nu-Lec policy that all technical bulletin rules that are required for the CAPM to be DNP3 level 2 compliant are implemented.
2) The following data types are not used by the CAPM:
   - File transfer objects
   - String objects
   - Analog input floating point and analog output floating point objects
   - Variable arrays objects
   - 8-bit unsigned integer objects

Point list – extract

The ACR – counter point part of the point list is included here as an example.

ACR – counter point

W series support is indicated below by a 'Y'. If indicated as 'N' then value is always 0.

DNP3 implementation

Binary counters

Static object: Object 20 variation 05 – 32-bit binary
                                        counter without flag

Request Function Codes: 01 – Read, 07 – immediate freeze,

                                        08 – immediate freeze, no ack, 09 – freeze
                                        and clear
                                        10 – freeze and clear, no ack

Frozen counters

Static object: Object 21 variation 9 – 32-bit frozen
                                        counter without flag

Request function code: 01 – read

ACR Counter Points					
DNP ID	Name	W Series	Min	Max	Units
0	KWH Cumulative Note 1	Y	0	2147483647	KWH
1	Source Outages Note 2, 3	Y	0	2147483647	Counts
2	Source Outage Duration Note 2, 3	Y	0	2147483647	Seconds
3	Load Outages Note 2, 3	Y	0	2147483647	Counts
4	Load Outage Duration Note 2, 3	Y	0	2147483647	Seconds

Note

1. This accumulates the total kWH flowing through the ACR. If the CAPM is set for power flow unidirectional then the cumulative total increases irrespective of the direction of power flow to show the total power that has passed through the device. If the CAPM is set for bi-directional power flow then the cumulative total can increase or decrease reflecting the nett power flow.
2. Resetting any outage counter via a protocol counter reset command will result in the resetting of all outage counters.
3. The power flow direction (source/load designation) is determined by the user. Refer to power flow direction binary input for status and binary output for control.

Appendix D

Practicals

SESSION 1: MODBUS PROTOCOL

Overview

The Modbus protocol is still one of the most popular protocols used in the world today and is used extensively in industrial automation and SCADA systems. It is interesting to compare this with the DNP3 protocol used later on in the exercises. It is preferable to use a PC setup a protocol analyzer with two active serial ports to monitor the messages (request and response). This is possible by using the existing comport on the PC along with an add on com port in the form of either a PCMCIA card or USB com port device.

In this practical we will use two computers connected by a Laplink cable to simulate the transfer of data from an RTU to the monitoring computer. Therefore we will only need one com port to monitor data in one direction.

Procedure

The hardware required for this practical is as follows:

- Two personal computers running Windo-ws 95/98/ME/XP/2000/NT
- One Laplink cross over cable (two 9-pin connectors/two 25-pin connectors) for RS-232

The software required is as follows:

- IDC's Modbus software running on both PCs
- IDC's protocol analysis software tool (PAT) running on one PC

Hardware setup

- Boot up both computers
- Connect the ends of the Laplink cable to the com 1 port on each computer.

Software setup

- Load up the Modbus program on both PCs.
- Execute Modbus and set the one PC to master device using the F10 key to toggle the setting. Set the other up as the slave.
- Confirm the Modbus communications setup by hitting the F11 key on both computers.
- Select 9600 baud and 8 data bits and no parity (why is no parity selected?).
- Press the page/down key on the slave and set the coils A and B as 1s.
- Press the page/up key to return to the main page.

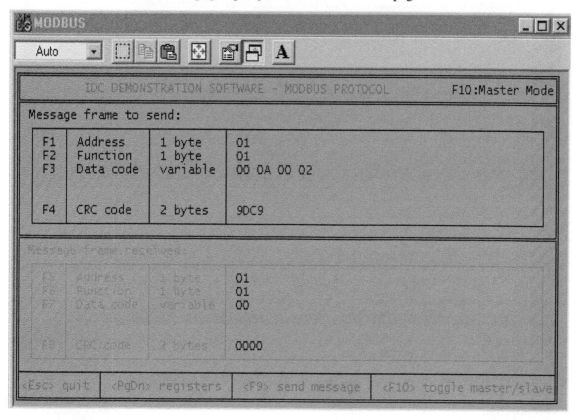

Test procedure

1. Create a protocol message on the master device by selecting the F3 function key. Key in 000A0002. This selects the read coil function code (F2 - 01) to read 2 points starting at address 0A hexadecimal.

Note: This function allows the host to obtain the ON/OFF status of one or more logic coils in the target device. The data field of the request consists of the offset address of the first coil (A) followed by the number of coils to be read (2)(A and B). The data field of the response frame consists of a count of the coil bytes followed by that many bytes of coil data.

1. Press the F9 key on the master and then follow the screen prompts.
2. Verify that the correct data was transferred between both PCs as shown.
3. On the slave computer exit out of the Modbus software.
4. Run the PAT software on the slave computer
5. Set up the PAT software to match these parameters using the Port settings.

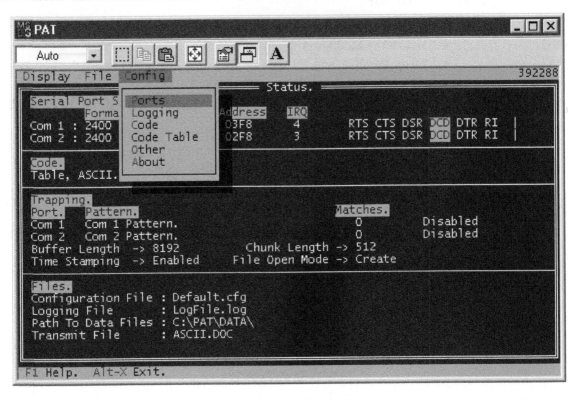

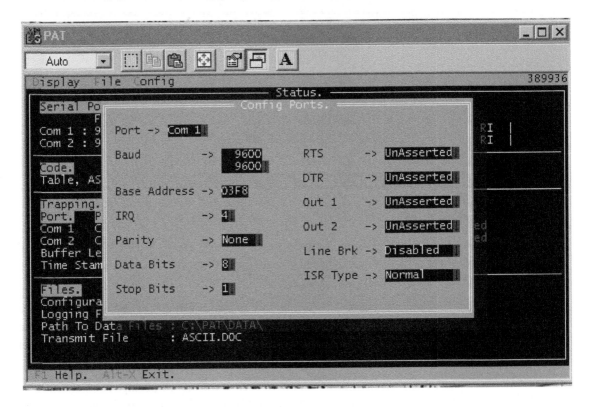

1. Set up the PAT PC to Monitor to monitor the port.
2. Calculate the cyclic redundancy check (CRC-16) code by hitting F4.
3. Now dispatch the message from the master to the slave by hitting the F9 function key on the Modbus master.
4. The coil data bytes are packed with one bit for the status of each consecutive coil. The least significant bit of the first coil data byte conveys the status of the first coil read. If the number of coils read is not a multiple of eight, the unused data in the byte will be padded with zeros. Note that the least significant bit of the data byte in the response of the slave (03 or 0000 0011) contains the status of coil A (00011) and the next to the least significant bit indicates the status of coil B (00011). The target device's response indicates both coils are either ON or OFF depending on whether a one (1) is considered ON or OFF in the system.
5. Confirm what you see with the PAT is the same as the protocol request message sent down the link between the Modbus master and the PAT software.

Hint: Are you looking at the data in hexadecimal?

Conclusion

As can be seen this is a very simple protocol that is easy to setup and run. It is however rather limited in its functionality and only has the data link layer defined; hence the need for a protocol such as DNP3 which has a well structured data link and application layers (with a pseudo-transport layer as well).

SESSION 2: SETTING UP A NETWORK

Overview

The first network based practical is for setting up a PC network and testing it at the physical and data link layer (or from a TCP/IP perspective – the network interface layer). This requires the network to be cabled up.

Procedure

Equipment

- 6 notebook computers all with Windows 95 /98 running
- A 10Base T hub (preferably an 8 port 10BaseT hub)
- 6 by 10BaseT cables
- NDG software installed on each PC
- Windows 95/98 operating system software installed on each PC
- Associated power supplies for both the 6 computers and the hub.

Setting up the network is the foundation of all Ethernet practicals in this course. Six computers will be connected to one or more hubs using the 10BaseT cables. Power for the computers and hub/s will be on an as needed basis. The network will be set up as a star/ hub system. This is one of the most used systems in industry.

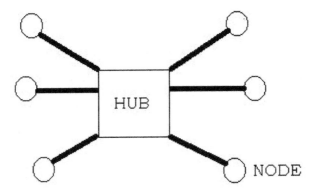

Electrically Parallel Ethernet Star

Note: Remember that even though the network has a hub in the system, the NODES or computers are all **physically** wired in parallel.

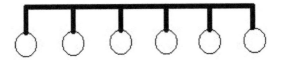

Parallel Ethernet Bus

Objectives

- To show how a basic Ethernet network is setup
- To demonstrate the physical layer with an Ethernet network
- To implement TCP/IP on an Ethernet network
- Define and change the IP address on a computer
- To be able to share information from one computer to another
- To verify the setting and if needed troubleshoot the network

Hardware/software required

No less than one laptop computer per three users
One two or three Ethernet hubs
One PCMCIA Ethernet card per computer (two for the router)
One adapter cable for each Ethernet card (except the Ambicom card, it uses a special cable)
At least one 10BaseT cable per computer
Windows software (Win95 for all computers except the router)
Windows NT installed on the routing computer

Implementation/setting up the network

Plug in power supplies into the computers (**do not** turn them on yet)
Carefully plug in the adapter cables into the PCMCIA cards
Plug in the 10BaseT cables into the PCMCIA adapters and into the HUB/s

Hub connections

Plug in the hub power supplies (they should now have power)
Turn on the computers and let them boot up.

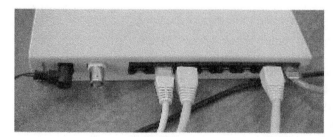

Hub Connections

When the computer asks you to log on use guest.

After boot up, double click on the Network Neighborhood icon

The screen should look something like this but the computer names will be different.

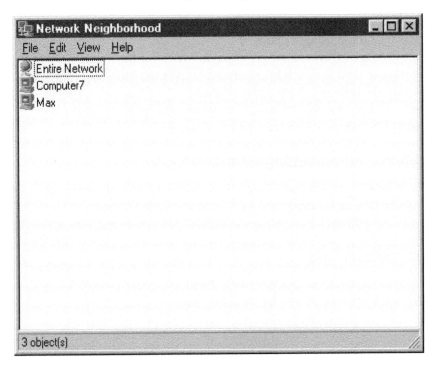

This shows that there are two computers on the network. The third computer is the router. It is not shown because the server setup is not installed on the routing computer.

All WIN95 computers on the network should be displayed. If you cannot see all of the computers then you will need to troubleshoot the system.

Troubleshooting the network

1. Turn off the computer that cannot be seen.
2. Verify that the 10BaseT cables are connected at both ends.
3. Verify that the PCMCIA card is inserted completely.
4. Verify that the hub is powered up and the lights are on.
5. Turn the computer back on again. Once the computer is booted up, log on using the correct password.
6. On the other computers click refresh under the view pull down menu.
7. If the computer still doesn't come up then you will need to continue with the next section and setup TCP/IP.

Implementation/setting up TCP/IP

Click on the START button on the bottom of the screen and go to settings.

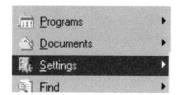

Click on Control Panel.

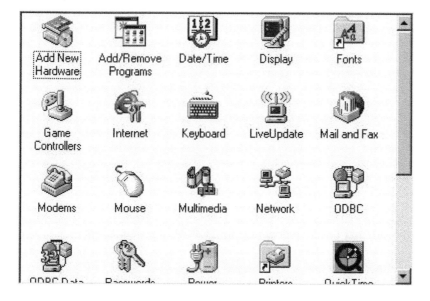

In the Control Panel click on Network icon

The screen should change to

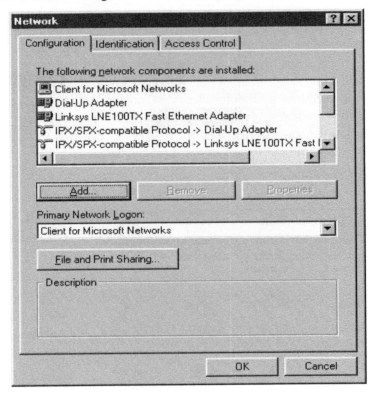

Use the side bar to move down to the TCP/IP Ethernet Adapter.

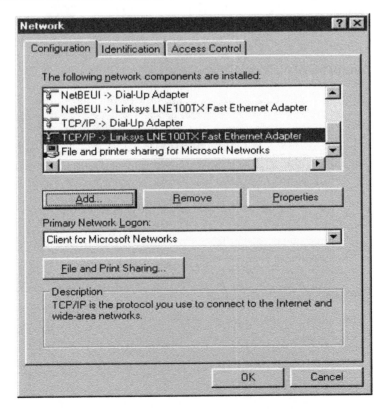

Click once on the TCP/IP Ethernet Adapter and then click on Properties. The screen should change to…

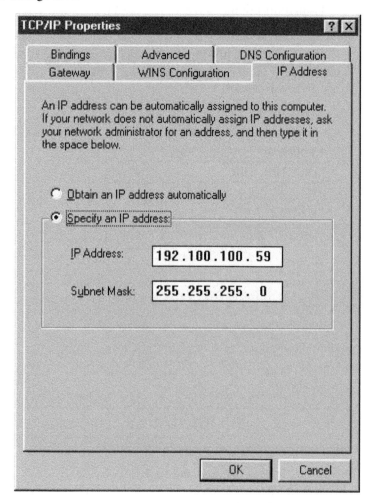

Specify an IP address and type in the correct IP address and Subnet Mask as listed below.

Computer1   192.100.100.1
Computer2   192.100.100.2
Computer3   192.100.100.3
Computer4   192.100.100.4
Computer5   192.100.100.5 (this is the router computer)
Computer6   192.100.100.6

The Subnet Mask for all computers is 255.255.255.0
Then click on the GATEWAY tab at the top of the window. The window will change to..

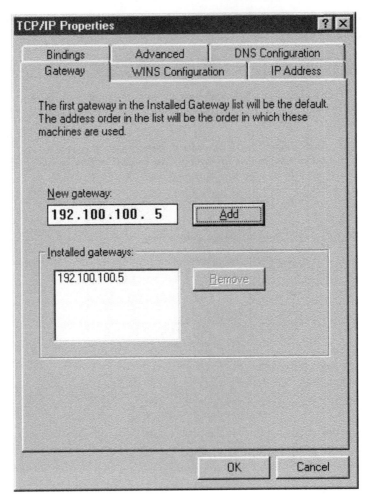

Type in the new default gateway as shown and then press the Add key. Then close the window by pressing the OK key and then OK again in the IP Address window.

Windows will then ask if you wish to reset the computer. Click on the YES key. The computer will then reset and boot up again. Remember to put the correct password in when Windows asks.

Note: If your computer did not have TCP/IP on it then it would ask you to insert the Windows 95 disk. It would then load it from the disk.

Go into the Network Neighborhood and verify that you can see your computer listed there. (Except for the routing computer (Computer5).)

In the C:\windows directory there is a program called Winipcfg. Run this program and verify the settings of your computer. If anything is wrong then you will need to start over setting up TCP/IP at **1.4**.

Implementation/sharing files

To setup file sharing go into the IP setup as outlined in 1.4. When you get to the Network window select File and Print Sharing as shown on the next page.

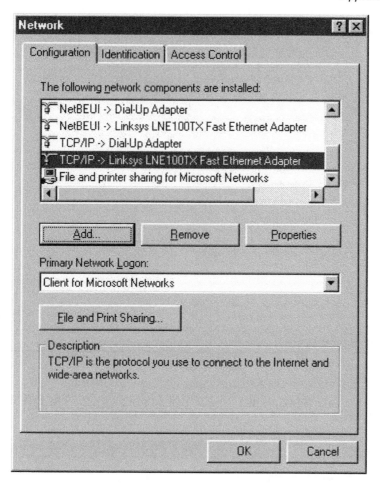

Click on the File and Print Sharing button. The following window will pop up…

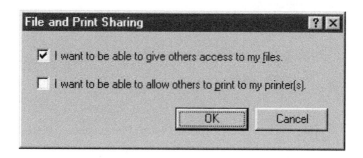

Select the 'I want to be….' line and then click on OK. Then OK again in the Network window. When Windows ask if you want to reset the computer select NO for the moment.

Go to the PAT directory in Windows Explorer. Highlight the PAT directory by clicking on it once.

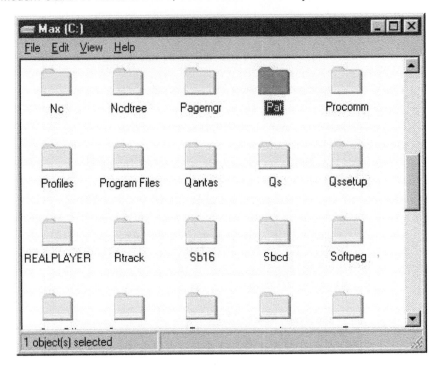

Then right click on the PAT directory and choose Sharing.

Setup the Pat Properties as shown. Click Apply then OK. The PAT directory icon should look like this.

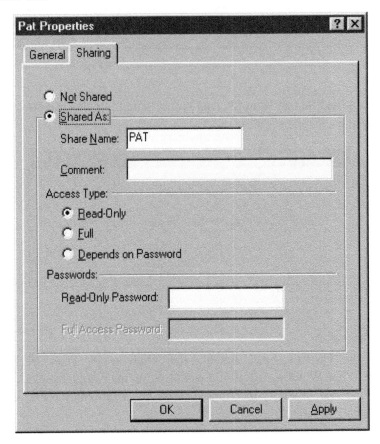

Pat

Now reset the computer. When the computer resets go to Network Neighborhood and click on someone else's computer. Notice that the Pat directory is shown as being available for sharing. Verify that you can copy a file from someone else's PAT directory.

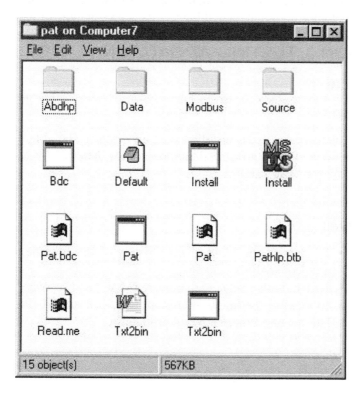

Run Pat by clicking on the PAT icon.

Pat

Press Enter and then the space bar. Notice that the Pat software does not support a mouse. One of the dangers of sharing is that sometimes it is possible to get access to a computer through the back door of a program. Can you do this in Pat?

Conclusion

Setting up an Ethernet network is important in understanding TCP/IP. The physical layer of the network has to be working correctly before anything else can be done. Once the network is working the user can then concentrate on the other layers of the OSI model with respect to Ethernet. In this practical we saw how the network was physically wired. In the following practicals we will set up other layers of the network with respects to the OSI model. We also saw how to troubleshoot a physical network. This practical also included changing TCP/IP settings and sharing files. Now that the physical side is out of the way the next practical will demonstrate to the delegate the data link layer on an Ethernet network.

SESSION 3: TESTING AT DATA LINK LAYER AND TCP/IP

Practical 1

Overview

Once the network has been installed it is important to be able to interpret the packets being sent on the Ethernet frames being sent at the data link (or MAC) layer and identify the hardware (or MAC) addresses.

Objectives

- To identify the main characteristics of the Ethernet frame using a typical protocol analysis package.
- To distinguish between hardware (MAC) and software (or IP) addresses.
- To identify the layering concept (e.g. OSI and TCP/IP model) as applied to Internet and Ethernet based protocols.

Hardware/software required

- 6 notebook computers all with Windows 95 running
- One 10BaseT hub
- 6 by 10BaseT cables
- NDG software – specifically the packet analyzer (PacketBoy)
- Windows 95/98
- Associated power supplies for the hub.

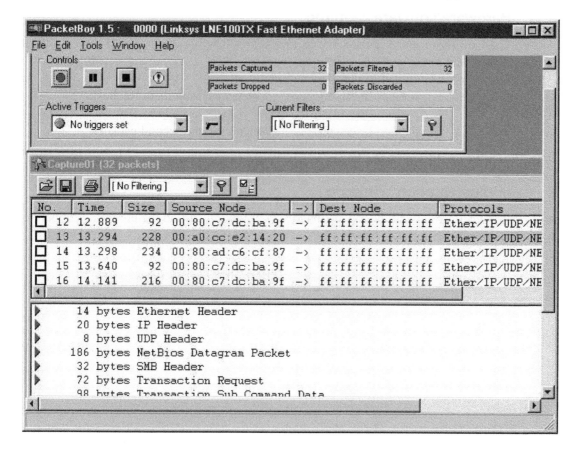

Practical 2

Overview

In the course of implementation, use and maintenance of an Ethernet network it is often necessary to investigate what is happening in the network. Many tools are available for this investigation. Some of the most popular ones are Windows diagnostics (Winipcfg), WinChat, Ping, ARP and NDGs' PacketBoy.

Objectives

This practical is designed to demonstrate to the delegate the procedures and some software packages needed to interpret what's going on in the network.

1. Winipcfg to verify the setup of the computer.
2. WinChat is a chat program for networks.
3. Pinging will be used to verify network communication.
4. ARP will be used to get the MAC address of the other computer.
5. NDG's PacketBoy will be used to interpret very detailed information on traffic flow within the network.

Hardware/software required

The hardware needed is the same as Practical 1. The hardware should be setup the same as Practical 1.

The software needed is as follows

- Ping
- ARP
- Winipcfg
- NDG's Packetboy

Implementation/Winipcfg

In My Computer and the top left-hand side of the screen find the program Winipcfg in the windows directory.

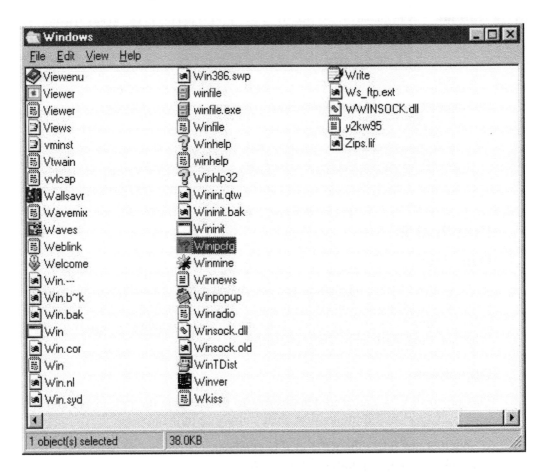

Double click on the Winipcfg program. The screen should change to..

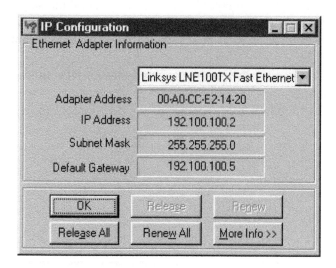

This shows the status of the computer setup with regards to the network. You might want to write this information down for future reference.

Implementation/WinChat

Using Winchat

To run the Winchat program and click on My Computer and find the Chat directory. Click on the Winchat program under the Chat directory.

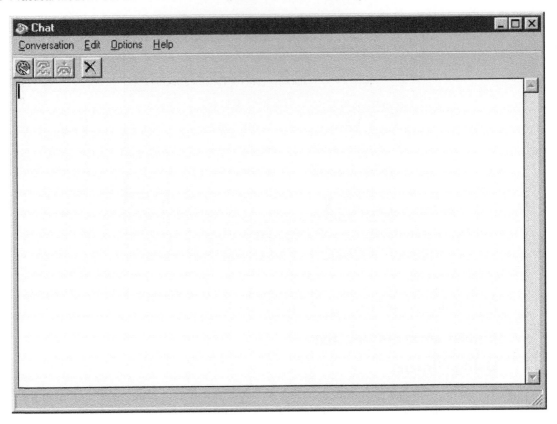

To 'dial' another computer click on Conversation then Dial on the pull down menu at the top. Type in the name of another computer. You may hear a beep. (If the sound is turned on your computer and the other computer is running the Winchat program.) Click on the 'off hook' icon or answer the call under the Conversation pull down menu. You can now 'talk' to the other computer by typing in the box on the screen.

Implementation/Ping

Verify that your computer can see the other computers by going into Network Neighborhood.

Once you are satisfied that you are connected to the network go to the DOS prompt by selecting the Go to Dos ICON in the Programs menu.

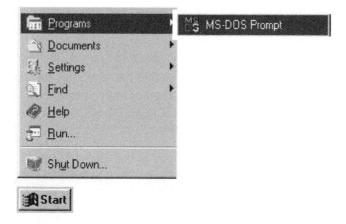

At the Dos prompt type in the IP address of another computer on the Network.

C:\Ping 192.100.100.XX

If you get something like below then recheck the IP address you are pinging and verify that the computer you are pinging is online.

```
C:\>ping 192.100.100.3

Pinging 192.100.100.3 with 32 bytes of data:

Request timed out.
Request timed out.
Request timed out.
Request timed out.

C:\>_
```

The response should look something like this.

```
C:\>Ping 192.100.100.3

Pinging 192.100.100.3 with 32 bytes of data:

Reply from 192.100.100.3: bytes=32 time=2ms TTL=32
Reply from 192.100.100.3: bytes=32 time=1ms TTL=32
Reply from 192.100.100.3: bytes=32 time=1ms TTL=32
Reply from 192.100.100.3: bytes=32 time<10ms TTL=32

C:\>_
```

Notice that the reply starts with giving the IP address you pinged (192.100.100.3) and the number of bytes (32) in the Ping. Then where the reply came from (192.100.100.3) again, how many bytes again (32) and the time (< 2 ms) each response took to come back. TTL is time to live equals 32. This number would decrease if the response went through a router.

Note: The Ping will only work on one network.

Implementation/ARP

ARP (address resolution protocol) is used to find the MAC (media access control) physical address of the Ethernet card of another computer on the network. It will also tell the user the route the packets took for a response. The ARP is used after a Ping. First Ping an IP address of another computer as shown below.

(Note: You can use a different address)

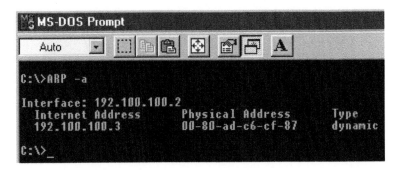

Then type the following..

The Interface is your IP address. The Internet Address is the source of the response and then its Physical Address. The Type is the type of IP allocated addressing. Dynamic means that the ARP list will not be held forever. After a few minutes the ARP will need more traffic to update its live list.

Note: The Pinging and ARP will also be used in Practical 3 (Subnet masking).

1.1 3.7 Implementation/PacketBoy

The NDG's PacketBoy software program is just one of a suite of programs that allow the network user or manager a view of what is happening on the network. PacketBoy shows detailed information about every aspect of the packets that are being sent back and forth between computers.

IMPORTANT NOTICE:

Before starting the PacketBoy software it is necessary that all computers are connected to the hubs and the hubs are connected together.

PacketBoy can be found under the NDG Software menu in programs.

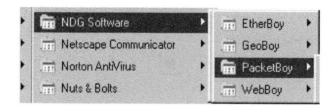

When you click on PacketBoy the screen should change to ....

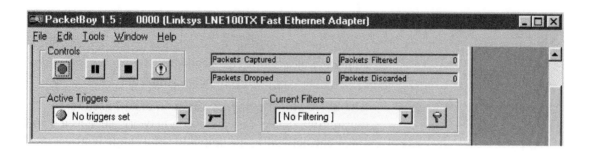

Clicking on the red dot. This will start the packet recording process. Do not press it yet.

The instructor will have one computer Ping another computer, at the same time the delegates will press the red button. After the successful Ping you should see an increase in the number of packets being captured by PacketBoy.

The screen should again look like the picture on the next page.

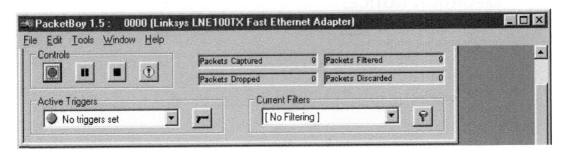

Click on the square button

The Screen should change to ..

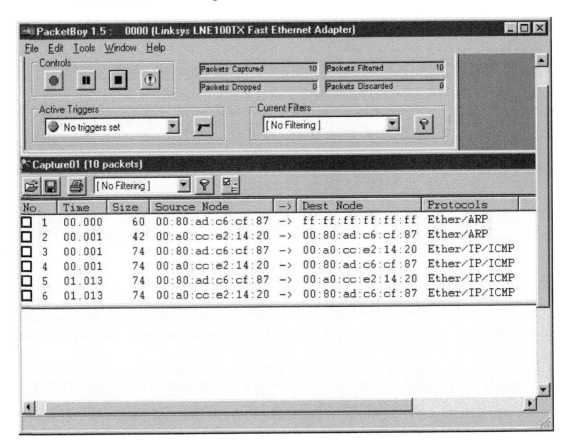

These are the packets that were recorded by PacketBoy. It is showing 6 of 10 packets that were received.

- They are numbered 1 to 6.
- Next is the time since the start of the first packet.
- Then the size in bytes is shown.
- Next is the MAC address of the source of the transmission.
- Then the destination MAC address.
- The protocol used is listed on the far right. Click on number 1.

(This is request (Ping) from the even numbered computer.)

The screen should change to:

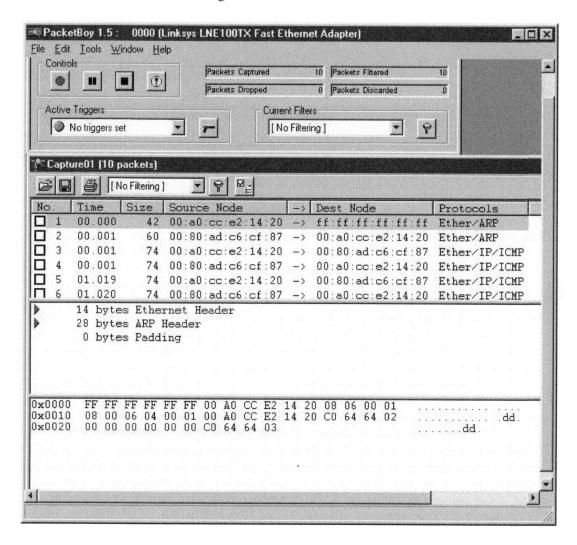

Note: You may have to rearrange the windows within the PackBoy window for optimum viewing.

The center section defines in English what is in packet number 1. It says that there are..

14 bytes in the header of the packet

28 bytes in the ARP header (data area)

0 bytes of padding

The bottom section is the hexadecimal and ASCII value of the information in the packet.

Click on the ARP header. The screen will change to

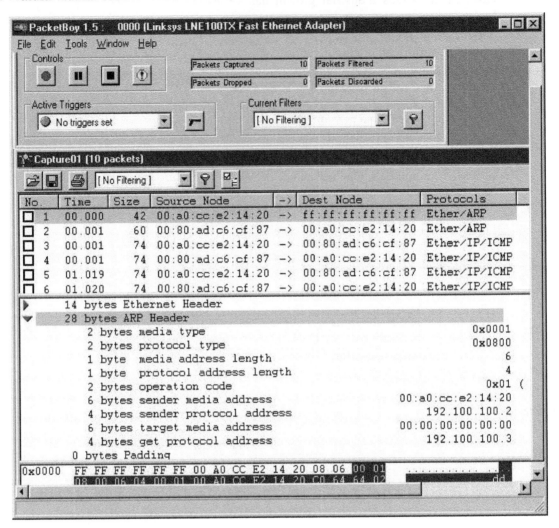

This shows the details of the ARP header (data). This was the original Ping from IP address 192.100.100.2 to 192.100.100.3. Notice that the Dest. Node at the top is ff.ff.ff.ff.ff.ff. This is because the pinging computer did not know the MAC address of 192.100.100.3.

Notice all 00:00:00:00:00:00 in the target media address line. Computer 3 then responds in the next packet (number 2)

Click on packet number 2 and note that the sender and destination information reverses. This is the response from the odd computer. Also note that the sender knows the MAC address of the destination computer. How?

1.2 3.8 Conclusion

These four programs are very simple but yet give us a great wealth of information on what is going on in the network. The Winipcfg tells us about the setup of our computer. Ping tells us we are able to 'talk' to another computer. ARP gives us the MAC address of the other computer and NDG's PacketBoy allows us to have an intimate view of the communications on the network.

PRACTICAL SESSION 4
TOPIC: EXAMINATION OF RTU CONFIGURATION SOFTWARE

Overview

In this practical the use of configuration software for a general purpose RTU supporting DNP3 is examined. A simple read transaction from the RTU is carried out and the in-built protocol analyzer is used to examine the transaction at each protocol layer.

Procedure

- Load up the Hunter Watertech configuration software on your PC.
- Plug in the RS-232 cable into the computer and PORT 1 on the RTU
- Use the Communication \ Communication Settings menu to configure the following:
  - Com Port: COM1
  - Baud rate: 9600
  - 8 Data bits, no parity, 1 stop bit
- Go to the Diagnostics screen and select (tick) the upper five Display Filter levels (in preparation for doing a time read from the RTU). Clear the display using the Display Control Clear button.

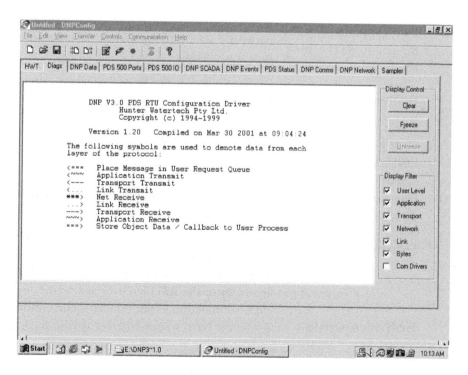

- Examine all screens of the configuration software and consider what each performs. Take your time doing this and look in detail at the available drop down menus.
- When the instructor brings the RTU to your PC, upload the time from the RTU using the menu path Transfer\Get RTU Time

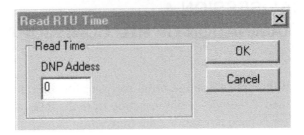

- Click on Get Time under the Transfer Menu at the top of the screen
- Set the address for 0 as show above.
- Examine the upload transaction in detail and note the information displayed for each level of the transaction.

PRACTICAL SESSION 5
TOPIC: USE OF DNP PROTOCOL ANALYSER WITH RTU

Overview

This exercise is to show communications between a Citect master station and a DNP3 RTU device, using a protocol analyzer to observe transmissions.

Hardware needed

Laptop running Win98
RS-232 to RTU cable
Hunter WaterTech 500 RTU

Software needed

Citect
Config from Hunter Watertech
DNP3 Citect drivers – DNPDriverV10406000
Citect DNP3 project – DNPC500.ctz
Citect.ini – This is information needs to be added to the existing Citect.ini in the Citect directory

Hardware setup

- Connect up PC to RTU Port 1 with supplied cable
- Connect power supply to the RTU

Software setup

Run the Hunter Watertech Config software.

DNPConfig

Click on the Diags button and the following screen will come up.

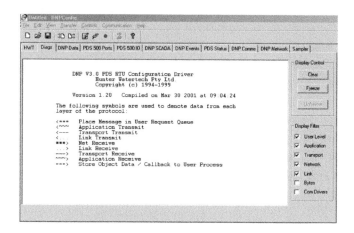

Clear the screen by pressing the clear button on the right.
Click on Transfer at the top of the screen and then press Get RTU Time.
Put in the address 100 and then press OK.

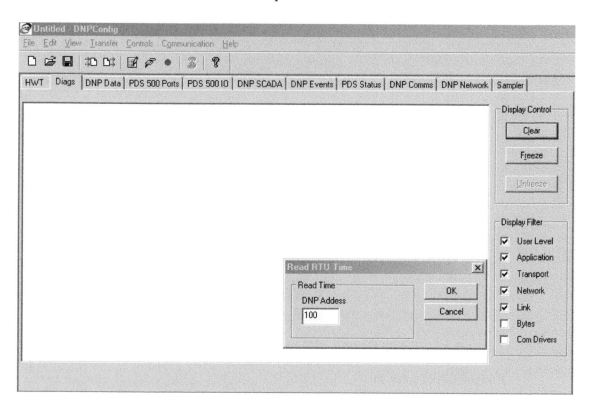

The screen should show the following.

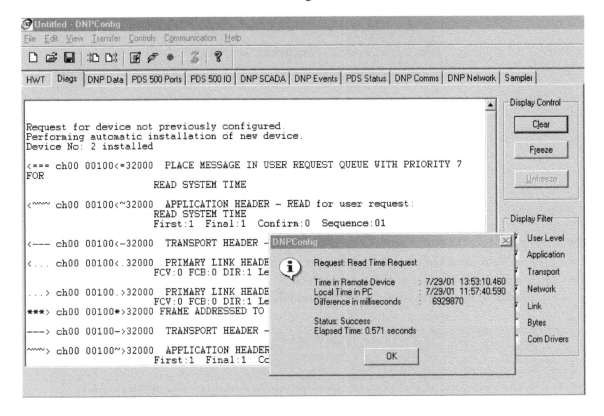

This indicates that the computer is talking to the RTU. Exit out of the Config software and add the information in the Practical Citect.ini file to the existing Citect.ini file.

citect

- Check with the instructor to see if this has already been done.

Run the DNP3 Driver installation software.

DNPDriverV...

- Check with the instructor to see if this has already been done.

Run the Citect software.

CTEXPLOR

The screen should change to..

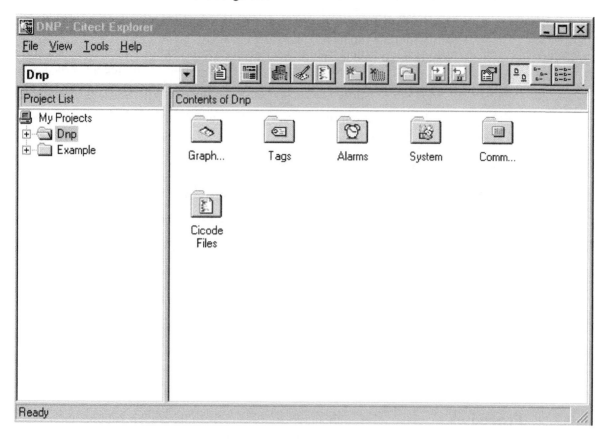

Once in the Citect program load the DNP RTU project by clicking on FILE then run. The screen should change to..

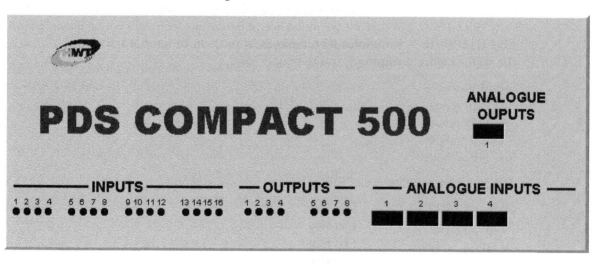

Procedure and observations

- Use the Citect screen to verify that the outputs can be turned on and off.
- Verify that the inputs are operating correctly.
- Note that the analog inputs show values.

Additional exercise:

If time permits, set up the diagnostic display of RTU and use this to observe traffic on the network.

PRACTICAL SESSION 6
TOPIC: RADIO PATH DESIGN PROBLEM

Overview

It is necessary to consider all the issues from designing the radio system to configuring the DNP protocol when setting up a complete system. In this exercise we use a radio path design program to design a radio link.

Equipment required

- Notebook computer
- Teledesign software program

Procedure

Master site

Site A – to co-ordinate the pumping of water from the 5 RTUs; each at an approximate distance of 40 km away from the master site.

Five RTU's sites – Boreholes with tanks next to them to temporarily store the water before pumping it to the master site.

Site B Borehole
Site C Borehole
Site D Borehole
Site E Borehole
Site F Borehole

The path between Site A and Site B has the following profile.

0 km	220 m	Flat Dry
5 km	150 m	Flat Dry
10 km	120 m	Flat Dry
15 km	120 m	Flat Dry
20 km	130 m	Flat Dry
25 km	130 m	Flat Dry
30 km	110 m	Flat Dry
35 km	120 m	Flat Dry
40 km	150 m	Flat Dry

Assume that the Site A (master station) to the Site B RTU radio link is problematic and needs to be investigated. You are advised that Site A to Site B is the only one that needs investigation for optimum antenna heights and the other radio telemetry issues. The other RTU sites are fine.

Problem 1 – Calculation of antenna heights

Execute the Teledes program within DOS in your Teledes folder.
Press the space bar and the following screen will appear.

- You first run the 'Terrain Analysis' to input the terrain data as described above.
- Enter the data for the path profile above by going to 'Sheet' and then Enter.

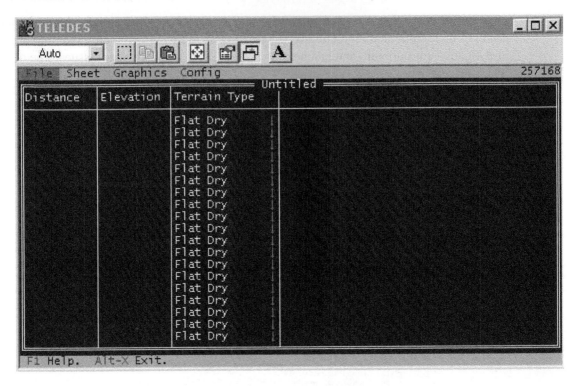

- The program calculates this using the 'Antenna' option under 'graphics'. You first need to select the appropriate frequency using the 'Config Other' settings.
- The 'Antenna' menu allows you to fix EITHER end of the link at a particular height and it will calculate the necessary height at the other end.
- Assume neither antenna is fixed by leaving both fields blank and press 'Enter'.
- Program now calculates both antenna heights. Write these down along with the site elevations and the path length.

Site elevations _____

Path length _____

(Note: Fix antenna at A (main) at say 24 m, then calculate antenna heights at RTU.)

Problem 2 – Calculation of availability

Exit 'Terrain analysis' and go to 'Radio Link Design'

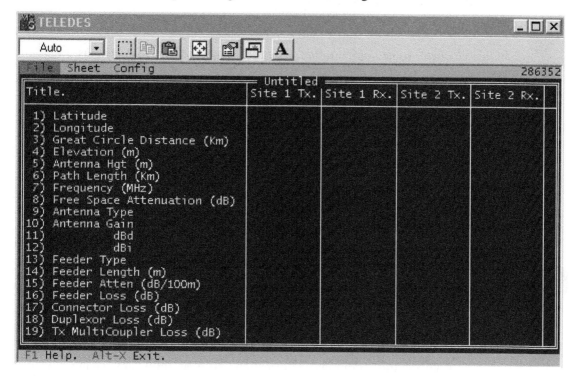

Here we design the equipment needed to meet our availability requirements.

To do this properly you need data sheets for the various items of equipment and the various frequencies etc. The answer is given in the 'A-B' sheet which you access via the 'Load' menu under this program. You can then explore the sheet using the 'Sheet' 'Enter' command.

Experience has indicated that a fade margin of 30 dB provides a good design guideline for achieving a reliable link. What fade margin have you calculated for this radio system?

Radio data for Sites A and B

Frequencies TX1 450.025MHz, TX2 454.725 MHz
Antenna data:
          Main = Sidemount dipole SUI-4C (omnidirectional) Gain 6dB
          RTU = Yagi Y409e gain 12 dB
Feeder cable RG214 Coax loss @ 450 MHz = 16 dB/100 m
Feeder length = Antenna height + 5 m
Duplexer insertion loss = 0.6 dB
Transmitter power A = 2 W RTU = 1 W
RX sensitivities (microvolts)
Main (A) RSL = 0.25   12 dB SINAD = 0.3 μV
RTUs   RSL = 0.3 μV   0.35 μV

PRACTICAL SESSION 7

TOPIC: DNP CONCEPTS

Overview

In this practical, some configuration issues are examined for DNP systems.

A DNP3 SCADA system is to be setup to provide control over a water supply system comprising two remote borefields and a town reservoir. This system is to be modelled on the example in the text shown for Port Hedland TWS System.

Part 1. RTU numbering and message routing

Examining the system block diagram determine the following:

1. Determine which RTUs will be required to carry out message routing functions.
2. Make up your own block diagram and identify these RTUs.
3. Determine an assignment of RTU numbers which may be used to facilitate effective routing of DNP messages.

Investigation of the system requirements shows that each borefield operates as a 'control zone' in which the bores in that field are operated so as to maintain the level in the borefield reservoir. To increase system security the control of this is carried out from the PLCs at the borefield reservoir locations.

- Given this additional information, do you think any changes would be required to accommodate this system?
- Do you think that the RTUs at the remote reservoirs would operate as masters to the borefield RTUs, or would peer–peer communications be used?

Part 2. System Loading

How do you think you might calculate the message loading for this system on the individual radio paths? How are you going to quantify the message loading (bits, bytes, frames, per unit time?)

The following data is provided as a basis for making an estimate. Use this data to carry out an estimation of traffic on the various parts of the network. Control actions are not accounted for in the following data. Allow a 10% loading for these and error margin in your calculations.

Network Loading Assumptions

Item	Data / Frequency	Note
Background scan of static points of RTUs	Once per 4 hours	Carried out sequentially as a background operation
Borefield RTU	8 x analog input 12 x status input 4 x digital output 2 x register output Average events: • Class 1: 1 per hour • Class 3: 10 per hour • Analog Class 3: 20 per hour	Class 3 are buffered up to 25 items before transmission Class 1 are buffered up to 5 items before transmission
Pump Station / Reservoir	40 x analog input 100 x status input 6 x counter input 30 x digital output 15 x register output Average events: • Class 1: 10 per hour • Class 3: 40 per hour • Analog Class 3: 50 per hour	As above

Communications channels

This system is using 900 Mhz radio channels to provide full-duplex paths. The data radios used will provide a 9.6 kbps link capacity. Alternative data radios are available that can operate at 19.2 kbps capacity if required. Using this information, can you determine which types of radio will be required?

Given the buffering of class 1 and class 3 messages specified, can you determine approximately how many messages per hour are going to be generated from a borefield area and pass over the main trunk links to the town's SCADA system? Given this information, do you think that the intermediate repeater sites should be continuously operated, or should they be operated only when messages come through? The transmitter key-up time is 400 ms.

General issues

Buffering of events

The RTU local data is assigned in groups to DNP classes. The configuration screen will display the additional 'Buff Event' and 'Trig Event' options. These determine the behavior of the reporting of events from the RTU. The difference between these is that the buffered events are stored for periodic transfer to the master, whereas the trigger events are sent immediately using a DNP3 unsolicited response. This is a mechanism provided by PDS RTUs for optimizing the use of limited bandwidth communications systems.

How do you think you might use these options in configuring the borefield RTUs?

DNP events

What level of application layer timeout would you configure for the master station? Why would you need to increase this level if operating over a radio or landline system?

_____

_____

_____

In order to minimize network congestion consecutive messages are inhibited for a set time to allow other devices to use the network (Min_Unsol_Event_Tx_Delay). What sort of time would you select for this system for each RTU?

_____

Similarly when an event happens at a site, this will often trigger a series of other events, so a short time delay can also be set to allow all changes to be included in the one transmission (event notification delay). What sort of event notification delay would you select for this system?

_____

Confirmation and retries

When a message is sent from a DNP device, the device will wait for a confirmation message sent back from the destination device. Data to be transmitted is broken down into fragments (application level) and then again down into frames (data link layer). At both of these layers, timeout and number of retries applies so that the RTU can determine if the message was received and recover if not.

The data link layer has parameters for each port called data link retries and data link confirm timeout. The data link confirm mode is usually set to Sometimes which means to only apply link confirm (with retries) to the data link layer when the original message has more than one frame in a fragment. If a message is small and takes no more than one frame, then the timeouts at the data link layer are not necessary because the application layer timeout will be checking the same data. It can also be set to never and always.

What would you set these RTUs to for data link retries, data link confirm timeout and data link confirm mode? How would you decide?

Data link retries _____

Data link confirm timeout _____

Data link confirm mode _____

2. IEC 60870-5-101 Packet Analysis Exercises

Objective:

This information and the practical exercises are intended to provide the delegate with a practical understanding of the IEC 60870-5-101 packet by providing information specific to packet interpretation.

Introduction:

IEC 60870-5-101 packets are output from a protocol analyser as hexadecimal data. Sometimes these hex values need to be converted to decimal or binary values. The number of bytes in a datagram is an example of a value in a 101 packet that needs to be changed to decimal. Sometimes binary data is needed as in the flag settings within the application layer portion of a packet. Another part of the structure of the packet is the positioning of the most significant and least significant bytes within two bytes of data. When data needs to be represented by two bytes, such as an address, the least significant byte is placed first and the most significant byte is place second. An example of this is...

Common Address – AA00 hex (as shown in the data stream)
Common Address – 00AA hex (as normally written, least significant byte first)
Common Address – 170 decimal (after converting to decimal)

And

Common Address – 0200 hex (as shown in the data stream)
Reversed to 0002 hex (as normally written, least significant byte first)
Converted to Decimal 2 (after converting to decimal)

Zero (0) is not allowed as an address.

Link Layer Message Formats:

Single control character

0xE5   Control character
Used for message acknowledgements

Fixed length messages

	S	C	A	A	CS	E
Hex example	1	4	0	0	4A	1
	0	9	1	0		6
LPDU						

S   Start character – always 0x10 in fixed length messages
C   Control character
A   16 bit Outstation address, LSB first – this example is 0x0001
CS Checksum, a single byte accumulation of the values of C+A+A.
E   End character – always 0x16 in all messages.

Variable length messages

Variable length messages

	LPCI							APDU	LPCI	
	S	L	L	S	C	A	A	1. ASDU	CS	E
Hex example	6 8	1 1	1 1	6 8	7 3	0 1	0 0	67 01 06 00 00 00 00 55 69 10 0D 13 01 01	D2	1 6
	LPDU									

S   Start character – always 0x68 in variable length messages
L   Length character which specifies the length in octets (bytes) of the ASDU+C+A+A
L   Repeat of previous
S   Repeat of previous
C   Link control character
A   16 bit Outstation address, LSB first – this example is 0x0001
CS Checksum, a single byte accumulation of ASDU+C+A+A

Control Field:

Interpret using details in Chapter 9.4.4.1 (Page 218 onwards)

ASDU Structure:

ASDU

Data Unit Identifier	Type ID	
	Variable Structure Qualifier	
	Cause of Transmission	
	Common Address of ASDU	
Information Object 1	Information Object Address	
	Information Elements	
	Time Tag	
	Information Object	

For each Information Object Type (Type ID) the sequence of bytes, Variable Structure Qualifier, Causes of Transmission, Information Object Addresses and the Information Elements are described as shown in the following examples:

3.1.1.1.1

3.1.1.1.2 Examples of Various Type Codes

3.1.1.1.3 Type 1

INFORMATION OBJECT TYPE:	**1**
CODE:	M_SP_NA_1
DESCRIPTION:	Single point information without time tag
VALID WITH SQ:	0, 1
Information Object for SQ = 0	(Sequence of Information Objects)

Information Object Address								
IV	NT	SB	BL				SP I	SIQ

Information Object for SQ = 1 (Sequence of Information Elements)

Information Object Address 1								
IV	NT	SB	BL				SP I	SIQ, Information Element 1
			.....					
Information Object Address N								
IV	NT	SB	BL				SP I	SIQ, Information Element N

Valid Cause of Transmission Codes

<2>	Background scan
<3>	Spontaneous
<5>	Requested
<11>	Return of information caused by remote command
<12>	Return of information caused by local command
<20>	Interrogated by station interrogation
<20 + G>	Interrogated by group G interrogation, G= <1..16>

Notes

SIQ – Single-point information with quality descriptor.

Type 2

INFORMATION OBJECT TYPE: 2
CODE: M_SP_TA_1
DESCRIPTION: Single-point information with time tag
VALID WITH SQ: 0
Information Object for SQ = 0 (Sequence of Information Objects)

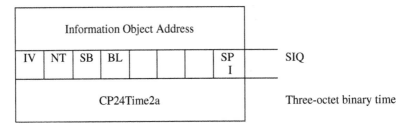

Valid Cause of Transmission Codes

<3> Spontaneous
<5> Requested
<11> Return of information caused by remote command
<12> Return of information caused by local command

Notes

SIQ – Single-point information with quality descriptor.

3.1.1.1.4 Type 3

INFORMATION OBJECT TYPE: 3
CODE: M_DP_NA_1
DESCRIPTION: Double-point information without time tag
VALID WITH SQ: 0, 1
Information Object for SQ = 0 (Sequence of Information Objects)

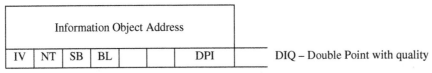

Information Object for SQ = 1 (Sequence of Information Elements)

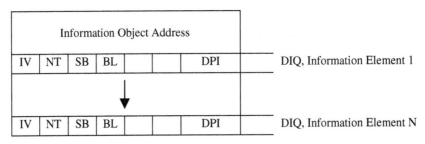

Valid Cause of Transmission Codes

<2>   Background scan
<3>   Spontaneous
<5>   Requested
<11>   Return of information caused by remote command
<12>   Return of information caused by local command
<20>   Interrogated by station interrogation
<20 + G> Interrogated by group G interrogation, G = <1..16>

Notes

DIQ – Double-point information with quality descriptor.

3.1.1.1.5 Type 10

INFORMATION OBJECT TYPE: **10**
CODE: M_ME_TA_1
DESCRIPTION: Measured value, normalised value with time tag
VALID WITH SQ: 0
Information Object for SQ = 0   (Sequence of Information Objects)

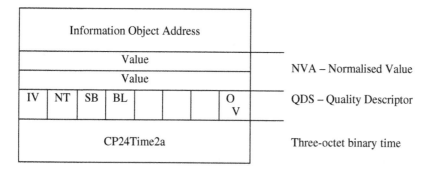

Valid Cause of Transmission Codes

<3>   Spontaneous
<5>   Requested

Notes

NVA – Normalised value.

3.1.1.1.6 Type 11

INFORMATION OBJECT TYPE: **11**
CODE: M_ME_NB_1
DESCRIPTION: Measured value, scaled value
VALID WITH SQ: 0, 1
Information Object for SQ = 0 (Sequence of Information Objects)

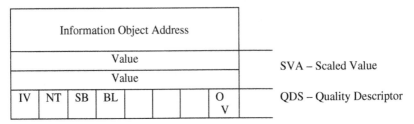

Information Object for SQ = 1 (Sequence of Information Elements)

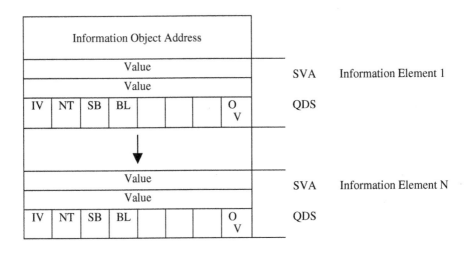

Valid Cause of Transmission Codes

<2>	Background scan
<3>	Spontaneous
<5>	Requested
<11>	Return of information caused by remote command
<12>	Return of information caused by local command
<20>	Interrogated by station interrogation
<20 + G>	Interrogated by group G interrogation, G = <1..16>

Notes

SVA – Scaled value.

3.1.1.1.7 Type 14

INFORMATION OBJECT TYPE: **14**
CODE: M_ME_TC_1
DESCRIPTION: Measured value, short floating point number with time tag
VALID WITH SQ: 0
Information Object for SQ = 0 (Sequence of Information Objects)

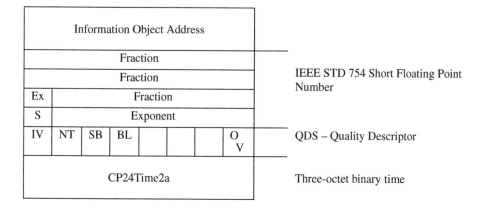

Information Object Address							
Fraction							
Fraction							
Ex	Fraction						
S	Exponent						
IV	NT	SB	BL				O V
CP24Time2a							

IEEE STD 754 Short Floating Point Number

QDS – Quality Descriptor

Three-octet binary time

Valid Cause of Transmission Codes

<2>   Background scan
<3>   Spontaneous
<5>   Requested
<11>   Return of information caused by remote command
<12>   Return of information caused by local command
<20>   Interrogated by station interrogation
<20 + G>   Interrogated by group G interrogation, G = <1..16>

Notes

IEEE STD 754 – Short floating point number.

3.1.1.1.8 Type 100

INFORMATION OBJECT TYPE:	**100**
CODE:	C_IC_NA_1
DESCRIPTION:	Interrogation Command
VALID WITH SQ:	0

Information Object for SQ = 0 (Sequence of Information Objects)

Information Object Address

QOI – Qualfier of Interrogation

Valid Cause of Transmission Codes

<6>	Activation
<7>	Activation Confirmation
<8>	Deactivation
<9>	Deactivation Confirmation
<10>	Activation Termination

3.1.1.1.9 Type 103

INFORMATION OBJECT TYPE:	103
CODE:	C_CS_NA_1
DESCRIPTION:	Clock synchronisation command
VALID WITH SQ:	0

Information Object for SQ = 0 (Sequence of Information Objects)

Information Object Address

CP56Time2a

Seven Octet Binary Time
(date and Clock time in milliseconds)

Valid Cause of Transmission Codes

<3>	Spontaneous
<6>	Activation
<7>	Activation Confirmation

3.1.1.1.10 Information Elements:

General Type Symbol	Description
Process	
SIQ	Single-point information with quality descriptor
DIQ	Double-point information with quality descriptor
BSI	Binary state information
SCD	Status and change detection
QDS	Quality descriptor
VTI	Value with transient state indication
NVA	Normalised value
SVA	Scaled value
R32-IEEE STD 754	Short floating point number
BCR	Binary counter reading
Protection	
SEP	Single event of protection equipment
SPE	Start events of protection equipment
OCI	Output circuit information of protection equipment
QDP	Quality descriptor for events of protection equipment
Commands	
SCO	Single command
DCO	Double command
RCO	Regulating step command
Time	
CP56Time2a	Seven octet binary time
CP24Time2a	Three octet binary time
CP16Time2a	Two octet binary time
Qualifiers	
QOI	Qualifier of interrogation
QCC	Qualifier of counter interrogation command
QPM	Qualifier of parameter of measured values
QPA	Qualifier of parameter activation
QRP	Qualifier of reset process command
QOC	Qualifier of command
QOS	Qualifier of set-point command
File Transfer	
FRQ	File ready qualifier
SRQ	Section ready qualifier
SCQ	Select and call qualifier
LSQ	Last section or segment qualifier
AFQ	Acknowledge file or section qualifier
NOF	Name of file

File Transfer	
NOS	Name of section
LOF	Length of file or section
LOS	Length of segment
CHS	Checksum
SOF	Status of file

Miscellaneous	
COI	Cause of initialisation
FBP	Fixed test bit pattern, two octets

The format of each of these information elements is defined as shown in the following examples:

SIQ   Single point information

SIQ is single point information with quality descriptor. The status bit itself is bit 0. The 4 highest bits provide the quality information per the key below.

7	6	5	4	3	2	1	0
IV	NT	SB	BL				SPI

Key
SPI   Status ON
BL   Blocked
SB   Substituted
NT   Not topical
IV   Invalid

DIQ   Double-point information

The DIQ is double-point with quality. The quality bits are as previously defined, and the four states of the two status bits are given in the key following.

7	6	5	4	3	2	1	0
IV	NT	SB	BL			DPI	

Key - DPI Code
<0>   Indeterminate or intermediate state
<1>   OFF
<2>   ON
<3>   indeterminate state

Key – Status Bits

BL   Blocked
SB   Substituted
NT   Not topical
IV   Invalid

QDS   Quality Descriptor

The quality descriptor may be used to provide the same quality information for analog and counter values as is included with the single or double-point with quality information elements. In addition it has an overflow bit OV.

7	6	5	4	3	2	1	0
IV	NT	SB	BL				OV

Key - Bit
OV   Overflow
BL   Blocked
SB   Substituted
NT   Not topical
IV   Invalid

SVA   Scaled value

This is used to transmit values where a fixed decimal point position is defined. Values are in the range −32768 to +32767. The range of the decimal points are fixed parameters, set in the system database. For example, a value of 39.5 amps may be transmitted as 395 where the resolution is fixed at 0.1 amp.

7	6	5	4	3	2	1	0
15			Value I16				0

Key
I16   Value I16[0..15] $<2^{15}..+1-2^{-15}>$

R32   Short floating point number

The short floating point number is a 4-octet number defined by IEEE Standard 754. It is made up of a fraction, an exponent or power of 2, and a sign bit.

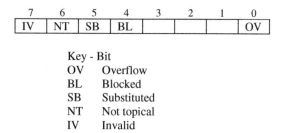

Key
F   Fraction   UI23[0..22] $<0..1-2^{-23}>$
E   Exponent   UI[23..30] $<0..255>$
S   Sign   0= Positive, 1 = Negative

Interpretation:

Case	Interpretation
F=<0>, E=<0>	Value = <0>
F non-zero, E=<0>	Non-normalised number Value = $(-1)^S \times 2^{E-126} \times (0.F)$
F non-zero, E <1..254>	Normalised number Value = $(-1)^S \times 2^{E-127} \times (1.F)$
F=<0>, E=<255>	Value = $(-1)^S \times$ infinity
F non-zero, E=<255>	Not a valid number

Note that a normalised number is one in which has been scaled to the form 0.1xxxx so that it falls between 0.1 and 1.0, and then multiplied by 2 to give 1.xxxx. This removes the leading '1' to the right of the radix point, which is redundant because it is always a 1.

BCR   Binary counter reading

	7	6	5	4	3	2	1	0	
Octet 1	7								0
Octet 2	15			Counter I32					8
Octet 3	23								16
Octet 4	31								24
Octet 5	IV	CA	CY			SQ			

Key
I32   Counter value I32[0..31] $<-2^{31}..+2^{31}-1>$
SQ   Sequence number UI5[32..36] <0..31>
CY   Carry
CA   Counter adjusted
IV   Counter valid

SCO   Single command

This is a command to operate a single output. Bits 2 to 7 are the Qualifier of Command sub-field. This is used for other commands also.

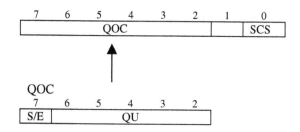

Key - Command
SCS   Single command state BS1[0] <0..1>
      <0> = Command OFF
      <1> = Command ON

Key - QOC Qualifier of Command
QU   Qualifier UI5[2..6] <0..31>
      <0>   = No additional definition
      <1>   = Short pulse duration
      <2>   = Long duration pulse
      <3>   = Persistent output
      <4..8>   = Reserved for further standard definitions
      <9..15>   = Reserved for selection of other predefined
      functions
      <16..31> = Reserved for special use (private range)

S/E   Select / Execute BS1[7] <0..1>
      <0>   = Execute
      <1>   = Select

An important feature of this command is that it has two forms depending on bit 7, the select and the execute form. The select form is used when select before execute operation is required. This is also known as two-phase command operation.

CP56Time2a – Seven Octet Binary Time

Seven octet binary time is used for clock synchronisation. Note that although Days of the Week are defined, these are not used and are set to zero.

7	6	5	4	3	2	1	0	Octet	Range
Milliseconds ms								1 2	0 .. 59,999 ms
		Minutes						3	0 .. 59 min
			Hours					4	0 .. 23 h
Day of week = 0			Day of month					5	0, 1 .. 31
				Month				6	1 .. 12
Year								7	0 .. 99

CP24Time2a – Three Octet Binary Time

This is typically used for time tags of information objects. It is the first three octets of the seven octet binary time element.

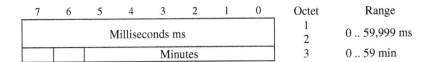

CP16Time2a – Two Octet Binary Time

This is used for elapsed times such as for relay operating time. It is the first two octets of the seven octet binary time element.

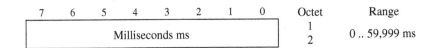

QOI   Qualifier of Interrogation

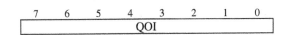

Key
QOI   Qualifier of command UI8[1..7] <0..255>
        <0>   = Not used
        <1..19>   = Reserved for future standard definitions
        <20>   = Station interrogation – global
        <20+N>   = Interrogation of group G, where G = <1..16>
        <37..63> = Reserved for future standard definitions
        <64..255> = Reserved for special use (private range)

3.1.1.1.11

Communication 1

Interpret the following 60870-5-101 format message, assuming Station address length (2), Common Address length (1) and an Information Object Address length of 3 octets.

68 11 11 68 73 01 00 67 01 06 00 00 00 00 55 69 10 0D 13 01 01 D2 16

How long is the message?   What is the checksum?

What is the Control Byte?   Interpret the Control Byte:

Pri/Sec=   FCB=   FCV=

What is the Function Code?   What does this mean?

What is the Station Address?
What is the Type Code and its meaning?

Interpret the Variable Sequence Qualifier:

What is the Cause of Transmission?

What is the Common Address?   What is the Information Object Address?

Interpret the meaning of the Information :

Communication 2

Interpret the following data stream from the same 60870-5-101 system as communication 1. Assume a structured Information Object Address of 3 octets.

68 0B 0B 68 73 02 01 64 01 06 00 00 00 00 14 EF 16 E5 68 25

25 68 53 02 01 0B 05 14 01 01 00 05 12 00 00 01 00 01 74 0D

00 01 00 02 0B 00 00 02 00 02 01 00 00 03 00 02 00 00 00 AA 16

How many Messages are there?

Explain the message sequence:

For each message identify the following, as appropriate:

Control byte:

Function Code:

Station Address:

Type code:

Variable Sequence Qualifier:

Cause of Transmission:

Common Address:

Information Object Address(es)

Data Values:

Quality Descriptor (QDS)

Communication 1 Answer

Interpret the following 60870-5-101 format message, assuming Station address length (2), Common Address length (1) and an Information Object Address length of 3 octets.

68 11 11 68 73 01 00 67 01 06 00 00 00 00 55 69 10 0D 13 01

01 D2 16

How long is the message?   17 (0x11)   What is the checksum?   D2

What is the Control Byte? 73   Interpret the Control Byte: 01110011
Pri/Sec=   Pri   FCB=1   FCV=1

What is the Function Code? 03   What does this mean? User data, Confirm expected

What is the Station Address?   1   (0x0001)

What is the Type Code and its meaning? 0x67 (103) = Clock Synchronisation

Interpret the Variable Sequence Qualifier: 0x01 = One object

What is the Cause of Transmission? 0x06 = Activation

What is the Common Address? 00   What is the Information Object Address? 00 00

Interpret the meaning of the Information : CP56 Time Object (55 69 10 0D 13 01 01)

55 69 = 0x6955 milliseconds = 26.965 seconds

0x10 = 16 minutes

0x0D = 13 hours

0x13 = Day = 19

01 = Month = January

01 = Year assume 2001

Communication 2 Answer

Interpret the following data stream from the same 60870-5-101 system as communication 1. Assume a structured Information Object Address of 3 octets.

68 0B 0B 68 73 02 01 64 01 06 00 00 00 00 14 EF 16 E5 68 25

25 68 53 02 01 0B 05 14 01 01 00 05 12 00 00 01 00 01 74 0D

00 01 00 02 0B 00 00 02 00 02 01 00 00 03 00 02 00 00 00 AA 16

How many Messages are there?   Three

Explain the message sequence: 1. Interrogate command (type 100) COT Activate
2. Single byte acknowledgement (E5)
3. Response (Type 11, COT Global Interrogation)

For each message identify the following, as appropriate:

Control byte:	0x73	0x53
Function Code:	FC=3 (FCB=1, FCV=1)	(FCB=0,FCV=1),FC=3
Station Address:	0x0102 = 258	0x0102 = 258
Type code:	0x64=100	0x0B = 11
Variable Sequence Qualifier: 01		05 = Five objects
Cause of Transmission: 06 (Activate)		0x14=20 (Global Interrogate)
Common Address: 00 (N/A)		01
Information Object Address(es) 00 00 00 (N/A)		See below
Data Values:		See below
Quality Descriptor (QDS)		0x14=20

Structured addresses	05	00 01	Data 0x0012= 18	QDS= 00
	01	00 01	Data 0x0D74= 3444	QDS= 00
	02	00 01	Data 0x000B= 11	QDS= 00
	02	00 02	Data 0x0001=1	QDS= 00
	02	00 03	Data 0x0000=0	QDS= 00

CITECT PRACTICAL

For Citect Version 5.4 Edit 1

Objective

The Citect practical is designed to give you an introduction to using the Citect software to talk to a RTU using DNP3. This is accomplished by helping you set up, design and run a working SCADA system. The system when running will display a main menu with a test button. You will be able to push the button and view a light that will indicate the position of a switch on the RTU. You will design the SCADA system from the ground up. Three indications will tell you how many polls have happened, how many switch changes have occurred and how many errors have happened. You will define an alarm page and a hardware page to display errors.

Citect Design Information

The Citect package is set up in a page format. Each page has to be opened, defined, and saved to a project. The pages used in this practical are kept simple because of time constraints.

The flow of the project will be as follows. (NOTE the software **must** be set up in the following order.)

Hint – If you have any problems press the F1 key on the keyboard. This will show you the help screen.

(1) Opening a New Project

Open a Citect by clicking on the Citect icon on the Desktop. Click on File then New Project.

   Type NEW. If this name is all ready used then put in one of your choosing. The screen should appear as follows on the next page... (Add in the name **NEW**)

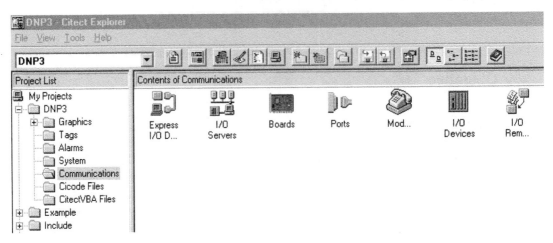

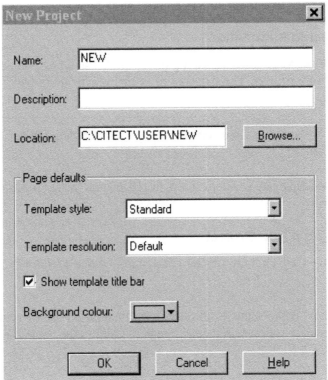

Then Click on the OK button. <u>Do Not Press Return</u>. The "NEW" project is now created.

(2) Defining Communications

In Citect Explorer click on . Set the screen up as shown.

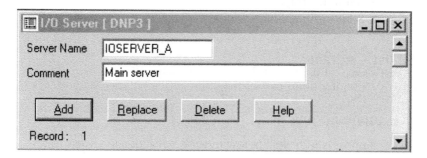

Next click on the 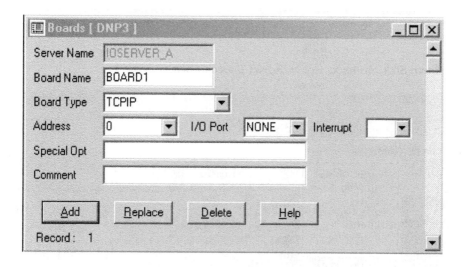 Boards and set up as shown.

Next click on the Ports and set up as shown.

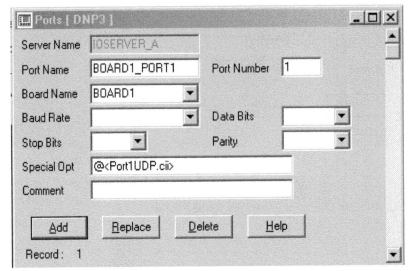

Next click on the   I/O   and set up as shown.
                    Devices

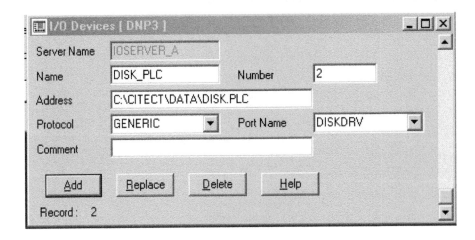

(3) Defining Tags

Variable Tag

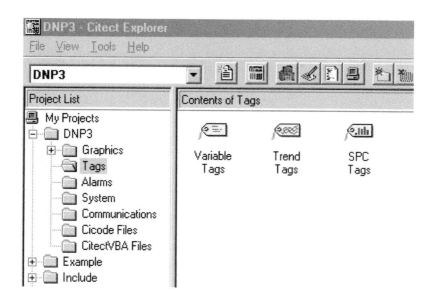

In the Citect Explorer click on Variable . Set up the seven Variable Tags as shown and after
                                        Tags
the information is entered press Add. **Do Not Press Return**.

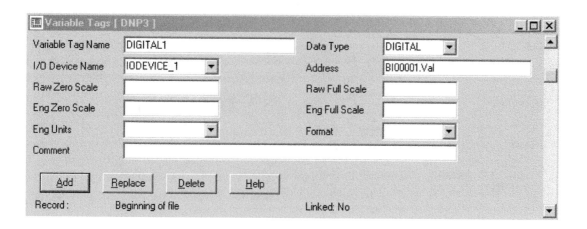

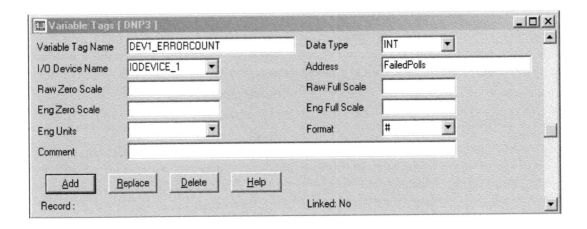

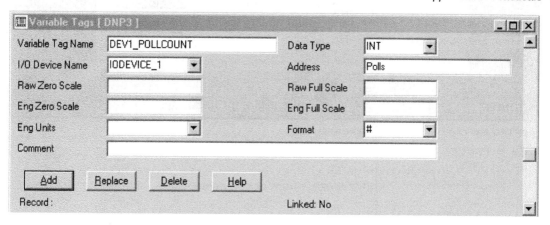

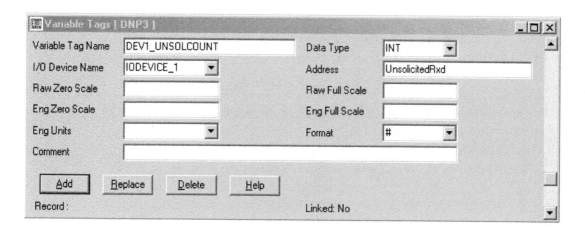

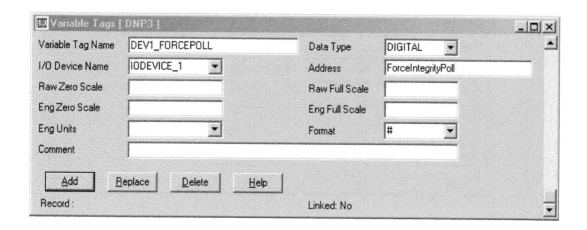

Time Stamped Alarm Tags (found under Alarms in the project editor.)

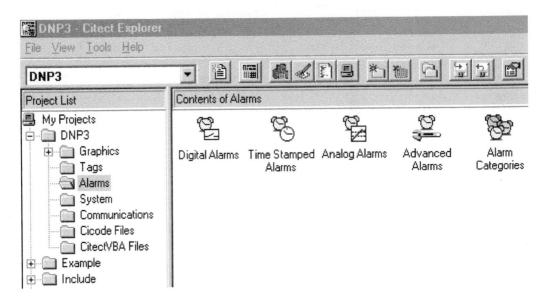

Click on the Time Stamped and setup the page as shown.
Alarms

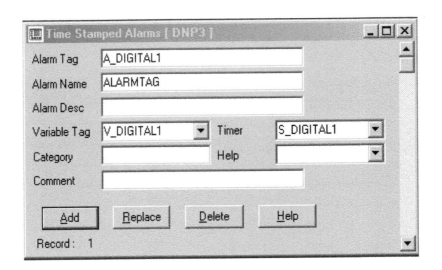

(4) Creating the Graphic Pages

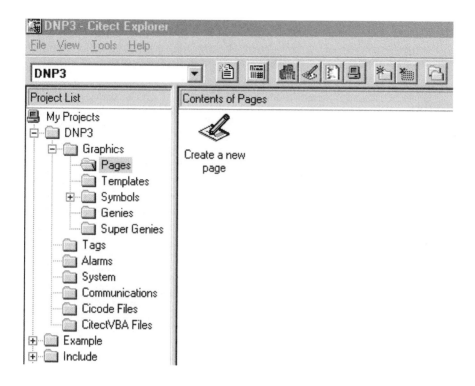

Click on the Create a new page and create three pages. Select the alarm page and click on OK.

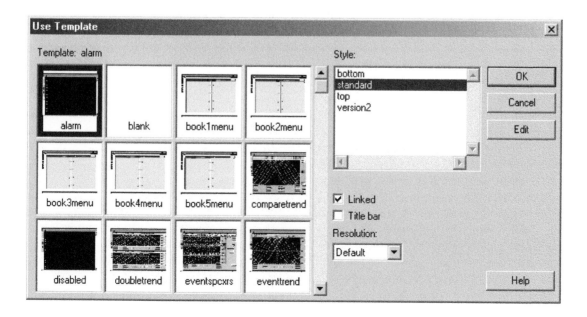

When the page has opened save the page with the name Alarm.
Then create two more pages using the Normal and the Hardware templates.
Name the Normal page TEST and the Hardware page Hardware.

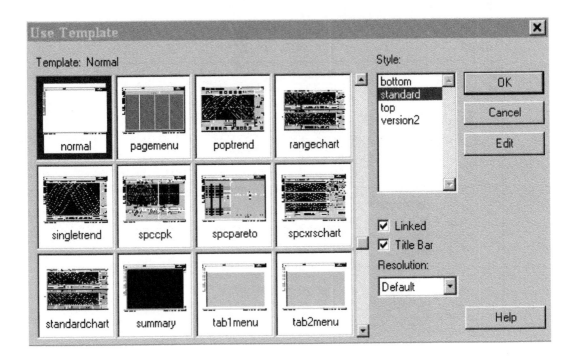

When all three pages (ALARM, TEST and HARDWARE) have been saved open the "TEST" page and place the button and text as shown on the page. Once the page has been created save the page.

(5) Building the Test Page

The Test Page will look something like this when it is done.

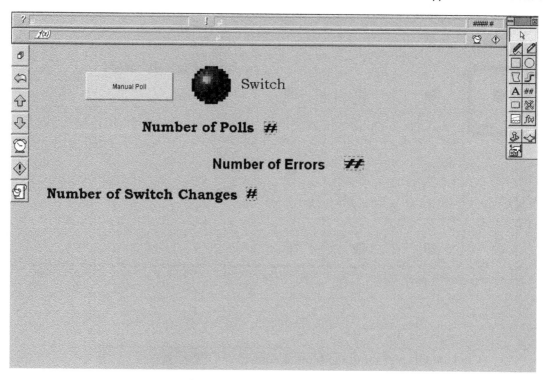

Use the menu 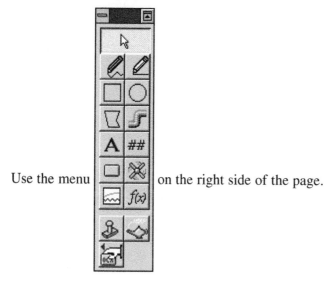 on the right side of the page.

Click on the small rubber stamp icon to select the light.

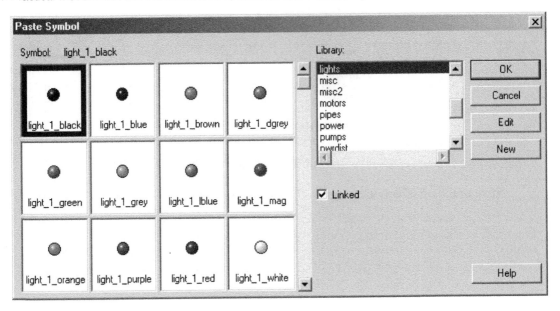

Click on OK and setup the light as shown.

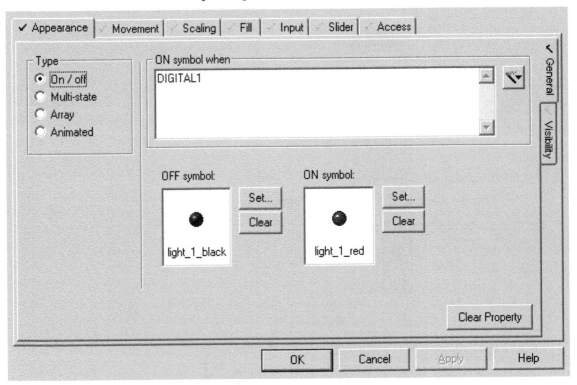

Click on the A 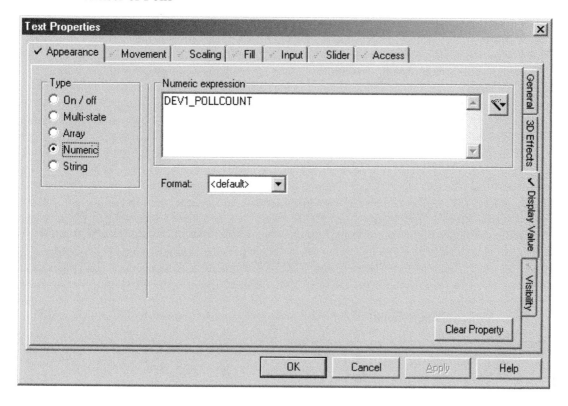 to insert the text on the page and the # to inset the count information. Set op the text and counts as shown.

Number of Polls

Number of Errors

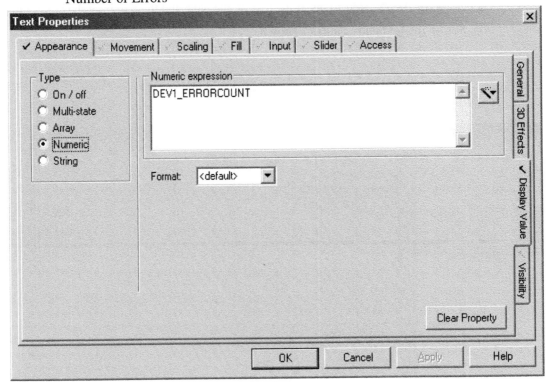

Switch Change Count

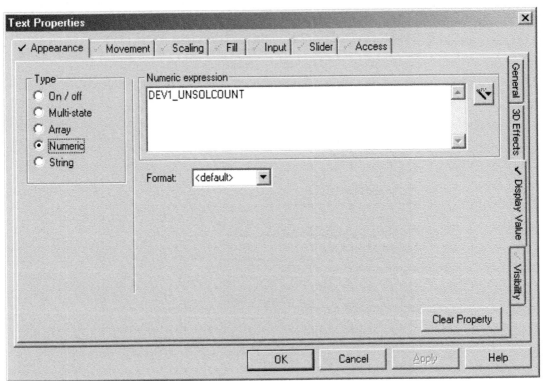

When finished with the Test setup, save the page and Compile and Run the project.

When the project has been ran the Menu page should come up and look like this.

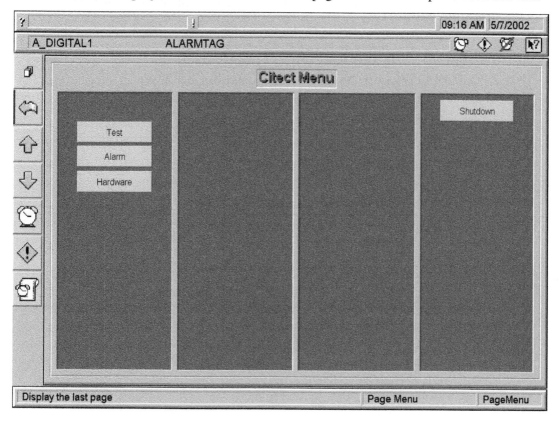

Clink on the Test button and the Test page should come up. After a few seconds the numbers should be seen and when the switch on the RTU is changed the light should change from red to black or from black to red. Red indicates that the switch is in the on position. If there is an allarm click on the flashing clock at the top of the page and the alarm page should come up.

Note: While this is happening the packetboy software can be used to view the data that is passing over the network.

DNP3 Protocol Packet Analysis
Instructors Answers

Communication 1

056408C40300A200EA80C5C5171E4405641044
A2000300D57EDEC58100003402070 1880288DA

What are the two start bytes?	____05____	____64____
How many packets are there?	____2____	
What are the last CRC's of each packet?	____1E44____	____88DA____
What are the addresses?	____0003____	____00A2____
What are the lengths of the packets?	____8____	____16____

What are the Control Bytes for the packets.____C4____ ____44____ Hex
<u>11000100 01000100</u> Binary

The First Packet	Bits	The Second Packet	Bits	
A to B	___1___	B to A	___0___	
From the Pri/Sec	___1___	From the Pri/Sec	___1___	
FCB / Res	___0___	FCB / Res	___0___	(FCB)
FCV/ Ignored	___0___	FCV / Ignored	___0___	
First bit of Function	___0___	First bit of Function	___0___	
	___1___		___1___	
	___0___		___0___	
	___0___		___0___	

What is the Function?

1. User Data No Reply Needed   2. User Data No Reply Needed

What is the Transport Layer Header information in the first packet?

___C5___ Hex   =   ___11000 0101___   Binary

FIN   FIR   Sequence

___1___ ___1___   ___0___ ___5___

Is there more than one fragment? ___NO___

056408C40300A200EA80C5C5171E4405641044A
2000300D57EDEC58100003402070188 0288DA

What is the Transport Layer Header information in the second packet?

___ D5___ Hex = ___1101 0101_____ Binary

FIN   FIR   Sequence

___1___   ___1___   ___1___ ___E___ Decimal _____30_____

Is there more than one fragment? ___NO___

What is the Application Layer Header information in the first packet?

___C5 ___ Hex = ___1100 0101 ___ Binary

FIR   FIN   Confirm   Sequence

___1___   ___1___   ___0___   ___0___ ___5___

What is the Function Code of the first packet? ___1 7___

What is the Function of the first packet?   Delay Measurement Request

What is the Application Layer Header information in the second packet?

___C5___ Hex = ___1100 0101___ Binary

FIR   FIN   Confirm   Sequence

___1___   ___1___   ___0___   ___0___ ___5___

What is the Response Function Code of the second packet? ___81___

What are the two bytes of Internal Indication? ___00___   ___00___

What is the Response Object Group?   ___34___Hex ___52___ Decimal

What is the purpose of the second packet? ___Time Measurement Response___

What is the Variation of the Object group? ___02___

What is the Qualifier byte? ___07___

What is the Range value? ___8___ Bits

What is the delay time in seconds? ___.648___ **Hint: LSB / MSB in Decimal**

Communication 2

05640DC405001A006378C6C601010200003F3806056
451441A0005004F65DFC681000001020300003F0081
018101BB390181010181818101818101010101010117
AC010101010101010101010101010101BBC301010
1010101010101010101010101BBC30101010101010
10101010101E481

What are the two start bytes?	___05___	___64___
How many packets are there?	___2___	
What are the last CRC's of each packet?	___3806___	___E481___
What are the addresses? ___0005___	___001A___	
What are the lengths of the packets?	___13___	___81___ Decimal

05640DC405001A006378C6C601010200003F3806056
451441A0005004F65DFC681000001020300003F0081
018101BB390181010181818101818101010101010117
AC0101010101010101010101010101010101BBC301010
10101010101010101010101010101BBC30101010101010
10101010101E481

What are the Control Bytes for the packets. ___C4___   ___44___ Hex
1100 0100 0100 0100 Binary

The First Packet	Bits	The Second Packet	Bits	
A to B	__1__	B to A	__0__	
From the Pri/Sec	__1__	From the Pri/Sec	__1__	
FCB / Res	__0__	FCB / Res	__0__	(FCB)
FCV/ Ignored	__0__	FCV / Ignored	__0__	
First bit of Function	__0__	First bit of Function	__0__	
	__1__		__1__	
	__0__		__0__	
	__0__		__0__	

What is the Function?

1. User Data No Reply Needed   2. User Data No Reply Needed

05640DC405001A006378C6C601010200003F3806056
451441A0005004F65DFC681000001020300003F0081
018101BB390181010181818101818101010101010117
AC0101010101010101010101010101010101BBC301010
1010101010101010101010101010101BBC30101010101010
10101010101E481

What is the Transport Layer Header information in the first packet?

____C6____ Hex = ____1100 0110____ Binary

FIN FIR Sequence

____1____ ____1____ ____0____ ____6____

Is there more than one fragment? ____NO____

What is the Transport Layer Header information in the second packet?

____DF____Hex = ____1101 1111____ Binary

FIN FIR Sequence

____1____ ____1____ ____1____ ____F____

Is there more than one datagram / fragment? ____NO____

05640DC405001A006378C6C601010200003F3806056
451441A0005004F65DFC681000001020300003F0081
018101BB390181010181818101818101010101010117
AC01010101010101010101010101010101BBC301010
10101010101010101010101010101BBC30101010101010
10101010101E481

What is the Application Layer Header information in the first packet?

___C6___ Hex = ___1100 0110 _____ Binary

FIR	FIN	Confirm	Sequence
__1__	__1__	__0__	__6__

What is the Function Code for the first packet? __01__

What is the function of the first packet?   __READ_____

What is the Object byte for the first packet? __01__

What does it mean? _____Binary Input_____

What are the Variation, Qualifier and Range for the first packet?   __02__ __01__ __00__3F__

What is the Range in Decimal?   __00__   to   __63__

What is the Application Layer Header information in the second packet?

___C6___ Hex = ___1100 0110__ Binary

FIR	FIN	Confirm	Sequence
__1__	__1__	__0__	__6__

What is the Response Function Code for the second packet? __81__

What are the Internal Indications for the second packet? ___0___ ___0___ ___0___
___0___

What is the Response Object Group? ___01___Hex

What is the purpose of the second packet? ___Binary Input Response___

What is the Variation of the Object group? ___02___ It meaning? ___Static Values___

What is the Qualifier byte? ___01___

What is the start of the data in Hex? ___00___ to ___3F___ Decimal ___00___
___63___

What is the data? Hint 81 = 1 and 01 = 0

See Data In Example Below

DI1 = 81 = 01
DI0 = 01 = 00
DI2 =
CRC = BB39

Digital Input Status Request 26 to 5

[15:13:3] 05 64 0D **C4 05 00 1A 00**<
Data Link Header [DIR] [PRM]
User Data (No Confirm) Length 13 Dest 2 Source 170 crc:63 crc:78
C6< **Transport Header** Fin:1, Fir:1, Seq:06
C6 01 01< **Application Data DI Stat request** AC Fir:1 Fin:1 Con:0 Seq:06 Object 1
02<Vart'n 2> **00**<Qual 00 > **00**<Start 0> **3F**<Stop 63> crc:38 crc:06 <—

05640DC405001A006378C6C601010200003F3806

Digital Input Status Response 5 to 26

[15:13:3] 05 64 51 **44 1A 00 05 00**<
Data Link Header [PRM]
User Data (No Confirm) Length 81 Dest 170 Source 2 crc:4F crc:65
DF< **Transport Header** Fin:1, Fir:1, Seq:31
C6 81 00 00 01< **Application Data DI Stat response** AC Fir:1 Fin:1 Con:0 Seq:06 [IIN Clear] [IIN Clear] Object 1
02<Vart'n 2> **01**<Qual 01 > **00 00**<Start 0> **3F 00**<Stop 63>
81<DI 0, Flag [OnLine.], Val: 1>
01<DI 1, Flag [OnLine.], Val: 0>
81<DI 2, Flag [OnLine.], Val: 1>
01<DI 3, Flag [OnLine.], Val: 0> crc:BB crc:39
01<DI 4, Flag [OnLine.], Val: 0>
81<DI 5, Flag [OnLine.], Val: 1>
01<DI 6, Flag [OnLine.], Val: 0>
01<DI 7, Flag [OnLine.], Val: 0>
81<DI 8, Flag [OnLine.], Val: 1>
81<DI 9, Flag [OnLine.], Val: 1>
81<DI 10, Flag [OnLine.], Val: 1>
01<DI 11, Flag [OnLine.], Val: 0>
81<DI 12, Flag [OnLine.], Val: 1>
81<DI 13, Flag [OnLine.], Val: 1>
01<DI 14, Flag [OnLine.], Val: 0>
01<DI 15, Flag [OnLine.], Val: 0>
01<DI 16, Flag [OnLine.], Val: 0>
01<DI 17, Flag [OnLine.], Val: 0>
01<DI 18, Flag [OnLine.], Val: 0>
01<DI 19, Flag [OnLine.], Val: 0> crc:17 crc:AC
01<DI 20, Flag [OnLine.], Val: 0>
01<DI 21, Flag [OnLine.], Val: 0>
01<DI 22, Flag [OnLine.], Val: 0>
01<DI 23, Flag [OnLine.], Val: 0>
01<DI 24, Flag [OnLine.], Val: 0>
01<DI 25, Flag [OnLine.], Val: 0>
01<DI 26, Flag [OnLine.], Val: 0>
01<DI 27, Flag [OnLine.], Val: 0>
01<DI 28, Flag [OnLine.], Val: 0>

01<DI 29, Flag [OnLine.], Val: 0>
01<DI 30, Flag [OnLine.], Val: 0>
01<DI 31, Flag [OnLine.], Val: 0>
01<DI 32, Flag [OnLine.], Val: 0>
01<DI 33, Flag [OnLine.], Val: 0>
01<DI 34, Flag [OnLine.], Val: 0>
01<DI 35, Flag [OnLine.], Val: 0> crc:BB crc:C3
01<DI 36, Flag [OnLine.], Val: 0>
01<DI 37, Flag [OnLine.], Val: 0>
01<DI 38, Flag [OnLine.], Val: 0>
01<DI 39, Flag [OnLine.], Val: 0>
01<DI 40, Flag [OnLine.], Val: 0>
01<DI 41, Flag [OnLine.], Val: 0>
01<DI 42, Flag [OnLine.], Val: 0>
01<DI 43, Flag [OnLine.], Val: 0>
01<DI 44, Flag [OnLine.], Val: 0>
01<DI 45, Flag [OnLine.], Val: 0>
01<DI 46, Flag [OnLine.], Val: 0>
01<DI 47, Flag [OnLine.], Val: 0>
01<DI 48, Flag [OnLine.], Val: 0>
01<DI 49, Flag [OnLine.], Val: 0>
01<DI 50, Flag [OnLine.], Val: 0>
01<DI 51, Flag [OnLine.], Val: 0> crc:BB crc:C3
01<DI 52, Flag [OnLine.], Val: 0>
01<DI 53, Flag [OnLine.], Val: 0>
01<DI 54, Flag [OnLine.], Val: 0>
01<DI 55, Flag [OnLine.], Val: 0>
01<DI 56, Flag [OnLine.], Val: 0>
01<DI 57, Flag [OnLine.], Val: 0>
01<DI 58, Flag [OnLine.], Val: 0>
01<DI 59, Flag [OnLine.], Val: 0>
01<DI 60, Flag [OnLine.], Val: 0>
01<DI 61, Flag [OnLine.], Val: 0>
01<DI 62, Flag [OnLine.], Val: 0>
01<DI 63, Flag [OnLine.], Val: 0>
crc:E4 crc:81 —>

056451441A0005004F65DFC681000001020300003F0081018101BB39018101018181 81018
18101010101010117AC010101010101010101010101010101BBC3010101010101010101
010101010101BBC3010101010101010101010101E481

Other Examples...

Delay Measurement Request 161 to 3

[15:13:3] 05 64 08 **C4 03 00 A2 00**<
Data Link Header [DIR] [PRM]
User Data (No Confirm) Length 8 Dest 2 Source 170 crc:EA crc:80
C5< **Transport Header** Fin:1, Fir:1, Seq:05
C5 17< **Application Data DelayMsur request** AC Fir:1 Fin:1 Con:0 Seq:05 crc:1E
crc:44 <—
056408C40200AA00EA80C5C5171E44

Delay Measurement Response 3 to 161

[15:13:3] 05 64 10 **44 A2 00 03 00**<
Data Link Header [PRM] **User Data** (No Confirm) Length 16 Dest 170 Source 2 crc:D5
crc:7E **DE**< **Transport Header** Fin:1, Fir:1, Seq:30
C5 81 00 00 34< **Application Data DelayMsur response** AC Fir:1 Fin:1 Con:0 Seq:05
[IIN Clear] [IIN Clear] Object 52 **02**<Vart'n 2> **07**<Qual 07 > **01**<Count 1> **88 02**<Sec:
0.648> crc:88 crc:DA —>
05641044AA000200D57EDEC5810000340207018802088DA

No Master Confirmation Needed:

Master Confirmation Request 170 to 2

[15:13:3] 05 64 08 **C4 02 00 AA 00**<
Data Link Header [DIR] [PRM]
User Data (No Confirm) Length 8 Dest 2 Source 170 crc:EA crc:80
C2< **Transport Header** Fin:1, Fir:1, Seq:02
C2 00< **Application Data Mastr Con request** AC Fir:1 Fin:1 Con:0 Seq:02 crc:A6
crc:BE —>

Read a Byte of Data From the Slave:

Read Data Request 170 to 2

[15:13:3] 05 64 0B **C4 02 00 AA 00**<
Data Link Header [DIR] [PRM]
User Data (No Confirm) Length 11 Dest 2 Source 170 crc:BA crc:13
C1< **Transport Header** Fin:1, Fir:1, Seq:01
C2 01 50< **Application Data Read request** AC Fir:1 Fin:1 Con:0 Seq:02
Object 80 **01**<Vart'n 1> **06**<Qual 06 > crc:D0 crc:64 <—

Read Data Response 2 to 170

[15:13:3] 05 64 11 **44 AA 00 02 00**<
Data Link Header [PRM]
User Data (No Confirm) Length 17 Dest 170 Source 2 crc:32 crc:CB
DB< **Transport Header** Fin:1, Fir:1, Seq:27

E2 81 00 00 50< **Application Data Read response** AC Fir:1 Fin:1 Con:1 Seq:02 [IIN Clear] [IIN Clear]

Object 80 **01<**Vart'n 1> **00<**Qual 00 > **00<**Start 0> **0F<**Stop 15> **00<** [IIN Clear] **00<** [IIN Clear] crc:E9 crc:8E —>

Setting The Time on the Slave:

Set Time Request 170 to 2

[15:13:3] 05 64 12 **C4 02 00 AA 00<**
Data Link Header [DIR] [PRM]
User Data (No Confirm) Length 18 Dest 2 Source 170 crc:40 crc:44
C4< **Transport Header** Fin:1, Fir:1, Seq:04
C4 02 32< **Application Data Set Time request** AC Fir:1 Fin:1 Con:0 Seq:04 Object 50
01<Vart'n 1> **07<**Qual 07 > **01<**Count 1>
05 B7 05 A4 E8 00<30-Aug-2001, 15:10:50.629> crc:2B crc:B7 <—

Set Time Response 2 to 170

[15:13:3] 05 64 0A **44 AA 00 02 00<** **Data Link Header** [PRM]
User Data (No Confirm) Length 10 Dest 170 Source 2 crc:7F crc:BA
DD< **Transport Header** Fin:1, Fir:1, Seq:29
C4 81 00 00< **Application Data Set Time response** AC Fir:1 Fin:1 Con:0 Seq:04 [IIN Clear] [IIN Clear] crc:72 crc:64 —>

DNP3 Protocol Packet Analysis

Objective:

This information and practical is intended to provide the delegate with a practical understanding of the DNP3 packet by providing information specific to packet interpretation.

Introduction:

DNP3 packets use hexadecimal as a language. Sometimes these hex values need to be converted to decimal or binary values. The number of bytes in a datagram is an example of a value in a DNP3 packet that needs to be changed. In the packet, the length value is given in hexadecimal but we count in decimal, therefore the length needs to be converted to decimal. Sometimes binary data is needed as in the flag settings within the Application Layer portion of a packet. The eight bit hexadecimal values that represent the flag will need to be converted into binary. Another part of the structure of the packet is the positioning of the most significant and least significant bytes within two bytes of data. When data needs to be represented by two bytes, such as an address, the least significant byte is placed first and the most significant byte is place second. An example of this is...

Address – AA00 Hex (as shown in the data stream)
Address – 00AA Hex (as normally written, least significant byte first)
Address – 170 Decimal (after converting to decimal)

Or

Address – 0200 Hex
Reversed to 0002 Hex
Converted to address 2 decimal

Structure of the Packet

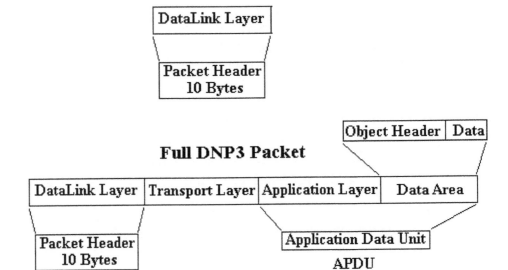

The type of packet sent determines the overall structure of the packet, but the packets can be divided up into two basic types.

1. Datalink layer only
2. Datalink / Transport / Application Layer combinations

The Datalink layer in both examples contains the Message Header. This header always contains only 10 bytes of data. The Transport layer contains a transport header and the Application Layer contains the object header and the data. Following is an example of a Datalink layer only packet.

Resetting the Link:

This example shows the packets of data that are sent from the master to the slave and then from the slave to the master to reset the communication link. This is always done when a DNP3 system is first started.

First the master sends a "reset the link" command to the remote device and then the device responds with an acknowledgement of the reset. The actual data stream in hexadecimal would look like this…

056405C00200AA00A76E05640500AA0002003F42

At fist glance this data might seem to be unintelligible, but it can easily be decrypted. The first step is to divide the data stream into packets. Start by finding the sequence **0564**. This is the unique sequence of start bytes for all DNP3 packets. The data would then look like this…

Packet From the Master   Packet From the Slave
056405C00200AA00A76E   **0564**0500AA0002003F42

All DNP3 packets end in a two byte CRC. The CRC and the start bytes can also be removed from the packet.

0564   05C00200AA00   **A76E**   **0564**   0500AA000200   **3F42**

The data that is left is Block 0 Packet 1 and Block 0 Packet 2…
Note: larger packets may have multiple blocks.

05C00200AA00   0500AA000200

Because of the small size of the data sent, these packets are obviously just Datalink Layer packets. Working from the right end of each of the packets the destination and source addresses are removed.

Packet 1	Destination	Source	Packet 2	Destination	Source
05C0	0200	AA00	0500	AA00	0200

It can be seen that in packet 1 the data is being sent to 0200 from AA00. The bytes are then reversed to read 0002 and 00AA. The addresses are then converted into decimal and thus become… Packet 1 from address 170 (the master) to address 2 (the slave) and in the second packet from address 2 (the slave) to address 170 (the master).

The data that is left is the length and control bytes of the packet. The length as seen in both packets happens to be 05 Hex. This value is converted to decimal and becomes 5. (Notice that the highest value possible is FF hexadecimal, which is 255 decimal) There are then five bytes in the packet, not including the CRC, the start bytes and itself. These five bytes in this case are 1 byte of control byte, 2 bytes of destination address and 2 bytes of source addressing.

The data that is left is the control byte

Packet 1 Control   C0
Packet 2 Control   00

The control byte provides for the control of the data flow over the link.

We see the control byte can be interpreted as such...

C0 = 1100 0000   **00** = 0000 0000   therefore...

The First Packet   The Second Packet

A to B	1	B to A	0	
From the Pri/Sec	1	From the Pri/Sec	0	(1= Primary, 0 = Secondary)
FCB / Res	0	FCB / Res	0	
FCV/ Ignored	0	FCV/ Ignored	0	
First bit of Function	0	First bit of Function	0	
	0		0	
	0		0	
	0		0	

Reset the Link   Acknowledgement

Notice: the two least significant bits denote the datalink functions (if any) of the packets.

If a protocol analyzer was used to look at the previous packets it might interpret the data as such.

Reset Link Command From 170 to 2

Started at 30-Aug-101 15:13:1, protocol DNP 3.0 —>
[15:13:3] **05 64 05 C0 02 00 AA 00**<
Data Link Header [DIR] [PRM]
Reset Link (Confirm) Length 5 Dest 2 Source 170 crc:**A7** crc:**6E** <—
056405C00200AA00A76E

Reset Command Acknowledgement From 2 to 170

[15:13:3] **05 64 05 00 AA 00 02 00**<
Data Link Header
Ack Length 5 Dest 170 Source 2 crc:**3F** crc:**42** —>
05640500AA0002003F42
Next we are going to look at a more complicated packet. The "disabling unsolicited response" packet is a very common packet that is used to put the DNP3 system into a master/slave only mode. This guarantees that there are no collisions within the system. It also makes the system more deterministic. (we know who talks to whom and when)

Disabling Unsolicited Responses From the Slave:

056411C40200AA0010D7C0C1153C02063C03063C0406944305640A44AA0002007FBAD
AC1810000A393

Again the first thing is to separate the data into packets.

056411C40200AA0010D7C0C1153C02063C03063C04069443
05640A44AA0002007FBADAC1810000A393

Then remove the start characters and last CRC's.

Packet 1   11C40200AA0010D7C0C1153C02063C03063C0406

Packet 2   0A44AA0002007FBADAC1810000

Next remove the first eight bytes from the left as this is Block 0.

11C40200AA00**10D7**   Block 0 Packet 1

0A44AA0002007**FBA**   Block 0 Packet 2

Since all other blocks have a maximum of 16 Bytes of data and 2 bytes of CRC, divide the rest of the data in each packet into blocks of 18 bytes.

C0C1153C02063C03063C0406   Block 1 Packet 1

ADAC1810000   Block 1 Packet 2

In both Block 0's remove the last 2 bytes of CRC

11C4<u>0200AA00</u>   **10D7**   Block 0 Packet 1

0A44<u>AA000200</u>   **7FBA**   Block 0 Packet 2

The last four bytes on the right are the addresses. This shows that packet 1 went again from the master 00AA to the slave 0002 and that packet 2 went from the slave 0002 to the master 00AA.

The data that is left is the length and control bytes.

11C4   Block 0 Packet 1
0A44   Block 0 Packet 2

The lengths are (11Hex) 17 bytes for packet 1 and (0A Hex) 10 bytes for packet 2

The control bytes for each packet tell us the following…

C4 = 1100 0100   **44** = 0100 0100   therefore…

The First Packet		The Second Packet		
A to B	1	B to A	0	
From Pri/Sec	1	From Pri/Sec	1	(1= Primary, 0 = Secondary)
FCB / Res	0	FCB / Res	0	
FCV/ Ignored	0	FCV/ Ignored	0	
First bit of Function	0	First bit of Function	0	
	1		1	
	0		0	
	0		0	
User Data (no Confirm)		User Data (no Confirm)		

Next we look at Block 1 of Packet 1 (Transport + Application Data)

C0C1153C02063C03063C0406   Note that since this Block is 16 bytes or less the CRC
has been already removed.

The first byte on the left is the Transport Header (C0).

C0 = 1100 0000

FIN	FIR	Sequence
1	1	00 0000

This tells us that this packet is the first and last packet in this sequence and therefore it is
not fragmented. We then know that the rest of the packet is an Application Layer Block.

C1153C02063C03063C0406

The first byte on the left is the Application header (C1).

C1 = 1100 0001

FIR	FIN	Confirmation	Sequence
1	1	0	0 0001

This tells us that this packet is the first and last packet in this sequence and therefore it is
not fragmented at the Application Layer level. It also tells us that this packet is sequence
number 1.

153C02063C03063C0406

The next byte on the left (**15**) tells us that this packet is sending a function code that disables
the unsolicited message capabilities of the slave. This can be seen under Func. Code under
Request Header under Message Header under APCI on the DNP APDU sheet. (0X15)

3C02063C03063C0406

The next byte on the left (3C) is part of the object header. 3C Hex is converted to 60 Decimal because the object group ranges are in Decimal. Object Group 60 can be seen as class objects on page 147 in the book.

02063C03063C0406

02 is the objects variation "Class 1 Data" under group.

063C03063C0406

06 is the qualifier of the object and can be decoded by using the DNP APDU sheet provided. Notice that 06 is "No Range Field"

3C0306 3C0406

The Disable Unsolicited Request is made within this packet for all 3 classes of data. Notice that the next three bytes only differ from the last three bytes by 03 in the middle...

Last One   3C**02**06
This One   3C**03**06
Next One   3C**04**06

These three variations account for the three classes within the 60 Group.

Now we will look at the response from the slave with Block 1 Packet 2

DAC1810000

DA again is the Transport Header

DA = 1101 1010

FIN	FIR	Sequence
1	1	01 1010 (26)

C1810000

C1 The first byte on the left is the Application header (C1).

C1 = 1100 0001

FIR	FIN	Confirmation	Sequence
1	1	0 - No Confirm	0 0001

This tells us that this packet is the first and last packet and therefore it is not fragmented. It also tells us that this packet is sequence 1.

Notice that the Transport and Application layer sequences are different and that the Application layer sequence on both packets match.

810000

The last three bytes are in the Response Header under Message Header under the APCI on the DNP APDU sheet.

81 indicates a Response Function Code (0X81). The last four 0's indicates no Internal Indications.

If a protocol analyzer was used to look at the previous packets it might interpret the data as follows.

Disable Unsolicited Request 170 to 2

[15:13:3] 05 64 11 **C4 02 00 AA 00**<
Data Link Header [DIR] [PRM]
User Data (No Confirm) Length 17 Dest 2 Source 170 crc:10 crc:D7
C0< **Transport Header** Fin:1, Fir:1, Seq:00
C1 15 3C< **Application Data DisUns request** AC Fir:1 Fin:1 Con:0 Seq:01 Object 60
02<Vart'n 2> **06**<Qual 06 > **3C 03 06 3C 04 06** crc:94 crc:43 <—

056411C40200AA0010D7C0C1153C02063C03063C04069443

Disable Unsolicited Response 2 to 170

[15:13:3] 05 64 0A **44 AA 00 02 00**<
Data Link Header [PRM]
User Data (No Confirm) Length 10 Dest 170 Source 2 crc:7F crc:BA
DA< **Transport Header** Fin:1, Fir:1, Seq:26
C1 81 00 00< **Application Data DisUns** response AC Fir:1 Fin:1 Con:0 Seq:01 [IIN Clear] [IIN Clear] crc:A3 crc:93 —>

05640A44AA0002007FBADAC1810000A393

Packet Interpretation Practical

Objective:

The objective of this practical is to give the delegate the opportunity to decode some examples of real DNP3 packets. These packets have been captured from a real working system.

Equipment needed:

A Computer or calculator that can convert Hexadecimal to Decimal and Binary

Procedure:

Follow the instructions on the following sheets. Use the book as required. Pages are mentioned throughout the practical. Use the DNP APDU short cut sheet. And use the calculator as provided under Application in Windows. If any help is needed consult the instructor.

Interpretation Practical:

Below is a typical communication between two DNP3 devices. Decode the packets and determine what kind of communication is taking place. Answer the question as requested.

Communication 1

056408C40300A200EA80C5C5171E4405641044
A2000300D57EDEC58100003402070188O288DA

What are the two start bytes?   _____   _____

How many packets are there?   _____

What are the last CRC's of each packet? _____ _____

What are the addresses?   _____ _____

056408C40300A200EA80C5C5171E4405641044
A2000300D57EDEC581000034020701880288DA

What are the lengths of the packets? _____

What are the Control Bytes for the packets. _____ _____ Hex
_____Binary

The First Packet	Bits	The Second Packet	Bits	
A to B	_____	B to A	_____	
Primary/Sec	_____	Primary/Sec	_____	
FCB / Res	_____	FCB / Res	_____	(FCB)
FCV/ Ignored	_____	FCV / Ignored	_____	
First bit of Function	_____	First bit of Function	_____	MSB
	_____		_____	
	_____		_____	
	_____		_____	LSB

What are the functions of the packets?

Packet 1. _____   Packet 2. _____

What is the Transport Layer Header information in the first packet?

_____ Hex = _____ Binary

FIN	FIR	Sequence
_____	_____	_____

Is there more than one fragment? _____

056408C40300A200EA80C5C5171E4405641044A
2000300D57EDEC5810000340207018800288DA

What is the Transport Layer Header information in the second packet?

_____ Hex   =   _____   Binary

FIN   FIR   Sequence

_____   _____   _____

Is there more than one fragment? _____

What is the Application Layer Header information in the first packet?

_____ Hex = _____ Binary

FIR   FIN   Confirm   Sequence

_____   _____   _____   _____   Decimal _____

What is the Function Code of the first packet?_____

What is the Function of the first packet?_____

What is the Application Layer Header information in the second packet?

_____Hex = _____ Binary

FIR   FIN   Confirm   Sequence

_____   _____   _____   _____   Decimal_____

What is the Response Function Code of the second packet? _____

What are the two bytes of Internal Indication? _____   _____

What is the Response Object Group? _____Hex   _____ Decimal

What is the purpose of the second packet? _____

056408C40300A200EA80C5C5171E4405641044A
2000300D57EDEC581000034020701880288DA

What is the Variation of the Object group? ⎯⎯⎯⎯

What is the Qualifier byte? ⎯⎯⎯⎯

What is the Range value? ⎯⎯⎯⎯

What is the delay time in seconds? ⎯⎯⎯⎯ **Hint: LSB / MSB in Decimal**

Communication 2

05640DC405001A006378C6C601010200003F3806056
451441A0005004F65DFC681000001020100003F0081
018101BB39018101018181810181810101010101010117
AC010101010101010101010101010101BBC301010
1010101010101010101010101BBC30101010101010
10101010101E481

What are the two start bytes? _____ _____

How many packets are there? _____

What are the last CRC's of each packet? _____ _____

What are the addresses? _____ _____

What are the lengths of the packets? _____ _____ Decimal

05640DC405001A006378C6C601010200003F3806056
451441A0005004F65DFC681000001020100003F0081
018101BB39018101018181810181810101010101010117
AC0101010101010101010101010101010101BBC301010
1010101010101010101010101010101BBC30101010101010
10101010101E481

What are the Control Bytes for the packets. _____ _____ Hex _____ _____ Binary

The First Packet	Bits	The Second Packet	Bits	
A to B	_____	B to A	_____	
Primary/Sec	_____	Primary/Sec	_____	
FCB / Res	_____	FCB / Res	_____	(FCB)
FCV/ Ignored	_____	FCV / Ignored	_____	
First bit of Function	_____	First bit of Function	_____	MSB
	_____		_____	
	_____		_____	
	_____		_____	LSB

What are the Functions of the packets?

1. _____ 2. _____

05640DC405001A006378C6C601010200003F3806056
451441A0005004F65DFC681000001020100003F0081
018101BB390181010181818101818101010101010117
AC010101010101010101010101010101BBC301010
10101010101010101010101010101BBC30101010101010
10101010101E481

What is the Transport Layer Header information in the first packet?

_____ Hex = _____ Binary

FIN   FIR   Sequence

_____   _____   _____ Hex _____ Decimal

Is there more than one fragment? _____

What is the Transport Layer Header information in the second packet?

_____ Hex = _____ Binary

FIN   FIR   Sequence

_____   _____   _____ Hex _____ Decimal

Is there more than one datagram / fragment? _____

05640DC405001A006378C6C601010200003F3806056
451441A0005004F65DFC681000001020100003F0081
018101BB390181010181818101818101010101010117
AC010101010101010101010101010101BBC301010
1010101010101010101010101BBC30101010101010
10101010101E481

What is the Application Layer Header information in the first packet?

_____ Hex = _____ Binary

FIR   FIN   Confirm   Sequence

_____   _____   _____   _____

What is the Function Code for the first packet? _____

What is the function of the first packet? _____

What is the Object header for the first packet? _____

What does it mean? _____

What are the Variation, Qualifier and Range for the first packet? ____ ____ ____ ____

What is the Range in Decimal? _____ to _____

What is the Application Layer Header information in the second packet?

_____ Hex = _____ Binary

FIR   FIN   Confirm   Sequence

_____   _____   _____   _____

What is the Response Function Code for the second packet? _____

What is the Response Object Group? _____ Hex

What is the purpose of the second packet? _____

What is the Variation of the Object group? _____ It meaning? _____

What is the Qualifier byte? _____

What is the RANGE of the data in Hex? _____ to _____ Decimal _____ to _____

What is the data? Hint 81 = 1 and 01 = 0

DI0 = _____

DI1 = _____

DI2 = _____

DI3 = _____

CRC = _____   _____   _____   _____

_____

_____

_____

_____

_____

_____

_____

_____

Digital Input Status Request 26 to 5

[15:13:3] 05 64 0D **C4 05 00 1A 00**<
Data Link Header [DIR] [PRM]
User Data (No Confirm) Length 13 Dest 2 Source 170 crc:63 crc:78
C6< **Transport Header** Fin:1, Fir:1, Seq:06
C6 01 01< **Application Data DI Stat request** AC Fir:1 Fin:1 Con:0 Seq:06 Object 1
02<Vart'n 2> **00**<Qual 00 > **00**<Start 0> **3F**<Stop 63> crc:38 crc:06 <—

05640DC405001A006378C6C601010200003F3806

Digital Input Status Response 5 to 26

[15:13:3] 05 64 51 **44 1A 00 05 00**<
Data Link Header [PRM]
User Data (No Confirm) Length 81 Dest 170 Source 2 crc:4F crc:65
DF< **Transport Header** Fin:1, Fir:1, Seq:31
C6 81 00 00 01< **Application Data DI Stat response** AC Fir:1 Fin:1 Con:0 Seq:06 [IIN Clear] [IIN Clear] Object 1
02<Vart'n 2> **01**<Qual 01 > **00 00**<Start 0> **3F 00**<Stop 63>
81<DI 0, Flag [OnLine.], Val: 1>
01<DI 1, Flag [OnLine.], Val: 0>
81<DI 2, Flag [OnLine.], Val: 1>
01<DI 3, Flag [OnLine.], Val: 0> crc:BB crc:39
01<DI 4, Flag [OnLine.], Val: 0>
81<DI 5, Flag [OnLine.], Val: 1>
01<DI 6, Flag [OnLine.], Val: 0>
01<DI 7, Flag [OnLine.], Val: 0>
81<DI 8, Flag [OnLine.], Val: 1>
81<DI 9, Flag [OnLine.], Val: 1>
81<DI 10, Flag [OnLine.], Val: 1>
01<DI 11, Flag [OnLine.], Val: 0>
81<DI 12, Flag [OnLine.], Val: 1>
81<DI 13, Flag [OnLine.], Val: 1>
01<DI 14, Flag [OnLine.], Val: 0>
01<DI 15, Flag [OnLine.], Val: 0>
01<DI 16, Flag [OnLine.], Val: 0>
01<DI 17, Flag [OnLine.], Val: 0>
01<DI 18, Flag [OnLine.], Val: 0>
01<DI 19, Flag [OnLine.], Val: 0> crc:17 crc:AC
01<DI 20, Flag [OnLine.], Val: 0>
01<DI 21, Flag [OnLine.], Val: 0>
01<DI 22, Flag [OnLine.], Val: 0>
01<DI 23, Flag [OnLine.], Val: 0>
01<DI 24, Flag [OnLine.], Val: 0>
01<DI 25, Flag [OnLine.], Val: 0>
01<DI 26, Flag [OnLine.], Val: 0>
01<DI 27, Flag [OnLine.], Val: 0>
01<DI 28, Flag [OnLine.], Val: 0>

01<DI 29, Flag [OnLine.], Val: 0>
01<DI 30, Flag [OnLine.], Val: 0>
01<DI 31, Flag [OnLine.], Val: 0>
01<DI 32, Flag [OnLine.], Val: 0>
01<DI 33, Flag [OnLine.], Val: 0>
01<DI 34, Flag [OnLine.], Val: 0>
01<DI 35, Flag [OnLine.], Val: 0> crc:BB crc:C3
01<DI 36, Flag [OnLine.], Val: 0>
01<DI 37, Flag [OnLine.], Val: 0>
01<DI 38, Flag [OnLine.], Val: 0>
01<DI 39, Flag [OnLine.], Val: 0>
01<DI 40, Flag [OnLine.], Val: 0>
01<DI 41, Flag [OnLine.], Val: 0>
01<DI 42, Flag [OnLine.], Val: 0>
01<DI 43, Flag [OnLine.], Val: 0>
01<DI 44, Flag [OnLine.], Val: 0>
01<DI 45, Flag [OnLine.], Val: 0>
01<DI 46, Flag [OnLine.], Val: 0>
01<DI 47, Flag [OnLine.], Val: 0>
01<DI 48, Flag [OnLine.], Val: 0>
01<DI 49, Flag [OnLine.], Val: 0>
01<DI 50, Flag [OnLine.], Val: 0>
01<DI 51, Flag [OnLine.], Val: 0> crc:BB crc:C3
01<DI 52, Flag [OnLine.], Val: 0>
01<DI 53, Flag [OnLine.], Val: 0>
01<DI 54, Flag [OnLine.], Val: 0>
01<DI 55, Flag [OnLine.], Val: 0>
01<DI 56, Flag [OnLine.], Val: 0>
01<DI 57, Flag [OnLine.], Val: 0>
01<DI 58, Flag [OnLine.], Val: 0>
01<DI 59, Flag [OnLine.], Val: 0>
01<DI 60, Flag [OnLine.], Val: 0>
01<DI 61, Flag [OnLine.], Val: 0>
01<DI 62, Flag [OnLine.], Val: 0>
01<DI 63, Flag [OnLine.], Val: 0>
crc:E4 crc:81 —>

056451441A0005004F65DFC681000001020100003
F0081018101BB3901810101818181018 181010101
01010117AC010101010101010101010101010101
BBC3010101010101010101010101010101BBC3
010101010101010101010101E481

Other Examples...

Delay Measurement Request 161 to 3

[15:13:3] 05 64 08 **C4 03 00 A2 00<**
Data Link Header [DIR] [PRM]
User Data (No Confirm) Length 8 Dest 2 Source 170 crc:EA crc:80
C5< **Transport Header** Fin:1, Fir:1, Seq:05
C5 17< Application Data DelayMsur request AC Fir:1 Fin:1 Con:0 Seq:05 crc:1E
crc:44 <—
056408C40200AA00EA80C5C5171E44

Delay Measurement Response 3 to 161

[15:13:3] 05 64 10 **44 A2 00 03 00<**
Data Link Header [PRM] **User Data** (No Confirm) Length 16 Dest 170 Source 2 crc:D5
crc:7E **DE< Transport Header** Fin:1, Fir:1, Seq:30
C5 81 00 00 34< Application Data DelayMsur response AC Fir:1 Fin:1 Con:0 Seq:05
[IIN Clear] [IIN Clear] Object 52 **02**<Vart'n 2> **07**<Qual 07 > **01**<Count 1> **88
02**<Sec: 0.648> crc:88 crc:DA —>
05641044AA000200D57EDEC5810000 34020701880288DA

No Master Confirmation Needed:

Master Confirmation Request 170 to 2

[15:13:3] 05 64 08 **C4 02 00 AA 00<**
Data Link Header [DIR] [PRM]
User Data (No Confirm) Length 8 Dest 2 Source 170 crc:EA crc:80
C2< **Transport Header** Fin:1, Fir:1, Seq:02
C2 00< Application Data Mastr Con request AC Fir:1 Fin:1 Con:0 Seq:02 crc:A6
crc:BE —>

Read a Byte of Data From the Slave:

Read Data Request 170 to 2

[15:13:3] 05 64 0B **C4 02 00 AA 00<**
Data Link Header [DIR] [PRM]
User Data (No Confirm) Length 11 Dest 2 Source 170 crc:BA crc:13
C1< **Transport Header** Fin:1, Fir:1, Seq:01
C2 01 50< Application Data Read request AC Fir:1 Fin:1 Con:0 Seq:02
Object 80 **01**<Vart'n 1> **06**<Qual 06 > crc:D0 crc:64 <—

Read Data Response 2 to 170

[15:13:3] 05 64 11 **44 AA 00 02 00**<
Data Link Header [PRM]
User Data (No Confirm) Length 17 Dest 170 Source 2 crc:32 crc:CB
DB< Transport Header Fin:1, Fir:1, Seq:27
E2 81 00 00 50< Application Data Read response AC Fir:1 Fin:1 Con:1 Seq:02
[IIN Clear] [IIN Clear]

Object 80 **01**<Vart'n 1> **00**<Qual 00 > **00**<Start 0> **0F**<Stop 15> **00**< [IIN Clear] **00**<
[IIN Clear] crc:E9 crc:8E —>

Setting The Time on the Slave:

Set Time Request 170 to 2

[15:13:3] 05 64 12 **C4 02 00 AA 00**<
Data Link Header [DIR] [PRM]
User Data (No Confirm) Length 18 Dest 2 Source 170 crc:40 crc:44
C4< Transport Header Fin:1, Fir:1, Seq:04
C4 02 32< Application Data Set Time request AC Fir:1 Fin:1 Con:0 Seq:04 Object 50
01<Vart'n 1> **07**<Qual 07 > **01**<Count 1>
 05 B7 05 A4 E8 00<30-Aug-2001, 15:10:50.629> crc:2B crc:B7 <—

Set Time Response 2 to 170

[15:13:3] 05 64 0A **44 AA 00 02 00< Data Link Header** [PRM]
User Data (No Confirm) Length 10 Dest 170 Source 2 crc:7F crc:BA
DD< Transport Header Fin:1, Fir:1, Seq:29
C4 81 00 00< Application Data Set Time response AC Fir:1 Fin:1 Con:0 Seq:04 [IIN
Clear] [IIN Clear] crc:72 crc:64 —>

Index

Printed and bound by CPI Group (UK) Ltd, Croydon, CR0 4YY

03/10/2024

01040334-0018